Ja Nigel + Ursula

Suffering and Glory

The Church from the Apostles to Constantine

— PATRICK WHITWORTH —

With Love from

Patrick **Sacristy Press**

Sacristy Press
PO Box 612, Durham, DH1 9HT

www.sacristy.co.uk

First published in 2018 by Sacristy Press, Durham

Sacristy Limited, registered in England & Wales, number 7565667

British Library Cataloguing-in-Publication Data
A catalogue record for the book is available from the British Library

Paperback ISBN 978-1-910519-80-6
Hardback ISBN 978-1-910519-92-9

To our brothers and sisters in the Armenian Apostolic Church.

The first nation to believe.

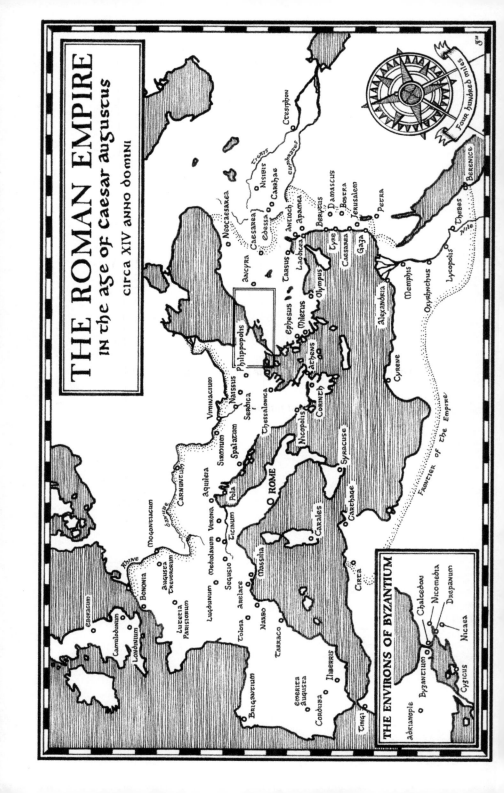

THE ROMAN EMPIRE
in the age of Caesar augustus
circa XIV anno domini

THE ENVIRONS OF BYZANTIUM

Four hundred miles

Foreword

Preserved in the Frankfurt Bible Museum is a remarkable inscription from the ruins of the ancient city of Priene in modern-day Turkey. It reads, "The birthday of the god has brought glad tidings to the world". The god in question is the divine Augustus, Emperor of the Roman World.

St Luke appropriates this imperial propaganda and applies it instead to the birth of Jesus Christ in a remote part of one of the territories ruled by a client king of the Romans.

In the mid-40s AD, when Paul was preaching in cities like Perge, whose ruined splendour can still astonish, it must have seemed obvious that the future belonged to the Emperor and his regime. In Paul's lifetime, the Empire was still expanding and moving towards its second century apogee under the five good Emperors. It was in these circumstances that Paul preached the gospel of Jesus Christ and prophesied that the future would belong to the followers of a Jew crucified under the Roman Governor, Pontius Pilate.

It was an audacious claim, but it came to pass. Having sketched the political context, Patrick Whitworth tells the story of the growth of the early Christian community. Eschewing speculation, he provides a clear narrative interspersed with pithy accounts of the most significant Christian teachers in the period which culminated in the advent of the first Christian Emperor, Constantine.

It is a story that is particularly relevant to a time when Christendom is a fading memory and the Christian community is struggling to discover where the Spirit is leading in a global culture described by the late Ernest Gellner as "Consumer Unbeliever International".

It is characteristic of the English Reformation to appeal to the authority of the "ancient fathers" in the manner of the Book of Common Prayer.

It must be confessed, however, that there is widespread ignorance even among those preparing for the ordained ministry of the way in which the teachers of the Apostolic Age read the Bible and strove to make the gospel accessible in terms of contemporary thought.

Patrick Whitworth offers an introduction to this seminal period of the Christian community and material for further study. He writes in a way that is accessible and relevant to all Christians, but in the process he also demonstrates that the tradition of the learned parish priest, one of the glories of the Church of England, is alive and well.

Richard Chartres
Former Bishop of London

Preface

When the Apostle Paul knelt on the beach at Miletus, a notable Greek and then later Roman colony, with the Ephesian Elders at the end of his third missionary journey, he knew the shape of things to come. Taking his leave of them, and knowing he would never see them again, he warned of "fierce wolves" who would come among them and others who would "distort the truth", seeking to draw them away from their faith in Christ, as he had taught them. This was a prophecy that came true.

Within a few years of this leave-taking Paul would be executed in Rome. The persecution of Christians under the Emperor Nero would begin. Far from evangelising the Roman world from a position of human strength, the church would be seemingly weak and vulnerable. The persecution of the church would continue for another 250 years, until it abruptly came to an end under Constantine. During that time, persecution ebbed and flowed, coming to a high tide of suffering during the reign of Diocletian. Then, with the accession of the Emperor Constantine, it abated and ceased. Over those 200 and more years, not only was there fierce persecution from *outside* the church, but there were also strong *internal* challenges as well. The church, which was still being formed in both its beliefs and practices, faced dangerous challenges from various quarters: Gnosticism sought to envelop Christianity in a larger religious system in which Jesus was just one more emanation of a supreme being; Marcion sought to denigrate the Old Testament, making it unrelated to the New Testament; there were early rumblings about the reality of the Trinity and, at the end of this period, the greatest heresiarch (heretic) Arius emerged in Alexandria, to preach that Jesus was not God. It was a turbulent period.

In these pages we will meet great figures of the early church, like Ignatius of Antioch, who eagerly went to his death in Rome, fed to lions. Polycarp was martyred and burnt in Ephesus. Justin, although appealing to the Emperor as an Apologist, was executed. The great Irenaeus, a Greek-speaking Bishop of Lyons, gave the first full defence of Christianity against Gnosticism and an exhilarating description of Christianity as restoring our true and full humanity. We shall observe Tertullian, the marvellously eloquent and rapier-tongued defender of Christian orthodoxy, and the godly Cyprian, Bishop of Carthage. And then, after the greatest persecution of the church since Nero or Decius (AD250), in the reign of Diocletian, we will follow the sudden *volte-face* of the Empire's religious policy under Constantine and the beginning of religious tolerance. When all seemed set fair, the severest threat to the integrity and power of Christianity emerged with Arius, who denied the full divinity of Christ. This spurred Constantine to intervene and summon the bishops to the Council of Nicaea at his summer palace. The survival, and indeed expansion, of the church during a period of exceptional challenge can only be accounted for by the grace of God and the power of his word which the Apostle Paul had commended to its leaders on the sandy beach of Miletus.

Suffering and Glory: The Church from the Apostles to Constantine is in fact the first of a trilogy, charting the church's life from the Apostles till the end of the fifth century. The other two titles are *Three Wise Men: The Cappadocian Fathers and the Struggle for Orthodoxy* and *Constantinople to Chalcedon: Shaping the World to Come*. My hope is that these three books *together* faithfully chart the progress of the church in these early turbulent centuries of its life, against the background of events in the Roman Empire. They have been written over four years and not without the help and encouragement of many people.

I am especially grateful to Professor Mark Edwards of Christ Church Oxford (my old college or house, I should say) for guiding me through the period in terms of reading, and also for reading this and each of the manuscripts and keeping me from too many blunders. Any mistakes are entirely mine. I would like to thank Benedict Books for helping with the early stages of proofreading and Sacristy Press for taking on the project and for patiently seeing it through; my thanks also go to Richard

Chartres, who generously wrote the foreword to this book, soon after stepping down from his distinguished ministry as Bishop of London. Thank you too to Richard and Sarah Parry for accompanying Olivia and myself to Armenia, while a Velvet Revolution took place in the spring of 2018. Finally, I would like to thank my wife Olivia, who has wonderfully supported me in the project over the last five years of research and writing, while leaving my last parish, All Saints Bath Weston, and settling into a new home and area for "retirement". She tells me she has not noticed too much let up, but instead the take up of new projects. But meal times have been well seasoned with yet another discussion about the challenges facing the church in its first few centuries of life, and now.

Patrick Whitworth
The Feast of St Perpetua and St Felicitas of Carthage, 7 March 2018

Contents

Foreword v
Preface vii
Abbreviations xii

Part One: The Apostolic Age 1
The Roman Empire and Judea in the Age of Augustus 3
Expansion and Persecution 39
The Formation of the Church 75

Part Two: Defence, Definition and Exploration 111
Defenders of the Faith: Justin and Clement 113
Gnosticism and Irenaeus 143
North Africa: Tertullian and Cyprian 173
Meanwhile, in Rome 207
Origen in Alexandria and Caesarea 224

Part Three: Reform and Revolution 267
Diocletian: Reform and Persecution 269
Constantine and the Roman Revolution 289
The Road to Nicaea 309
Conclusion 332

Chronology 342
Dramatis Personae 345
Notes 354
Bibliography 380
Index 383

Illustrations

Map of the Roman Empire in the age of Augustus iv
Map of Constantinople after its foundation by Constantine 351
Genealogy of the Imperial Family 352
Genealogy of the family of Herod the Great 353

Abbreviations

ACO . . . . *Acta conciliorum oecumenicorum:* E Schwartz

CD . . . . *Civitatis Dei:* Augustine

CEP. *Contra epistulam Parmeniani:* Augustine

CCL . . . . *Corpus Christianorum, Latina*

CSEL. . . . . *Corpus scriptorum ecclesasticorum*

GCS . . . . Die Griechische Christliche Schriftsteller

FC. . . . . Christiani Fontes

FOTC . . . . *Fathers of the Church*

HE. . . . . *Historia Ecclesiastica:* Eusebius

PG. . . . . Migne's *Patrologia Graeca*

PL . . . . Migne's *Patrologia Latina*

NAPNF . . . . *Nicene and Post-Nicene Fathers*

SC . . . . *Sources Chretiennes*

TCAH. . . . . *The Cambridge Ancient History*

Part One: The Apostolic Age

CHAPTER 1

The Roman Empire and Judea
in the Age of Augustus

By any stretch of the imagination the story of the growth of the Christian faith from the birth of Jesus, in an obscure part of the Roman Empire, to becoming the faith of the Emperor Constantine and the religion of the Empire is unparalleled in human history. But it is even more exceptional when we consider, in this book, how utterly weak and vulnerable the church was for most of that time: suffering, during these years, intense persecution for long periods of time, and beset continually by false teaching and dissension. The threats of persecution, Gnosticism and then Arianism might well have extinguished the church's witness in the Roman world, but it was able to call upon the courage of an Ignatius or a Polycarp, as well as on the resolute and lucid explanations of the faith by the likes of Irenaeus, Tertullian or Athanasius, to burnish and defend its message of grace, forgiveness and salvation to humankind. These leaders are comparatively well known, but they led a noble army of women and men of whom we know next to nothing, but whose faith prevailed in the most severe testing. Judging by the Catacombs in Rome, this army of saints was sizeable, faithful and brave. The story began in the unlikeliest of ways in a stable or inn in Bethlehem, in or around 4 BC, where the infant Jesus was threatened from birth by the local king, but was welcomed and worshipped by shepherds and Magi alike. This is the story of what happened to belief in Jesus Christ from that time on, and the impact it had on the world.

Jesus was born in or close to 4 BC, and into a world that had been shaped by Augustus Caesar (27 BC–14 AD). Herod also died in 4 BC, but was alive at the time of the birth of Jesus (see Matthew 2:2). The massacre of the innocents commanded by Herod was of children aged two years and younger (Matthew 2:16), and presumably the birth of Jesus occurred some months before Herod gave this command, in which case Jesus' birth would have been at least several months before the death of Herod in 4 BC. Furthermore, it is commonly accepted that the Magi may have arrived in Bethlehem several months after the birth of Jesus. Their arrival precipitated Joseph and Mary's flight to Egypt (Matthew 2:13).

Adding all these facts and projections together, it is not too far-fetched to suppose that the special conjunction of the stars in 7 BC, which may have triggered the Magi's search for a new king, also gives us an approximate date for Jesus' birth. The Magi could well have been Zoroastrian stargazers or astrologers, and their study of the stars was the evidential reason for their mysterious and enthralling journey.[1]

Seemingly contradictory evidence for the date of Jesus's birth is then given by the careful historian Luke, who places the birth after a decree by the Provincial Governor of Syria, Quirinius, who gave an order that the population of Judea should register for taxation in their hometowns (Luke 2:2). From other sources, we know that Quirinius did this in AD 6 after Herod's son Archelaus had been deposed and Syria's governor now directly administered Judea. From these sources we know that Quirinius called for a census for purposes of taxation in AD 6,[2] but if this was the census referred to by Luke it would mean that it did not take place until Herod had been dead for ten years.

In interpreting this inconsistency between Matthew's account, which places Jesus' birth date firmly in Herod the Great's reign, and Luke's account, which is dated by classical sources to AD 6, it is likely that either the census, which had taken place earlier, was wrongly attributed to Quirinius, or that there was an earlier census which had taken place, but which, in the public mind (from which Luke may have gained his facts), had become associated with Quirinius, a man greatly despised by the Jewish population once direct rule over Judea had been established from Syria.

It is thus more likely that Jesus was born around 5/6 BC. His crucifixion took place under Pilate's prefecture, which was from AD 26–36. If Jesus was in his early thirties when crucified, the crucifixion would have taken place in the earlier part of Pilate's unhappy prefecture. Whatever the precise dating, what we may be sure about is that the world that Jesus was born into had been powerfully shaped by Augustus and Herod and by the interlocking and often conflicting cultures of the Jewish and Greco-Roman worlds. Both Augustus and Herod are mentioned in the narratives of Christ's birth; they and their successors were to shape the Apostolic Age to come.

In 5 BC, Augustus had been *Princeps* or Augustus for 22 years. In January 27 BC, the Senate had sought a new title (*cognomen*) to express the authority (*auctoritas*) of Octavian (Augustus' birth name). Debates took place in the Senate in Rome between 13 and 16 January that year, both praising Octavian Caesar for his achievements and seeking a suitable title for him. The word which had to be avoided at all costs was "King", for Rome had turned its back on monarchy after the Tarquins, when in 509 BC their cousin, another Brutus, made the people swear a collective oath that "they would never allow again a single man to reign in Rome".[3] The tradition of the republic, pursued thereafter, remained singularly powerful in the Roman mind, however much Julius Caesar, or previously Sulla, may have suborned it.

A kind of power dance was performed between the Senate and Augustus, in which he was offered ever more powerful titles, much like his adoptive father, Julius Caesar, but which he ostentatiously rejected; only to be offered an equal or greater power, but under a different name. Not for him the titles Dictator or King; he wanted something else. Eventually Senator Plancus, a one-time supporter of Mark Antony, proposed that the title Augustus be given to Octavian. Henceforward, he would be titled Imperator Caesar Augustus *divi filius*. No one had been given such a title before, not even his great uncle Julius Caesar. There was more than a hint of the divine about the phrase *divi filius* (son of God) and a sense of seeking the divine will for Rome, as stated by one of her earliest and most revered poets, Ennius.[4]

These titles displayed the almost unassailable authority Augustus had gained in the years since the assassination of Julius Caesar by Brutus and

Cassius during the Ides of March in 44 BC. Augustus was to reign supreme for a further 41 years till AD 14, by which time he was 76 years old. His sheer longevity in power made his era unique: his age was to Rome what the Victorian age was to Britain, although Augustus' power, unlike that of the British constitutional monarch, was untrammelled.

Augustus's rise to power was partly due to his name and family, partly due to good fortune, and partly due to his calculating use of violence and terror to avenge the death of his adoptive father, Julius Caesar. He was the warlord turned *eminence grise*, the avenging instrument of Mars turned embodiment of the State. But at first his ascendancy was anything but certain. By 44 BC, the events of the previous years had left Rome deeply shaken, facing another period of bloodletting, civil war and uncertainty.

Julius Caesar

Julius Caesar's career was meteoric. He combined extraordinary talent, personal magnetism and charm, brilliance as a general, and utter ruthlessness as a commander with political ambition second to none. Added to this was his lineage, which was of the most purple, linked to an eloquence that never deserted him. He had taken a course of rhetoric from Apollonius Molon of Rhodes, "the greatest living exponent of the art",[5] was both hard—sleeping with his troops in Gaul on frozen ground,[6] and flamboyant, the biggest dandy in town when flaunting his power and bribing his way to the top. He practically seized the honorific post of *pontifex maximus* through bribes.[7]

From the spring of 58 BC, Julius Caesar had had three governorships: one of the northern part of Italy, a second of the Balkans and lastly of southern Gaul. For ten years he was to be both Governor of these vast provinces and Magistrate of Rome, one of the city's chief offices,[8] amassing in the process very great wealth and unlimited freedom of action. His campaigns were on a devastating scale, involving, it is thought, the loss of life of a million men.[9] From the Mediterranean in the south to the Rhine in the north, and from the Alps to Britain, countless tribes had been broken on his sword, but he was not at the end of his ambition. The money he had at his disposal from his campaigns in Gaul was almost as great as the state treasury itself. Suetonius tells us that Caesar exacted an annual tribute of 40 million sesterces.[10] Yet men of equal talent and wealth, Pompey and Crassus, blocked his path to the very top. He looked now for a second consulship, the premier position in the Roman hierarchy, held with one other consul in what was called the *cursus honorum*, the Roman political pecking order of the Republic's offices of state, or the racetrack to the top.[11]

The two other powerful figures in the firmament of Roman power were Pompey and Crassus. In 67 BC, Pompey, then only 23 and a kind of Roman Alexander the Great, had been given a command that embraced the entire Mediterranean. Pompey proceeded to conquer present-day Turkey, and, having defeated King Mithradates VI, took his Pontic Kingdom, which included Armenia (extended in those days to include much of present-day Turkey), and also secured the eastern Mediterranean seaboard and the country of Syria.

Pompey also extended Roman power forcibly into Israel itself. When a civil war developed between the sons of Queen Alexandra Salome, the Hasmonean ruler of Jerusalem, Pompey eventually intervened on the side of Hyrcanus II after Salome's death. After a siege, Pompey took Jerusalem in 63 BC. He entered the Temple and violated the Holy of Holies. He then incorporated Judea into the Empire. Later, in 40 BC, Herod the Great secured from Augustus the right to rule Judea as a client ruler of Rome.

Pompey, like Caesar, had hugely extended the power of the Empire, and together with Crassus and Caesar, sought to dominate Rome. Yet in 50 BC, Crassus, immensely wealthy, but not as victorious militarily as either Pompey or Caesar, sought fame by going to fight a campaign against the Parthians on the eastern edge of the Empire. The Parthians ruled an empire which was a successor to the Persians and which stretched from the Indian Ocean to the Tigris and beyond. Their methods of warfare were anathema to those following the infantry tactics of Rome. Their lightly clad horsemen, swift in advance and retreat, wheeled and darted like their lethal arrows. They were effeminate and unpredictable in comparison with Rome's well-toned masculinity with its cumbersome columns, but were nevertheless deadly and effective.[12] Thus, in 53 BC, on a baking plain in Mesopotamia near the border town of Carrhae, Crassus and his legions were wiped out. Three legions were annihilated, the Eagles—silver representations of the holy bird of Jupiter—were seized and Crassus himself was killed. It was to be one of the worst defeats for the Roman army until Augustus's overconfident commander, Publius Quinctilius Varus, lost three legions in the bogs and woods of Germany between the Elbe and the Rhine in AD 9.[13] Crassus's loss was a body blow to Rome, a grievous shock, but it also left only two *imperators* in the field, both with their sights set on complete authority. In December 50 BC, one of the consuls went to Pompey's villa outside Rome, and, presenting him with a sword, charged him to wield it against Caesar in the interests of the Republic.

Caesar was not prepared to back off, however, and on 10 January 49 BC, together with his legions, he crossed the Rubicon, a small river south of the Alps. For the next four years there was civil war, with its almost infinite cost to the Republic. Cicero could scarcely choose between the two: "I am fond of Curio, a Tribune in support of Caesar, I wish to see Caesar honoured in the manner which is his due, and as for Pompey, I would lay down my life for him—all the same, what really counts with me is the Republic itself ".[14] Cicero was committed to the *res publica*, but unsure how to discern what was best in the conjunction of such warring parties. It was a dilemma faced by many, but the lives of thousands would now be ground down between the millstones of the ambition of these two men. Pompey, cast as the defender of the Republic, left Rome and crossed over to Epirus in central Greece, where he gathered his forces and waited for Caesar.

The battle took place on 8 August 48 BC at Pharsalus in central Greece. Pompey was reluctant to engage Caesar, but the senators with him wanted a fast and crushing victory. Despite much smaller forces, Caesar's superior tactics and hardened legionnaires proved decisive in victory. Pompey was defeated and put to flight. This left Caesar in control of the Empire, but it was a tragic victory.

Looking at the defeated legions at Pharsalus, Caesar reportedly said, "They brought this on themselves. They would have condemned me regardless of all my victories—me Gaius Caesar—had I not appealed to my army for help".[15] But the cries of the Roman wounded and the piles of the Roman dead told another story: a story of fratricide, of civil war and of the bitterest grief. To the remnant of Pompey's army, Caesar showed his celebrated clemency, and in particular to Marcus Brutus, the much-admired senator and ally of Pompey. But although Brutus was spared, he was never to be reconciled. It would be less than four years before he and Cassius plunged their knives into Caesar for betraying the Republic and taking to himself powers that no Roman should possess.

Pompey fled first to Mytilene to meet his wife Cornelia and then on to Egypt, where a renegade Roman on the beach at Alexandria ignominiously murdered him, with the full consent of Ptolemy XIII, who stood watching. "Pompey, drawing his toga over his face with both hands, endured them all [the stab wounds], nor did he say or do anything unworthy, only gave a faint groan".[16] When Caesar arrived in pursuit of Pompey, and was given Pompey's pickled head, he wept. It was no fit end for a great Roman general who had received three Triumphs from his compatriots. Caesar despised the Ptolemies, but nevertheless found consolation in the bed of Cleopatra and in giving her a son, Caesarion.

After a brief respite in Egypt with the allurements of the Nile and Cleopatra, civil war continued for Caesar until 45 BC, but now in Spain. At the end of the conflict Caesar rewarded his army with 24,000 sesterces for each soldier, while the veterans were given land on which to retire, and every citizen was given ten pecks of grain and ten pounds of oil.[17] Caesar also gave Rome great games and spectacles for its entertainment[18] and planned a vast new Temple of Mars. He conducted a new census.[19] He brought the Senate up to strength. But still the question remained: how should he rule? As a king, or as a consul or tribune of the people? What title should he have?

On 15 February 44 BC, a festival called the *Lupercalia* was celebrated, recalling the early days of Rome and how Romulus and Remus were suckled by a she-wolf. The *Luperici*-men, dressed only in loincloths, and among whom was Mark Antony, one of Caesar's chief lieutenants, processed through Rome on a February night. Loyal Mark Antony offered Caesar, who was seated on a golden throne on the Rostra, a symbol of kingship, a diadem entwined in laurel. To great applause Caesar refused it.[20] But still "from that day forward he lay under the odious suspicion of having tried to revive the title of king".[21] Over 60 conspirators now planned his assassination. Among them was Cassius, who complained to Brutus in Shakespeare's *Julius Caesar*, "Why, man, he (Caesar) doth bestride the narrow world, like a colossus, and we petty men walk under his huge legs, and peep about to find ourselves dishonourable graves".[22] Rome was not meant to have such a belittling colossus, so they planned *his* death.

Despite auguries of his impending doom, Caesar continued his programme as usual. Suetonius records how a little bird called a king wren flew into the Assembly Hall of Pompey, carrying a sprig of laurel in its beak, and was pursued by a swarm of birds that tore it to pieces.[23] To the pagan mind such premonitions were hints of a predestined fate. On the day of his assassination Caesar derided Spurinna, the haruspex or soothsayer, as a false prophet. "The ides of March have come," Caesar said to Spurinna. "Aye, they have come but they have not yet gone," replied Spurrina.[24]

On 4 March, Caesar was killed with 23 stab wounds. When Brutus delivered his blow, Caesar said in Greek, "You too my son?"[25] His was, as Shakespeare says in Mark Antony's speech, "the unkindest cut of all".[26] But if the blows were designed to end ambition for "Brutus says he (Caesar) was ambitious",[27] they did not. The assassination inaugurated a further 14 years of civil war, until Mark Antony and Cleopatra lay dead in Alexandria.

Caesar's will was read out soon afterwards in Antony's house. He posthumously and surprisingly appointed Gaius Octavius as his heir, giving him three quarters of his estate and the rest to his sisters and three grandsons. A day was set for his cremation on a large pyre on the Campus Martius. The clothes he was murdered in hung on a pillar above the pyre. Antony said little. A recent decree of the Senate was read out, voting Caesar all human and divine honours. He was made immortal in death, in a way that he had not been allowed in life. Women threw their jewellery onto the funeral pyre. The mob turned on the houses of Brutus and Cassius. A twenty-foot column of Numidian marble was erected in Caesar's memory and on it was inscribed the words, "To the Father of his Country".[28] It is said that Caesar wanted a quick death. The day before his murder he dined with Marcus Lepidus, and the dinner party subject was "the best sort of death". Caesar had said, "Let it come swiftly and unexpectedly". He was 55 years old when he died. On the first day of the funeral games, organised by Octavian, a comet appeared in the sky and remained a week. Almost all of the assassins would be dead within three years, but the unrest and civil war was to last much longer.[29]

Gaius Octavian

Gaius Octavian had a clear task: to avenge the death of his adoptive father, Julius Caesar. He was 18 years old when Caesar was killed and he was to be like the avenging Mars, whose temple he would later build in the heart of Rome, completing that of Julius Caesar, only far more splendidly.

He was born on 23 September 63 BC. His mother, Atia, was married to Senator Gaius Octavius. Her 37-year-old uncle was Julius Caesar, who was doubtless a visitor to their spacious house on the Palatine in Rome. Seven days after the birth of Octavian, on 30 September, a ceremony of purification was held, culminating in sacrifices, to rid the child of any evil influences.[30]

As so often in Rome, the times were tense. Cicero was the consul and ambitious Catiline was once again passed over for that most prestigious office. Joining with other disaffected senators and soldiers, Catiline planned to wrest power for himself and his co-conspirators, but was exposed by Cicero before the Senate, arrested and executed—even though Julius Caesar argued for clemency.[31] In 59 BC, Atia's uncle, Julius Caesar, was made consul and it seemed that family fortunes were in the ascendency, but Caius Octavius, on his way back from a campaign in Macedonia, fell ill and later died in his house in Nola.[32] Octavian was only four. Julius Caesar now had to begin a ten-year absence from Rome which he spent subduing Gaul. Octavian's grandfather, Marcus Atius Balbus, may have died soon after 59 BC, the date of his last public appointment.

At the age of seven, Octavian had begun his education. He would have been assigned to observe a senior male relative; to exercise, ride and train in the Campus Martius; and also to be tutored by a *grammaticus*, learning the Greek and Latin classics by heart. Rome remained restless,

while Pompey and Caesar mostly soldiered abroad. The aristocratic
and highly charismatic figure of Publius Clodius Pulcher sought power
directly from the people of Rome, alternately mesmerising and provoking
them. But other events were brewing which would lead fatefully to civil
war. Octavian was taken from Rome while the strife grew worse. He
stayed outside Rome in the villa of his new stepfather, Phillipus, where
his education continued. Aged 12, he spoke elegantly at his grandmother
Julia's funeral. (Julia was the sister of Julius Caesar.)

Octavian was also given his first rewards by Caesar, and the hint
of greater honours to come. With the defeat of Pompey at Pharsalus,
and the election of Caesar as consul and then dictator in 48, 46 and
44 BC successively, Octavian was drawn increasingly into the limelight.
He was rewarded with ceremonial military honours, and his pleas for
clemency for his friends, who had fought with Pompey, were granted.[33]
But suddenly, with the assassination of his great uncle and patron,
everything changed.

At the time of Caesar's death, Octavian was in Macedonia with the
legions preparing to go on campaign with Julius Caesar, this time to
pacify the Parthians. But two weeks later a letter from his mother arrived,
telling him of Caesar's death. He set out immediately, and by 10 April,
having sailed to Brundisium, arrived back in Rome.[34]

There was deep uncertainty in Rome. Cassius and Brutus kept away
from the Senate, fearing for their safety. Mark Antony was the consul
most in charge; the suffect consul replacing Caesar was Dolabella.
Cicero's was an influential voice in the Senate, counselling moderation,
but wanting above all the supremacy of the *res publica*. Octavian went to
Naples from Rome and took soundings from the veteran soldiers there.
Rome festered and waited. No one wanted chaos. Caesar's legislation had
been confirmed on 17 March.[35] The direction of the future needed to be
set out, and sooner or later a new guiding force must emerge.

Octavian returned to Rome in May to prepare for the funeral games,
which were to be held in July. Antony was already recruiting from among
the veterans, and so too gradually did Octavian from among Julius
Caesar's soldiers, both officers and men. By September, Octavian, now 19,
had recruited 3,000 men, who were once part of the Seventh and Eighth
Legions. He had no shortage of money from his father's will with which

to recruit soldiers. Antony, who had been away from Rome, returned, and tried to persuade newly-arrived legions from Greece to follow him. But he handled them badly, even executing some of their centurions for insubordination. Finally, when these legions, the *Legio Martia* and the Fourth, left Brundisium, they declared for Octavian, or Caesar as they already called him.[36] The myth of the young returning hero, like Achilles from Troy, was still strong in the public mind, and Octavian's name, youth, money, and bearing commended him to the legions as a new Achilles or Aeneas, of whom Virgil would soon write. They would march for him and this willingness was a game changer.

Mark Antony now tried to turn the Senate against Octavian, but the attempt was inconclusive. Instead, he took his soldiers north to Gaul. Meanwhile, Cicero gave tentative backing to Octavian, and the Senate despatched its consuls, Hirtius and Pansa, along with Octavian and his legions and Decimus Brutus, to engage Antony. They did so in a two-day encounter at Mutina (present-day Modena) following a battle at Forum Gallorum a week before on 14 April. The fighting was fierce and in difficult marshy terrain, with no outright winners; the consuls, Hirtius and Pansa, were killed. The armies retreated. Rome felt relief, but in truth the situation was as confused as ever. Cassius and Brutus both had armies in the field, and likewise Antony. Nevertheless, the campaign was the making of Octavian, however slight his overall contribution (Mark Antony accused him of ineffectiveness). He was elected consul at age 19 on 19 August 43 BC, having more than won his spurs. He was formally recognised as the heir to Julius Caesar. The next 16 years would turn that proclamation into a reality, through warfare, terror and the ruthless pursuit of ultimate power.

The Roman Republic once more had a triumvirate: Octavian, Mark Antony and Lepidus—not taking account of forces led by Brutus and Cassius. Purges began, and proscriptions, like those that had taken place under Sulla, a previous dictator, re-occurred. This meant that lists were put up in Rome of those who were proscribed and they were hunted down and murdered if they had not already committed suicide. The most illustrious of those proscribed in these death lists was Cicero, the former consul, who was killed by soldiers commanded by the Triumvirate. Cicero's right hand and head were brought to Rome and nailed to the

Rostra. This was the revenge of Mark Antony in particular.[37] Before these morbid artefacts were pinned to the Rostra for all to see, they were brought to Mark Antony, who at the time was dining with his wife Fulvia, for inspection. Both abused Cicero's memory and scorned his life. Nor was Octavian innocent of such revenge, but "once this [the proscriptions] had been decided upon he carried it out more ruthlessly than either of them".[38] Some were even proscribed simply because they were wealthy, and the Triumvirate needed to pay the troops. This was the "Terror" of the revolution they had set in motion.

The bloodletting and purge completed, Octavian and Mark Antony went east to confront the forces assembled by Brutus and Cassius. Once again an important battle was to be fought in Greece. The Liberators, Brutus and Cassius (the assassins of Caesar), had a very strong force of 20 legions, and cavalry besides some 90,000 troops they had recruited in Asia. They crossed the Hellespont and took up position at Philippi in Macedonia. Octavian and Mark Antony moved their forces from Italy to Apollonia close to the *Via Egnatia* that led to Philippi. They had smaller numbers than the Liberators, some one-third fewer, but Antony was, on the surface anyhow, a confident and swashbuckling leader, at least for the present. The first day's fighting on 3 October ended in stalemate. Octavian was ill, once again incapacitated in a major campaign, and unable to command, giving Brutus and his troops the upper hand. Yet both armies, after fierce fighting, disengaged to strengthen their positions. When fighting recommenced on 23 October, the Triumvirs held better ground. Octavian's soldiers, many trained by Julius Caesar, steadily overwhelmed the Liberators' less experienced troops. Soon they were put to rout. Brutus, sensing disaster, took his life. Octavian considered his adoptive father avenged.

Soon relations between Octavian and Mark Antony deteriorated. Octavian wrote ribald poetry about Fulvia and Antony's sexual relations.[39] But Fulvia died in 40 BC and Mark Antony married Octavian's sister, Octavia. An uneasy truce existed between them, while the threat of Sextus Pompeius, Pompey's son, grew. He was based in Sicily, had strong naval power and enforced a food blockade of Italy. A temporary halt to the blockade was called through the Treaty of Misenum, in return for an amnesty over further proscriptions. War with Sextus broke out again in

37 BC. Caesar had rebuilt his navy and hired some ships from Antony's own fleet. In Agrippa, Octavian found a very capable commander, an engineer, a loyal lieutenant, and much later a son-in-law married to Julia. Naval engagements followed, and with difficulty Octavian landed legions on Sicily and, despite some very close calls, defeated Sextus with Agrippa's support.

Octavian was inexorably, if not entirely smoothly, eliminating his rivals. At the same time he had found a woman who would nurture and support him for the rest of his life. Her name was Livia and he was deeply in love with her. Ironically, given his later legislation against adultery and his exacting treatment of his daughter Julia, Livia was at the time another man's wife, and what is more, pregnant with her husband's second child when she left him; no doubt commanded to do so by Augustus, who always took what he wanted. Livia was Claudian by blood, but descended from the more patrician side of the family. She was more prestigious and talented than her husband, Claudius Nero. Livia's father had fought with the Liberators, had been proscribed, and had taken his own life.[40] Her first child was Tiberius Claudius Nero, the future emperor, and her second child, born after her separation from Claudius Nero, was Drusus, born in 38 BC. Livia's husband had also rebelled against the Triumvirate, causing the family (including Tiberius) to escape to Greece, where they hid in Sparta, narrowly escaping capture. After the amnesty effected by the Treaty of Misenum, they returned to Rome. Their lands were confiscated and they were vulnerable. Livia was pregnant, young and beautiful, and she caught Caesar's eye. Octavian was married to Scribonia, already his second wife. Scribonia was pregnant and later that year gave birth to a daughter, the self-willed and latterly wayward Julia, Octavian's only child. In 39 BC, Octavian and Livia were betrothed after her husband obligingly divorced her, which one could do under Roman law simply by saying "take your things for yourself". Octavian and Livia were to reign and live together for 53 years. No other imperial couple could match them for longevity, mutuality or like-mindedness. Theirs proved a formidable and supremely powerful partnership.

If Octavian's emotional and interior life was settled by his love for and marriage to Livia in 38 BC, his imperium or rule was soon to be supremely established. The next eight years would see him deal with

Sextus Pompey, campaign successfully in Illyricum against the Dalmatae, and finally turn on his rival Mark Antony in that final lair of cornered contenders, Alexandria. Mark Antony had sought to reverse the defeat of Crassus against the Parthians, but his campaign had faltered and then failed. His Armenian allies let him down and the Roman columns were once again harried and rendered helpless by the Parthian mounted archers. By contrast, Octavian's campaign in Illyricum was successful: he retook previously captured standards, took much plunder, and returned triumphant to Rome. He was given a Triumph and in 33 BC was elected consul for a second time. His authority was now well established. At the same time, great building projects were begun in Rome: a new Forum; a rebuilt Senate House; a new temple to Venus; a water system that boasted 700 new cisterns, 500 fountain heads and 130 water towers; an aqueduct named after Octavian's daughter Julia, and a giant mausoleum—all masterminded by the ever loyal and supremely talented Agrippa, a kind of military Brunel of his age. Together the "collective grandeur and sheer scale of the projects" was prodigious.[41]

In the summer of 32 BC, after a barrage of propaganda, and knowing such a declaration would encompass Antony also, the Roman Republic formally declared war on Cleopatra. Agrippa began to harry Mark Antony's bases in Greece, since he was Cleopatra's ally in arms. Antony trusted to his large navy and army, but they were all too vulnerable to the lightning attacks planned by Agrippa on Mark Antony's forces. Agrippa was able to blockade Mark Antony's fleet in its harbour at Actium in northwest Greece with his own well-schooled fleet, fresh from defeating Sextus Pompey. The fleets engaged, and apart from some 70 or 80 ships, which broke through with Cleopatra and Antony, Mark Antony's navy and thousands of troops were lost.

Shakespeare captures Mark Antony's infatuation with Cleopatra, which was said to have cramped his martial skills and blunted his strategic capability, thus:

> Egypt (Cleopatra), thou knew'st too well
> My heart was to thy rudder tied by the strings,
> And thou shouldst tow me after: o'er my spirit
> Thy full supremacy thou knew'st, and that

Thy beck might from the bidding of the gods
Command me . . .

Antony and Cleopatra, Act III Scene II

Defeated at Actium, the couple fled to Alexandria to await their fate. Antony committed suicide, but it was a lingering death. Cleopatra took poison atop her tomb, which was filled with treasure like that of an Egyptian pharaoh. Even at the last Cleopatra considered switching her allegiance to Octavian. She pleaded with the victor in a final, and perhaps only, meeting.[42] She was not an enemy of Rome, more a chancer and survivor. It was not to be, however. Octavian had no use for her and he needed her money. The venom from asps took its course and despite a doctor's attempt (perhaps supplied by Octavian) to assuage the effect of the poison, she died. Caesarion, Julius Caesar's son by Cleopatra, was also killed. Octavian stayed on to gather the treasure and put his troops to work to restore the waterways of the Nile Delta so that it would flourish again as a corn bin, but now for the Empire. Famine in Rome was to be avoided at all costs and with foresight Octavian made Egypt, along with Carthage, the breadbasket of the Empire.

Octavian was now triumphant. All his rivals were vanquished; he was master in the stable house of *his* Empire. "The underlying motive for every campaign was to avenge Caesar and keep his decrees in force".[43] Caesar had been avenged, but more than that, Octavian was unassailable. He had defeated Sextus Pompey and Antony, and had stripped Lepidus of power (in 36 BC). In 30 BC, he was voted in for his fourth consulship, which was now virtually an annual occurrence. In 29 BC, he was awarded a triple Triumph in Rome for campaigns against Brutus and Antony in Illyricum. Horace, who had taken part in the Battle of Philippi and was now tethered firmly to his patron Maecenas—Octavian's friend and Minister of the Arts but without portfolio—longed for the peace that now broke out. Horace then cried: "Let the drinking begin".

No one could remember a time when the Republic had not been threatened by violence: "So much conflict and death had battered their political ideals, dislocated old ties of friendship and alliance, and even curbed the aristocrats' instinctive ambition. The senators, like the rest of the population, wanted peace more than they wanted anything else".[44]

Octavian was just 34 years old. The Augustan age had begun in all but name. Two years later, in 27 BC, the Augustan age began in earnest with the conferral by the Senate of the name Augustus on Octavian.

The Age of Augustus

For the next 41 years Augustus and Livia would hold the reins of power. The years of bloodshed were over, provided Augustus's authority was not put to the test. Instead, the age of the arts, construction, consolidation, censuses, Augustan morality and family life and, for the most part, military supremacy in the north, near east and even in Parthia, was assured. The tag *Pax Romana* was a reality. This rolled-out authority, which touched every area of Roman existence, was now based on Augustus's unquestioned command of the legions. He commanded 60 legions (this was later reduced to about 27), near on a quarter of a million troops. He also commanded untold wealth: so much cash was injected into the economy that the historian Cassius Dio said interest rates in Rome fell on his return from 12 to 4 per cent.[45]

The Augustan age was marked by a number of characteristics: the formation of a court based around the Emperor's family, and the search for a successor proclaimed by the Emperor. This strategy was made possible by the ancient Roman power of *paterfamilias*, whereby complete control of the family went to the senior male therein; by the choreography of power between Emperor and Senate in which the Senate vested power in the Emperor, who gave the semblance of power to the Senate along with the illusion that it was still the guardian of the *Res Publica*; by the flourishing of the arts, especially literature, building work and theatres under the patronage of the Emperor and his court; by the formation of a moral culture underpinned by the values of the Emperor and the court; and lastly, through complete control of the army and provincial administration which created the lasting shape of the Empire until its implosion in the fifth century. We begin with the army and the way it was controlled by the Emperor.

By the end of the civil war, the army was about 60 legions in strength. In the imperial period, a legion consisted of 4,800 soldiers divided into ten cohorts of 480 each, and in each cohort there were six centurions commanding 80 men each. In the Augustan army there were some 1,560 centurions.[46] As at the end of any prolonged war, the army was greater than was needed for normal security and so would be reduced to about 27 legions. Augustus, as he was from 27 BC, and during his seventh consulship, paid off the veterans. Keeping them favourably disposed towards him was an important part of his strategy in order that a usurper later on might not suborn them. To this end, every adult male citizen was given 400 sesterces. Furthermore, 1,000 sesterces went to each of the 120,000 veterans who were established in veteran colonies around the Empire and Italy.[47] To be a veteran, one had to fulfil 16 years of service.[48] In Italy alone, according to Suetonius, Augustus personally founded 28 veteran colonies.[49] Thereafter, the dispositions of his forces were such that the legions were distributed in various provinces, but especially on the borders of the Rhine and in Syria and the East, which continued for generations to be flashpoints of the Empire, facing as they did the German tribes and the Parthians, as well as disaffected Jews and Syrians. One fleet was stationed at Misenum, in the Bay of Naples. Augustus garrisoned the Praetorian Guard in Rome under the command of the Prefect of Rome, like Sejanus during the reign of Tiberius. The Praetorian Guard was made up of German soldiers amongst others, until the defeat of the legions by the German tribes under Varus, at which point they were no longer welcome or trusted.[50] In all, Augustus could count on about 130,000 soldiers to police and defend the Empire. It was a relatively small number of forces to defend such a vast area, and in some areas, such as between the Rhine and the Elbe, its size had to be increased at great cost. But given the discipline and traditions of the legions, they were still the finest fighting machines that existed. Nevertheless, the raw power of the German tribes and the tactics of the Parthian mounted archers remained a constant threat.

The administration of the Empire depended on a number of regional centres of power, the revival of various institutions after the years of civil war, the flourishing of trade in a new *Pax Romana*, and the increasing power of Rome over more stable provinces. The Empire was subject to a census overseen by the ever-active Agrippa. When completed, the census indicated a grand total of 4,063,000 citizens; their property and status were duly recorded, which was an extraordinary administrative achievement, predating the Domesday Book by a thousand years.[51] The Senate was both slimmed down and given renewed influence, but remained firmly under the authority of the Emperor. The Senate increasingly became the preserve of the very wealthy, with qualification for entry increased to ownership of a million sesterces. Egypt, Gaul, Syria and the Spanish Peninsula were put under the charge of the Emperor, since all these areas were far from settled. Legates were sent where Caesar could not go himself.[52] Augustus was himself to campaign in Spain for the best part of two years from 26–25 BC, ensuring Roman power against tough adversaries. Once again, he was seriously ill, but survived to be voted another Triumph by Rome, which he declined. "The effective declaration that he had no need of personal glory since he had already won so much was more powerful than yet another parade through the heart of Rome".[53] More honours and prestige were to come Augustus's way when the Eagles, taken when Crassus was defeated by the Parthians, were returned to Rome, following a general amnesty between Parthia and Rome and King Phraates IV and Augustus.[54] Nothing accorded Augustus more honour than their return, coins were minted and a triumphal arch was constructed in celebration of the repatriation of these precious symbols of Roman power. Nor was Augustus lacking in writers to further bolster his reputation.

The Augustan age was a golden age for Roman and Latin literature. The beginning of Octavian's ascendancy coincided with the demise of Cicero, the greatest of Rome's statesmen and writer-philosophers. He was the one who made Plato known to the Latin mind and whose works were to have such a profound effect on many, not least Augustine of Hippo, whose reading of *Hortensius* when still in Carthage helped him turn his back on the Manichee religion.[55] The *impresario* of the arts during Augustus's long reign was Augustus's close confidant and minister, Maecenas. Although Maecenas never took on Roman magistracy, nor became a member of the Senate, he nevertheless had remarkable freedom of action due to the implicit support of Augustus. He often deputised for Augustus when the latter was away on campaigns, and his wealth was such that he was well able to support talented and aspiring writers. It was

Maecenas who took Horace into his circle after the Battle of Philippi, when Horace fought for Brutus. (Maecenas had met Brutus earlier, on a visit to Athens, where Horace was then studying art at the Academy.) Horace was the son of a freed slave who had managed to own property and estates in Venusia in northeast Italy. He was a talented and versatile poet—both charming and lofty in style—and his iambic poetry, odes and epodes were to comprise some of the most graceful and appealing of all Latin poems. Alongside Homer, Virgil was the great poet of the age. He too was drawn into Maecenas's circle and encouraged to write poetry. The *Georgics* chronicled in poetic form life on the farm, perhaps reminiscent of Virgil's early life spent on his family estates in northern Italy, before these lands were confiscated by Augustus for the purposes of founding a veteran colony. Virgil's most famous piece was the epic poem *The Aeneid*, which tells of the return from Troy of Aeneas, whose descendants, Romulus and Remus, would found Rome. The poem encapsulates many of the themes of the Augustan age: the re-affirmation of the foundation of Rome; the piety of Aeneas, who put the greater destiny of his people before his own wishes by leaving for his greater calling and the Carthaginian Queen Dido, who had fallen passionately in love with him. Modelled on Homer's *Illiad*, the poem reveals, as Homer did, the reality and necessity of war, but also its awful cost.[56] "Less gregarious than the *bon viveur* Horace, Virgil spent much of his time closeted away on one of his estates, tinkering with the poem and modifying or rejecting line after line".[57] In 19 BC, he accompanied Augustus to Athens, but caught a fever and died. He was 52 years old. Virgil, Horace Lucius Varus and Propertius were part of this golden age of poets. One other younger contemporary, who marched to a different drum, or indeed, who strolled to a more swooning theme, was the poet Ovid.

If Virgil pointed to the cost and art of war in the context of an epic and heroic journey, Ovid wrote about the art of love in *Ars Amatoria*, and about the means of seduction and the adventures of the pagan gods in *Metamorphoses*. If Virgil was in keeping with the more hypocritical piety of the Augustan age, Ovid was far more of a free spirit. In the end he was sent into exile by express command of Augustus. The reasons for this have perplexed scholars for ages, but it could well be that, having in 18 BC passed the Julian Marriage Laws that punished adultery in the cause of producing stable marriages and a higher birth rate among the equestrian class, Augustus felt Ovid's writing did not encourage fidelity or productivity. He was thus banished in AD 8 to the isolated Black Sea town of Tomis, where he remained until his death in AD 17 or 18. He yearned for the sophistication and stimulation of Rome, he pined for his third wife who was left in Italy, and he wrote of his deep sadness and isolation in his final work *Tristia*. He was out of kilter with the morals of the age, which had been designed if not exemplified by Augustus, whose own family life was fraught with the very pitfalls against which he tried to legislate.

The family of Julius Caesar was to dominate the life of Rome and the Empire for about 120 years. More than most, the family spawned a rash of divorces, adoptions, jealousies, triumphs, murders, rivalries, conspiracies, banishments, suicides and cruelties. It was a twisted tale of machinations, victories and tragedies, which we must briefly tell as the backdrop to a contrasting way of life exhibited by another king, one born in poverty in Bethlehem, whose own family of disciples would come to change the world.

As we have seen, Julius Caesar made Octavian his heir.[58] Octavian followed the way of many noble families in seeking dynastic advantage and political influence through marriage. Suetonius tells us that Octavian first cemented his connection with Mark Antony by marrying Antony's stepdaughter, Claudia—the daughter of Fulvia's first marriage to Publius Clodius.[59] The marriage did not last. Octavian, well known in his early years for his many relationships, for which Antony lampooned him in a famously ribald way, divorced Claudia, who was anyhow barely of marriageable age. Octavian, who had quarrelled with his mother-in-law, Fulvia, divorced Claudia to marry Scribonia (who had already been married to a consul by whom she had a child).

Although Scribonia was herself of noble birth and well connected, when the vulnerable but beautiful Livia, who came from one of the most prestigious families of the Republic, arrived in Rome following her escape from Greece, she proved irresistible to Octavian. She was blue-blooded, beautiful and not yet 20. The chemistry between them was such that they both quickly divorced (or in the case of Livia, was divorced by her husband, Tiberius Nero). Both women were already pregnant. Scribonia gave birth to Julia and Livia to her second son Drusus (38 BC), whose older brother by four years was Tiberius. Livia had given birth to Tiberius when just 16 and now she was only 20 when she married for the second time.

In the end it was Scribonia and Livia's children by their previous husbands who were to provide the heirs in the house of Caesar, as in turn their children and grandchildren were adopted by Octavian. Although Octavian and Livia were lovers and their marriage was the one around which the Empire was built, they were childless (the only child they had died soon after birth). As with the Tudors in sixteenth-century England, the problem of succession became the critical factor in the administration of the Empire, which had become a monarchy in all but name.

The search for an heir was attended by tragedy. Augustus's only daughter, by his second wife Scribonia, was Julia. Julia was high-spirited, sophisticated, profligate and promiscuous. Octavian (or Augustus), alternately spoiled and punished her, goaded by Livia, who was a scheming and contemptuous stepmother. At the age of 14, Julia was married to Marcus Claudius Marcellus, but after his death in suspicious circumstances Augustus arranged her marriage to Agrippa, who was 25 years older than her. Julia was then only 18 years old. While married to Agrippa, who was Augustus's faithful and loyal army and navy commander, chief civic engineer and public works manager, Julia seemed contained. She had five children by him in seven years: two sons, Gaius and Lucius, who were duly adopted by Augustus, as well as two daughters, including Agrippina, later to become the wife of Germanicus, the darling of Rome, and a third son, Agrippa Postumus. In 11 BC, when she was 27 and after the death of Agrippa, Julia was forced to marry Tiberius, the older son of Livia. At last Livia had the dynastic marriage of her choice, uniting her eldest son with Augustus's only daughter. In order for this to happen, Tiberius was commanded to divorce his wife, Vipsania, whom he loved. Julia despised the moody and taciturn Tiberius. Not surprisingly, the marriage did not work. Julia lived an increasingly dissolute life with many lovers, famously saying, when accused of being unfaithful to Agrippa: "I only take on passengers after the cargo-hold is fully loaded".[60] Tiberius longed to see his former wife, whom he had been banned from seeing. Tiberius and Julia had no children.

As the years went by, the question of an heir became more pressing. Julia had had three sons by Agrippa. The older two, Gaius and Lucius, were adopted by Augustus and brought up in his household. They were capable and talented young men. Yet after the death of their father, Agrippa, in 12 BC, and the failing marriage of their mother to the resentful Tiberius, they fell increasingly under the influence of Augustus and Livia. In 9 BC, Tiberius's beloved brother Drusus suffered wounds that became gangrenous, and despite a heroic ride by Tiberius to reach him on the borders of Germany, across hundreds of miles of virtually unconquered territory, Drusus died.[61] Tiberius, worn down by soldiering, depressed by the loss of Vipsania, and seeking solitude and opportunity for reflection and academic study, refused any further commands or involvement with Augustus's plans and, to the horror of Augustus and Livia, went into self-imposed exile on Rhodes. Further tragedy was to follow. With the arrival of the laws against adultery, enacted by the Senate in 18 BC at the instigation of Augustus, who sought to regulate marriage and increase the birth rate among the nobility, Julia herself became vulnerable to arrest because of her liaisons. So it was that she was arrested in 2 BC for adultery and banished to a small island, Pandateria, off the coast of Italy. It was virtually a prison, being no longer or wider than two kilometres. She was forbidden male company and wine; nor could she see her children. Worse was to come. In AD 2, her second son Lucius died of sickness in Gaul, when only 15 years old.[62] Then, two years later, his older brother Gaius, the apple of the Emperor's eye and his heir, died of wounds inflicted by an assassin while fighting the Armenians. His wounds also turned gangrenous and he died on 21 February AD 4. The news broke "like a thunderclap" in Rome.[63] Augustus reluctantly made Tiberius his heir: the stolid, conservative, moody and reclusive soldier who preferred army tents to the sophisticated society of Rome. Not given to play-acting, nor able to recognise a joke if he heard one, Tiberius would at first bring uncertainty, then resentment, and at last revulsion to the hearts of Romans. As Augustus himself said of Tiberius, "Poor Rome, due to be ground by such slow moving jaws".[64]

In AD 2, after eight years on Rhodes, Tiberius returned to Rome in time for the banishment of Julia. In AD 10, he once again took up arms against the Germans, and after a Triumph in Rome, was on hand when

Augustus weakened and died in his villa at Nola, near Naples. Augustus was 75 years, 10 months and 26 days old.[65] The coffin was taken from Nola to Rome, travelling at night to avoid the August heat. Escorted by Lictors dressed in black, and with a military guard, the coffin took two weeks to reach the "eternal city". Sometime during the cortege's slow procession, a centurion galloped up to report that what Caesar had commanded had been done.[66] The youngest son of Julia, Agrippa Postumus, in exile first in Sardinia and then in Planasias, had been murdered. The succession was to be Claudian after all, that is, from Livia's great family, although she was adopted into Augustus's family in his will. It was probably at her instigation that Postumus had been killed. The Senate met following the Emperor's cremation and, on 17 September AD 14, Augustus was declared a god and Tiberius his successor.

Judea

Some years before, in Herod's kingdom and around 5 BC, another king was born in Bethlehem. In a little over 300 years his followers would turn the world upside down. If Augustus and the *Pax Augusta* set the scene internationally for the birth of Christ, Herod and his family were responsible for the local political climate in Judea. Judea was a multi-layered political, religious and cultural society with complex origins, diverse connections and a religious life quite distinct from anything else in the Roman Empire. It was a Jewish, Hellenic and Roman mix.

Judea was the ancient homeland of the Jews, but their national life had been chequered, to say the least. In about 440 BC, under Ezra the scribe, and Nehemiah the re-builder of the ancient walls of Jerusalem, Jewish life in Jerusalem had begun anew. The Northern Kingdom had been re-settled by the Assyrians (see 2 Kings 17:24–41), leading to an ethnic and religious mix in what came to be called Samaria, which was populated by hybrid Samaritans. Because of their diversity and religious "impurity", Samaritans were despised by the Jews of Judea, as is made clear in several of the gospel stories (see John 4:9 and Luke 10:25–42).

Later, Samaritans would only be specifically included in the church by a sovereign act of the Spirit (Acts 1:8; Acts 8:14–17).

If Assyrian resettlement of the Northern Kingdom of Israel had led to its ethnic and religious impurity, other nations from the fourth century BC would trample over Judea, subjecting its people to various degrees of occupation. Alexander the Great is reported to have visited the city after his conquest of Gaza in 332 BC.[67] The whole of the Near East would come under Greek influence and power and, in the carving up of these territories, Judea would form part of the Ptolemaic section of the Greek Empire. It was Ptolemy, one of Alexander's principal generals, who deported thousands of Jews to Egypt, following the wars between the local inhabitants and his forces. These Jews were settled in Alexandria. His successor Ptolemy II favoured the Jews and freed thousands of Jewish slaves and encouraged the Jewish High Priest to send the Jewish Tanakh (a Hebrew acronym for the Law, the Prophets and the Writings) to the Alexandrian community for translation into Greek. It was this translation, by the supposed 70 scholars, that became known as the *Septuagint*. Furthermore, it was this translation that became a cornerstone of the Jewish scriptures and eventually the Christian Bible, leading to its dissemination throughout the Greek and then the Roman world.[68]

Ptolemaic sovereignty over Jerusalem was not to last. Joseph the Tobiad, reportedly a descendant of Zadok the Priest and a client ruler of Jerusalem, was confronted by a new force in the Near East.[69] This new military star in the person of the Seleucid King Antiochus III defeated Joseph the Tobiad and the Ptolemaic Empire, taking control of the city. Antiochus was popular with the Jews. He promised to repair the Temple, to repopulate the city, and to give them autonomy in their government. Simon the High Priest took over control of the city as High Priest. He was a priest-prince, and under his aegis the city thrived, but again not for long. Antiochus IV, who was a Nero to his father's Augustus, checked by the growing influence of Rome in the West after the defeat of Hannibal, expanded east to take easy pickings from the treasury of the Temple in Jerusalem. Antiochus IV's ambitions were great. He secured victory over the Ptolemaic Empire, and by 170 BC had conquered Egypt. Jerusalem rebelled under the leadership of Jason and his ally, Hyrcanus the Tobiad

Prince from Jordan, but Antiochus IV or Epiphanes (as he was called) retook Jerusalem, deported 10,000 Jews, entered the Holy of Holies, desecrated the Temple and stole its holy and precious artefacts.[70]

When an old priest called Mattathias, father of five sons, was called upon to sacrifice to Antiochus in a village south of Jerusalem, it was the spark for resistance, which began the uprising led by the Maccabees (literally Latin for hammer/s). By 164 BC, Judah, the third of the five sons, had conquered all of Judea and Jerusalem apart from the newly built Seleucid fortress called the Acra. War continued for 20 years between the Seleucids and the Maccabee brothers: first Judah the Hammer, then Jonathan the Diplomat—who sought to play off the Romans and the Ptolemies against the Seleucids—and finally Simon. In 141 BC, Simon captured the Seleucid fortress, Acra, in Jerusalem. Simon was successful until assassinated by his son-in-law,[71] whereupon his third son, John, took up the cause of the Maccabees. John's second son, Alexander, succeeded him in what had become by then a Greek-Jewish kingdom. Alexander's two sons, Hyrcanus II and Aristobulus II, would fight for the crown. Their mother Salome asked for the help of Pompey The Great, the new power in the region. Pompey intervened in Jerusalem, destroying its fortifications, abolishing the monarchy, breaking down the Maccabean kingdom and appointing Hyrcanus as High Priest with Antipater of Idumea (the former territory of the biblical Edomites, many of whom had converted to Judaism under Hyrcanus) as his Chief Minister. Antipater's son Herod married (among at least ten others) Mariamme, the granddaughter of Hyrcanus II. We know him as Herod the Great.

Herod the Great

Herod's rise to power depended on the support of the *Princeps* in Rome, but after the murder of Julius Caesar and the formation of the Triumvirate of Octavian, Lepidus and Mark Antony, it was some time before it was clear who was in the ascendancy. Antony was the Roman Commander in the East, and thus closest geographically to Herod.

Naturally, Herod pinned his hopes on Mark Antony's star, while at the same time seeking to eliminate a Maccabean pretender to the throne of Judea—Jonathan, Mariamme's older brother. Herod, now married to Jonathan's sister Mariamme, plotted Jonathan's murder. He invited him to his palace in Jericho and, while he was swimming in Herod's pleasure pools at night, Herod's henchmen drowned him.[72] News of Jonathan's death was reported to Cleopatra and Antony, who invited Herod to Syria, intending to assassinate him. Herod survived the encounter, however, as well as a later meeting in 34 BC, when both Antony and Cleopatra came to Jerusalem after a campaign against the Parthians.

For all Herod's kow-towing to Antony and Cleopatra, it was becoming clear that Octavian was gaining in strength. After Antony and Cleopatra's defeat at Actium and their later suicides in Alexandria, Herod realised he must settle with Octavian if he was to have any power in Judea. At a fateful meeting with Octavian on the island of Rhodes, he asked Octavian to consider not whose friend he had been (i.e., Antony's), but what kind of friend he had proved to be. On this basis Octavian accepted him and appointed him as a client ruler of Rome in Judea, as well as of swathes of Jordan, Syria and Lebanon.[73] Extraordinarily, Herod was to become a close friend of both Agrippa and Octavian.

Next to Augustus, Herod would become the greatest builder in the Empire. He rebuilt the Maccabean Palace opposite the Temple, which became known as the citadel, and called one of its towers after his executed wife, Mariamme. Outside Jerusalem he constructed a new artificial harbour at Caesarea. He built a new city at Sebaste—to be called Sebasteni—where many of his veteran soldiers were settled.[74] The region was later a recruiting ground for Roman soldiers, and the soldiers who executed Jesus were almost certainly drawn from there.

The most famous of all Herod's building projects was the rebuilding of the Second Temple. A thousand priests were trained as builders. The stones used to build the Temple were massive, with one stone in the tunnels beneath the Temple weighing 600 tons.[75] Herod created a three-acre platform held up by these huge foundation stones, which were built onto the rock below. The Court of the Gentiles opened onto the Court of Women, which in turn opened onto the Court of Israel, and finally the Court of Priests. Within the Court of Priests stood the sanctuary, the

Holy of Holies, where the sacrifices were performed. It was within these precincts that Jesus taught, and where he was brought as an infant for his circumcision and presentation (Luke 2:21, 22–40). When the Temple was complete, Herod presented for sacrifice 300 oxen.[76] He had reached the apogee of his power, but the internal divisions of his family and his gargantuan appetite for power, sex and food proved fatal.

During his reign, Herod paid numerous visits to Rome to maintain his relationship with Augustus and keep his source of power fresh and strong. He sent his sons to be educated in Rome.[77] He gained the support of Augustus in obtaining shipments of grain from Egypt in a time of famine in the 20s BC. He went to meet Agrippa and Augustus whenever they were travelling in the East. In 15 BC, Agrippa and Julia, his new wife and the daughter of Augustus, visited Jerusalem. Yet despite all this patronage from the imperial family, the cracks in his own family could not be papered over. Princes Alexander and Aristobulus, the two sons of Mariamme—Herod's wife who was executed on Herod's orders for conspiring against him—could not forgive him for his treatment of their mother. Then a third son by his first wife Doris, Antipater, was equally embittered by his father's neglect.

When Augustus was asked to judge between them, as to who should succeed Herod, he attempted a reconciliation between all three and Herod. Herod then decided that all three should share the kingdom. The legacy of Herod's family life was not so easily smoothed over, however. The Maccabean side of the family were in mortal struggle with Herod's Idumean side: thus Alexander and Aristobulus were pitted against Antipater, Salome (Herod's sister) and Doris (Herod's first, but divorced, wife). A conspiracy by Alexander to kill Antipater was uncovered, whereupon the two brothers were arraigned for trial in Beirut. Sentenced to death, Alexander and Aristobulus were taken back to Judea and garrotted. Antipater became Herod's heir, but died in 4 BC, leaving the kingdom to progeny of Herod's third wife, Malthace: Archelaus the Ethnarch, who ruled in Judea but only until AD 6, and Herod Antipas (the Tetrarch of Galilee and Perea).

In 4 BC, Herod died, having only recently heard of the threat of another king in Bethlehem, then only a few weeks or months old. Herod's death was as grotesque as much of his life: "His body started to ooze clear fluid, he could scarcely breathe, a vile stench emanated from him, and his genitals swelled grotesquely until his penis and scrotum burst out into a suppurating gangrene that then gave birth to a seething mass of worms".[78] Eighteen years later, in much more peaceful circumstances, Augustus died in AD 14 near Naples, and his heir Tiberius Claudius Nero succeeded him.

The Age of Tiberius

It had been a long and winding road to Tiberius's eventual succession. The previously adopted sons of Augustus, Gaius and Lucius (the children of Julia and Agrippa) had already died—young, popular and deeply mourned by Rome. Then, with Postumus, the youngest son of Julia and Agrippa, still surviving, and hence a possible heir, Livia turned her husband's heart against the young boy, first banishing him to exile on the island of Planasia, and then, in order to prevent his succession, having him murdered when Augustus died.

Tiberius now fulfilled his mother Livia's ambition of having a Claudii on the Emperor's throne. Her oldest son ruled the Empire, but it was not a role he discharged easily. Reading out Augustus's will in the Forum he broke down and handed the document over to his son Drusus to finish.[79] Not for Tiberius the insouciant enquiry made by Augustus on his deathbed: "Have I played my part in the farce of life creditably enough?"[80] For Tiberius, the business of being Emperor was not a charade or a piece of enacted theatre, but the serious fulfilment of the values of the Roman Republic, only now in the age of Emperors. Tiberius's role became more demanding when, on 17 September AD 14, he and his adoptive father were declared *divi filius*, although Tiberius studiously avoided being called divine. In response, Tiberius addressed the Senate to say that he wanted to live like a private citizen.

Apart from the years of seclusion which Tiberius spent on the island of Rhodes (6 BC–AD 2), he proved an exacting and demanding general. He conducted campaigns in Pannonia (12–9 BC), then in Germany (9–7 BC).

Further campaigns in Germany were to follow, not least in reversing the disastrous loss of the legions under Quinctilius Varus in AD 9. Tiberius was to be Emperor for 23 years until AD 37. His reign can be divided into two contrasting halves. The first ten years he took the path of the dutiful Emperor, seeking to keep to the values of the Republic, but in the new age of imperial power. He decreased the power of the plebs and increased that of the Senate.[81] He was happy to bask in the reflected limelight of his nephew and adopted son, Germanicus, his brother Drusus's oldest son. Germanicus was the darling of the Roman populace. Like Absalom, he had gorgeous locks, was a brilliant and inspiring general, and gained his spurs and a Triumph in AD 17 after campaigning on the Rhine. Furthermore, he wrote poetry in Athens and attended lectures there on his way to the East in AD 17. He was devoted to his wife Agrippina, who travelled with him to Germany and then to the East. She gave birth on the island of Lesbos to her youngest, Agrippina II, who was later the Emperor Claudius's wife and the mother of Nero. Agrippina was of fiery and martial spirit, and had reportedly rallied the Roman troops in Germany to her husband's cause. Tacitus, recalling the moment when she rallied the troops to hold a bridge over the Rhine, wrote: "A woman of heroic spirit, she assumed during those days the duties of a general, and distributed clothes or medicine among the soldiers, if they were destitute or wounded".[82] She was the youngest of Agrippa and Julia's children.

The early success of Tiberius's reign was soon overshadowed by tragic events. In AD 19, Germanicus died of illness in Antioch, reportedly cursed at the behest of the jealous Prefect of Syria, Calpurnius Piso. Later, the Senate in Rome tried Piso, but one night, after sending his wife to bed, he committed suicide in his dressing room. Agrippina had by then arrived with the urn of Germanicus's ashes at Brundisium on the toe of Italy, now the focus of Rome's shattered hopes. Tacitus records that when she "descended from the vessel with her two children, clasping the funeral urn, with eyes riveted to the earth, there was a universal groan".[83] Sincerely mourning and heartbroken, she nevertheless knew how to play the part of the grieving and wronged widow to maximum effect, while Tiberius held himself in remote and stoic indifference to scenes of grief. She was accompanied by a weeping following of mourners back to a distraught and grieving Rome. Then, in AD 23, Tiberius's own son, Drusus, died. The earlier aspirations of Tiberius to be "worthy of my forbears, careful of the Senate's interests, steadfast in danger, and fearless of such resentment as I may incur in serving the public good" now foundered.[84] With no wife, since Julia had been banished and then virtually starved to death by her resentful mother-in-law, Livia, and for whom Tiberius had no regard anyway, given her promiscuous life[85], and separated from Vipsania, the one he truly loved years before, his emotional and political life became more and more disjointed, his pleasures more and more exploitative of others and his frame of mind a mixture of abandonment and guilt.

In AD 27 he retired to the island of Capri, hardly ever returning to Rome, and relying on the scheming and capricious Praetorian Prefect Sejanus to manage affairs there. It was a fatal and fateful decision. With so much power and so little business, he surrounded himself with young boys and girls from the equestrian class who became his playthings: some were trained to swim between his legs and lick his genitals.[86] Tiberius had been one of the greatest commanders of Roman forces, but now he had reduced himself to frustration, and to a cycle of guilt, detachment and impotent exasperation at the intrigues of his court. He was not suited to playing the part of a *roi soleil* at court; he was better accustomed to sleeping rough with his troops on the borders of Germany or Illyricum. He was tight-fisted,[87] and his stinginess turned eventually to rapacity, happy to tax, but not to spend. He gained no satisfaction from his family. At odds with his mother, the Augusta Livia, alienated from his dissolute son, Drusus, and cajoled by his demanding daughter-in-law, Agrippina, he sought isolation and immersion in his pleasure gardens in Capri; and greater and greater dependence on the Praetorian Prefect Sejanus.

Sejanus wanted power and, seeing the gap between what Tiberius wanted the Senate to be, and what it in fact was, saw his opportunity to alienate Tiberius further and further from the Senate and make Tiberius more and more dependent on him. But with others like Agrippina standing in the way of his ambition, and seeking to raise her children as potential Caesars, Sejanus began a scheme to isolate Agrippina and cow the Senate. He brought Senators to trial on charges of disloyalty to the Emperor or *maiestas* (ambition for majesty, amounting to treason), and sought to isolate Agrippina. Sejanus deceitfully warned her that Tiberius was trying to poison her. Believing him, she refused all food at

Tiberius's table, only to inflict a deep slight on him, and receive his lasting animosity. Her sister Julia, the granddaughter of Augustus, died in exile, banished for breaking the adultery laws,[88] and then both Agrippina and her older son Nero were banished to offshore gaols; in Agrippina's case to the same island where her mother had been banished and later died. At Sejanus's instigation, another son, Drusus, was imprisoned in the Palatine in Rome and Tiberius ordered Caligula, the youngest, to Capri.[89] There he imbibed the worst of the excesses practised by his great-uncle Tiberius, but was beyond the reach of the ambitious and scheming Sejanus.

By AD 31, Sejanus hoped that he was near to his final *coup d'état*. His plan was to destroy Agrippina's family, marry the Emperor's niece Livilla (daughter of his brother Drusus, sister of Germanicus), and with the *Princeps*'s support place himself in the position of likely successor. If Caligula had put himself out of reach at the court in Capri, Sejanus believed that with the warm support of Tiberius, of which he had been given ample evidence, it was only a matter of time before he put himself in the position of heir. Agrippina was under house arrest in Camapania, Nero banished, and Drusus imprisoned in Rome. When a letter arrived from Tiberius in the autumn of AD 31, making him *tribunicia potestas*, a magistracy of great power, Sejanus went to the Senate to receive the applause of the senators. While he was seated there, however, a further letter from the Emperor was read out by Memmius Regulus, and far from being praised, Sejanus was criticised and condemned. He was led out to prison. On the same afternoon, the Senate met again and voted for his execution. Like Haman in the biblical story of Esther, his ambition had threaded a noose around his neck. Livilla, his intended bride, was locked up in a room and starved to death. A purge was carried out and bodies piled high in the Forum. Twenty senators, all supporters of Sejanus, were executed in a single day. His schemes had been made plain to the Emperor by Antonia, the grandmother of Caligula. Such meddling with the imperial family warranted death.[90]

The conspiracy and ensuing terror were in part the result of Tiberius's self-imposed exile in Capri. Yet the exile became an imprisonment in his mind: on many occasions he would journey to Rome only to wander in the countryside beyond it. As Tacitus wrote, "He often landed at points in the neighbourhood [by Rome], visited the gardens by the Tiber, but went

back again to the cliffs and to the solitude of the sea shores, in shame at
the vices and profligacies into which he had plunged so unrestrainedly; in
the fashion of a despot he debauched the children of free-born citizens".[91]
By AD 37, he had become a figure of myth. He had alienated the plebs
with his haughty treatment; he had terrorised the Senate by his purges
following the conspiracy of Sejanus, washing the Gemonian Steps with
blood that cried out. (The Gemonian Steps on the Capitoline Hill were
where the bodies of executed criminals were flung, the name associated
with *gemere*—to moan.) Worst of all, he had raised a young teenager
in the cruel extremes of the lifestyle of Capri. Caligula survived the
experience by silent complicity, but he stored up a way of behaving which
would surpass even his great-uncle's cruel acts of terror and humiliation.
His was an education from which even Rome would shrink and through
which it would be deeply traumatised.

Somewhere between AD 28 and 33, a crucifixion took place in a
troublesome part of the Empire, Judea, and more specifically in its capital,
Jerusalem, a crucifixion which would change the world. The crucified
"criminal" was called Jesus of Nazareth. On the wooden cross on which
Jesus was crucified, the charge was pinned on the orders of the Roman
Prefect, Pontius Pilate, who had been appointed by Tiberius.[92] It read
"Jesus of Nazareth, King of the Jews" (John 19:19). Judea was well known
to Tiberius, not so much from visits he himself had made, as from visits to
his courts in Rome and Capri by his son Drusus's friend, Herod Agrippa.[93]
It was nevertheless unlikely that Tiberius heard about the difficult trial
that Pilate faced when jealous rulers of the Jews brought Jesus of Nazareth
before him.

The crucifixion of Jesus, followed by the resurrection, were events
which would change history. Two hundred and eighty years later,
the Roman Empire under the Emperor Constantine would adopt the
Christian faith as the imperial religion. It is this story, from the execution
of its founder to the adoption of the Christian faith by the Empire, that
we tell here.

The world Jesus was born into was shaped by the reign of Augustus
and his heir Tiberius, by the client king of Rome—Herod the Great, his
heirs and family—and by the Jewish religious leaders of the day and the

institution of the Temple. Luke tells us that John the Baptist began his preaching in the Judean desert in the fifteenth year of Tiberius, AD 29 (Luke 3:1), when Jesus was "about thirty years old" (Luke 3:23). Jesus would interact with all these authorities, but spoke of another kingdom and suggested himself, obliquely, as another king (Luke 19:28–44). He announced this kingdom at the outset of his ministry (Mark 1:15). He described what it was like in terms of the Old Testament scriptures (Luke 4:17–19; Isaiah 61:1, 2) and never ceased describing it in parables (Mark 4:33, 34). He demonstrated the presence of the kingdom with miracles too many to number (John 20:25), in which the sick were cured, the possessed freed, the lame healed, the blind given back their sight, and the dumb their voice. He drew huge crowds from the region of Galilee, and these he fed miraculously and also taught (Mark 6:30–44, 8:1–10).

Throughout the narratives of the gospel, Jesus interacted with the Roman authorities. His birth at Bethlehem, rather than Nazareth, was because of an order of a provincial governor that his father, Joseph, should go to his hometown to be registered for taxation (Luke 2:1–3). In going there, Joseph fulfilled the prophecies of the Old Testament that the Messiah would be born in Bethlehem, the town of David (Matthew 2:3–6). In the course of his ministry Jesus met centurions: one he praised for his great faith, which he said he had not found in all Israel (Luke 7:1–10), the other supervised his crucifixion and yet called him a Son of God (Mark 15:39). Roman soldiers were a common sight in Judea. There were four legions in the province of Syria,[94] and probably one in Judea. Roman soldiers had the right to make a passer-by carry their luggage. Jesus said if asked to go one mile carrying a soldier's luggage, one should go two instead (Matthew 5:40). When Jesus saw a Roman execution party escorting a prisoner carrying his cross, he told his followers that if they wanted to follow him they too must pick up the cross (Matthew 10:38) and go wherever he led. When asked about paying taxes to Caesar, Jesus asked for a coin bearing Caesar's image and told them to pay their taxes to Caesar, but also to give to God what rightly belonged to him (Luke 20:20–26). Jesus called tax collectors like Matthew, who were working for the Romans, to follow him (Matthew 8:9). And lastly, when the Roman governor asked him if he was a king, Jesus replied that his kingship was not of this world or else his followers would fight for him

(John 18:28–19:16, especially 18:36). Jesus's take on power was that the powerful should serve the weak and that "whoever wants to be great among you must be your servant, and whoever wants to be first must be slave of all" (Luke 22:26; Mark 10:43). This was the kingdom that Jesus proclaimed and died for, so that by faith any might enter. The reality of the kingdom was endorsed when on the third day he rose again.

If the Romans in the stories of the gospels were impressed by Jesus's courage, recognised his innate authority, and were challenged by his evident power, the Jewish leaders, especially the Scribes and the Pharisees, wrestled with how to respond to him—a man who seemingly came from outside their institutions, yet had evident authority and power, like none of their teachers (Mark 1:27), and who made them so jealous that they engineered his death. Again and again they questioned him about his pedigree, his teaching, his authority: where did it come from? (Luke 20:1–8; John 7:25–32). As with the Romans, Jesus challenged the Jewish leaders' authority, but found them implacably hostile towards his incipient claims to forgive sins (Mark 2:5), to be Lord of the Sabbath (Mark 2:28) and most of all, his indirect claim to the divine name (John 8:58).

The common people heard him gladly, but the Pharisees, with just a few exceptions (e.g. Nicodemus in John 3), did not. They had appointed themselves the guardians of Judaism and the Law. They were the descendants of the *Hasidim*, another branch of the even stricter Qumran Community and Essenes, who had withdrawn from normal society to prepare the way of the Lord.[95] Their training was long, their position in society respected, but self-promotion and self-congratulation had taken hold of them. In a blistering attack on their values, recorded in Matthew 23, Jesus says they "travel over land and sea to win a single convert, and when he becomes one, [they] make him twice as much a son of hell" (Matthew 23:15). They tithed mint, dill and cumin, but neglected the more important matters of the law—justice, mercy and faithfulness. "You should have practised the latter, without neglecting the former. You blind guides! You strain at a gnat and swallow a camel" (Matthew 23:23–24). Through his invective, which highlighted the emptiness of their spirituality, Jesus provoked the Jewish religious leaders' hostility. Many of them were the rulers of the Jews, and members of the Sanhedrin along with the Chief Priests. It was these who set about plotting his death (John 11:45–57).

The other powers Jesus offended or provoked were the Herodian rulers of Galilee and the Temple authorities, who were under the direction of the High Priest. Herod the Great's son Herod Antipas, the Tetrarch of Galilee, was the client ruler of the Romans in northern Judea. It was he who married his brother Philip's wife, Herodias, having divorced his Nabatean wife of many years. It was this marriage between Herodias and Herod Antipas that John the Baptist strongly criticised, for it contravened Jewish law (see Leviticus 18:16 and 20:21), and for which criticism he was imprisoned at the Perean fortress of Herod at Machaerus, east of the Jordan,[96] and then ignominiously executed (Matthew 14:1–12; Mark 6:14–29) at the request of Salome, who, prompted by her mother, Herodias, had bewitched Herod with her dancing. Josephus records Herodias's brother, Herod Agrippa, was a friend of the imperial family, especially of Tiberius's great nephew, Gaius (Caligula), although there was little love lost between Herodias and her brother. Herod Agrippa was a stirrer of trouble, a heavy gambler and a wastrel. For his part, Jesus had little direct dealing with Herod Antipas, but he was aware of his animosity. His disciples told him, "Leave this place and go somewhere else. Herod wants to kill you". Jesus responded by saying of Herod, "Go tell that fox, I will drive out demons and heal people today and tomorrow, and the third day I will reach my goal" (Luke 13:31, 32). Jesus was only to meet this Herod in the final days of his life, when it seemed that the ever inquisitive and facile Herod was glad to have an audience with Jesus at Pilate's request, although he treated him as if he were a magician, asking him to perform miracles on demand (Luke 23:5–12). Jesus would not play Herod's games, so Herod resorted to mocking him instead, and returned him to Pilate.

Finally, Jesus recognised that the welfare of the Temple, and indeed the city itself, were to be short-lived. He was under no illusions about their fate. At the top of an incline before the road went down the Mount of Olives, he stopped and wept over the city (Luke 19:40–44). The city—its governing authorities at least—had not recognised, let alone welcomed, the peace that he had come to bring, and instead put their trust in a system which was passing and corrupt, and which would be blown away.

Jesus's relationship with the Temple, as used by the priests, was more than ambivalent. It was one of deep disappointment. The Temple should have been a house of prayer, but had become a den of robbers (Matthew 21:12–17; Mark 11:12–19; Luke 19:45–48; John 2:12–22). It should have been a place of mercy, but had become a moneymaking machine. It raised its own taxes (Matthew 17:24–27), and had its own currency and rate of exchange. It looked as if it would last forever, but all its edifices would be pulled down and just a few vast stones in the foundation platform left, which now form the Wailing Wall (Mark 13:1–2). What had been built over 46 years would be destroyed in months. Contrastingly, Jesus would be killed on a cross outside Jerusalem and in three days the temple of his body would be raised to life, indestructible and eternal (John 2:20–25).

What the Apostles understood gradually after the resurrection was that Jesus had come to inaugurate a new kingdom quite unlike any systems of power in the world, whether found in the capricious lives of the imperial family in Rome, in the Empire's representatives around the Mediterranean, in the Senate House on the Capitoline Hill, or among the guardians of Judaism—Scribes, Priests or Pharisees. Entrance to this kingdom was by faith in the Christ of God; it involved following this king in the power of the Spirit. What Peter proclaimed to the crowds on the day of Pentecost was to be made known throughout the world: "Let all Israel be assured of this: God has made this Jesus, whom you crucified, both Lord and Christ" (Acts 2:36). It was a message to be made known "to the ends of the earth" (Acts 1:8c), in the hope and knowledge that one day "every tongue (would) confess that Jesus is Lord" (Philippians 2:11). This would involve a titanic struggle with the rulers of empires already in existence or others still to come. It was now the role of the church to confront and transform the culture of the Empire in the years ahead.

CHAPTER 2

Expansion and Persecution

The momentum for the mission of the church was given at Pentecost. The dominical command to engage in worldwide mission was given at the end of Jesus's ministry, just before the Ascension (Matthew 28:19–20), when he commanded the Apostles to go into all the world and preach the gospel. As Jesus promised, the Apostles who waited in Jerusalem were "clothed with power from on high" (Luke 24:49).

The newly formed church was empowered for mission. The effect was immediate. The Holy Spirit was now manifest "as a violent wind" among them, filling the house where the Apostles were sitting, a ball of flame separated into tongues of fire resting on each of them (Acts 2:1–3). Immediately, they spoke in other tongues or languages as the Spirit gave them utterance (Acts 2:4), conferring unity in the Spirit where hitherto there had been division.[97] Once again the effect was immediate. Pilgrims in the city of Jerusalem from all over the Jewish Diaspora heard them speaking in their own languages: "Parthians, Medes and Elamites, residents of Mesopotamia, Judea and Cappadocia, Pontus and Phyrgia and Pamphylia, Egypt and the parts of Libya near Cyrene; visitors from Rome (both Jews and converts to Judaism); Cretans and Arabs" (Acts 2:9–11). These pilgrims from an area greater than the Empire itself were amazed and wondered what it could mean. They were principally astonished by the wonder of the communication itself: "Utterly amazed, they asked: 'Are not all these men who are speaking Galileans? Then how is it that each of us hears them in his own native language?'" (Acts 2:8). What is clear is that this message given to the Apostles was indeed for all nations, or at the very least, in the minds of the hearers, for the Jews,

X

converts or God-fearers living in communities in the Mediterranean basin and the Near East.

When Peter stood up and explained the meaning of the message, culminating in the proclamation: "God has raised this Jesus to life, and we are all witnesses of the fact. Exalted to the right hand of God, he has received from the Father the promised Holy Spirit and has poured out what you now see and hear" (Acts 2:32–33), the bystanders were no longer simply amazed at the *means* of communication (each one hearing in his own language), but also at the *content* of the message. "'Brothers, what must we do?' They asked". About three thousand were baptised in the name of Jesus Christ for the forgiveness of sins and to receive the gift of the Spirit (Acts 2:38–42). And so the primitive church was formed in Jerusalem, as well as in the *diaspora*.

The church in Jerusalem had been formed quickly. Its leaders were the Apostles, initially with Peter as chief spokesman and leading apostle. Later, this leadership passed to James, the brother of the Lord (see Galatians 2:9 and Acts 15:13: The Council of Jerusalem). The family of Jesus, including his mother and brothers, were also part of the community (Acts 1:14). The characteristics of the church were the practice of a common ownership, devotion to the Apostles' teaching and prayer, the breaking of bread in homes, and visibility in public places, especially the Temple (Acts 5:12; 6:42), where wonders and miraculous signs were performed, principally by the Apostles (Acts 2:42–44; 4:32–34), and where many priests believed (6:7b).

Corporate life was strongly defended by the Apostles, both in relation to sharing of property and provision for the widows (Acts 5:1–10 and 6:1–7). Any pretence or hypocrisy in relation to financial gifts was judged harshly, as in the case of Ananias and Sapphira (Acts 5:1–10), while sacrificial giving, as in the case of Barnabas, a Levite from Cyprus and later associate of Paul, was greeted with thanksgiving (Acts 4:36, 37). What proceeded from faith was good, but that which was deceitful was quickly condemned. In such a way the fear of the Lord seized the church (Acts 5:11).

The witness of the church in Jerusalem consisted in miraculous events, leading to the proclamation of the gospel, which in turn led to persecution, awe, and a widening circle of influence. A classic example of the miraculous linked to proclamation was the incident of the healing of the cripple at the Gate Beautiful (Acts 3:1–24). From an incontrovertible act of power in which a cripple regained the full use of his legs so as to walk and leap, Peter proceeded to preach that Jesus was the Messiah and Prophet promised by Moses ages ago (Acts 3:22, Deuteronomy 18:15, 18–19). As the Jews would find the reality of a crucified Messiah an anathema, Peter centred his address on the reality of the resurrection and the evidence of the cured cripple. Indeed "by raising him (Jesus) from the dead, God had reversed the death sentence passed upon him, together with all that death sentence implied".[98] Even as Peter and John, the leading Apostles, were teaching this they were arrested, imprisoned overnight, and tried by the Jewish leaders, who charged them not to speak or teach in the name of Jesus, a command they could not possibly obey (Acts 4:18–19).

Proclamation and powerful healings continued (Acts 5:12–16), and persecution increased (Acts 5:17–18), but an angel released Peter from prison (Acts 17:19). Peter and John appeared before the Sanhedrin, which wished to kill them, but Gamaliel's wise advice prevailed: if this preaching was true and from God, nothing could stop its effect (Acts 5:35–39).

The church in Jerusalem was to face increasing pressure, both internally from social divisions, and externally from greater persecution. Internally, the church consisted of Hellenist and Hebrew (Palestinian) Jews. The former had assimilated Greek culture, spoke in Greek and probably originated from the Jewish Diaspora of Greek-speaking colonies of the Roman Empire. In contrast, the Palestinian or Hebrew Jews spoke in Hebrew or Aramaic. Those who spoke Semitic languages believed themselves purer than their Greek brethren. As a result, the Greek Jewish widows were neglected in the daily food distribution (Acts 6:1). The Apostles called for seven deacons to be selected to deal with this situation. Among the seven were two notable leaders: Stephen and Philip, both of Greek-Jewish background. Stephen was drawn from a synagogue called the Synagogue of the Freedmen, which comprised Jews drawn from Cyrene and Alexandria (present-day Egypt and Libya respectively), as well as from Cilicia and Asia (Acts 6:9). Stephen was accused, like Jesus, of speaking against the Temple and against the Law, when he said that Jesus would destroy the Temple and change the customs given by Moses. Such claims were considered incendiary (Acts 6:13, 14). Stephen was charged before the Sanhedrin, but in a long speech drawn from Jewish history, demonstrated that Jesus was the one promised to succeed the Patriarchs and Moses—their lives had not been confined to one place and nor now was Christ's. God does not live in buildings made by human hands; he is present with his people and in effect the Temple was redundant. This enraged Stephen's hearers and they stoned him, laying their clothes at the feet of a Pharisee called Saul.

The persecution of the church increased as its mission continued from Jerusalem to Judea, to Samaria, and to the whole world (Acts 1:8). Only the Apostles remained in Jerusalem, while a great many others were scattered through Samaria and Judea (Acts 8:1). As a result of the persecution, the message spread. Philip took the gospel to Samaria, and following a successful mission there, Peter and John went to pray for the gift of the Spirit to be given them (Acts 8:15). Simon sought to buy this blessing, giving the church a new sin—simony (Acts 8:19–24)—which is essentially defined as the attempt to buy the gift of the Spirit or a position in the church.

After the encouragement of a vision (Acts 10:9–23), and following considerable persuasion and much choreography by the Spirit (see Acts 10:1–48), Peter then preached the gospel to Cornelius, another God-fearing centurion Gentile. At last, the mystery hidden for ages had been revealed: "This mystery is that through the gospel the Gentiles are heirs together of one body, and sharers together in the promise in Christ Jesus" (Ephesians 3:6).

The church in Jerusalem welcomed the Gentile converts, concluding, "So then, God has granted even the Gentiles repentance unto life" (Acts 11:18). Later, c.AD 50, a church council was called in Jerusalem, where it was decided that the Gentile church need not observe the Torah, but was nevertheless to "abstain from blood, from meat of strangled animals and from sexual immorality" (Acts 15:29), thus distinguishing Christianity from Judaism.

The gospel, through the severe mercy of persecution and through the urging of the Spirit to cross new barriers, had gone from Jerusalem, to Judea, then to Samaria, but finally must go to the ends of the earth. Thomas, according to Eusebius, took the message to Mesopotamia and to India, according to the Syrian, St Ephrem. But one man especially was called to take this step of going to Gentile nations, at least in the narrative of Acts. He was Saul, soon to be Paul.

The Apostle Paul

In his own words Saul was "a Hebrew of Hebrews; in regard to the law, a Pharisee, as for zeal, persecuting the Church; as for legalistic righteousness, faultless" (Philippians 3:5b, 6). It was a bold claim and probably true, although he later came to recognise that even he was not without his failings in relation to the Law, conceding, "I do not understand what I do. For what I want to do I do not do, but what I hate I do".[99] At the time he had set out from Jerusalem to Damascus with letters of authority from the High Priest[100] in order to arrest followers of the Way and put them in gaol, he was sure of his own cause and his zeal for it was limitless—until, that is, he had a vision of Christ.

The bright light, the voice of Christ, the immediate sense that this was a theophany, the loss of sight and the sudden realisation that Jesus was none other than the Messiah, re-ordered all his thinking, re-constituted all his previously held presuppositions, and changed forever the direction of his life and zeal. No wonder he needed solitary withdrawal, and the loss of physical sight meant that his inner sight was entirely re-focussed (Acts 9:8, 9). No wonder he suffered a loss of appetite and denied himself all sustenance while he digested the implications of this event. Through the good offices of Ananias, who bravely received Saul into the church by baptism, praying for him to receive back his sight and be filled with the Holy Spirit (Acts 9:17–19), Saul became one of the brethren. It appears from a conflation of Paul's own words in Galatians and the story of Paul's early ministry in Acts (see Acts 9:19b–25) that he remained in the area of Damascus for some time, spending three years in Arabia (Galatians 1:16), where he may have been instructed by the Lord, and also preaching in the Nabatean kingdom.[101] He then returned to Damascus, preached in the synagogues, and escaped from the hostile Jews, abetted by the Ethnarch of Damascus, who represented the Nabatean King Aretas (2 Corinthians 11:32). He was let down in a basket through a window in the city wall and made the first of many escapes of the coming years (see 2 Corinthians 4:8–11 and 11:16–33). It was then that he went to Jerusalem on a short visit of 15 days, was introduced to Peter and James (Galatians 1:18 and Acts 9:26–29) and then, partly because of the hostile reaction of the Jews to his presence in Jerusalem, went back to Cilicia and Tarsus (Acts 9:30 and Galatians 1:21). He was to remain there for 14 years (Galatians 2:1).

During this long interlude in Cilicia, Paul was no doubt active in preaching and teaching, and was known to the church. This period may have lasted from c. AD 37–43, when he received a vision telling him to go to Jerusalem.[102] This time Barnabas was with him, and he now invited Paul to the flourishing church at Antioch.

Christians from Cyprus and North Africa had started the church in Antioch, and it was to be one of the foremost centres of Christianity for the next 400 years. It does not appear to have been an apostolic initiative (see Acts 11:19–21), but began after the persecution of the church in Jerusalem, the stoning of Stephen, and the dispersal of Christians from Jerusalem and Judea. It was a mega church: "a great number of people had believed", and the further ministry from Barnabas resulted in a further "great number" turning to the Lord (Acts 11:21). Clearly, the church at Antioch was a great resource for mission and in need of apostolic teaching at a time when none of the New Testament scriptures had been written. The presence and teaching of Paul, now at least 17 years into his ministry, was vital for the church's development, but after a year, and through prophetic urging (see Acts 13:1–3), Paul and Barnabas were set aside for a new type of mission altogether.

The first of Paul's missionary journeys, conducted with Barnabas and John Mark, was to relatively familiar territory. Barnabas was from Cyprus and they made Salamis, the large colony on the eastern side of the island (near present-day Famagusta), their first port of call (Acts 13:4–12). From there they went through the interior to Paphos, where the governor or pro-consul, Sergius Paulus, came to faith on seeing the temporary blindness visited on the sorcerer Elymas by Paul, as a result of his opposition to Paul's message.[103]

The journey then proceeded north by ship to Perga in Pamphylia, and to cities in Phyrgia and Galatia (Acts 13:13–14:28). The method of working became established. Paul would go first to the synagogue, where he would address the congregation, and then, if thrown out of the synagogue by irate Jews, which was often the case, to an after-meeting with a mixture of sympathetic Jews, God-fearers and Gentiles. In the synagogue at Pisidian Antioch, Paul spoke at length to the congregation in what can be seen as a classic address to a synagogue audience (Acts 13:16–43). He briefly rehearsed Israelite history, and then demonstrated that God had fulfilled his promises to the nation by sending Jesus, whom he raised to life after his crucifixion at the hands of the rulers in Jerusalem. But now he concluded, "Forgiveness of sins is proclaimed to you. Through him everyone who believes is justified from everything you could not be justified from the Law of Moses" (Acts 13:38–39).

In Pisidian Antioch, Iconium especially, and in Lystra, they met great interest, but also, and particularly in Lystra, violent opposition (see Acts 13:44, 49; 14:1, 19). Paul escaped with his life in Lystra, where he was dragged out of the city and stoned. Being Paul, he got back on his feet and re-entered the city. Going on to Derbe, he won there "a large number of disciples" (Acts 14:21). They had met with mixed reactions initially: the pagans all but worshipping them as gods (Acts 14:18) and the opposing Jews whipping up hatred against them (Acts 14:19–20). Nevertheless, churches were started in most of the cities of Phyrgia, Galatia and Pamphylia. The church had expanded in the face of strong opposition. Paul revisited these new Christian communities, summarising his message as follows: "We must go through many hardships to enter the kingdom of God" (Acts 14:22). He and Barnabas appointed "elders", or leaders, and "with prayer and fasting" committed them to the Lord (Acts 14:23). The church had started in a region where for the next 600 years it would remain strong. It would expand yet further in the second missionary journey to territories unfamiliar to Paul.

After the completion of the first journey into the interior of Asia (present-day Turkey), Paul reported back to the church at Antioch what God had done through them. We are told then that Paul stayed at Antioch "a long time" (Acts 14:28).

Having at the Council of Jerusalem cleared up issues relating to the Law and circumcision and whether new Gentile converts should observe these (Acts 15), Paul decided to revisit the communities established in the first missionary journey. A sharp dispute with Barnabas arose over whether to take John Mark, Barnabas's cousin, with them. John Mark had turned back early in the first missionary journey, after the visit to Cyprus (Acts 13:13). Barnabas favoured giving his cousin a second chance, but Paul, with eyes only on the effectiveness of the mission, refused. Barnabas separated from Paul, along with John Mark. Later, Paul and John Mark were reconciled (see Colossians 4:10), and it is often suggested that John Mark was the author of the second gospel, being a close friend of Peter and present in Rome with him (1 Peter 5:13).

The second missionary journey began with Paul revisiting the churches in Cilicia and Syria, and in Galatia and Phyrgia (Acts 15:41; Acts 16:9). A new team was formed, including Silas and Timothy. Timothy, of mixed Greek (paternal) and Jewish (maternal) parentage, was circumcised by Paul, not for reasons of salvation, but so that he would be more acceptable to Jewish audiences both locally and further afield (Acts 16:1–3). They delivered to the communities the verdict of the Council of Jerusalem by which the churches were encouraged and strengthened.

Unable to preach the word in Asia (we are not told what the precise hindrance was), they struck west through present-day central Turkey to Dorylaeum and Mysia, the coastal province that includes Troy (Troas) and which many know as the Gallipoli peninsular. Luke is adamant that Paul was prevented by "the Spirit of Jesus" from entering Bithynia to the north: the province, together with Pontus, that abuts the Black Sea (Acts 16:6–7). During the night Paul was called in a vision by a man dressed in Macedonian clothing to "come over and help us" (Acts 16:10). Momentously, the gospel was now to be preached in Europe for the first time. Having immediately taken a ship via the Greek island of Samothrace, Paul and his companions arrived at Neapolis, the port close to the Roman colony of Philippi. Here the first European church was to be founded.

The European part of the second missionary journey took in some of the principal towns of Greece: Philippi, Thessalonica, Athens and Corinth. Christian communities were to be established in each of these, although no record of a church in Athens exists from Pauline or other early church correspondence. Where synagogues were known to exist, as in Thessalonica, Berea, Athens and Corinth (see Acts 17:1–3; Acts 17:10b; Acts 18:4, 5), Paul went to them first, always reasoning with the congregation from the scriptures that Jesus was the Christ. There were always mixed, but nonetheless fruitful, results. The Thessalonian Jews were particularly vociferous and violent in opposition, but "some of the Jews were persuaded" (Acts 17:4) as well as a large number of God-fearing Greeks and not a few "prominent women" (Acts 17:4). In Berea, where the people were "more noble in character" than the Thessalonians, many Jews believed, together with some "prominent Greek women and many Greek men" (Acts 17:12). In Athens, we do not hear of any Jews joining the church, whereas in Corinth, the synagogue ruler Crispus "believed" (Acts 18:8). In every church, except possibly Athens, there were Jews and Greeks present, and often the Greek women were from prominent families.

Other themes common to the second missionary journey to Greek cities were: Paul's use of pagan literature and poetry in preaching; his sensitivity to pagan places of prayer, worship and philosophical debate; his involvement in power encounters with opposing spiritual or demonic forces; and his encounters with the Roman magistrates and law. It is worth following these themes in the different cities where they presented themselves in both the second and third missionary journeys of Paul.

Where there was no synagogue in a town, Paul sought other places to speak and meet others, whether in prayer or for religious or philosophical discussion. So, in Philippi he went to a place of prayer by a river outside the city gate of the town (Acts 16:13). It was there that he met Lydia, a businesswoman and dealer in purple.[104] At Athens, Paul made for the place where the Areopagus met, as well as the forum or market place, having been to the synagogue (Acts 17:17). The Areopagus was a mixture of a philosophical debating chamber and a town council; typical of Athens, it was a mingling of culture with civic power. In Ephesus, he hired the debating hall of Tyrannus, having previously been to the synagogue (Acts 19:9). In all these places he evangelised the population, by announcing the good news, dialoguing with those who engaged with him, and explaining in less Jewish terms the salvation that Jesus brought.

There is a noticeable change of style in Paul's presentation of the gospel to pagan or Greek audiences. Whereas with the Jews he could argue from the commonly respected scriptures, which Christians call the Old Testament, that Jesus was the Christ, to a pagan audience these scriptures were unfamiliar, and the expectation of the coming of a Messiah was generally unknown. With great sensitivity and intellectual elasticity, Paul therefore started from what was familiar to them as pagans. Nowhere was this more clearly seen than in Athens. His spirit was provoked by the many temples—there were probably far more temples in Athens than in any other town he would have visited (Acts 17:16). However, he found one inscription with which he was able to begin his preaching. This was a temple erected for the worship of *An Unknown God* (*Agnosto Theo*) (Acts 17:23). Paul thus began his address with the compliment that the Athenians were very religious, even worshipping this unknown God (hedging their religious bets, if you like), then went on to say, "Now what you worship as something unknown I am going to proclaim to you" (Acts 17:23).

His proclamation centred on the Jewish/Christian doctrine of creation, in terms of which God created everything, and thus cannot be restricted to human, man-made temples. Paul quoted two Classical poets in support of these ideas. His point was that God is greater than all his creation, and should not be confused with his creation. Rather than being confined to particular temples, God was everywhere. Quoting Epimenides—as attributed by the ninth-century author Ishodad—a poet from Crete, he says, "For in him we live and move and have our being". Paul takes a pagan insight, first expressed in a poem to Zeus, and applies it more truly to God. It is a classic case of a human, and in this case expressly pagan, insight being *baptised* by Paul into Christian theology and indeed into scripture. Furthermore, Paul quotes Aratus, a poet from his home region of Cilicia, who wrote of Zeus, "we are also his offspring".[105] Once more Paul says these words are only true of the God and Father of us all. Paul then goes on to say that this same Father of us all has sent Jesus into the world and given notice of final judgement by bringing him back from the dead (Acts 17:31), and therefore all should repent.

Spoken in Greek, in which Paul was fluent, and quoting Classical poets, beginning with an association with one of the Athenian temples, and with other allusions to Platonic thought (e.g. Plato's *Euthyphro*), Paul's address was a master class in the evangelism of a pagan audience: some sneered, but others wished to hear more (Acts 17:32). An influential member of the Areopagus called Dionysius believed (Acts 17:33).

Along with Paul's addresses to Jews and God-fearers in the synagogues, and his addresses to chiefly pagan audiences, other features of his missionary activity were "spiritual power encounters" in several of the cities he visited, notably Philippi and Ephesus. As Paul explained in his epistle to the Ephesians, "Our struggle is not against flesh and blood, but against the rulers, against the authorities, against the powers of this dark world and against the spiritual forces of evil in the heavenly realms" (Ephesians 6:12). It was not surprising to him or to the world in which he lived that he should encounter spiritual opposition to his presence and preaching, in the same way that Jesus whom he served had done (Mark 1:21–28; Mark 5:1–20). For Paul, pagan worship was connected to the worship of demons (see 1 Corinthians 10:20), a view that was widely held by the early church and demonstrated often by Augustine in his work, *City of God*.[106] During Paul's visit to Philippi, a slave girl, with a spirit of divination, accosted him and shouted out frequently: "These men are servants of the most high God, who are telling you the way to be saved" (Acts 16:17). After a while Paul became troubled by her behaviour, and cast out the evil spirit, but was brought by her owners before the magistrates and charged with "advocating customs unlawful to Romans" (Acts 16:21). After being severely flogged, Paul and Silas were imprisoned by the magistrate. In Ephesus, similar exhibitions of spiritual power were evident. Extraordinary miracles of healing were performed through handkerchiefs which Paul had touched and which were then taken to the sick (Acts 19:11, 12). Seven sons of Sceva, a Jewish chief priest, set up a business of casting out evil spirits in the name of Paul and Jesus. Coming upon a man with an evil spirit, they sought to restore him, but seeing their lack of real faith and sincerity the evil spirit overpowered them and gave them a beating. When this event became known in Ephesus, the name of Jesus was held in high honour (Acts 19:13–18). The effect was to turn many people away from occult practices, of which there were a great number in the city (Acts 19:19–20). Furthermore, Paul's preaching of Christ led to a wholesale abandonment of the worship of the pagan goddess Diana at Ephesus, thereby threatening the livelihoods of the silversmiths who made representations of her to sell (Acts 19:23–29). It is not surprising that Paul's preaching had such an impact on the culture and economy of these cities and, consequently, on several occasions he found himself appearing before the magistrates.

A final feature of Paul's second and third missionary journeys was therefore his interaction with the courts. In Philippi, Paul was brought by complainants before the magistrates. The decision of the magistrates seems to have been largely influenced by the crowd, so that without much enquiry as to the legalities of the case, Paul and Silas were beaten and thrown into prison (Acts 16:23). Later, when an earthquake had effectively released them, the magistrates sent officers of the court to release them, perhaps thinking better of the summary justice they had been given without warrant the previous day (Acts 16:35). Stating that both he and Silas were Roman citizens, Paul requested that the magistrates themselves come and take them from prison and escort them out of town (Acts 16:37).

The regional court in Corinth gave Paul quite different treatment. Following a reassuring vision, Paul stayed in Corinth for 18 months and had a very effective ministry in this large and populous city. Yet the Jews there remained implacably opposed to his teaching and brought a case to Gallio, the pro-consul or governor of Achaia, the important Greek province of the Roman Empire. Gallio was the older brother of Seneca, the closest adviser and tutor to Emperor Nero.[107] Gallio refused to hear the case, making an interesting judgement in which he said, "If you Jews were making a complaint about some misdemeanour or serious crime, it would be reasonable for me to listen to you. But since it involves questions about words and names and your own law—settle the matter yourselves. I will not judge such things" (Acts 18:14–15). However, the studied indifference of Gallio to what he thought of as only an internal Jewish religious dispute was not to last. Civic unrest in Ephesus at the diminution of the silversmiths' business once again brought Paul's activity into the civic-legal sphere, although the town clerk's invitation to the craftsmen to bring charges against Paul in the courts was not taken up (Acts 18:35–41). In Jerusalem, further civic unrest led to Paul's arrest and protracted trials in Caesarea (Acts 22:29). By the end of the second missionary journey (*c.*AD 52) it had become evident that the interaction of Christianity and the Roman judicial system was inconsistent (as cases normally came up in connection with rioting among Jews, or in Ephesus because of pagan reaction to the gospel). Ten years later, a more settled prosecution and persecution of Christians through the courts seems to have developed. Some of this was due to imperial policy, which came to see Christians as convenient scapegoats for the ills of Rome: because of their refusal to take part in pagan worship; their dislike of the games and military service; their unwillingness to contemplate worship of the Emperor and their alienation from other Jews.

Changes in Rome

Tiberius died on 16 March AD 37, which would have been just a few years after the death and resurrection of Jesus. It is quite possible that Paul's conversion dates from AD 34,[108] in which case Paul's ministry covered most of the lives of the next three Caesars. They were all descended by adoption from Julius Caesar, but were genetic descendants of Livia, Augustus's wife, and her illustrious family of Claudians. So they came to be called the Julio-Claudians. As an imperial lineage they were to continue until the death of Nero in AD 68.

Tiberius's successor had been prepared by him on the island of Capri. As Tiberius himself said, "I am rearing them a viper in Rome's bosom".[109] Suetonius records how the adopted heir of Tiberius, Caligula, was the youngest son of the great Germanicus, the paragon of Roman virtue. But unlike his father, Caligula was fond of using his power to humiliate. He loved watching torture and executions, and he abandoned himself nightly to the pleasures of feasting and scandalous living, sometimes disguised in a wig and a long robe. It is an arresting thought to recall that the great Apostle Paul was in the deserts of Arabia preparing himself for his world-changing ministry, while Caligula, meaning "little boots" (a diminutive given to him by the Roman soldiers when his mother Agrippina brought him as a two-year-old to the German legions where his father was fighting), was cavorting and indulging in excesses of all kinds on the island of Capri.

At first there was ecstatic rejoicing at the succession of the new Emperor after the last few sterile years of Tiberius's rule, in which his abdication of active government almost allowed the Praetorian Prefect Sejanus to usurp him. A great deal of sacrificing and feasting went on in the first three months of Caligula's reign.[110] The treasury was full, donatives were splashed out, even Caligula's ostracised uncle Claudius was raised to the consulship. Caligula forswore *maiestas* (treason trials), executions and putting in place networks of informants, at least initially. But when Caligula fell seriously ill eight months into his reign, his two closest advisers looked around for a potential successor. The only real choice was Gemellus, the 18-year-old grandson of Tiberius.

When Caligula recovered, first Gemellus, then Macro, who had taken over as Prefect from Sejanus, and Silanus, Caligula's father-in-law, were forced to commit suicide. Caligula now realised the full extent of his power, which, worst of all, was allied to the visceral genius of a cruel tyrant. When his favourite sister Drusilla died, a vortex of grief was added to his desire to dominate, and the Emperor Caligula was handed an emotional reason for his vindictiveness. Such vindictiveness was fuelled by his frightening ability, common in tyrants, to unearth and expose to public ridicule the hypocrisies or foibles of others, and with a terrifying precision lay bare their wishes for mocking inspection. These traits were the stock-in-trade of the bully, but in Caligula's case were greatly refined and allied to unassailable power. Such destructive characteristics in the Emperor were soon to come to define the terror in Rome.

Caligula determined to humiliate the Senate. Although he had said that all the paperwork in connection with *maiestas* had been destroyed, this was untrue. He began to resurrect these trials, and pick off those he thought his enemies, or simply humiliate them *pour encourager les autres*.

In AD 39, aged 27, he burnished his credentials further with the decision to go to war. He marched north to take command of the legions on the Rhine. He appointed Galba his commander in place of the all-too-accommodating Gaetulicus.[111] Caligula managed a number of successful sallies against the Germans and was hailed no less than seven times as *imperator*. However, while away, news filtered back to him of a conspiracy to depose him, led by one Lepidus, a close friend of Caligula, who had seduced both his sisters, Agrippina and Julia Livilla. Lepidus was executed and both sisters were exiled. When Caligula returned to Italy, he scorned Rome and the Senate and made first for the Bay of Naples and the popular town of Baiae, where he proceeded to ride across a pontoon stretching out across the bay to Puteoli, which was then covered with a road. When the Emperor eventually arrived in Rome, he humiliated the Senate. He threw money at the crowds to win their support. He surrounded himself with an armed Praetorian Guard recruited from Germany. He proposed to the Senate that the next consul be his horse, Incitatus. It was a cruel satire bordering on madness, born of insane jealousy and suspicion.

Caligula now settled down to a reign of terror, sexual exploitation and self-indulgence. His house on the Palatine was filled with hostages from the noblest houses, whom he subjected to sexual outrage.[112] He molested Marcus Lepidus Mnester, the pantomime dancer, Valerius Catullus, a young man of consular family, and many others.[113] Women who attended his banquets were inspected and "he would send for whoever pleased him best and leave the banquet in their company".[114] His eating was excessive also, even to the point of dissolving valuable pearls in vinegar and then drinking the mixture.

He squandered 2,700 million sesterces and a great deal of treasure beside.[115] Terror continued in those around him and paranoia in the mind of the Emperor, who constantly feared conspiracy or assassination. It was a paralysing mixture of emotions. Then the very thing he feared, and had provoked, came about. Walking down a corridor in the August House on the way back from games performed in the name of Augustus in January AD 41, he was brutally assassinated. The Emperor, with Claudius and Asiaticus leading the way, was confronted by officers from the Praetorian Guard, who sliced into him with their swords and then turned on his wife Caesonia and their daughter, who were bending over his severed body. Extraordinarily, Claudius, the limping, stammering, twitching and dribbling son of Drusus and the grandson of Mark Antony, who had been rejected for his physical weakness by his mother Antonia, became Emperor. From AD 41 to 56, while Paul was for the most part planting churches in the Empire, Claudius took the imperial reins. This 50-year-old man, whom his mother called a "freak",[116] and whom the

Senate despised, became Emperor. He was the choice of the crowds and, more importantly, of the Praetorian Guard.

Claudius was shrewd, calculating and bookish. He had survived in Caesar's household almost because of his anonymity and his obvious weakness. He looked like nobody's rival, and no Emperor in the making, and he inadvertently became *Princeps*. Because of his obvious physical vulnerability, he was in constant fear of assassination, and so surrounded himself with soldiers. If Caligula had emptied the coffers, Claudius was to fill them again, with able freedmen working as bureaucrats in an emerging civil service in the Emperor's sprawling house on the Palatine. One of his freedmen, a civil servant called Callistus, was the equivalent of Chancellor of the Exchequer. He knew how to make his master rich, and himself at the same time. Another talented freedman, Pallas, whose administrative ability was like that of a Wolsey or a Cromwell in Henry Tudor's court, was also given opportunity to shine. He was completely loyal to Claudius and was also given over to pursuing Claudius's interests. The third Claudian mandarin to make up a triumvir of imperial administrators was Narcissus, a well-named wheeler-dealer, ever able to fix the Emperor's interests.

But Claudius's court, like those of his predecessors, was soon full of jealousies and rivalry. Agrippina and Julia Livilla were summoned back from exile. Claudius's young and beautiful wife Valeria Messalina was jealous of the influence and charms of Julia Livilla. There were some early conspiracies led by General Silanus and a former consul named Paetus.[117] But these were either discovered or, as in the case of Silanus, did not successfully raise the legions against the Emperor. Both were executed, Paetus at his own hand, following the example of his wife.

But, like Caligula before him, Claudius's greatest propaganda coup was to go to war. In AD 43, he decided to invade Britain. Roman forces had been there in the days of Julius Caesar and invasion had been considered since, but a wholesale subjugation had not been attempted. Now, assisted by four legions, Claudius was to lead the invasion—in fact, he went after the invasion and his generals had already mopped up the opposition, but Claudius came to receive the plaudits of a "conquering hero". The thought of fighting in Britain stirred memories of the defeat of the legions under Varus in Germany. The tribes in Britain were barbaric. They painted their bodies. They had unspeakable customs and strange religious leaders, called Druids, who were reported to make human sacrifices. On the day of invasion the Channel was calm for the crossing and the transports landed in the Thames estuary on the north side, advancing to the capital Camulodunum, which was easily taken by so great a force. Thirty chieftains, some from as far away as Orkney, sought a treaty with the Emperor. Then, 16 days after first setting foot in Britain, Claudius decided to go back to Rome; his enemies there could not be left to make mischief, and perhaps he preferred Roman comforts to the exigencies or deprivations of Britain.

He would return to Rome a hero. In honour of his success, the infant son of his wife Messalina was named Britannicus—an obvious tribute to his military campaign! By AD 51, eight years later, his legions had defeated Caratacus, the legendary British leader who had outwitted the legions for a decade. Captured and brought to Rome, Caratacus was famously spared by Claudius after a speech he made in front of the Emperor, an event which was later frequently depicted in art. Flushed with military success, although he was only in Britain for 16 days, and at that after the fighting, and laden with the spoils of war, Claudius determined to win prestige. He began great building projects to benefit the people, including two new aqueducts; he drained the Fucine Lake to reclaim land; he developed the Aventine hill in Rome and greatly extended the grain harbour at Ostia.[118] In all, these projects employed some 30,000 men and took 11 years to complete.

Yet for Claudius, as with most Emperors, his greatest foes were of his own household and family. At the best of times Claudius was insecure because of his disabilities and his rejection as a child, but now he suffered the humiliation of his wife, Messalina, marrying, or purporting to marry, the very handsome Gaius Silius, and thus bringing shame on her family, including Britannicus and Octavia. Not content with her antics with the dancer and actor Mnester, she had now thrown all caution to the winds. Claudius, hearing of her actions, took refuge with the Praetorian Guard, who quickly executed the conspirators and Messalina herself. Her actions had tarred the whole family, including Britannicus. Into the vacuum of his need for affection and strength stepped none other than Claudius's niece, Agrippina the younger. "She had the niece's privilege of kissing and caressing Claudius, and exercised it with notable effect on his passions". After obtaining Senate approval, the wedding took place right away in AD 49.[119] Agrippina did not hang about. Claudius then formally adopted her son Nero, who was married in AD 53, aged 16, to Octavia, Claudius's daughter. When Claudius died on 13 October AD 54, Nero became the last of the Julio-Claudian emperors. With Seneca, a former lover of Agrippina, as his tutor and mentor, and Burrus as her appointee as the Prefect of the Praetorian Guard, Nero's mother had started as she meant to go on, ruling the Empire through her son. Yet in the end Nero had other plans.

At the same time, from AD 52 onwards, a new movement was to spread around the Empire, first in Asia and then in Europe. Its pioneer missionary was a Roman citizen, one Paul of Tarsus.

The Expansion of the Church

Paul's missionary journeys took place for the most part during the reigns of Claudius and Nero. He taught the church at Antioch for at least a year before he was sent with Barnabas on his first missionary journey (Acts 13:2). Luke tells us that this period was marked by a severe famine throughout the Roman world and took place during the reign of Claudius (AD 41–54; Acts 11:27). It was a period which saw the spread of the church through Paul's missions, but also through the travel and witness of ordinary Christians throughout the Empire, even to Rome itself.

We know that there was a sufficiently significant Christian community in Rome for Suetonius to refer to it when telling us that, due to rioting between Jews and Christians in Rome, Claudius expelled from the city a body of Jews who followed *Chrestus*.[120] Among those expelled were Priscilla and Aquila (Acts 18:2). Since Paul met Priscilla and Aquila in Corinth following their expulsion and during Gallio's governorship of Achaia (AD 51–52; see Acts 18:12), the expulsion probably occurred around AD 49, as it was something that had happened recently.

Paul was next in Corinth in AD 56, and it is from there that he *may* have written his Epistle to the Romans. It is clear from the greetings at the end of the Epistle[121] that much of the community in Rome had by then been re-constituted.[122] After the Passover in AD 57, Paul and his companions began his final voyage to Jerusalem via Philippi, Troas and Miletus. He was keen to reach Jerusalem by the feast of Pentecost (Acts 20:5–16). He met, taught and said goodbye to the Ephesian elders at Miletus in an emotional farewell (Acts 20:13–38). Then, by way of Cos, Rhodes and Patara, and passing to the south of Cyprus, Paul, Luke and his companions arrived at Tyre, staying there for seven days with the disciples (Acts 21:3–7). From there he went via Ptolemais to Caesarea, where they finally disembarked. They stayed at Caesarea with Philip the Evangelist and his four unmarried, prophesying daughters (some 20 years after Philip's appointment with Stephen as one of the seven: Acts 6). From there, Paul went to Jerusalem against much advice, including that of the prophet Agabus, who predicted that arrest and imprisonment awaited him in Jerusalem (Acts 21:10–14). For Paul, Agabus's prediction was no reason for *not* going to Jerusalem. Whatever awaited him, the Lord's will ought to be embraced. They stayed in Jerusalem at the home of Mnason, an early disciple from Cyprus (Acts 21:16).

What is clear, simply from recounting this journey, is how extensive the Christian community was by AD 57. In most of these towns and ports there were considerable networks of Christians. Indeed, just 25 years after the resurrection of Jesus there was a plethora of churches in the Empire. Other communities, those recalled in epistles written by Peter, for instance, existed near the Black Sea in Pontus and Bithynia (1 Peter 1:1). Now a new phase in the life of the church was about to begin with the arrest of Paul and his transfer to Rome.

Paul's Arrest, Trials and Journey to Rome

Paul was warmly received in Jerusalem by the brothers in the church there (Acts 21:17). Without delay he went to greet James and the other elders of the church. On the one hand, they were impressed by the work he had done among the Gentiles, but on the other, they were nervous about his attitude to the Mosaic Law, especially since there were literally thousands of Jewish Christians in Jerusalem who "were zealous for the Law" (Acts 21:20). Unless Paul showed himself loyal to the Law of Moses, they feared trouble. Paul had already written passionately to the Galatian Christians about not returning to the Law (see Galatians 3:1–14). A scheme was thus devised whereby Paul might show himself loyal to the Jewish Law and so not give offence to the many Jewish Christians in Jerusalem who believed in Jesus, but still held the Mosaic Law precious (Acts 21:19). The plan was that Paul would accompany four men who had made a Nazirite vow to the Temple. He would show solidarity by going with them to the Temple, paying their expenses, and purifying himself, thereby demonstrating his high regard for what they were doing (Acts 21:17–26). However well-intentioned the idea was to make Paul acceptable to his Jewish brethren, and to the Jews of the city, it did not succeed.

Paul was a marked man. A group of Jews from Asia, who knew of his missionary work there, whipped up the crowd and said that he spoke against the nation, the Law and the Temple (Acts 21:28). They also spread a rumour that he had brought a Greek into the Temple, presumably into the Court of the Jews (Acts 21:29). In no time there was a disturbance. Paul was seized in the Temple precincts, dragged from the Temple, and was about to be stoned and beaten to death when a Roman Commander, Claudius Lysias, intervened by arresting him (Acts 23:26). Paul spoke Greek to the commander and, asking permission to speak to the infuriated crowd, addressed them in Aramaic (Acts 21:37–40).

Paul spoke to the Jerusalem crowd, recounting the story of his conversion. They were quiet and attentive until he recalled the moment that the Lord sent him to preach to the Gentiles. At this they became enraged (Acts 22:22). Once again, the Roman commander intervened and was about to have Paul flogged when Paul said he was a Roman citizen. The centurion desisted, and in order to find out more about the charges against Paul, asked the Sanhedrin to hear his case. When he appeared before the Sanhedrin, Paul exposed their divisions by emphasising that he was a Pharisee, and that he was being tried for his belief in the Resurrection (Acts 23:6). This statement precipitated a row between the Pharisees and the Sadducees, as the latter did not believe in the possibility of resurrection.

Paul was once again in Roman custody. Then, when a nephew of Paul's warned the Roman commander of an assassination plot against him, Paul was given a military escort of 470 soldiers to take him to the more Roman coastal town of Caesarea (Acts 23:21). He was then sent to the Governor of Judea, who was Felix.

Paul's stay in Caesarea lasted over two years (AD 57–59). It is quite possible that, during this period, Luke, who had accompanied Paul back to Jerusalem (see Acts 20:14; 21:15–16), researched his own gospel and published it soon after, to be followed by the book of Acts a few years later.[123] Paul was kept in prison in Caesarea, but in quite an open way. He was able to receive friends and gifts (Acts 24:23). He had been transferred for trial to the Governor of Judea, Antonius Felix, by Lysias, the Roman Commander or Chiliarch in Jerusalem (Acts 24:22). Felix was the Procurator of Judea and married to Drusilla, a Jewess and the daughter of Herod Agrippa I.[124] Felix's older brother was Pallas, a senior administrator in the household of the Emperor Claudius. There were imperial links here, and news of this new Jewish movement may well have travelled from Caesarea to the heart of the imperial household.

Felix had an interest in Judaism (having a Jewish wife), but also in the *Way*—the epithet given to Christianity (Acts 24:14). Soon after Paul's arrival in Caesarea, a heavyweight delegation came down from Jerusalem, including the High Priest, Ananias, other elders of the people—probably members of the Sanhedrin—and their own lawyer, Tertullus (probably a Greek or Roman). The case against Paul that Tertullus presented was that he was a deliberate troublemaker, breaking a peace that had lasted a number of years (Acts 24:2). Tertullus flattered Felix by saying that this peace was due "to your foresight (bringing) reforms to the nation" (Acts 24:2), for which Tertullus expressed himself profoundly grateful.

Paul's defence was that he was not a troublemaker. He had not sought trouble in the Temple when he was arrested, far from it. Paul had brought money for the poor, and it was seditious Jews from Asia who had stirred up trouble (Acts 24:12–20). As he had previously testified before the Sanhedrin, his hope was in all that was promised to his ancestors, now fulfilled in Jesus and in his resurrection from the dead. Once again, as in Ephesus and in Philippi, the charge had more to do with public order than blasphemy, which would be the charge against Christians later. The case was adjourned until the Roman Commander Lysias arrived, but apart from one or two private conversations between Paul and Felix—when Felix hoped for a bribe (Acts 24:26)—nothing further happened. Paul remained in prison for another two years.

With the appointment of a new governor, Festus, the Jewish leaders again raised the case against Paul and a proposal was made that he be tried in Jerusalem. At this point Paul, exercising his right as a Roman citizen,[125] appealed to Caesar. When Festus heard this, he famously said, "You have appealed to Caesar, to Caesar you will go" (Acts 25:12).

There was one more appearance, if not in an actual courtroom, in which Paul appealed to Caesar. And this was before Festus and his friend King Herod Agrippa II, the grandson of Herod the Great, and his sister Berenice. Festus had asked for a second opinion on Paul from the young Jewish king. Herod Agrippa II had succeeded his father aged 17, but was given a diminished territory by Claudius because of his inexperience. This consisted of the former tetrarchies of Philip and Lysanias.[126] In this his lengthiest speech, before Agrippa, Berenice and Festus, Paul recounted his conversion on the road to Damascus, the heavenly vision he was given, the fact that the coming of Jesus, his death and resurrection, was no less than what Moses and the prophets predicted, and the means of bringing enlightenment to both Jew and Gentile alike (Acts 26:19–23). At this point Festus accused Paul of being out of his mind, demented by his great learning, and in a short time trying to make Festus a Christian. Paul replied: "Short time or long—I pray God that not only you but all who are listening to me today may become what I am, except for these chains" (Acts 26:32).

Agrippa advised Festus that, but for Paul's appeal to Caesar, he might have been released. Paul was then handed over to yet another centurion, Julius, from the Imperial Regiment, to be escorted to Rome (Acts 27:1). After an eventful, vivid sea journey involving "an unscheduled shipwreck" in Malta, which was consequently evangelised—and described in one of the most dramatic accounts of a turbulent voyage across the Mediterranean found in ancient literature (Acts 27 and 28)—Paul found himself in the capital of the Empire in the final years of Nero's vicious and capricious rule.

Nero's Rome

When Paul arrived in Rome in February AD 60,[127] Nero had been Emperor for less than six years. Nero was the younger son of Agrippina the younger and Domitius Ahenobarbus. Nero's mother took after her own resilient and fiery mother Agrippina the elder, wife of Germanicus, who had been the darling of Rome.

It was Agrippina the elder who had arrived at Brindisium with the urn of her husband Germanicus's ashes in AD 19 after his untimely death in Antioch. Germanicus was the grandfather of Nero. Agrippina the younger had, as noted, married her uncle Claudius, and subsequently successfully sidelined Claudius's son, Britannicus, in favour of her own son, Nero. Nero's father, Domitius Ahenobarbus, was descended on his mother's side from Mark Antony, as was Agrippina, making them cousins.

If Nero's mother was highly ambitious for him, as her marriage to her uncle, the Emperor Claudius, had made clear, his father was a hard and cruel man. Suetonius says "he was wholly despicable".[128] He deliberately killed a boy who was in the way of his chariot one day, and killed a freedman in his employment for not drinking enough.[129] Nero's infancy and childhood had been anything but stable, with his uncle Caligula banishing his mother when he was three, his father dying in the same year, and he himself being brought up by his aunt, Domitia Lepida. His ancestry and childhood generated deep insecurity and the need for applause and constant approval (stemming from what psychiatrists would today describe as "anxious attachment"), feeding a disposition to cruelty and ambition bequeathed by his parents and family. Add to this the fact that at the immature age of 16 he became Emperor of the greatest

Empire of the early modern era, without in any way having to prove himself, then it was a recipe for perverted government. His unlimited power became bound to whimsical caprice in an unholy alliance of terror. As Miriam Griffin says, "young emperors (like him and Gaius Caligula), with no clear mandate from their predecessor to rule, and no achievements to justify their assumption of power, had difficulty in finding a *persona*".[130] At the beginning of Nero's rule there was cause for hope, but when restraint was cast off, disaster beckoned.

Nero's rule began in AD 54. The next four years, if not promising, were not in themselves disastrous. He gave Claudius a lavish funeral[131] and his speech, crafted by Seneca, was well received. But the struggle from the outset, as Nero perceived it, was to break free from his mother Agrippina's control. On the day of his accession, the password among the Praetorian Guard was "*The best of mothers*". Nero was repeatedly reminded that he was only Emperor because of her manipulation of the power structures of the Empire, not least of Claudius himself.

If Agrippina was his *eminence grise* (not to say *noire*), Seneca was Nero's long-suffering and stoic tutor, appointed by Claudius and Agrippina to guide his steps. He was Nero's speechwriter and adviser, and at first his steadying influence was beneficial. Early on, Nero gave an important speech to the Senate that was no doubt crafted by Seneca, in which he said, like Caligula before him, that he would henceforward desist from treason or *maiestas* trials, would curb bribery in the imperial household and in the courts, and would generally enhance the powers of the Senate.[132] Under Seneca's guidance, Nero seemed to recognise that, "The Principate as a system of government could only remain efficient and secure if it had the consent and co-operation of the senatorial order: the price demanded of the Emperor was respect for constitutional forms, deference to the Senate as a body, and opportunity for ambitious members of the upper orders".[133]

If there were some positive beginnings to Nero's government, the darker side was never out of sight. His relationship with his mother was always strained. Chafing against his marriage to Octavia, Claudius's serious-minded daughter, he found a mistress from his household slaves called Acte. This infuriated Agrippina. She in turn threatened that he could lose his position to his stepbrother Britannicus, which only made

Britannicus more than ever an object of Nero's cruelty and vengeance. He frequently sodomised Britannicus[134] and then prepared to kill him. Inviting Octavia and Agrippina to dinner, he quite probably poisoned Britannicus in their presence, pretending when the latter was in the throes of death that he was suffering an epileptic fit.[135] The body was quickly despatched and cremated so no enquiry could be made into the cause of death. For onlookers, the motive was obvious, even if the final evidence was not forthcoming.

With the removal of Britannicus, Nero's position as *Princeps* was strengthened. Agrippina was sidelined and removed from the imperial household. There was no clear heir waiting in the wings. Another of the restraining cords on Nero's behaviour had been removed, and he began a round of lavish entertainment, pleasing the plebs by distributing extravagant gifts as prizes. Nero lived for spectacle upon spectacle, luxuriating in the praise and popularity of the people, as only the insecure do. He staged youth games, chariot races galore, stage plays, gladiatorial shows; and at all of these events prize upon prize was showered upon the crowd: anything from a bird to a ship was indiscriminately given.[136]

In AD 58, four years into his rule, Nero fell in love again, this time with a woman of senatorial standing, and no slave girl. Her name was Poppaea Sabina.[137] She was exquisitely beautiful and well able to joust verbally with Nero and indulge his passions: "The radiance of Poppaea's charisma exemplified everything that Nero most admired about woman".[138] Poppaea was married to a close friend of Nero, Otho, whom Nero banished to Lusitania on the Atlantic coast of Spain. Octavia, Nero's wife, cousin and the daughter of Claudius, was humiliated by Nero's flaunting of his love for Poppaea. As long as Burrus, who was the Prefect of the Praetorian Guard, an appointee of Claudius, was in post, Octavia was safe, although not for long.

The restraining influences on Nero continued to unravel. He was determined to rid himself of the influence of his mother, Agrippina, with her increasingly bizarre mood swings and overriding desire to exercise control over Nero, even as he made clear his own desire to be rid of her influence and presence. After seeing a collapsing boat in a play in Rome, Nero asked for a replica to be built at Baiae, the popular coastal resort town north of Naples. Then, after dinner at his villa there, Nero escorted

Agrippina to her newly-made yacht with his words echoing in her head: "For you I live and it is thanks to you I rule".[139] Not far from the shore, the roof of the room on deck where Agrippina reclined fell in, and she found herself thrown into the water. Swimming away from the boat, and understanding the evil conspiracy behind its design, she made it to shore, where she was rescued by fishermen. The next day she sent word of her survival through her freedman, Agerinus, knowing full well that it had been Nero's intention to kill her. Nero consulted Burrus and Seneca about what to do, both of whom were aware of Nero's intent. They refused to countenance the murder of Germanicus's daughter, but Anicetus, a centurion of the guard, took matters into his own hands. Taking a column of troops, he surrounded Agrippina's house, and entering it, found her at the back in a dimly lit room with a single slave girl. "The assassins closed in round her couch, and the captain of the *tireme* first struck her head violently with a club. Then, as the centurion bared his sword for the fatal deed, presenting her person, she exclaimed 'Smite my womb', and with many wounds she was slain".[140]

Rome was shocked by the news of this matricide. Nero was relieved, even ecstatic, to be free of his mother's influence. Close associates like Seneca and Burrus, although not willing accomplices, were tarred with the brush of assassination. Seneca even had to write a piece of self-exculpation on Nero's behalf for the Senate. Elsewhere in the Empire there was trouble, with Queen Boudicca raising 80,000 troops from the Iceni and other tribes to challenge Roman rule in Britain, while the Legate Suetonius Paulinus campaigned in North Wales and Anglesey. Four legions were detailed to Britain and eventually pacified the British after suffering heavy losses. All told, nearly 100,000 troops perished from all sides in a bloody campaign around London, St Albans and Colchester, of which by far the greater part were British. Boudicca herself committed suicide in the end. A victory for Suetonius was a victory for Nero, whatever the cost. The plebs in Rome revelled in yet more games and prizes. It was into this febrile and fetid city, besmirched by Nero, that the Apostle Paul arrived via the Appian Way in AD 60.[141]

Paul's sea voyage from Caesarea had been dramatic. The ship was driven for 14 days by a hurricane-force storm from Crete to Malta (Acts 27:13–44). Eventually, it was beached in Malta on a sandbank, and the ship's company of 276, under the leadership of Centurion Julius of the Imperial Regiment, survived (Acts 27:36). A new ship of Alexandrian origin, with figureheads of Castor and Pollux, was chartered in Malta, and Paul arrived in Italy via Sicily (Acts 28:12). Some brethren escorted him from Puteoli to Rome, meeting more brethren at the Three Taverns near the Forum of Appius (Acts 2:15). A house was then put at Paul's disposal, where he met Jewish leaders: "From morning to evening he [Paul] explained and declared to them the Kingdom of God and tried to convince them about Jesus from the Law of Moses and the Prophets" (Acts 28:23b). He was under armed guard, but had considerable freedom and remained for two years in this loose captivity.

It is quite possible that Paul was given an earlier initial trial. In 2 Timothy, Paul refers to a trial from which he escaped further punishment: "At my first defence no-one came to my support, but everyone deserted me. May it not be held against them. But the Lord stood at my side, and gave me strength so that through me the message might be fully proclaimed and all the Gentiles might hear it. And I was delivered from the lion's mouth" (2 Timothy 4:16–17). Eusebius, a church historian from the fourth century (c.260–339), believed that the phrase "delivered from the lion's mouth" may well have referred to Nero. He writes, "the reference being apparently to Nero, because of his bestial cruelty".[142] It is possible that after this trial Paul was "on bail" and even able to travel, going to Spain (Romans 15:28) and Crete (Titus 1:5). Or alternatively, he was able to travel to both of those places before his first trial, which was followed by closer imprisonment (Philippians 1:12–14), and a more serious later trial at which a sentence of execution was passed.

At any rate, the years between AD 60 and 64, during which time Paul was awaiting final trial, saw an increasing decline in Nero's government. Having murdered his mother, his rule became ever more capricious and tyrannical. In AD 62, the restraining figure of Burrus, the Prefect of the Praetorian Guard in Rome, died of throat cancer.[143] Nero's wife Octavia was banished and the new prefect, Tigellinius, was ordered to kill her. False evidence was extracted from a tortured female slave about Octavia's alleged adultery with a slave and she was duly convicted. Rome protested at her impending execution, knowing of both her innocence and pedigree, so instead she was banished to Pandateria, where she was later ignominiously killed. Nero then married Poppaea, who was equal to his excesses: she bathed in asses' milk to enhance her complexion, had her mules shod with gold, and luxuriated in beauty treatments.[144] Nero revelled in the scandals he created, titillated the crowds with his excesses, and planned ever more shocking spectacles, like the one in which he dressed as a woman in order to enact a sham marriage to a freedman. Last of all, he demeaned his office by singing on stage to his own accompaniment on the lyre. These were performances he took so seriously that he went on exacting diets and strengthened his diaphragm by placing weights on his chest. It was not surprising to the stoic pagans of Republican Rome, therefore, that on 18 July AD 64 the great city suffered its worst fire. In their minds, the wrath of the gods had been enflamed by Rome's virtue-less tyrant. Nero, however, had other theories.

The fire destroyed between a quarter and a third of the city: street after street of tenement buildings, where Rome's crowded population squeezed out a living, became heaps of ash. It took six days to bring the blaze under control. In the end, both pauper and Emperor had suffered losses, but who or what was to blame? Nero encouraged the population to think that the fire had been deliberately started and spread: had not hooded figures been seen flitting around the city starting and encouraging fires? Who did Nero blame but a class of Jews called Christians who held views and beliefs most un-Roman? Thus Tacitus writes, "Nero fastened the guilt and inflicted the most exquisite tortures on a class hated for their abominations, called Christians by the populace. Christus, from whom the name had its origin, suffered the extreme penalty during the reign of Tiberius at the hand of one of our Procurators, Pontius Pilate."[145] Despite this execution of its founder, the movement spread, re-emerging in Judea, and was even present in Rome. "An immense multitude were convicted",[146] some were torn apart by dogs, some cruelly crucified in different positions and, perhaps worst of all, some were tarred with pitch and set alight as human torches, illuminating the gardens Nero had opened to the public. At the end of this gargantuan orgy of punishment and persecution, in which Jerome says 979 were killed,[147] Tacitus ruefully concludes that, "even for criminals who deserved exemplary punishment, there arose a feeling of compassion; for it was not as it seemed, for the public good, but to glut one man's cruelty, that they were being destroyed."[148] And it was very likely that, in this vortex of persecution, both Paul and Peter lost their lives, martyred for their Lord. They joined an ever-increasing number of martyrs in this first substantial wave of persecution which would go on for the next two centuries and more.

Some four years later, in AD 68, Nero would be assassinated: he had made so many enemies and his style of rule was an unsupportable scandal to both the republican and military traditions of Rome. Before then, the fire had given Nero an extraordinary opportunity to rebuild, and being Nero, still only 28, he conceived of a building project worthy of a megalomaniac, the Golden House. It would consist of elegant facades, spacious and impressive living quarters, and great works of art scattered throughout. In the entrance hall or atrium would be a huge statue of himself, 120 feet tall, with the head alone four metres high, and fashioned out of bronze in the workshop of Zenodorus.[149] As the Golden House was being conceived and built, Nero took to treading the boards in Naples, taking 5,000 cheerleaders with him to fill the seats and fill out the applause. Humiliating sex games and executions continued in Rome. One family member, Aulus Plautius, was first raped then put to death and even Nero's beloved wife, Poppaea, for whom he had sacrificed Octavia, was attacked by an angry Nero, who stamped on and kicked her when she was pregnant until she died.[150] Appalled by what he had done, he arranged a funeral which was both munificent and tawdry, and later found a male look-alike of Poppaea, nicknamed Sporus, who was castrated and taken as a "lover".

A conspiracy to be rid of Nero was hatched around Gaius Calpurnius Piso, descendant of Gnaeus Piso, the Prefect of Syria who had been made responsible for the death of the beloved Germanicus. But the plot was given away by a freedman in the house of Scaevinus, who told the Emperor's guard about some quite literal sharpening of knives. Piso panicked because of Nero's popularity with the Roman people. He took his own life and the plot was abandoned. A purge of all associated with this assassination attempt followed, including Seneca, who was commanded by the Emperor to take his own life. Although Seneca had been obsessed with a good death throughout his life, when it came to it, his death was a protracted business: with cuts to his wrists, ankles and even behind his knees, before his blood and life drained away.[151] Although Nero embarked on a purge, there were stirrings of revolt in the military further afield. The military Prefect and Praetorian Governor of Gaul, Vindex, informed Nero during the Ides of March AD 68 of his rebellion against him and of his support for Galba, the Governor of Spain. Then the commander of the forces in Germany, loyal to Nero, marched south and defeated Vindex near Besancon. Now Galba showed his hand and took up the rebellion against Nero. Galba declared himself a servant or legate of the Senate. Nero was in serious difficulty. Galba was a hardened soldier, a veteran of the German front, and the Praetorian Governor of Spain, one of the great provinces of the Empire. Then Otho, the former husband of Poppaea, gave his allegiance to Galba. When Petronius, commander of the North Italian legions, also gave his loyalty to Galba, Nero panicked. He left the Golden House in Rome with Sporus, taking quantities of poison with him, and made for Phaon's villa outside Rome. There he heard that the Senate had declared him a public enemy. Numbed by the suddenness of this reversal, Nero wept, but soon the sound of approaching hooves stopped outside the villa. Nero took his dagger and drove it into his neck, and with his death ended the dynasty of Julius Caesar and Augustus. A time of great turbulence followed, with three Emperors succeeding one another in AD 68 in swift succession: Galba, Otho and Vitellius, until another general, Vespasian, returned from the Jewish War, started the new and shorter dynasty of the Flavians.

The Jewish Rebellion

During Nero's reign, the Empire had faced challenges to its hegemony in both East and West. There was nothing unusual in that. For almost all its life, the Empire would face danger from the German tribes in the north and from the Parthians in the east. Already, Roman legions had suffered serious defeats: Varus, who lost three legions to Arminius at the Teutoborg Pass in AD 9,[152] and earlier Crassus, who also lost three legions to the Parthians at Carrhae in 53 BC.[153] Honour had eventually been restored with the return of the Eagle standards and defeat thus avenged, but these were deep blows to a culture predicated on military success. During Nero's reign, considerable resources were expended on the defeat of Boudicca and the Iceni in Britain. Armenia had been subjugated, and its client king, Tiridates, sumptuously entertained and crowned by Nero. However, the most serious rebellion came late in his reign: the Jewish rebellion of AD 66.

Judea was frequently a place of revolt against imperial power. It had been so under the Maccabees, who had deeply resented the offence given to Judaism by Antiochus Epiphanes, and it was again restless under the Romans during the first century AD. The triggers for the revolt were punitive taxes, religious offence given to the Jews in Caesarea, and the desecration of the Temple by the Roman Governor of Jerusalem, Florus, who seized money from the Temple treasury and killed many Jews, further enflaming relations.[154] Agrippa II and his sister Berenice tried to mollify the incensed crowd in Jerusalem, reasoning that a rebellion against Rome could never succeed,[155] but they did not convince the Zealots or the Sadducees. Chaos came quickly to the region. The Jewish community was slaughtered in Caesarea. Jewish leaders emerged in Galilee, Edom and Jerusalem. Often rivals, these leaders were unable to make common cause. So, with the region seething with dangerous discontent, the Roman Provincial Governor in Syria, Cestius Gallus, took the Legio XII Fulminata into Judea to quell the rebellion. After initial success, the legion was ambushed at Beth Horon by Jewish rebels led by Eleazar ben Simon, with the loss of 6,000 legionnaires and the legion's Eagle. At this point, Nero gave his general Vespasian the order to suppress the revolt. Little did Nero know that Vespasian would be his eventual successor and the founder of a new dynasty.

Vespasian, 57 years old and a veteran soldier, travelled overland from Achaia, via the Dardanelles, to Antioch, despatching his son Titus to Alexandria to fetch the XV Legion.[156] Already the initial success of the Jews against Cestius had been reversed, when Roman cavalry under Antonius had held and defeated successive charges by the Jewish rebels at Askelon, where two of their principal leaders, John and Silas, had been killed.[157] The Jews, Josephus says, lost 10,000 at Askelon, followed by a further 8,000 in a later attempt to retake the town. Vespasian, now commanding from Antioch, sent Roman reinforcements to Antonius, consisting of 6,000 infantry and 1,000 cavalry, and Titus, marching at great pace, arrived at Ptolemias with the XV Legion. Three legions were now assembled, consisting of the Fifth, the Tenth and the Fifteenth, as well as other forces committed by client rulers of Rome in the area and additional cohorts. Josephus tells us that the total force was 60,000 strong.[158]

Vespasian continued his advance into Galilee, besieging the town of Jotapata, where Josephus, the later writer of the Jewish histories, was commanding Jewish forces. When all seemed lost, Josephus advised his compatriots to surrender rather than commit mass suicide. Vespasian put Josephus in custody, but Josephus's prophecies that the siege would be successful for the Romans, and that greater glory awaited Vespasian in the future, persuaded the general to treat him kindly.[159]

Vespasian's advance continued along the coast, taking Caesarea, and then deeper into Galilee, where stiff resistance was offered by the Jews at Gamala, and then on to Gischala, in northern Galilee, which quickly capitulated.[160] Eventually, a path was cleared for the assault on the capital Jerusalem itself. Jerusalem was the penultimate stand of the Jewish Rebellion (the last desperate stand being at Masada), but the Jews there were seriously divided about the right course of action. Zealots from Galilee, under their leader John of Gischala, took refuge in the Temple itself, while Ananus, the newly appointed leader of the priestly party, and High Priest himself, raised a force to clear the Zealots out of the Temple area. After a rallying speech by Jeshua, another High Priest, a fierce battle ensued against the Zealots.[161] Then the Zealots made a pact with the Idumeans, and entered the city from the south, overwhelming the priestly party and killing Ananus and thousands beside.[162] Some of the Zealots deserted to another commander, Simon ben Giora, so there was now a three-way battle inside Jerusalem, even as the Roman legions approached its walls.[163] Eventually, these Jewish parties united to prepare Jerusalem to meet a common and much more deadly foe.

Even as the Jews prepared Jerusalem for the oncoming onslaught of Roman power, Roman imperial politics intervened to change the command of the Roman forces in Judea. The year AD 69 was the year of the four Emperors alluded to in Revelation 13:3, recorded as a vision on the island of Patmos by John the Divine, almost 30 years later (c. AD 94).

John spoke of "a fatal wound" in the Empire: this was the year in which Nero committed suicide and then Galba, Otho and Vitellius succeeded to the purple in swift and bloody succession. Each Emperor was in turn proclaimed such by the legions under his command: Galba by the Spanish legions, while the Praetorians in Rome chose Otho, who had previously assassinated Galba, and the German legions proclaimed for Vitellius, who marched on Rome, defeating Otho, who then committed suicide.[164] The troops in the East, hearing of Vitellius's seizure of the Empire for himself, resented his arrogance and usurpation. First, the Third legion in Pannonia under Antonius Primus, almost unknown to Vespasian, declared him Emperor, then the legion in Alexandria under the Prefect Tiberius Alexander[165] and finally the four legions in Syria and Judea swore allegiance in person.

Almost a quarter of the Roman forces had declared for Vespasian. Taking up his cause, the troops that were loyal to him marched on Rome while he went to Alexandria to secure grain and await the outcome. There was little opposition to Vespasian's troops. Vitellius was hunted down by the mob, stripped half naked, dragged through the streets and killed on the Gemonian Steps, and his body thrown into the Tiber.[166] The Senate declared Vespasian Emperor. His father gave Titus the command of the legions in Judea for the final assault on Jerusalem, which was not long in coming.

It is Luke's gospel especially that expresses grief over the predicted siege and destruction of Jerusalem. When Jesus rode into Jerusalem, receiving the praise of the people, we are told that he stopped and made an awful prophecy over the city:

> As he approached Jerusalem he wept over the city and said "If you, even you, had only known on this day what would bring you peace—but now it is hidden from your eyes. The days will come upon you when your enemies will build an embankment against you and encircle you and hem you in on every side. They will dash you to the ground, you and the children within your walls. They will not leave one stone on another, because you did not recognise the time of God's coming to you."
>
> *Luke 19:41–44*

Later, answering the disciples' observations about the beauty of the Temple, Jesus said:

> "As for what you see here, the time will come when everyone of them will be thrown down" and "when you see Jerusalem being surrounded by armies, you will know that its desolation is near. Then let those who are in Judea flee to the mountains, let those in the country not enter the city. For this is the time of punishment in fulfilment of what has been written. How dreadful it will be in those days for pregnant women and nursing mothers! There will be great distress in the land and wrath against this people. They will fall by the sword and will be taken as prisoners to all nations. Jerusalem will be trampled on by the Gentiles until the times of the Gentiles are fulfilled."
>
> **Luke 21:6, 20–24**

What was prophesied, and then recorded by Luke, probably after the destruction of Jerusalem, was dreadfully fulfilled. The siege would last seven months from February to August AD 70. With three legions encircling the city to the west and a fourth on the Mount of Olives to the east, they surrounded the city, enforcing a complete siege. A wall was constructed around the city in April. No food could enter, and a population of probably several hundred thousand faced starvation. Platforms were constructed from which the city walls might be effectively attacked. Within the city, the Jewish Zealots were divided between two leaders, John and Simon. Starvation soon drove the besieged to desperation: old men were beaten for their crusts, wives robbed their husbands, mothers ate their babies, others were tortured, others still, bringing weeds and plants from forays into the areas outside the walls, were robbed on their return.[167] Deserters were crucified mercilessly around the city; some preferred capture to starvation. By May (Artemisios, in the Macedonian Lunar Calendar Josephus used), some of the siege towers were ready to be positioned.[168] Eventually, the need to assault the fortress Antonia in Jerusalem could no longer be avoided. The attack was made, led by a Syrian, Sabinus, spurred on by Titus's address to the troops, and followed by a centurion, Julian from Bithynia. Despite fierce resistance from the

Jews, the Antonia was eventually taken and destroyed. By now fire was engulfing the Temple next door. Titus had no wish to see this great edifice, which he wanted for a pagan temple, destroyed. Josephus was called on to address the defenders as a Jew, albeit a Jew now working for the Romans. He appealed for the sanctuary to be spared. But his words were flung back in his face and his appeal was disdained because of his betrayal.[169] The final bitter struggle for the Temple Mount ensued. Molten silver was hurled at the wooden gates. The Temple began to burn from Jewish and Roman attacks alike. Titus could not prevent it, try as he might, and Josephus depicts the scene of unrestrained violence and war in a lurid description:

> Yet more terrible than the din were the sights that met the eye. The Temple hill, enveloped in flames from top to bottom, appeared to be boiling up from its very roots; yet the sea of flame was nothing to the ocean of blood, or the companies of killers to the armies of killed; nowhere could the ground be seen between the corpses, and the soldiers climbed over heaps of bodies as they chased the fugitives.[170]

The Temple treasury melted along with all its wealth and fine clothes. A further 6,000 women and children perished in the precincts. Still the Jews refused to surrender. In the end, John and Simon, their leaders, were captured, the former taken into lifelong imprisonment and the latter as an exhibit in the Triumph at Rome. Josephus concludes his account of the siege with an overview of the history of Jerusalem, "Neither its long history, nor its vast wealth, nor its unparalleled renown of its worship sufficed to avert its ruin". So ended the siege of Jerusalem.[171]

Few Christians could have remained in the city. The leader of the church in Jerusalem, James the Lord's brother, had already been martyred.[172] Eusebius also records James's martyrdom from stoning and clubbing by his fellow Jews under the Sanhedrin.[173] With the killing of their leader in Jerusalem just before the siege, and presumably the persecution of Christians by the Zealots in the city during the siege, the church there would either have perished or been left with just a very few survivors. Some may have escaped before the siege to other parts of Judea, such as Pella.[174]

In Rome, Vespasian became Emperor; a refreshingly straightforward army commander turned Emperor after the extreme insecurity and violence of Nero's Rome. Vespasian's rule from AD 69–79 was unexceptional; except for the stability it gave the Empire after the final years of Nero's reign and the years of civil war which followed it. After another fire in Rome, a number of building projects were started, not least of which was the Coliseum.[175] Suetonius's verdict on Vespasian was, "He was from first to last modest and restrained in his conduct of affairs".[176] Vespasian was succeeded by his well-liked son, Titus, the vanquisher of the Jews. Skilled with sword and pen, Titus embodied the virtues of a Roman. Brought up by Claudius with his son Britannicus, he was well connected in the former imperial family. His rule was cut short by illness, however, and he died just two years after taking up his position as Emperor. It was on his watch that Mount Vesuvius destroyed Pompeii, the great luxurious centre of Campania.

The final and least noble of the Flavian dynasty was Domitian. Overshadowed hitherto by his more talented and better-educated brother Titus, he was determined to show his mettle. His rule signalled a regression to some of the worst features of Nero's rule: lavish entertainment of the plebs; arbitrary executions of senators;[177] capricious violence and provocative and scandalous personal behaviour. He ignored the principles of the Republic, preferring to centralise power under his personal rule. He elevated the worship of the Emperor with a resulting persecution of Christians and Jews. He successfully consolidated the power of the Empire in Dacia and the Low Countries. Not surprisingly, with such assertive, not to say obsessive, tendencies (he was, for instance, neurotic about his baldness and was irritated by the sound of oars, so was towed at some distance from a rowing boat), he neither won friends nor influenced people for good. He was assassinated in AD 96 and was succeeded, with the support of the Senate, by his senior civil servant, Nerva, who ruled for a brief two years.

The Age of Augustus was now over. The Empire settled into being led by generals rather than by politicians. It was in this atmosphere that the church began its second century since the birth of Christ, with a mixture of maturity but great vulnerability.

CHAPTER 3

The Formation of the Church

By the end of the first century AD, the church was becoming established across a wide area of the Mediterranean and the Near East, albeit often in vulnerable groups. In the second century, there would be evidence of Christianity spreading through the Roman Army, as far north as Hadrian's Wall, and as far east as Persia. Paul's missionary journeys, together with the movement of Christians across the Empire and the work of other Apostles, such as Peter, John and Thomas, accounted for some of this expansion. Churches formed through a multitude of means, but with the same essential core.

When Paul recounted the founding of the church in Thessalonica, he recalled how the Word of God came to them in the power of the Spirit and through the lips of the Apostle. The seed of the Word and the power of the Spirit gave birth to the church there, as indeed everywhere. Paul wrote that when "you received the word of God, which you heard from us, you accepted it not as the word of men, but as it actually is, the word of God, which is at work in you" (1 Thessalonians 2:13). He continued, "Our Gospel came to you not simply with words, but also with power, with the Holy Spirit and with deep conviction" (1 Thessalonians 1:5). The result was that these new converts—many of whom came directly from paganism, others from the Jewish faith or with the title "god-fearers" (see Acts 13:26)—became imitators of Paul (1 Thessalonians 1:6) and imitators of Christians they had not met, but who had experienced the same testing they had (1 Thessalonians 2:14). Churches in Judea, Thessalonica and elsewhere were birthed out of similar experiences of great testing and suffering, brought on them by their own kinsmen.

The stories of the founding of these first-century churches were different in each setting. In Corinth, while feeling weak and vulnerable in a worldly and commercial setting, Paul nevertheless founded a church in that city. He recounts how he came to Corinth in "fear and trembling", determined to know nothing but "Jesus Christ and him crucified" (1 Corinthians 2:1–4). The church in Rome was not begun by an Apostle, but by ordinary Christians. The church in Antioch was started by Greeks from Cyprus and Jews from Jerusalem (Acts 10:19–20). In Alexandria, the church was begun, so tradition has it, by the preaching of Mark, possibly after the persecution of Christians in Rome under Nero. Peter could well have started the churches in Cappadocia, Pontus and Bithynia. He later wrote to these churches from Rome in his first epistle (1 Peter 1:1). The preaching of Paul began the church in Ephesus (Acts 19). In every case the church was founded where Christ was acknowledged as Saviour and Lord, and who then manifested his presence among them through the Holy Spirit, making a disparate group of believers into the body of Christ and filling their hearts with love for him, although they had never seen him (see Romans 8:15, 16; 1 Corinthians 12:12; 1 Peter 1:8).

By the end of the first century, leading churches existed in many of the main provinces of the Empire. At some point after the destruction of Jerusalem, the church there was re-founded, with Eusebius telling us that Symeon, the son of Clopas (either the Clopas of John 19:25 or Luke 24:18), was made leader or bishop of Jerusalem in succession to James, the Lord's brother. Further north in Antioch, the church was first led by Peter before his move to Rome, then by Evodius (AD 53–69)[178], and then by Ignatius, who was martyred during the reign of Trajan and whose influence we will study further. The churches around Ephesus, including those of Smyrna and Hierapolis, were important both in inspiring resistance to imperial pressure—as with Polycarp—but also in conveying the influence of John the Apostle, who was resident in the vicinity of Ephesus for many years. A line of tradition can be sketched from John the Apostle through Papias, the Bishop of Hierapolis close by Laodicea, to Polycarp and then Irenaeus.

Eusebius speaks of John being alive during the reign of Domitian and then exiled to Patmos. Irenaeus is quoted by Eusebius as saying that John was still alive during the reign of Trajan (AD 98–117).[179] To have survived till Trajan's reign would have made John a very old man, probably in his eighties.[180] In Rome, which had been at the centre of Nero's persecution, successive leaders or bishops were appointed. Peter was followed by Linus, Anenclatus by Clement, who shepherded the flock of God at Rome to the end of the first century. The final regional or provincial centre of the church in this period was at Alexandria.

Alexandria had become a centre of learning from the time of the Ptolemies, with its large Jewish community, extensive library and philosophical schools. We have no certain knowledge that the Christian community was planted there by Mark, Peter's close associate and the gospel writer, but we know the church came into existence there in the early part of the first century. We hear of a Bishop of Alexandria, one Annianus, dying after 22 years as Bishop of Alexandria in the reign of Domitian (AD 81–96).[181] This means that the church in Alexandria would have been formed in at least the AD 60s or before—not long after Paul's missionary journeys.

Another source concerning the early church in Alexandria is Philo, the Hellenistic Jewish philosopher. Philo was active in Alexandria from AD 20–50. He was a devoted Jew, but also wedded to classical Hellenism, and in particular Plato. What Philo sought to do was to show that the best of Greek philosophy, e.g., Platonism, was not at variance with the Hebrew scriptures—themselves translated into Greek—because wittingly or unwittingly these Greek ideas were themselves derived from Hebrew concepts evident in the scriptures. In fact, Philo attempted to do what Christian Alexandrian apologists, such as Clement of Alexandria, came to do in the second century, as we shall see.[182] Eusebius recalls Philo's admiration for the Apostolic Christians he met either in Rome or Alexandria. In particular, Eusebius tells us that Philo met Peter in Rome during the reign of Claudius, presumably following the return of Christians to the city after their expulsion, and there Philo experienced the spiritual life of what he calls their "therapeutic communities" in his *De Vita Contemplativa*, although these communities were hardly yet fully-fledged Christian ascetic communities. He was impressed by their absence of materialism, and their devotion to a discipline of prayer and fasting. Philo recalls:

Having first laid down self-control as a foundation for the soul,
they build the other virtues upon it. None of them would take food
or drink before sundown, as they hold that philosophy deserves
daylight but darkness is good enough for bodily needs. So to the
one they assign the day, to others a small part of the night. Some
think of food only once in three days—those in whom a greater
passion for knowledge is rooted; others delight and luxuriate as
they feast on the wisdom that richly and ungrudgingly supplies
their doctrines that they hold out even for twice the time, and
scarcely taste necessary food in six days, having accustomed
themselves to this.[183]

Philo was impressed by these spiritual disciplines, and by the seeming
vow of virginity taken by some of the women who "set their hearts not
on mortal children but on the immortal, which only the soul that loves
God can bring into the world".[184]

If Philo's descriptions accurately reflect these Christian ascetic
therapeutic communities in Rome or Alexandria in the reign of Claudius
(AD 41–54), then Christianity must have come to both Rome and
Alexandria earlier still. What we have by the end of the first century are
distinctive Christian communities with their own traditions, coloured
by their local context and forms of spiritual experience, with a strong
resonance of shared life and spiritual discipline. Five regional variations of
tradition or theology can be discerned by early in the second century, and
these can be characterised as follows: pragmatism in Rome, conservatism
in Antioch, asceticism and syncretism in Alexandria, Jewish-Hellenistic
emphasis in Ephesus and its surrounding churches, and an apocalyptic
tendency in Jerusalem. Later, Carthage would be added as another
provincial, regional church with a fierce and uncompromising spirituality.
The interactions of these traditions, which in part resulted from their own
regional and spiritual emphases, set up a dialectic, which came to shape
the development of the church in the next four centuries.

The Apostolic Fathers

One of the main influences we know of on the church from the end of the first century until the mid-second century was a group known as the Apostolic Fathers. They are responsible for a disparate collection of writings produced either towards the end of the Apostolic age or immediately afterwards. These writings existed before, during and after some of the principal books of the New Testament were fully established. The term "Apostolic Father" includes (generally speaking) 11 contributors whose works we will survey in this chapter. The term first occurs in the *Hodegos* of Anastasius, the seventh-century anti-Monophysite abbot of St Catherine's Monastery in the Sinai. Although in the end none of their writings would be included in the Canon of the New Testament, which was finalised by the end of the fourth century, some important codices like *Codex Sinaiticus* included writings by the Apostolic Fathers as if they were scripture.[185] At the end of the first and the beginning of the second centuries, these texts, which had circulated separately, as in the case of *The Shepherd of Hermas,* were widely read by churches. Indeed, several were more popular than some of the general non-Pauline epistles, but that changed after the closure of the Canon.

Some of the Apostolic Fathers' writings were grouped together in codices, as in the case of *Codex Alexandrinus*, which contained the New Testament, and 1 and 2 Clement. In 1627, the patriarch Cyril Lucar of Constantinople presented the fifth-century manuscript *Codex Alexandrinus* to King Charles I of England, from which the Royal Librarian, Patrick Young, published the *Epistles of Clement*, which were not available in the new translation of the Bible—the King James Bible— as they were not canonical.[186] *Codex Alexandrinus* is now exhibited in the British Museum.

Among the writings of the Apostolic Fathers are two letters, probably from Clement of Rome. They are called epistles, although the second letter is really a sermon. Since earliest times, the author has been thought to be Clement of Rome. Clement was the third Bishop of Rome after Linus (2 Timothy 4:21) and Anacletus and was thought to be an associate of Paul (Philippians 4:3). Eusebius assumed this,[187] and regarded him as the author of the epistle, but there are still some doubts about Clement's

authorship, for nowhere in the epistles is his position as Bishop of Rome
referred to. Indeed, some argue that the office of Bishop of Rome had
not yet been created. Some scholars suggest that the letter represents a
perspective advanced by just one of the "many house churches" in the
city, in an age when a variety of forms of Christianity were present in
Rome.[188] It is, in any event, difficult to reach back with any certainty into
a period so sketchily recorded.

The occasion for the letter called *1 Clement* was dissension in the church
in Corinth: a church which, as we can see from Paul's correspondence
with them, all too often fell into disunity (see 1 Corinthians 3:1–9).
Probably written between AD 95 and 96, it could well predate parts of
the New Testament, in particular Revelation and even St John's Gospel
itself.[189] The letter was directed at a rebellious group of younger church
members who had risen up against the presbyters and ousted them
from their position—*plus ça change plus c'est la même chose*. Clement
now wrote to the church, and in particular the perpetrators, urging
repentance, unity and the restoration of the evicted presbyters. The
opening greeting of the epistle demonstrates the temporary nature of
the church on earth in view of the persecution and hardship it was then
suffering. So Clement writes, "The church of God that temporarily resides
in Rome to the church of God that temporarily resides in Corinth".[190] The
writer goes on to explain that recent events which he describes as "sudden
and repeated misfortunes" had served to divert his attention from the
"matters causing disputes among you, loved ones, involving that vile and
profane faction stoked by a few reckless and headstrong persons to such
a pitch of madness that your venerable and renowned reputation has
been greatly slandered".[191]

Clement seems to think that their dissension is, in part, the result
of too much blessing, and to this effect he quotes Deuteronomy: "My
loved one ate and drank and became large and fat and kicked out with
his heels".[192] This blessing has the effect of producing not humility and
gratitude, as it should, but jealousy, envy, strife, faction, persecution and
disorderliness, war and captivity, "so the dishonourable rose up against
the honourable, the disreputable against the reputable, the senseless
against the sensible, the young against the old".[193] Clement calls on the
Corinthians to forswear jealousy of all kinds, giving examples not only

from the Old Testament, but more recently from the Apostle Peter's life, who "because of unjust jealousy bore up under hardships not just once or twice but many times. And having thus born witness he went to the place of glory that he deserved".[194] We do not know what Clement was specifically referring to here in connection with Peter, but it is quite probable that it was well known to the Roman church.

One aspect of the epistle, which is fascinating given its probable date, is the use of scripture as well as commonly held belief or tradition. The letter is heavily scripturally-based (mostly drawn from the Old Testament), with much of the narrative of the Old Testament quoted, along with copious references to Abraham, Lot, Moses, Rahab, Elisha, Elijah and Ezekiel.[195] Frequently, these Old Testament characters are called "hospitable",[196] meaning generous, with their hospitality commending them to God's mercy and protection. The Psalms are also quoted often. Alongside the use of the scriptures (i.e., the Septuagint, the Greek rendering of the Old Testament), Clement quotes sections of the Sermon on the Mount, as in the following passage: "Show mercy, that you may be shown mercy; forgive, that it may be forgiven you. As you do, so it will be done to you; as you give, so it will be given to you; as you judge, so you will be judged; as you show kindness, so will kindness be shown to you; the amount you dispense will be the amount you receive".[197]

If these are quotations from the Canonical Gospels of Matthew and Luke, it means that these gospels were circulating at least in the major churches by the end of the first century. On the back of such familiarity with the gospels, Clement can say, "For Christ belongs to those who are humble minded, not to those who vaunt themselves over his flock. The sceptre of God's majesty, the Lord Jesus Christ, did not come with an ostentatious show of arrogance or haughtiness—even though he could have done so—but with a humble mind, just as the Holy Spirit spoke concerning him".[198] Clement proceeds to give a full quotation of the Servant Song from Isaiah 53.[199] Clement had clearly grasped the nature of Christ's servant leadership, which he now looked to see expressed in Corinth.

Alongside Clement's familiarity with the synoptic gospels, there is also a reliance on the Pauline epistles in his letter, especially Paul's letter to Corinth,[200] as well as the Epistle to the Hebrews and, not surprisingly, 1

Peter. Like the writer to the Hebrews, Clement encourages his readers to consider those in the gallery of faith, such as Enoch, Noah and Abraham, as examples to follow, as recorded in Hebrews 11.[201] Of Abraham, Clement writes, "Because of his faith and hospitality, a son was given to him in his old age; and in obedience he offered him up as a sacrifice to God on one of the mountains that he showed him".[202] Faith and generosity were virtues to follow while rancour, bitterness and division, evidenced in the dispute in Corinth, were sins to eschew and repent of.

Undergirding the whole epistle is a rich theology which is indicative of the New Testament that Clement knew. Much of Clement's appeal to these tearaway usurpers of rightful authority in the church in Corinth was based on a deep understanding of the order and pattern God has given his people, firstly in creation, then in redemption, and lastly in the church, exhibited there by the presence of bishops and presbyters.[203] Clement tells his readers "we should gaze intently on the Father and Creator of the entire world and cling to his magnificent and superior gifts of peace and acts of kindness. We should observe him with understanding and look upon his patient will with the eyes of our soul".[204] Such gazing at the Father's rule in the created order will only show how peacefully the world is subject to his management. If such is the case in the created order, how much more should it be so in his new creation, the church. Clement concludes his argument by saying, "Let our children partake of the discipline that is in Christ. Let them learn the strength of humility before God and the power of pure love before God. Let them learn how the reverential awe of him is beautiful and great, and how it saves all those who conduct themselves in it".[205]

Furthermore, this attitude, he says, should reflect a reverence for "the Lord Jesus Christ whose blood was given for us. We should respect our leaders. We should honour the elderly [or the presbyters in some mss]; we should discipline our youth in the reverential fear of God; we should set our wives along the straight path that leads to good".[206] Clement holds before them a thumbnail sketch of true greatness: "Let a person be faithful, let him be able to speak forth knowledge, let him be wise in his discernment of words, let him be pure in deeds. For the more he appears to be great, the more he should be humble, striving for the good of all, not just for himself".[207] Here is the true leader. For

Clement it is "shameful, loved ones, exceedingly shameful and unworthy of your conduct in Christ, that the most secure and ancient church of the Corinthians is reported to have created a faction against its presbyters, at the instigation of one or two persons".[208]

Finally, he prays a prayer for the church that wonderfully exhibits the warm affection and godliness of his heart:

> We ask you, O master, to be our helper and defender. Save those of us who are in affliction, show mercy to those who are humble, raise those who have fallen, show yourself to those in need, heal those who are sick, set straight those among your people who are going astray. Feed the hungry, ransom the prisoners, raise the weak, and encourage the despondent. Let all nations know you, that you alone are God, that Jesus Christ is your child, and that we are your people and the sheep of your pasture.[209]

This letter must rank as one of the most comprehensive and clearly argued epistles in existence, to a church sundered by division to come back into line. It was apparently read in the Corinthian church till the mid-second century, according to Dionysius, and is cited by several of the early Church Fathers. It is also the first surviving instance of the church of Rome extending its influence over another church. Clearly, Rome already had a sense of its own authority.

What is known as the Second Letter of Clement to the Corinthians was probably written in the second century, and not by Clement at all. It is much less well attested than 1 Clement. A different author with a different style wrote it. It only exists in three manuscripts: *Codex Alexandrinus* (a fifth-century manuscript which misses a section from 12.5 to the end), *Codex Hierosolymitanus* (1056) and a Syriac manuscript of the New Testament dated from 1169.[210] It is not a letter at all, but a homily or sermon. Some scholars think it may have originated in Egypt and its high Christology and emphasis on truth from the outset may have been an answer to the Gnostic tendencies in Egypt in the second century. Others think that it came from Greece, possibly Corinth, as the author shows knowledge of the Isthmian Games, held in the first and third year of each Olympiad. It is an interesting document for showing us the sources available to the author and how he used them, and the issues with which he was concerned.

The homily was initially based on Isaiah 54, which is used in order to show the extent of the salvation that God has given. A restored presbyter following 1 Clement may have preached it in Corinth, but there is no certainty about this. It is clearly Christocentric, with the opening sentence setting the tone: "Brothers, we must think about Jesus Christ as we think about God".[211] Once again, there seems to be distinct knowledge of the synoptic gospels, with seemingly direct quotations from Matthew in particular.[212] In the homily there is a clear call to repentance and an invitation to prove faith by works. The writer very appropriately quotes Jesus as saying, "Not everyone who says, 'Lord, Lord' will be saved, but only the one who practices righteousness".[213] So the writer continues, "Having abandoned our temporary residence in this world, we should do the will of the one who called us and not fear departing from this world. For the Lord said, 'you will be like sheep in the midst of wolves'".[214] However, if this all seems familiar from the gospel account, the writer then quotes an unknown source in which Peter says to Jesus, "What if the wolves rip apart the sheep?"[215] The point being that there were either other sources available to the writer, or perhaps a different rendering of the gospel.

The overall message is a call to repentance and to demonstrate this in good works: guarding the flesh; giving God praise; pursuing virtue; not being double-minded; awaiting the Kingdom with love and righteousness; coming to the point of regarding neither female or male as such, but simply as fellow Christians;[216] and not being crowd-pleasers. Such is the Christian's calling, he says, and the way into it is through repentance.

Antioch and Asia

If 1 and 2 Clement give us evidence of Clement teaching in Rome in the early second century, and his care of another church in Corinth, as well as insight into the sources available to him from the embryonic origins of the New Testament, other churches in Asia were also influential at this time, with apostolic ministries. Antioch in Syria and the churches in and around Ephesus in the province of Asia were deeply influential in the development of the Christian faith in their regions and further afield. Defining elements of an eastern and western theology can also be discerned by the beginning of the second century, to which we shall return. Notable figures of these Asian churches were Ignatius, Papias and Polycarp. All, like Clement, were known as Apostolic Fathers, and their writings have come down to us in the collection known by the same name. Each of these leaders was well aware of the cost of being a Christian, and either faced martyrdom or recorded the deaths of close colleagues. Both Ignatius and Polycarp were martyred and Papias was close to many who were killed for their faith.

Ignatius was either the second or third Bishop of Antioch. In his commentary on Luke, Origen says he was the second bishop after Peter,[217] whereas Eusebius says he was the third bishop following Peter and Euodius.[218] Ignatius was arrested in Antioch in c.AD 108, probably with others, as part of a persecution of the Christians in Antioch, who were then taken to Rome for execution or, as Ignatius firmly believed, to be fed to wild animals there. Ignatius wrote a number of letters to churches while journeying under guard to Rome. These letters were to the Ephesians, Magnesians, Trallians, Philadelphians, Smyrneans and Polycarp himself. The main concern of Ignatius's correspondence was the unity of the church, which for him was found principally in obedience to the bishop, the rebuttal of false teaching—and in particular an incipient Gnosticism—and his own forthcoming death as a martyr. We shall follow these themes in his correspondence.

Ignatius's route to Rome was overland. He calls his guards "leopards", writing, "From Syria to Rome I have been fighting the wild beasts, through land and sea, night and day, bound to ten leopards which is the company of soldiers, who became worse when treated well".[219] This nickname of leopards for his guards was a premonition of what lay ahead. So he continued, "May I have the full pleasure of the wild beasts prepared for me; I pray they will be found ready for me. Indeed, I will coax them to devour me quickly—not as happens with some, whom they are afraid to touch".[220] His route took him from Antioch to Smyrna, where he met Polycarp, then to Troas, from where he sailed for Rome, being martyred midway through the reign of the soldier Emperor Trajan (AD 98–117), one of the so-called Five Good Emperors (as described by Machiavelli!). Along the way, conscious of the brevity of his life to come, he fired off urgent letters to the communities he passed by and to Polycarp, who in turn would follow his example.

To the Ephesians, he writes in warm terms. He calls them "a church foreordained from eternity to obtain a constant glory which is enduring and unchanging, a church that has been unified and chosen in true suffering" (recalling possibly Paul's epistle: see Ephesians 1:1–12 and its emphasis on predestination).[221] He praises the Bishop Onesimus, the presbytery and the deacons, as well as Burrhus and Crocus.[222] He seeks "symphonic unison" between the leadership and the church.[223] Taking submission to the bishop as a cardinal virtue, he says "we are clearly obliged to look upon the bishop as the Lord himself",[224] and to follow both his teaching and his warnings. Ephesus was subject to the visits of false teachers,[225] who were probably gnostic and docetic, meaning that they denied that Christ, the Logos, had really come in the flesh. In response, Ignatius re-enforces the truth of Jesus being the God-man by saying, "For there is one physician, both fleshly and spiritual, born and unborn, God come in the flesh, true life in death, from both Mary and God, first subject to suffering and then beyond suffering, Jesus Christ our Lord".[226] Carried away with his allegory of church-building, Ignatius writes:

> You are the stones of the Father's temple, prepared for the building of God the Father. For you are being carried up to the heights by the crane of Jesus Christ, which is the cross, using as a cable the Holy Spirit; and your faith is your hoist, and love is the path that carries you up to God. And so you are all travelling companions bearing God, bearing the temple, bearing Christ, and bearing

the holy things, adorned in every way with the commandments
of Jesus Christ.[227]

One of Ignatius's favourite words for himself, for a Christian, or for a
church, is God-bearer.[228]

In his next letter, to the Magnesians (Magnesia was on the Meander
in Turkey), Ignatius, as was his custom, praises their youthful Bishop
Damas and the presbyters, Bassus and Apollonius.[229] He pleads for unity.
He warns against reverting to Judaism.[230] Again, with a telling phrase,
he cautions them against "being snagged by the fish hooks of worthless
ideas".[231] Ignatius's next letter is to the Trallians, from Tralles. He had
met their Bishop Polybius in Smyrna and reckoned he had seen their
"entire congregation in him".[232] Again, to be subject to the bishop was to
live in the way of Jesus Christ; for the bishops and presbyters were like
the council of God and, typically, he goes as far as saying "apart from
these, a gathering cannot be called a church".[233] In other words, where
the bishop is, there is the church. He calls them to unity, and urges they
watch out for heresy.[234]

Ignatius's other letters to Asian churches or individuals, written from
Troas before he set sail for Rome, were to the Philadelphians, to the
Smyrneans and to Polycarp, the Bishop of Smyrna. Once again, Ignatius
praises their bishop, whose gentleness has amazed him and of whom he
says, "he is attuned to the commandments like a lyre to the strings".[235]
Ignatius's encouragements are by now familiar: they are to eschew evil
plants (false teaching), maintain unity, celebrate but one Eucharist
among themselves with the bishop and presbyters present,[236] love the
Old Testament prophets who predicted Jesus's coming,[237] and be cautious
of any Judaizers.[238] More than this, it seems that when Ignatius cried
out in a loud voice a prophetic word during worship: "Pay attention
to the bishop and the presbyter and deacons", he was asked where this
conviction came from.[239] Ignatius replied, "I knew it from no human
source; but from the Spirit (who) was preaching, saying, 'Do nothing
apart from the bishop; keep your flesh as the Temple of God; love unity;
flee division; be imitators of Jesus Christ as he is of his Father'".[240]

Ignatius also writes to the Smyrneans—with great praise for their
unity, sincerity and wisdom—and to their bishop, Polycarp.[241] In his

opening greetings he says their faith comes from the sufferings of Christ, and real sufferings at that, unlike the teachings of the docetic teachers. (Docetism means teaching that Jesus *seemed as if he came in the flesh,* but did not really—from *dokeo,* to seem.) He warns them to avoid false teachers, and to pay attention to the prophets and the gospels.[242] Ignatius then reflects on his forthcoming death in one of the amphitheatres of Rome with the extraordinary words, "To be near the sword is to be near God, to be in the presence of the wild beasts is to be in the presence of God—so long as it is in the name of Jesus".[243] Suffering and martyrdom have become in his spirit a sacrament of God's presence. He goes on to say that love and faith are everything and the test of true sincerity in teaching is whether they have "an interest in love, in the widow, the orphan, the oppressed, the one who is in chains or the one set free, the one who is hungry or the one who thirsts".[244]

Ignatius also wrote to Polycarp, who was the Bishop of Smyrna for a long time. He was martyred around AD 155, in his eighties. Ignatius may have been writing to him from Troas in *c.*AD 110, in which case Polycarp would have been in his early fifties when he received Ignatius's letter. Polycarp was to continue as bishop for a further 40 years until his own martyrdom. In his letter to Polycarp, after staying with him on his way through Smyrna from Antioch to Troas, Ignatius once again repeats his by now familiar themes of unity and love. He writes: "Gently bring those who are more pestiferous into subjection, stand firm against false teaching, don't neglect the widows, set slaves free through the common fund, encourage husbands and wives to love each other, let those who can remain celibate." It is essentially a pastoral epistle, ending with encouragement to send an emissary to Antioch, which had recently seen its own unity restored.[245]

All this should be done in the anticipation of the return of Christ: "Await the one who is beyond the season, the one who is timeless, the one who is invisible, who became visible for us, the one who cannot be handled, the one who is beyond suffering, who suffered for us, enduring in every way on our account".[246]

Finally, in anticipation of his arrival in Rome, Ignatius writes to the Roman church. He writes from Smyrna on 24 August, although which year we cannot be sure.[247] It is a letter full of anticipation of his death and martyrdom, and full of requests that he be ready for it. He asks that his death be like a libation to God and that he, the Bishop of Syria, be deemed worthy to be found at the setting of the sun (the West) after sending him from where it rises (the East).[248] He says to those in Rome, "coax the wild beasts, that they may be a tomb for me and leave no part of my body behind, that I may burden no one once I have died [presumably with burying him]. Then I will be truly a disciple of Jesus Christ when the world does not see even my body".[249] It a consistent theme in this epistle that in being made invisible (i.e., not even his body being seen), his faith and the Christian faith will be made more visible. So he says, "If I be found a Christian, I can also be called one and then be faithful—when I am no longer visible in the world. Nothing that is visible is good. For our God Jesus Christ, since he is in the Father, is all the more visible".[250] In invisibility he seeks immortality and the fulfilment of his faith. Ignatius is under no illusions, but nevertheless sees what awaits him in Rome as the attainment of life: "Fire and Cross and packs of wild beasts, cuttings and being torn apart, the scattering of bones, the mangling of limbs, the grinding of the whole body, the evil torments of the devil—let them come upon me, only that I may attain to Christ".[251]

The final two Apostolic Fathers to consider are Papias and Polycarp. Papias and Polycarp were contemporaries, each being a bishop in the same region of Asia: Polycarp of Smyrna, present-day Izmir, and Papias of Hierapolis, present-day Pamukkale. Pamukkale or Hierapolis is well known for its hot mineral, calcite-laden springs which contrasted with Laodicea, whose spiritual temperature was lukewarm, neither hot nor cold (see Revelation 3:1). Hierapolis reached its zenith in the second century, having been rebuilt after an earthquake, and its thermal waters were a steady attraction for visitors and citizens alike. It was here also that the evangelist, and one of the seven, Philip, last located in the New Testament at Caesarea (Acts 21:7), was martyred.

Papias lived between c.AD 60 and 130, and was Bishop of Hierapolis in the latter part of his life. Both Irenaeus and Eusebius record him as having met the Apostle John. Referring to Irenaeus's entry, Eusebius writes of him: "To these things Papias, who had listened to John and was later a companion of Polycarp, and who lived at a very early date, bears written testimony in the fourth of his books; he composed five".[252]

On the other hand Papias himself makes no such direct claim of having met the Apostle John.

Papias's most important contribution was a five-volume work entitled *Expositions of the Sayings of the Lord*. These, apart from a few fragments, are lost to us. But Eusebius, in his *History of the Church*, comments on it, telling us that Papias preferred an oral tradition to one that was written down, a common view in the ancient world. So Papias enquired whenever he could of the sayings of the Lord from "Andrew or Peter, or what Philip or what Thomas had said, or James, or John or Matthew or any of the other disciples of the Lord, and what things Aristion and the elder John, disciples of the Lord, were saying, for I did not suppose that what came out of books would benefit me as much as that which came from a living and abiding voice".[253] This comment is in itself an interesting reflection on authority and tradition in a period before the Canon of New Testament scripture was in any way fixed. Papias makes clear that, although he had little or no direct contact with the gospel writers or Apostles, he did have some with a secondary group of witnesses he calls the "Presbyters", and it was from these, along with John the Elder, the possible writer of Revelation, that he heard an oral tradition of Jesus's teaching which he incorporated into his five-volume work.[254]

Papias's interpretations of some of our Lord's sayings, and presumably the Book of Revelation, were extremely literal, not least when it came to teaching on the millennium—the expectation that Jesus would reign on earth for a thousand years, after a general resurrection, and that "(this) Kingdom of heaven will exist tangibly on earth".[255] Eusebius is caustic about Papias on this point as he would presumably be of any millenarian writing:

> He (Papias) says that after the resurrection of the dead, there will be a period of a thousand years, when Christ's kingdom will be set up on this earth in material form, I suppose he got these notions by misinterpreting the apostolic accounts and failing to grasp what they said in mystic and symbolic language, for he seems to have been a man of very small intelligence, to judge from his books.[256]

Thus, Eusebius showed he had little time for Papias. But Papias nonetheless had his followers, not least the great Irenaeus, who was also fascinated by the theory of a millennial rule of Christ on earth.

The final church leader from Asia who appears among the Apostolic Fathers is Polycarp himself. Ignatius met him in Smyrna on his way to Rome after his arrest in Antioch. The Christian church in Smyrna was no stranger to persecution and suffering from earliest times (Revelation 2:10), but it was to find its most celebrated martyr in Polycarp. Polycarp was described by both Irenaeus and Jerome as a hearer of the Apostle John.[257] Like others in the province of Asia, he had a strong exposure to the life and teaching of John, whose writings and theology were so influential. Apart from the account of his martyrdom, recorded by Irenaeus and circulated by the church at Smyrna to the Christians in Pontus, we have one of Polycarp's epistles, which form part of the writings of the Apostolic Fathers. It is addressed to the Philippians.

This letter to the Philippians is in part a cover letter to copies of Ignatius's correspondence to the Asian churches, for which they had asked. But it is more than just a complimentary slip attached to the great Bishop of Antioch's letters. It also addresses a number of issues in the Philippian church. The letter contains strong echoes, if not almost direct quotations, from Peter's first epistle (see 1 Peter 1:8). So he says, "Even without seeing him, you believe in him with an inexpressible and glorious joy that many long to experience".[258] There are also strong echoes of Paul's letter to the Ephesians, surprisingly few references to Paul's letter to the Philippians, and also quotations from John's first letter,[259] both of which must have been readily available to Polycarp.

The letter has five overall themes, which are as follows: a general encouragement to holy living;[260] an encouragement to the presbyters to be compassionate and caring;[261] a warning to those with gnostic tendencies; then, in a manner strongly reminiscent of John's epistle (see 1 John 4:2b), a warning to be aware of "those who do not confess that Jesus Christ has come in the flesh";[262] and lastly, a warning to a couple in the church with leadership responsibilities, involved in a fraud of some kind.[263] The letter was carried by Crescens to Philippi.

If this letter is in many ways unremarkable, the account of Polycarp's martyrdom remains one of the most vivid and moving accounts in early church literature of martyrdom, made all the more poignant because of his great age at the time of his death. The account of the martyrdom of Polycarp is in the form of a letter sent by the church in Smyrna to the church of Philomelium, in Phyrgia. It is written by one Marcion (not to be confused with the heretic who denied the necessity for the Old Testament scriptures). It is a martyrology, that is, an account of martyrdom that is in part didactic, showing how such suffering might be borne, and part inspirational, that is, showing how the grace of God sustained Polycarp right up to the end. The author seems to steer a middle course on the subject of martyrdom: on the one hand showing how to embrace bravely the consequences of a refusal to sacrifice to pagan deities or the Emperor, while on the other hand not glorifying in martyrdom for its own sake, as some extreme groups did. (For example, the Montanists in Phyrgia and later North Africa were known to volunteer for martyrdom; although some, like one Quintus, backed down and complied.[264])

The story of Polycarp's martyrdom is vivid and compelling. At the outset, the author or scribe, Pionius—who possibly copied the text from Irenaeus's own personal library edition, and which was subsequently included in seven manuscripts—gives a general introduction to martyrdom.[265] Such was their courage that,

> They (martyrs) endured even when their skin was ripped to shreds by whips, revealing the very anatomy of their flesh, down to the inner veins and arteries, while bystanders felt pity and wailed. But they displayed such nobility that none of them either grumbled or moaned, clearly showing us all that in that hour, while under torture, the martyrs of Christ had journeyed far away from the flesh, or rather, that the Lord was standing by, speaking to them.[266]

Some, like Germanicus, actually drew the wild beasts onto themselves, holding onto them as they were devoured.[267] But the crowd cried out, "Away with atheists [i.e., the Christians who would not serve the pagan gods]. Find Polycarp!"[268]

News of this renewed persecution of Christians had spread through the town and Polycarp, persuaded by the Christians, had gone into hiding;

first in one safe house and then another. Apparently, "three days before he was arrested, while praying, he had a vision and saw his pillow being consumed by fire. Then he turned to those with him and said 'I must be burned alive'".[269] The chief of police in Smyrna was uncannily called Herod. Polycarp was eventually found and taken to the amphitheatre, asking only for an hour to compose himself in prayer and offering his captors food and drink, all the time being encouraged to say, "Caesar is Lord", so that he might not face punishment.[270] As Polycarp entered the stadium, he heard a voice saying, "Be strong Polycarp, and be a man." The proconsul now tried to persuade him to swear "by the Fortune of Caesar, repent".[271] But famously Polycarp replied, "For eighty-six years I have served him, and he has done me no wrong, how can I blaspheme my king who saved me?" Polycarp was neither moved nor terrified by the proconsul's threat of turning the wild beasts on him. He was then threatened with burning, to which he replied that there were eternal fires to be frightened of, but not earthly ones. The proconsul's herald declared to the crowd that Polycarp had confessed himself a Christian (hardly surprising since he had been Bishop of Smyrna for 40 years!), whereupon the crowd shouted for his death. The crowd called for a lion to be set loose. The Asiarch replied that he had concluded the animal hunts, so a fire was proposed instead. Polycarp undressed, asked not to be tied to a stake in the pyre as he would remain in it of his own accord: "Leave me as I am; for the one who enables me to endure the fire will also enable me to remain in the pyre without moving, even without the security of nails".[272] Polycarp then prayed, "I bless you for making me worthy of this day and hour, that I may receive a share among the martyrs in the cup of your Christ, unto the resurrection of eternal life in both soul and body in the immortality of the Holy Spirit".[273] The fire was lit, and the flames did not so much consume him as surround him "like a vaulted room" in which bread was baked or gold or silver refined. A sweet aroma swept over the stadium. An executioner stabbed him. A dove was released and his blood extinguished the fire.[274]

After a dispute over his body, it was eventually cremated on the instructions of a centurion and the Christians reclaimed his bones. They were "more valuable than gems, more precious than gold".[275] He died on 23 February at 2pm, in the month of Xanthikos AD 155.[276] "He was not only an exceptional teacher but a superb martyr".[277] His death would inspire the church for centuries to come. Alongside the scriptures, the account of his martyrdom would be fuel for the church's witness.

Scripture and Other Writings

The formation of the Canon of the New Testament proceeded over a period of almost 400 years, although by the mid-second century AD much of the corpus of the New Testament was fixed.[278] Nevertheless, the period of time during which the Canon established itself, or was agreed by the church as directed by the Spirit, was a long one. It would be like the final edition of Shakespeare's work being decided in 2016, 400 years after his death.

The point is worth making, because it would be anachronistic to think otherwise. Most churches (let alone individual members) did *not* have a copy of the Bible in the fourth century. Equally, it would be a misapprehension to think that the whole of the New Testament was formed simultaneously across the Empire. It was a process proceeding at different paces and with different emphases across the church in the Empire—for that is where the church existed for most of the first five centuries. Some did have the whole New Testament as it developed, but these were wealthy churches in major cities. Only the Codex, as opposed to the scroll, was more widely used in the fourth century, but was still a very costly item. The scriptures would have been a treasured possession of the church, and its members would have gathered to hear them read and explained. Very few, except the very wealthy, would have had their own copy and many, like the Desert Fathers, would have had only a portion of scripture, such as the Psalms.

The main elements of the New Testament were *in situ* by the mid-second century, including Paul's epistles, the gospels, 1 Peter and 1 John. Again, the rate of assimilation of these writings into canonical status differed widely across the main churches of the Empire. It seems the Western Church quickly attested the authority, veracity and genuineness of the three Synoptic Gospels. These were probably written in Syria between AD 70 and 90, for a Greek-speaking Jewish community, possibly in Antioch. In which case, this was after the destruction of the Temple, about which teaching figures prominently in the latter discourses in Matthew 24. Sources for the gospels are generally thought to be Mark, Q and Matthew, and Luke's own sources, M and L. Earliest fragments of the gospel are from the end of the second century, called P4, and a larger fragment from the third century, called P37. But we can see from Clement of Rome's letter to Corinth that he had ready access to the record of Jesus's teaching, especially the Sermon on the Mount.[279] The content of the Gospel of Mark was mostly given to Mark by the Apostle Peter, with whom he lived in Rome (see 1 Peter 5:13). Irenaeus attests to this in his work *Against Heresies* III.1.2, saying:

> Matthew published a written Gospel for the Hebrews in their own tongue, while Peter and Paul were preaching the Gospel in Rome and founding the church there. After their passing, Mark also, the disciple and interpreter of Peter, transmitted to us in writing the things preached by Peter.[280]

Mark was quickly accepted as the spokesman for Peter and the Apostolic Fathers quoted from him.[281] In the same quotation, we are told by Irenaeus that Luke also wrote a gospel. This was probably written or published in Antioch in two volumes (Luke and The Acts of the Apostles) in the late first century between AD 80 and 100, also using Mark, Q and L (Luke's own source, perhaps researched during the years of Paul's imprisonment in Caesarea: see Acts 23–26).

Finally, John's gospel is generally dated the end of the first century, around AD 90, and may have been attached to a Jewish Johannine Greek-speaking community in Asia responsible for the gospel, the epistles and Revelation, which were soon embedded in the Eastern Church in Antioch and Alexandria. Of all the gospels, John's took longest to establish itself because it came out of a milieu of Gnosticism, which it sought also to rebuke. There are many papyrus fragments of John's gospel attesting to its significance; the earliest of these is the John Rylands' Papyrus, P52, from c.AD 130, containing verses from John 18 (John 18:31–33; 18:37–38).

Understandably, the gospel was not probably known in Rome for a little while and presumably had not reached Rome by the time of Clement's first letter, dated AD 95/96.[282]

By the late second century, and after a process of sifting out extraneous Gnostic gospels and Apocalyptic writings, four gospels were decided upon or authenticated themselves.[283] In particular, the Gnostic gospels, which mainly emanated from the East, had to be sifted out of circulation from among Orthodox churches. The Gnostic gospels seem to have been a desert industry, with most of the writings originating from Syria and Egypt, and then drifting west with Gnostic teachers. In 1945, on the east bank of the Nile, an entire Gnostic library from AD 400 was discovered. This included over 50 treatises in Coptic, collected into 13 codices and covering a thousand pages.[284] Thirty-nine of these 52 tractates, discovered at Nag Hammadi, are Gnostic in character and some, like the *Gospel of Thomas*, appear to have had close contact with the four gospels and probably came from Syria in AD 140.[285] During the struggle with the Gnostics and their principal teachers in the mid-second century, namely Basilides of Alexandria and Valentinus of Rome, the four gospels of the New Testament were validated and widely accepted. Irenaeus wrote that four was the perfect and God-given number for gospels:

> It is not possible that the Gospels can be either more or fewer in number than they are. For, since there are four zones of the world in which we live, and four principal winds, and since the church is scattered throughout the whole world . . . it is fitting that she should have four pillars breathing out immortality all over and revivifying men.[286]

Irenaeus goes on to draw parallels between the four gospels and the four covenants in the Bible (under Adam, after the Flood, with Moses and the New Covenant). It seems, however, that this system missed out the covenant with Abraham, and the one with the four living creatures in the Book of Revelation (4:6–9). For Irenaeus, four was therefore the perfect, universal number (as it is in the Book of Revelation: e.g., the Four Horsemen of the Apocalypse (Revelation 6), the four living creatures (Revelation 4:6–9), and the four descriptions of humanity as being from every nation, tribe, people and language (Revelation 7:9). For Irenaeus, four gospels would suffice to tell the story of Jesus perfectly.

The other collection that was to stand alongside the four gospels in an early formation of the Canon in the mid-second century was the Pauline epistles. The epistles were written, generally speaking, some twenty years earlier than the gospels, except for Mark, which was the earliest gospel. A collection of the Pauline epistles was made, and once their utility outside their immediate context became evident, they assumed a universal or catholic significance. The first solid evidence of there being a firm collection of Paul's epistles is provided by Marcion, the second-century heretic who denied that the God of the Old Testament was the Father of Jesus Christ. Marcion's collection (*c.*AD 140) consisted of the following letters in this order: Galatians, 1 and 2 Corinthians, Romans, 1 and 2 Thessalonians, Ephesians (known to Marcion as the Laodiceans), Colossians, Philippians and Philemon. This list, with Galatians at the head, perhaps demonstrated Marcion's theology and the premise that there was a discontinuity between Judaism and Christianity, or it may simply have been his attempt at a chronological ordering. Another list, called the "seven-churches edition", set in the order of the decreasing length of each epistle, also seems to have originated in the mid-second century.[287]

Paul's letters were used, not only by Marcion to try and prove his case, but more positively by several of the Apostolic Fathers: Clement of Rome, Ignatius of Antioch, Polycarp of Smyrna, and the author of 2 Peter. Later, in the second century, Clement of Alexandria, Irenaeus and Tertullian would also use these letters of Paul. It is clear that most Pauline letters were common currency by the mid-second century and had been "broadly valued in the preceding period as well".[288]

A final list of great significance was discovered by Ludovico Antonio Muratori in 1740 and came to be known as the Muratorian Canon. It comprises 85 lines of "barbarous Latin".[289] The codex that preserves the list is an eighth-century manuscript. The fragment itself probably dates from the late second century. It is not a Canon as such, but a list of mostly New Testament books with theological comment by the author. The author deals first with the gospels. Matthew is not mentioned, and is almost certainly omitted because of the fragmentary nature of the list itself, i.e., the Canon omits Matthew because the fragment begins *after* Matthew's gospel. The list then mentions both Mark and Luke as gospel writers—the latter is designated as a physician, an assistant to Paul, but not an eye-witness—and then John, who wrote after a period of fasting and only with the approval of the other Apostles, especially Andrew. The Book of Acts is mentioned followed by 13 of Paul's epistles (1 and 2 Corinthians, Ephesians, Philippians, Colossians, Galatians, 1 and 2 Thessalonians and Romans (in that order), then four epistles to three individuals: Philemon, Titus and Timothy, which were written out of personal affection, but nevertheless have universal application). Finally, the author includes two apocalyptic books: Revelation and Peter—probably 2 Peter. Works by Arisnoes, Valentinus and Miltiades, Marcion's book of Psalms, and Basilides were excluded. One work, which was much appreciated in the church of the late second century, but should not be read in church, according to the author of the Canon, was the popular *The Shepherd of Hermas*.[290]

Three works that were influential in the mid-second century are *The Shepherd of Hermas*, the *Didache* and the *Epistle of Barnabas*. Each was influential in the formation of the life and discipline of the early church. *The Shepherd* was probably written in the middle of the second century and was included in the list of works in the Muratorian Canon, but with the proviso that it not be read in church, as it was "composed quite recently in our times".[291] The writer of the Canon also says that Hermas's brother was Pope Pius, whose dates are around AD 140.

The Shepherd of Hermas is a piece of visionary and didactic writing featuring an angel instructing an ordinary Christian in a pastoral setting, which gave it wide appeal. In fact, it became the most popular non-canonical book in the church in the second and third centuries.[292] Hermas himself, probably not an office holder in the church and a resident of Rome, was a freed slave who became re-acquainted with his former owner, Rhoda, whose beauty and demeanour he much admired, even desired, when he saw her bathing one day in the Tiber. Later, in a vision, Rhoda reproved him for his lustful desire. The vision haunted him and drove him to repentance; and repentance is one of the chief themes of this book. As he reflects on his need of repentance, Hermas has a number of visions; and in the fifth of these an angelic figure called the Shepherd is revealed to him. In the remaining sections of the book, made up of commandments and parables, the Shepherd teaches Hermas how to live.

In the first vision, Rhoda accuses Hermas of his sin. At first he protests, but then begins to think, "If this sin is recorded against me, how can I be saved?"[293] He then sees an elderly woman "dressed in radiant clothes and holding a book in her hands". She, it seems, represents the church. She reproves him, not so much for his evil lust as for his failure to strengthen his own household in their discipleship. She then extols the Creator in a reading. In the second vision, he sees the same woman, who gives him her book, which he then copies. Once again he is encouraged to teach his wife and family the words of the book. In a third vision, Hermas is shown a tower being built by six young men, angels, who accompany the elderly woman. The tower is the church and is built with stones over water. Some of the stones represent baptism, while others represent Apostles, bishops and teachers.[294] Some are righteous, some are faithful, some need to repent, some are rejected.

This vision turns into a long and elaborate allegory about who might be included in the tower and whether repentance is available to those who have stumbled after baptism. The answer given is that after baptism there is but slight opportunity for repentance, hence the growing custom of postponing baptism to nearer death.[295] In the fourth vision, Hermas sees an enormous wild beast with a head like a ceramic jar. At the same time he sees a young woman dressed as a bride.[296] She interprets the meaning and significance of the beast as representing a time of trial coming on the church. The fifth vision reveals the Shepherd, "an eminent looking man dressed in shepherd's clothing wrapped with a white goat's skin around his waist, with a bag on his shoulder and a staff in his hand". He sits next to Hermas and says, "I have been sent from the most reverend angel to live with you for the rest of your life".[297] He then proceeds to teach Hermas the Commandments.

The Commandments form the second main section of the book and have to do with speaking truthfully, and with sexual purity: "If you keep thinking about your own wife, you will never sin".[298] The book also covers the correct treatment of a wife who has committed adultery, the limits of repentance, the importance of patience and the danger of irascibility, the influence of the angel of righteousness and the angel of wickedness on our lives,[299] the danger of double mindedness,[300] the avoidance of grief and the need to be clothed with cheerfulness,[301] how to discern true prophecy,[302] and finally, how to resist sins, "the chief of which is the desire for someone else's wife or husband, and for abundant wealth, with avoiding desire for many extravagant foods, drinking bouts, and many other such foolish luxuries".[303] Following these precepts, a person will "engage in righteousness and virtue, truth and fear of the Lord, faith and meekness, and every good thing like them. When you do these things you will be an acceptable slave of God and will live to him".[304]

The final section of *The Shepherd of Hermas* is the recounting of several parables by the Shepherd. Several of these are quite laborious allegories of the church, not unlike the vision of the church being built like a tower. The first parable is a call to live lightly in the foreign city of a Christian's earthly exile and to build up wealth, "by carrying out ministries for him".[305] There is another parable about an elm and a vine: the elm is like a rich person, strong, but not fruitful; the vine is like the poor, needing the strength of the rich (the elm) to grow upon, but fruitful nonetheless. Thus rich and poor find in each other a helpful and needed synergy.[306] A further parable describes the work of Jesus and the Holy Spirit in the field of God, clearing it and protecting it, and sowing it for a fruitful harvest. The longest two parables—the eighth and the ninth—which take up nearly half of this entire section, are about sticks from a willow tree and stones. The sticks of all kinds represent different types of Christians. Some are like apostates, some are withered, and some double-minded, some are slanderers, but some are green and promising. This parable of the sticks is like a variant of the Parable of the Sower, but more cumbersome and less clear.

Finally, the parable of the stones is similar to the earlier vision of the church as a tower over water; only this time the tower is surrounded by mountains which come to represent different types of people. In this parable, six men command virgins representing the holy spirits or virtues of the faith, such as simplicity, innocence, cheerfulness, holiness, truth, harmony and love[307], who build the tower[308] on a rock and gate (representing Christ). A great figure looming over the tower judges which stones should be used. Hermas watches virgins building the tower and is invited to stay with them: "You will sleep with us, but as brother, not a husband. For you are our brother, and we will be living with you from now on because we love you so much".[309] Inevitably, some stones are cast out because they are seduced by women "wearing black garments".[310] The angel of repentance gives them a final opportunity. In this way the tower is built.

Taken as a whole, *The Shepherd of Hermas* appears to be a folksy spiritual tale, high on revelation from the angelic Shepherd, but at variance with some teaching of the Epistles. Part of his purpose is to counteract the restriction of divine grace as posited by the letter to the Hebrews (see Hebrews 10:26). Perhaps his writing is closest to the epistle of James in tone, but has little of the limitless grace of God, which is so much a feature of Paul's writings. Nevertheless, *The Shepherd* remained a popular piece, and was even included in the *Codex Sinaiticus* in the late fourth century, influencing Origen in his writing. While an imaginative and visionary work, it had little of the succinctness and the significance of the *Didache*.

The discovery of the manuscript of the *Didache* was little short of a sensation, perhaps only surpassed by the discovery of the Dead Sea Scrolls. Philotheos Bryennios found it in the Library of the Holy Sepulchre in Jerusalem in 1873. There are two main manuscript sources. The first is the *Codex Hierosolymitanus* (dated 1056), which was the manuscript discovered by Philotheos Bryennios, and the second text is bound into the *Apostolic Constitutions*, a fourth-century church order manual. There are also three other fragments: a Greek papyrus found at Oxyrhynchus in Egypt, a fifth-century Coptic fragment, and finally an Ethiopian paraphrase used for Ethiopian Church order.[311]

The *Didache* refers to teaching given by the Twelve Apostles, which was then summarised by another writer in the form of a church manual. It may well have come from another unknown source, which is now lost. It covers four areas of church life: an ethical path known as the two paths, one of life and the other of death; a section on church ritual, e.g., how to fast, pray, baptize and celebrate the Eucharist;[312] a further section on how to deal with itinerant teachers, prophets and Apostles, refusing those who have come only to sponge, order food "in the spirit", or who stay longer than two days;[313] and a final short section on how to elect bishops and deacons.[314] It concludes with a discussion of what will happen in the final days.[315] Its special significance lies in how early it was circulating. It was probably written at the end of the first century AD in either Syria or Egypt. It is therefore in evidence at the end of the Apostolic age and possibly overlaps with some of John's works. It demonstrates how the ethical teaching of the gospels, especially the Sermon on the Mount, had permeated the life of the church and also how a pattern of church life was emerging quite clearly by then. It served to regulate church life and provide a path of spiritual development and discipleship.

The final two documents, which form part of the Apostolic Fathers and which impinge on the formation of the scriptures and the teaching of the early church, are the Epistle of Barnabas and the Epistle of Diognetus. The former is an attack on Judaism and the latter is an explanation to an enquirer, Diognetus, about the life and teaching of the church.

The relationship between Christianity and Judaism was fraught from the beginning. Initially, the church was strongly persecuted in Jerusalem. Paul argues in the epistles, especially in his letters to the Romans and Galatians, that observation of the Law cannot save a person (Galatians 3:15 and Romans 3:20). The Jews have the privileges of the Patriarchs, the Law, the Sabbath and circumcision, Paul argues, but none of these things can redeem them (Romans 9:1–9). Christ is the fulfilment of the Law and of what was promised to Abraham (Galatians 3:6–14), and through him there is redemption. One of the great questions was how the church should regard Judaism. Paul spelt this out to the Romans in chapters nine to eleven of his epistle, and the Council of Jerusalem spelt out how much of the Law Gentile converts must observe (see Acts 15:24–29). Despite this, the early church had a tempestuous relationship with Judaism. At one extreme was the outright heresy of Marcion, who rejected the God of the Old Testament as being a jealous tribal god whom he described as a demiurge, thereby betraying some gnostic tendencies as well. Marcion was a wealthy businessman and ship owner from the Black Sea whose father was a bishop and who later resided in Rome from AD 140. The church condemned him as a heretic, but his influence was extensive, as we shall see.

By contrast, Barnabas, the companion of Paul, was said to have written the letter bearing his name somewhere between the destruction of the Temple in Jerusalem and its rebuilding as a pagan temple by Hadrian.

It is commonly thought to have been written in Alexandria.[316] Like *The Shepherd of Hermas*, it forms part of *Codex Sinaiticus*. Barnabas is at pains to show how the Jews have misunderstood the Law they have been given and the calling which is theirs, and also the purpose of sacrifices. He generally spiritualises the commandments of the Law in a way that is not consistent with the purpose for which they were originally given. Thus he asks: "Did I command your fathers who came out from the Land of Egypt to offer whole burnt offerings and sacrifices to me? No, this is what I commanded them: let none of you bear a grudge against your neighbour in your heart, and do not love a false oath".[317] He goes on to describe the fast that God has chosen from Isaiah 58. Yet in fairness to the Jews, they were commanded to sacrifice a burnt offering daily (Leviticus 6:8–13). Barnabas then explains how Christ's sacrifice was a fulfilment of all that went before.[318] His method is consistent, even if at times his exegesis does not accord full value to the original purpose of the ceremonies and practices given to the Jews. Israel's reliance upon sacrifices, fasting, dietary laws and later temple worship cannot cover up their corruption of heart, hypocrisy and lack of charity or justice, he says. In other words, their practices cannot hide their hollow faith. In his final section, Barnabas turns to the "twin paths" of living. This formulation of Christian living had become common by the mid-second century, with echoes in the *Didache* (1:1), *The Shepherd of Hermas* (for example, chapters 36 and 38) and now in Barnabas (see 18, 19). The Two Paths' teaching consists of clear instructions on what to avoid (e.g., sexual immorality, pederasty, adultery, aborting a foetus[319]), along with things to do (e.g., "think about the judgement night and day" and "love like the apple of your eye everyone who speaks the word of the Lord to you"[320]). The black path will lead to destruction, the good path to being "glorified in the Kingdom of God".[321] It was firm teaching, but it is easy to see how it could tip over into a religion of works.

The final and, perhaps, the most delightful and illuminating of the works of the Apostolic Fathers is the Epistle to Diognetus. It was included in the works of the Fathers by Gallandi in the eighteenth century.[322] He thought it was written by Apollos (see Acts 19:1). The manuscript was not unearthed until 1436, when it was accidentally discovered by a young cleric in a pile of packing in a fish shop in Constantinople, from where it passed into the hands of the Dominicans.[323] This manuscript then found its way to Strasbourg, where it was destroyed by fire in the Franco–German war on 24 August 1870. By then other copies had been made, but the original was lost.

The letter is written to Diognetus, who has enquired about the Christian way, in much the same way Luke writes his gospel and Acts for Theophilus (Luke 1:3; Acts 1:1). It is an appeal to leave behind pagan idol worship.[324] It has little that is complimentary to say about Judaism and the observance of circumcision, the Sabbath, fasting or food laws.[325] Christians, the author goes on to say, in contrast to Jews, cannot be distinguished from others by their customs. Indeed, they live as resident aliens: "They live on earth but participate in the life of heaven".[326] The reason is because "the truly all powerful God himself, creator of all and invisible, set up and established *in their hearts* (my italics) the truth and the holy word from heaven, which cannot be comprehended by humans.[327] God revealed his plan in the fullness of time to his Son."[328] The author went on:

> But then, when the time arrived that God had planned to reveal his goodness and power (Oh the supreme beneficence and love of God!), he did not hate us, destroy us, or hold a grudge against us. But he was patient, he bore with us, and out of pity for us he took our sins upon himself. He gave up his own Son as a ransom for us, the holy for the lawless, the innocent one for the righteous, the righteous one for the unrighteous, the imperishable one for the perishable, the immortal one for the mortal. For what else could cover our sins but the righteousness of that one? How could we, who were lawless and impious, be made upright, except by the Son of God alone? Oh, the sweet exchange! Oh the inexpressible creation! Oh the unexpected acts of beneficence! That the lawless deeds of many should be hidden by the one who was upright, and the righteousness of one should make upright the many who were lawless![329]

The author then urges Diognetus to find this knowledge himself, to discover the Father and to follow God's ways in blessing his neighbour.

For happiness consists not in wealth and power, but in humble service, and above all, Diognetus is encouraged to live in grace.[330] It is a jewel of a letter.

In summary, by the mid-second century, a firm collection of canonical books had been established, but not yet all of what would become the New Testament had been agreed and assembled. A number of other authors, later to be called the Apostolic Fathers, had works circulating among the churches. If scripture, and to a lesser extent these other writings, were formative in the life and development of the church, they were established alongside a growing pattern of leadership. It was in this period that three orders of ministry, which were to shape the church, clearly emerged.

Orders of Ministry in the Church

In the church, as recorded and sketched by the Acts of the Apostles, there was already clear evidence of ministerial structure, albeit in a fluid form. All authority was derived from God and Christ (Matthew 28:18 and John 19:11), but the Apostles were given a particular authority in the life and mission of the church. Originally, there were eleven Apostles present in the upper room before Pentecost (Acts 1:13). Peter then announced the criteria for selecting a twelfth Apostle, to fill the place of Judas. The person was to have "been with us for the whole time the Lord Jesus went in and out among us, beginning from John's baptism to the time when Jesus was taken from us. For one of these must become a witness with us to the resurrection" (Acts 1:21, 22). Matthias was selected.

The Apostles then spearheaded the preaching of the gospel, firstly in Jerusalem and then in Judea (see Acts 2:14–41; 3:1–26; 5:12–16). They resided in Jerusalem (Acts 9:27; Galatians 1:18–19). Then, with the growing size of the community and the necessity to distribute food to the Hebrew and Hellenised (but Jewish) widows, a further group of deacons was appointed to serve at tables. The criteria for their appointment were that they must be "full of the Spirit and Wisdom" (Acts 6:3). Quite clearly, several among these deacons were gifted in both knowledge and evangelistic skill, notably Stephen and Philip (Acts 7 and Acts 8:4–40). In Acts 9, the conversion of Paul brings the arrival of the "last" Apostle (1 Corinthians 15:8), whose testimony of appointment was that he too had had an encounter with the risen Lord (Acts 9:5, 15, 16). Paul was eventually received by Peter and the Lord's brother James (Galatians 1, 18–19) and gradually welcomed as an Apostle into the churches at Jerusalem and Antioch (Acts 11:25–26).

The first rung in the structure of leadership in the early church was thus the appointment of Apostles, who then in turn appointed deacons (Acts 6:6) to help with the practical work of ministry, although some, as in the case of Philip and Stephen, were gifted in other ministries as well.

Two other insights about leadership became apparent in the early church. Firstly, Paul made it clear, as did Peter, that the Holy Spirit gifted the church for ministry (see Romans 12:6–8; 1 Corinthians 12–14; Ephesians 4:11–13; 1 Peter 4:10, 11). Hans von Campenhausen underlines this reality in the early church, emphasising the authority of the Spirit in the Pauline congregation.[331] The church also recognised this anointing by the Spirit for leadership, however fluid it may have been. Some presided or acted as helmsman (1 Corinthians 12:28), others were worthy of honour because of their labour in teaching in the church (1 Timothy 5:17), and those who thus laboured should be rewarded (1 Corinthians 9:9). In Corinth, leadership may have been fluid, shifting with the authority granted by the Spirit, but such fluidity was in the end acknowledged by the appointment of leaders who were either presbyters with the duty of oversight or guardians (*episkopoi*: Acts 20:28) or deacons. Paul was frequently involved in such appointments.

Evidence of an emerging pattern of leadership, which had traces in it of both eldership and oversight, is evident in the Acts of the Apostles and the Pastoral Epistles. In Antioch, there appears to have been a leading group of teachers and prophets (Acts 13:1). At the end of Paul's first missionary journey, he returned to the places he visited where churches had begun to appoint "elders ... in each church, and with prayer and fasting committed them to the Lord, in whom they had put their trust" (Acts 14:23). These elders were called *presbuteros* and they are frequently referred to as an order of ministry or spiritual leadership in Acts, the Pastoral Epistles and 1 Peter.

For Von Campenhausen, the development of a presbyteral system demonstrates a patriarchal system (i.e., the notion of fathers or elders) taking over from a purely pneumatic leadership,[332] but this need not be seen in such a rigid and conflicting way. What is more likely is that a form of leadership common to Judaism was now re-invigorated by the gifting of the Holy Spirit. Elders both emerged and were appointed in the early church. Thus in Jerusalem, alongside the Apostles, who were there until dispersed by persecution (see Acts 11:19, 12:1–4), a council of elders came into existence led by James the Lord's brother. Luke refers to this group as the Apostles and elders (Acts 15:4, 6). Furthermore, elders were appointed in Ephesus and it was this group that was summoned to meet Paul at Miletus (Acts 20:17) on his return to Jerusalem at the end of his third missionary journey. The elders or presbyters came to meet him in an emotional final meeting on the shoreline or beach at Miletus. Paul describes his own ministry among them, but he also refers to the responsibilities and oversight they have been given. The Holy Spirit has made them "guardians" of the flock and the Greek word for guardian used here is *episcopos,* from which we get the word bishop (Acts 20:28). In effect, presbyters were exercising an oversight, which later took on its own office as bishop. Equally, on several occasions in Paul's address to the elders, he spoke of the ministry or service (*diakonian*) they had received (Acts 20:24). Thus, within the one office of elder or presbyter, they exercised *together* the ministry of oversight and service, an important insight for the shape of future ministry. Gradually, it seems these three functions of elder, deacon and bishop were separated out into three identifiable offices. What began as separate ministries critical to the smooth functioning of the church moved to identifiable roles in the church. This gave both structure and hierarchy to the church's ministry, with the resulting dangers of abuse or authoritarianism.

In the Pastoral Epistles, Paul explains further the nature of church leadership, which appears initially to have been divided into two offices, the overseer or bishop (1 Timothy 3:1, which is singular) assisted by the deacons (1 Timothy 3:8, which are plural). Those who aspire to be bishop must be "above reproach, the husband of one wife, temperate, self-controlled, respectable, able to teach" (1 Timothy 3:2–3). Likewise, deacons are to be "worthy of respect, sincere, not indulging in much wine and pursuing dishonest gain" (1 Timothy 3:8). Added to these two orders was a further one called the ruling elders or *presbuteroi* (1 Timothy 5:17), who appeared to have a teaching and preaching ministry, being accountable to the overseer or bishop and supported practically by the deacons. Timothy himself, the overseer of the church at Ephesus, was equipped for his task at the time of his appointment or ordination by the Holy Spirit, and this was confirmed by prophetic words spoken over him (1 Timothy 4:14). The Epistle to Titus only confirms the arrangements spoken of to Timothy as typical of Paul's general practice when it came to forming a structure for church leadership. Once again he included as essential the appointment of presbyters in each community where there was a church (Titus 1:5). The qualities for being an elder were similar to those outlined in Timothy (see Titus 1:6–9). Furthermore, Paul includes in their remit the ministry of being an overseer or bishop. Again, this seems to suggest that the ministry of oversight or being episcopal is at some point separated out from part of the elders' responsibilities to being a particular office, now called a bishop. At some point at the end of the first century AD, this appears to have been the case. The writings of the Apostolic Fathers demonstrate this development.

In particular, the First Letter of Clement, the Letters of Ignatius, the Letter of Polycarp to the Philippians, and the *Didache* further demonstrate the developments of these three ministerial orders, but especially those of bishop and presbyter. Clement writes self-consciously as the Bishop of Rome to the church in Corinth, for which he holds some sense of oversight, commanding the regularisation of their affairs. He wants to see the re-instatement of ejected presbyters by young and fractious congregational members. Much of the epistle eulogizes examples taken from Old Testament scripture[333] demonstrating qualities that promote harmony and peace, such as humility, kindness, piety, obedience and faithfulness. For Clement, "audacity, insolence, and effrontery belong to those who are cursed by God: gentleness, humility, and meekness to those blessed by God".[334] In light of this, Clement writes, "we commit no little sin, if we remove from the bishop's office those who offer the gifts in a blameless and holy way".[335] Likewise, those who have removed presbyters commit no little sin. Clement argues and prays most beautifully for the re-instatement of those who have been wrongfully dismissed. He likewise prays for the establishment of harmony.[336]

Of all the Apostolic Fathers, Ignatius is the most convinced that the secret of a harmonious church is to be at one with your bishop. By the time he writes his letters in the early second century, c.AD 110, it seems that most churches have their own bishop, so that every town where there is a church has its bishop and probably a single congregation. To oppose the bishop is to oppose God, to be subject to the bishop is to be submissive to God.[337] Again to the Magnesians he writes, "Let there be nothing among you that can divide you, but be unified with the bishop and with those who preside according to the model and teaching of incorruptibility".[338] From the Trallians he calls for respect for the threefold order of ministry: "So too let everyone respect the deacons like Jesus Christ, and also the bishop, who is the image of the Father; and let them respect the presbyters like the council of God and the band of the apostles. Apart from these a gathering cannot be called a church".[339]

Finally, to the Philadelphians he says: "Do nothing apart from the bishop; keep your flesh as the Temple of God: love unity; flee division; be imitators of Jesus Christ as he is of the Father",[340] and to the Smyrneans, with their young Bishop Polycarp, he says: "Let the congregation be wherever the bishop is; just as wherever Jesus Christ is, there is the universal church".[341] No one could have had a higher view of the unifying effect of a bishop than Ignatius.

The *Didache* speaks of electing bishops and deacons, "who are worthy of the Lord, gentle men who are not fond of money",[342] but more space is given to discerning who is a genuine Apostle, prophet and teacher, and who is just a sponger.[343] It seems that, although the office of bishop and deacon exist (there being no mention of presbyter in the *Didache*), the threefold office is not fully developed by the time of the writing of the *Didache* (c.AD 100), at least in Syria, if that is where the *Didache* was first written. But a few years later, as both Clement and Ignatius show us, there is much greater definition of the roles of bishop, presbyter and deacon in Rome and Corinth. Understandably therefore, the rate of development of the threefold office varies across the Empire, and appears to have developed quite swiftly at the end of the first century.

By the mid-second century, the roots of the church appear well developed: the early stages of the Canon of the New Testament have been reached, especially in relation to the gospels and the Pauline corpus; other writings of the Apostolic Fathers are valued, but not given that final canonical accreditation; the expectation of persecution and martyrdom is common, and such an end is held in high esteem by the flock; the ministerial orders of the church are well advanced. By the mid-second century, more confident apologists of the church are challenging the Emperor, pagan culture and the Jews. To these individuals, and their contribution, we now turn.

Part Two: Defence, Definition and Exploration

CHAPTER 4

Defenders of the Faith: Justin and Clement

In *Decline and Fall of the Roman Empire,* Edward Gibbon wrote that the first part of the second century AD was "the period in the history of the world during which the condition of the human race was the most happy and prosperous".[344] If Gibbon was speaking of the stability and strength of the Roman Empire during that period, that may well be true. That the average inhabitant of the Empire, or the average Christian, was "most happy and prosperous" would probably represent wishful thinking rather than a reality. It had little truth for the Christian community, which suffered almost continuous threat.

What is undeniable is that the next 90 years, from the reign of Emperor Nerva (AD 96) to the death of Marcus Aurelius (AD 180), a period which included only six Emperors—two of whom, Marcus Aurelius and Lucius Verus, were Co-Emperors during the years AD 161–169—saw the Empire at its greatest and strongest. It may not have been a golden age in relation to the arts, as the Augustan Age had been, but it was a golden age with regard to the stability of the Empire and its rulers. Four Emperors—Trajan, Hadrian, Antoninus Pius and Marcus Aurelius—reigned for the best part of 90 years. They were four of the so-called "five good Emperors". Such strength and stability in the Empire was hardly ever to be seen again.

At the start of this period, Domitian, the last of the Flavian Emperors, was assassinated at the end of his increasingly tyrannical reign. A court official and loyal administrator, Nerva, succeeded him. Nerva's was a benevolent rule. He gave to the poorer Romans allotments of land worth 60 million sesterces. He sold some of the imperial treasures to raise funds. He abolished many sacrifices, horse races and games in order to reduce expenditure. He reduced taxation on the landowning classes and he promised not to execute senators.[345] For all these popular measures the Emperor Nerva did not have the support of the Praetorian Guard. The Guard was only compliant when Nerva adopted as his heir the military commander Trajan, who had recently won victories against the Germans. As a result of these victories, first Nerva and then Trajan took the title "Germanicus".

On 28 January AD 98, Nerva died, after only 18 months as Emperor. Trajan succeeded him, and in many ways Trajan was everything Nerva was not. Nerva had had a lifetime in imperial administration; Trajan was a soldier through and through. Nerva was 63 when he succeeded; Trajan was 45. Trajan had the firm support of the army; Nerva, for all his popular measures, did not have their backing.

In his rule as Emperor, Trajan was driven by a desire to re-enact the conquests of Alexander the Great.[346] Trajan's family originally came from Spain, although his family home was more recently in Umbria. His father had a distinguished career in the army, serving in Syria as a legion commander in Vespasian's army, which had confronted the Jewish rebellion of AD 66. As a young man Trajan served with his father in Syria, and was later transferred to Germany, where he was appointed Governor of Upper Germany. He was in Germany when Nerva died, and returned only slowly to Rome to claim his *imperium,* making the last part of the journey humbly and on foot as he entered the city.[347]

After his accession as Emperor, Trajan continued campaigning, firstly against the Dacians, whom he quelled, making a treaty with their leader Decebalus,[348] who was later executed after a further uprising against the Romans. Further campaigns followed in Petra, Arabia, against the Nabateans, and much later in Armenia and Parthia, regions that were frequently troublesome to the Roman Empire. However, the most revealing aspect of Trajan's reign in connection with the church was his correspondence with Pliny the Younger.

The letters of the younger Pliny form one of the great correspondences of the ancient world, surpassed in scope and depth only by those of Cicero, and a prequel to the great episcopal correspondence of Basil of Caesarea. His uncle, Pliny the Elder, was well known for his love of natural history as well as for dying while attempting to rescue a friend

from Pompeii during the eruption of Vesuvius in AD 79. Pliny delayed his
departure from Pompeii by drawing a bath, an action described as either
a means of calming down his friend, Pomponianus, or perhaps a means
of alleviating his own asthma. But his delayed departure meant that he
was overcome by toxic gases from Vesuvius and, by then a corpulent
man, he collapsed. Whatever the reason for the bath and delay, Pliny
the Younger inherited a large estate after his unmarried uncle's untimely
death and a change in his name indicates that he was also the adopted
son of his uncle. He carried on his uncle's literary habit, if not his love of
nature and botany.

Pliny the Younger started his career at the Roman Bar, in the Roman
Chancery Court, before entering into a magistracy, which was the first
rung of the *Cursus honorum*, during the reign of Domitian. He became
a *queastor*, an imperial official who conveyed messages to the Senate.
His career at the Bar resumed with the accession of Trajan, and he
proceeded to take on cases against officials suspected of corruption or
embezzlement. He brought a case against the Governor of Africa, Marius
Priscus. Today we might call him a Treasury lawyer, but all the while
he continued a prolific correspondence on a variety of subjects. It was
his appointment as an imperial legate to Bithynia and Pontus, where,
following the indictment of two previous governors, he was to conduct
an enquiry on behalf of Trajan, that brings him to our notice in relation
to the church.

Pliny consulted the Emperor frequently and Book Ten of his *Letters*
is devoted to this correspondence with the Emperor and his officials.
The subjects are various: there are letters about public works in Nicaea,
Byzantium and Nicomedia; petitions for citizenship for Pliny's doctor and
his family;[349] letters of congratulations on victories won, as in Dacia;[350]
enquiries into the administration of towns within these provinces;[351]
and letters about the Elder Citizens Club, which had burnt down in
Nicomedia and needed to be replaced.[352] Of such stuff local government
is made, both then and now, and it is amazing that the reach of the
Empire and the interest of the Emperor, and/or his officials, extended to
the baths, theatres, water supplies, gymnasiums and buildings of far-off
towns. These concerns demonstrate the values of the Empire: baths in
Pursa, a club for the elderly in Nicomedia, a theatre and gymnasium for

Nicaea,[353] and the creation of a reservoir in Nicomedia.[354] These projects emphasise the civic values of the Empire, values that knit together the social fabric of society. One group was left outside as exiles, however, as the Epistle to Diognetus notes, and subject to ongoing persecution—and this group was the Christians.

In Letter 96, Pliny raised with the Emperor the question of his treatment of the Christians.[355] Pliny (as a lawyer) genuinely wanted advice about a judicial issue which was arising frequently. Pliny admitted that he had not been present at the trials of Christians. But he knew that Christians of all ages, both the mature and the young, were being brought before the courts. He wanted to know if it was criminal simply to have the name of Christian, or whether there were crimes associated with that name.

Even if Pliny did not examine Christians, he nevertheless had them brought before him on charges. In such cases he asked them if they were Christians two or three times and, if they persisted, he warned them that they would be punished. If they continued to assert they were Christians, they would then be led away for execution. "For whatever the nature of their admission, I am convinced that their stubbornness and unshakeable obstinacy ought not to go unpunished".[356] It is a curious reason for punishing someone in a judicial system as sophisticated as that of the Romans. However, Pliny found that the number of cases did not abate, and pamphlets were circulated "which contain the list of a number of accused persons". Pliny therefore sought to establish the veracity of these lists by asking Christians so named to "repeat after me a formula of invocation to the gods and make offerings of wine and incense to your [the Emperor's] statue (which I ordered to be brought into the court for this purpose along with images of the gods) and revile the name of Christ".[357] Some who were accused did recant and reverenced the Emperor's statue and insisted the sum total of their guilt was to meet "regularly before dawn on a fixed day to chant verses alternately amongst themselves in honour of Christ as if to a god, and also to bind themselves by oath, not for any criminal purpose, but to abstain from theft, robbery and adultery, to commit no breach of trust, and not to deny a deposit when called to restore it".[358]

The church's treatment of people who had denied their faith in this manner was to become a major issue, especially in North Africa in the Donatist controversy. Others were stalwart in their confession of Christ. Pliny says he sought to extract the truth about Christian ceremonies by torture: "This [knowledge of Christian ceremonies] made me decide it was all the more necessary to extract the truth by torture from two slave women, whom they call deaconesses. I found nothing but a degenerate cult carried to extravagant lengths".[359]

Trajan's response to Pliny is both reassuring and cautious. He tells Pliny he is following the right procedure in his examination of Christians. He tells him that Christians must not be hunted down in a campaign, but if they are brought before Pliny and found guilty, then they should be punished. Those who confess in court that they are not Christians and who give evidence of this by offering prayers "to our gods" should be pardoned. Anonymous pamphlets accusing people of being Christians should not be heeded.[360]

This appears to have been Roman policy in general, with its enforcement varying in intensity, depending on regional governors and the attitude of the Emperor. The cardinal point is that refusal to burn incense to the Emperor's statue or to busts of the gods was considered blasphemy and a punishable offence, and this remained the case more or less until AD 313, and the arrival of Constantine and the Edict of Milan, which heralded tolerance for Christianity in the Empire.

Trajan died on his way back from Ctesiphon, having appointed Parthamaspates King over the Parthians.[361] He never reached Italy, dying in Cilicia from disease.[362] Before he died on 9 August AD 117, Trajan adopted Hadrian, the Governor of Syria, to be his successor.[363] On 11 August, Hadrian became Emperor and ruled until AD 138. He killed all potential rivals, remitted debts, held games, and was assiduous in his care of influential families, "visiting them twice or three times a day when they were sick".[364] He reinvigorated discipline in the army by his example: "He would walk as much as twenty miles in armour [in a day], he demolished dining rooms in army camps, he wore the humblest clothing and would visit sick soldiers in their quarters".[365] He travelled extensively: "Hardly any other *princeps* had travelled so quickly across so much territory".[366] He constantly inspected garrisons on the fringes of the Empire. Hadrian's rule was marked by energetic warfare to crush enemies such as the Moors, Britons, Jews, and Sarmatians, as well as insurgents in Libya and Egypt. Between AD 121 and 125, he went on a tour of his Empire, which included Gaul, Upper Germany, Raetia and Noricum.[367] His policy was essentially to secure the frontiers of the Empire and build fences or walls to keep the barbarians out. He did this in Dacia, Germany and Britain, and in Britain he initiated the building of Hadrian's Wall.[368] Back in Rome, a poet, Florus, wrote a piece of doggerel:

> I don't want to be Emperor, please
> To tramp around among the Britons,
> Or in the Scythian frosts to freeze.

To which Hadrian replied with wit:

> And I don't want to be Florus, please.
> To tramp about the pubs and bars,
> And get myself infested with fleas.[369]

Hadrian was an inveterate traveller and campaigner. His second tour began in AD 128, when he went via Sicily to Africa and Mauretania. In the *Augustan Histories* it is noted that his arrival in Africa was considered auspicious: "On his arrival it rained for the first time for five years, and for this reason he was highly esteemed by the Africans".[370] From Africa he went to his beloved Greece, for he was a lover of all things Greek. He travelled through Athens, which he richly endowed, to Ephesus, Syria, Palmyra and then Judea. In Judea he ordered the construction of a new city on the remains of Jerusalem, which had been destroyed by the Romans in AD 70. It was to be called Colonia Aelia Capitolina, a pagan city on a Jewish holy site. This, combined with the prohibition against circumcision among the Jewish population, meant unsurprisingly that Hadrian had another revolt on his hands. The Jews were united under a new heroic leader, Simeon Bar Kochba, "the son of a star", in a way they had not been when fighting Nero, Vespasian and Titus.[371] The two legions garrisoned in Judea were overwhelmed by Bar Kochba's rebellion.

A leading general, Julius Severus, was sent for. He was at that time governing Britain. Hadrian also returned from Egypt to the area after a fateful trip on the Nile in which he lost his lover, Antinous, who was drowned there in AD 130, and for whom Hadrian wept "like a woman".[372] Hadrian would set up innumerable statues of Antinous in Greek and Egyptian clothing, particularly at his great villa at Tivoli. Eventually, the Jewish rebellion was brought under control, after some 580,000 were killed.[373] By AD 136, the rebellion was over, Bar Kochba was dead, and Judea was re-named Syria Palaestina. It was as though Hadrian was trying to expunge all memory of the Jews from the land and it would not be until 1917 that Jews would regain a homeland under the Balfour Declaration. (A. J. Balfour was the British Foreign Secretary.) Hadrian was to rule for only four more years. He returned to Rome, where much of his time and energy was spent in finding and adopting a successor.

There is no disputing Hadrian's energy and range of interests. He loved to go on tour and travel. He enjoyed learning different customs and gaining knowledge from the places he went. He was at once hardy and cultured. He could endure cold and heat, and had great physical stamina:

> He was excessively keen on poetry and literature, in arithmetic, geometry, and [at] painting he was highly skilled—while as for his expertness in playing the cithara [a Greek lyre or guitar] and in singing he used to boast of it. He was in one person both stern and cheerful, affable and harsh, impetuous and hesitant, mean and generous, hypocritical and straightforward, cruel and merciful, and always in all things changeable.[374]

He took male lovers, notably Antinous, but was bisexual. He loved Greek culture and was a thoroughgoing philhellene. He was a great builder, restoring the Pantheon, which survives to this day, the Basilica of Neptune, the Forum of Augustus and the Baths of Agrippa. He was the first Emperor to wear a beard. His unpredictable nature was the result of having untrammelled power, of being able to do whatever he wanted, whenever he wished. He died in Baiae in Campania on 10 July AD 138, and his cremated remains were first buried in Cicero's villa at Puteoli. These were later transferred to the mausoleum in Rome, which would come to dominate the skyline along the Tiber, and is now known as the Castel Sant'Angelo. It is said that he was versifying even on his deathbed. He wrote, presumably of his soul or spirit:

> Little charmer, wanderer, little sprite.
> Body's companion and guest,
> To what places now will you take flight
> Forbidding and empty and dim as night?
> And you wont make your wonted jest! [375]

Hadrian's succession was problematic. He first chose Lucius Ceionius Commodus, but Commodus was so ill he could barely express his thanks in the Senate and then he died before Hadrian. Subsequently, Antoninus Pius, a wealthy aristocrat, was chosen as Hadrian's heir. Pius in turn had to adopt Lucius Verus (Commodus's son) and Marcus Aurelius. In a single piece of legislation, Hadrian decided the leadership of the Empire for the next 40 years.

Just as Trajan was so different from his elderly predecessor, the bureaucrat Nerva, so Antoninus Pius was different from the ever-active and inquisitive Hadrian. Antoninus was 51 when he succeeded. He only left Italy once in his lifetime, when he was proconsul in Asia for a year in AD 134–5.[376] He was a wealthy, well-educated senator with conservative tastes and little energy for change. His family had served the Flavians in the past as tribunes, but Pius was no soldier. Where Hadrian had been erratic in his loyalties, especially towards the end of his life, Pius remained fixed and steady. Preferred by the traditionalists in Rome to Hadrian, who had been apt to be too interventionist for their liking, Pius was considered a model of Roman pagan piety. "The style of Antoninus was that there was opulence without cause for reproof and frugality without meanness".[377] It was during Pius's reign that one of the foremost Christian apologists came to the forefront: his name was Justin Martyr.

Justin Martyr

Justin Martyr was born in Flavia Neapolis, ancient Shechem (Nablus today), in Samaritan territory in Judea.[378] His parents were most probably Greek-speaking. He was the first line of second-century apologists; others who followed were Tatian from Assyria (Turkey), Aristides and Athenagoras, as well as bishops like Theophilus of Antioch and Melito of Sardis.[379] Apologists had a number of aims. They wrote critiques of pagan culture demonstrating its shortcomings and inconsistencies. In some cases (e.g., Justin, Aristides and Athenagoras), they appealed directly to the Emperor for a cessation of persecution, pleading that Christians were the best of citizens. They showed up the erroneous nature of several heresies and asserted that Christianity was the true fulfilment of all that Judaism promised. They were therefore the first identifiable intellectual movement in the church which sought to reason for the Christian faith in the public space, engaging with Greek and Roman culture, imperial power, heresies and Judaism. It was an important development for Christianity, and although not successful in bringing about the end of persecution for almost another 200 years, it nevertheless demonstrated increasing intellectual confidence.

After his childhood and early schooling in Judea, Justin went to Ephesus for further training. It was here that he most probably began his studies in Greek philosophy—Plato and the Stoics in particular—and where he first wore the philosopher's cloak or *pallium*. In his seminal work, *Dialogue with Trypho the Jew,* Justin explains his own conversion to the Christian faith. While wearing his philosopher's garb, which identifies him as an intellectual bent on the search for truth, he is accosted in Ephesus by a Jew named Trypho, who has escaped from Judea after the rebellion led by Bar Kochba.[380] Justin proceeds to tell Trypho of his own spiritual journey and conversion. First, Justin says, he joined himself to a Stoic, "but having spent a considerable time with him and when I had not acquired any further knowledge of God (for he did not know himself, and said such instruction was unnecessary) I took myself to another, who was called a Peripatetic, and, as he fancied, shrewd".[381] So shrewd is he that, after a few days, he asks Justin for money, whereupon Justin leaves him. Next, Justin meets a Pythagorean. The Pythagorean insists on the need for music, astronomy and geometry. When Justin confesses to ignorance in these matters, he is dismissed. At this point Justin joins a "sagacious" Platonist philosopher in the city, with whom he progresses daily, making great improvements. "And the perception of immaterial things overpowered me, and the contemplation of ideas furnished my mind with wings, so that in a little while I supposed that I had become wise and, such was my stupidity, I expected forthwith to look upon God, for this is the end of Plato's philosophy".[382]

Then Justin has a "chance" meeting with an old man in some fields by the sea, where, he says somewhat whimsically, he is seeking solitude in order to think about philology. The conversation with the old man becomes serious, however, with the old man challenging him: "Do you not aim at being a practical man so much as being a sophist?" Justin replies, "What greater work is there than this, to show the reason which governs all, and having laid hold of it, and being mounted upon it, to look down on the errors of others, and their pursuits. But without philosophy and right reason, prudence would not be present to any man".[383]

The conversation leads to the Platonic view of the immortality of the soul and to the quest for a unifying knowledge that will explain all things. Is that not God, the old man asks, to which Justin readily agrees. But God cannot be known as though he were astronomy, music or arithmetic. Only the human soul *knows* and may have affinity with God. This soul part of man is not yet immortal or unbegotten; only God can give immortality since God alone is immortal and not subject to any kind of change or decay, as Plato makes plain in *Timaeus*.[384] The old man insists that only God can give life to the soul and has given notice of his truth through the prophets. So he says:

> There existed, long before this time, certain men more ancient than all those who are esteemed philosophers, both righteous and beloved by God, who spoke by the Divine Spirit, and foretold events which would take place, and which are now taking place. They are called prophets. These alone both saw and announced the truth to men, neither reverencing nor fearing any man, not influenced by a desire for glory but speaking those things alone

which they saw and which they heard, being filled with the Holy
Spirit.[385]

These prophets spoke of both the Creator God and his Son by the Spirit.
Justin is then told to pray "that the gates of light may be opened to you;
for these things cannot be perceived or understood by all, but only by the
man to whom God and his Christ have imparted wisdom".[386] Justin goes
on to say that "straightway a flame kindled in my soul; and a love of the
prophets, and of those men who are friends of Christ possessed me; and
whilst revolving these words in my mind, I found this philosophy alone
to be sage and profitable".[387] He was converted.

Having recounted his conversion to Trypho, Justin embarks on a
thorough and lengthy account of how the prophets of the Old Testament
prophesied about Christ, who was the Messiah. Like the Apostle Paul,
Justin tells Trypho there is only one God, who revealed himself to
Abraham, chose a people, gave the Law to Moses and then abrogated
the Law with something better, something greater:

> Now, law placed against law has abrogated that which was before
> it and a covenant which comes after in like manner has put an
> end to the previous one; and an eternal and final law—namely
> Christ—has been given to us, and the covenant is trustworthy,
> after which there shall be no law, no commandment, no
> ordinance.[388]

From then on Justin urges Trypho to hear the prophets who speak of
Christ, and to heed the Psalmist who predicted his coming and sufferings.
In particular, he turns to the Suffering Servant songs of Isaiah to show
the manner and purpose of Christ's sacrificial death, and the prophecies
from Isaiah that predicted his virginal conception.

Of the prophets he says:

> Some have reference to the first advent of Christ, in which he is
> preached as inglorious, obscure, and of mortal appearance: but
> others have reference to his second advent, when he shall appear
> in glory and above the clouds; and your nation shall see and

> know him whom they have pierced, as Hosea, one of the twelve
> prophets, and Daniel, foretold.[389]

Despite the clear predictions of Christ in the prophets, Justin tells Trypho that neither he nor his people "catch the spirit that is in them"[390] and that they misunderstand the meaning of circumcision, the Sabbath and sacrifices, all of which have their end or fulfilment in Christ. Furthermore, he argues, on many occasions in the Old Testament God manifested himself through a mediator, whether at the Burning Bush, through the encounters between God and the Patriarchs, or when Jacob wrestled, seemingly, with an angel of God at Peniel (Genesis 32:22–30). Each of these revelations of God is a prefiguring of the appearance of Christ.[391] Likewise, Jesus's death is frequently both prophesied and prefigured, not only by the prophets, principally Isaiah, and by the Psalmist as in Psalm 22, but also by Moses, who in prophetic action raises his arms in prayer for Israel, thereby becoming a "type" of the crucified Lord. This is a prefiguring of the Cross, as is the raising of the bronze serpent in the desert.[392]

Finally, Justin argues that the church and Christians are descendants by faith of Abraham and the community anticipated by Israel.[393] For Justin, it is Christ who called Abraham, though not yet incarnate, and it is Christ who struggled with Jacob at Peniel and both called and blessed him.[394] Christ is indivisible and inseparable from the Father, and through his various manifestations brings power and glory to Israel, whether in the call of Abraham, the angel struggling with Jacob, the fire in the Burning Bush, or the judgement on Sodom. Trypho ends the lengthy dialogue by saying that if Justin is continuing in Ephesus he will value further discussions. He wishes Justin well for his voyage, presumably to Rome, where the final part of Justin's life is to be lived.

Justin arrived in Rome during the reign of Antonius Pius (AD 138–161). He began to teach there and was an active and well-regarded member of the Christian community in the capital. Tatian, a later apologist, was one of his most well-known pupils, creating a harmony of the gospels which became a standard text in the Syrian Church in the third and fourth centuries, according to Ephrem. While in Rome, Justin wrote his *First*

Apology to the Emperor. Its purpose, as with all apologetics, was not only the defence of Christianity, but also an implicit criticism of paganism.

Justin sent his *First Apology* directly to the Emperor and called on him to judge the truth of what it said. At the outset, Justin recalls Plato's dictum that, "Unless both rulers rule and philosophise, it is impossible to make states blessed".[395] Justin proceeds to say it is unjust to punish Christians simply because they are Christians and not because of the reality and evidence of their lives. Like Socrates, who was killed for his "atheism", Christians are killed for repudiating demons (pagan gods), although they do believe in God. How can Christians be atheists who believe in the one true God? How can Christians be convicted for believing in God, when that belief does no harm?[396] Justin begins to show the hollow sham of gods that are man-made by craftsmen and put in temples for worship. Then, in a powerful section, Justin says that any sober-minded man will see that Christians worship rationally.[397] They give thanks for what God has created and do not need to offer sacrifices or libations to him. Rather, Jesus Christ is our teacher, says Justin, who was crucified under Pontius Pilate, the Procurator of Judea in the reign of Tiberius Caesar. And the madness of which we are accused is to call Christ the Son of the One True God when he was crucified by a Roman governor. Our critics, he says, "do not discern the mystery that is herein, to which, as we make plain to you, we pray you give heed".

The evidence for the truth, he continues, lies in changed lives:

> We who formerly delighted in fornication, now embrace chastity, we who formerly used magical arts, dedicate ourselves to the good and un-begotten God; we who valued above all things the acquisition of wealth and possessions, now bring what we have in common stock, and communicate to everyone in need; we who hated and destroyed one another, and on account of their different manners would not live with men of different tribe, now, since the coming of Christ, live familiarly with them, and pray for our enemies, and endeavour to persuade those who hate us unjustly to live conformably to good precepts of Christ, to the end that they may become partakers with us of the same joyful hope of a reward from god the ruler of all.[398]

Justin makes great play of the sexual standards of the Christian community, eschewing all lust towards women. He talks about the patience and gentleness of Christians, their willingness to be loyal citizens, and asks that Christians should be judged by their behaviour.

Justin also explains the hopes of Christians. The possibility of a resurrection body, he argues, is not so implausible when you consider that a human body arises from a small drop of seed placed in the womb. Indeed, he suggests that Christians are not departing far from heathen philosophers and poets such as Menander in saying that the creator is greater than the created and that the soul has immortality and will be judged for its bodily life on earth, being punished or rewarded accordingly.[399]

Justin then spends a good deal of his *Apology* on the status of Christ. He was born without sexual union (in a way not dissimilar to many of the progeny of the gods, such as Jupiter). The prophets, especially Isaiah and Moses, predict his coming and birth. His death and passion are likewise predicted. Furthermore, Plato, who Justin says used Moses as a source for his philosophy (a commonly-held view among early Christian teachers), predicts the death of Jesus by crucifixion. For Plato states in *Timaeus* that the soul was placed "crosswise in the universe".[400] In this way Plato intimates the cross will be a source of life and "gives the second place to the Logos which is with God, who he said was placed crosswise in the universe; and the third place to the Spirit who was borne upon the water".[401] Thus Plato imitates the truth of Moses and the Apostles.

Finally, Justin gives a vivid account of Christian worship and the use of the sacraments. He describes baptism as follows:

> As many as are persuaded and believe that what we teach is true, and understand to be able to live accordingly, are instructed to pray and to entreat God with fasting, for the remission of their sins that are past, we praying and fasting with them. Then they are brought by us where there is water, and are regenerated in the same manner in which we ourselves were regenerated. For, in the name of God, the Father and Lord of the universe, and of our Saviour Jesus Christ, and of the Holy Spirit, they then receive

the washing with water. For Christ said also, "Except ye be born again, ye shall not enter the Kingdom of heaven".[402]

This is a clear statement of the method of baptism and the accompanying doctrine of regeneration of which baptism is the symbol. Likewise, Justin says the Lord's Supper is called the Eucharist, "of which no one is allowed to partake but the man who believes that the things which we teach are true, and who has been washed with the washing that is for the remission of sins, and unto regeneration, and who is so living as Christ enjoined". In this supper "we have been taught", Justin continues, "that the food which is blessed by the prayer of His word, and from which our blood and flesh by transmutation are nourished, is the flesh and blood of Jesus who was made flesh".[403] Furthermore, Justin describes Sunday worship as follows:

> The memoirs of the Apostles or the writings of the prophets are read, as long as time permits; then, when the reader has ceased, the president verbally instructs, and exhorts to the imitation of these good things. Then we all rise together and pray, and as we before said, when our prayer is ended, bread and wine and water are brought, and the president in like manner offers prayers, and thanksgivings, according to his ability, and the people assent, saying Amen; and there is a distribution to each, and a participation of that over which thanks have been given, and to those who are absent a portion is sent by the deacons. And they who are well to do, and willing, give what each thinks fit; and what is collected is deposited with the president, who succours the orphans and widows, and those who, through sickness or any other cause, are in want, and those who are in bonds, and strangers sojourners among us, and in a word takes care of all who are in need.[404]

Thus, in an extraordinarily unchanging way, Christian worship is established by AD 150 with little change over the centuries to follow. It takes place on Sunday, the day of the creation of the world (Genesis 1:3) and the day of Christ's resurrection.

Justin's *First Apology* falls on deaf ears. The Roman philosopher Crescens continues to inveigh against Christians as "atheists",[405] while Justin is arguing that Christians are the people to reverse the corruption brought to the earth by wicked angels who make love to women, and whose progeny are demons who in turn encourage magical arts, fear, sacrifice, murder, adultery and "intemperate deeds".[406] Although there is some restraint sown into humanity through the seed of reason implanted by the *logos* (what Justin, and later Clement, call "the diffused word"), and which is expressed in poets or thinkers like the Stoics and Socrates, nevertheless the devil's aim is to both hate and destroy all who followed such precepts. Justin approves of both Heraclitus and Socrates (and his expositor Plato) and the Stoic poets, all of whom were popular in Rome.

All of these are examples of the existence of the "diffused word" or *logos* before the *Logos* fully and finally came in Christ. They exhibit the Word in part, but since their understanding of the Word is, as Justin argues, limited, they come to contradictory conclusions. Only Christ reveals the Word in its entirety, for he is *The Logos*.[407] Such approval of these giants of Greek philosophy is not enough to win the support of the Emperor, Antoninus Pius, or the Senate, to whom Justin addresses his *Second Apology*. Nor will Christians embrace vice for the sake of avoiding death. Indeed, Christians will, Justin argues, embrace virtue, which for them is allegiance to Christ, and will hold death in contempt.

Such was Justin's own fate as a martyr. Summoned by the Urban Prefect Rusticus, he refused to sacrifice to the statue of the Emperor, although failure to do so meant being scourged and beheaded. He and six others refused and were executed in Rome c.AD 150. Then, on the other side of the Mediterranean, in Alexandria, another apologist arose, even more wide-ranging and diffuse than Justin in his acquaintance with classical literature and philosophy, and likewise intent on showing the shortcomings of Greek culture and philosophy compared with the Word made Flesh.

Clement of Alexandria

Clement lived a little after Justin. In fact, he was probably born around the time Justin was executed in Rome, during the final years of the Emperor Antoninus Pius. He was to live through the years of Marcus Aurelius (AD 161–180), the Stoic philosopher Emperor and his egregious son Commodus (AD 180–192), who in terms of morality took Rome back to the days of Caligula and Nero.

Clement was educated for the most part in Athens, which had recently been favoured by Hadrian, who was renowned for his love of all things Greek. It seems that Clement had a pagan upbringing and at some point was converted to Christianity. His knowledge of classical literature was unsurpassed among the Early Church Fathers, and he brought to his Christian writing a profusion of classical allusions and examples.

At some point Clement moved from Athens to Alexandria, the centre of learning in the eastern Mediterranean. Since the time of the Ptolemies, who ruled there after the death of Alexander the Great, the city was known for its Greek, Egyptian and Jewish culture, which mingled together to form a rich intellectual diet. With the establishment of Christianity reputedly occurring after the preaching of St Mark, the city also became a leading centre of Christian worship and study. In particular, it became a city where scholars sought to explain religious views using Greek thought and forms. This was the case with Philo (25 BC–AD 50), a well-born and wealthy Alexandrian Jew who sought to explain the Hebrew scriptures and their tenets in Greek philosophical forms.

Clement had to hand the great Greek translation of the Hebrew Bible called the Septuagint (c.250 BC), which became the standard text of the Old Testament in the Greek-speaking world. Just as significant in terms of scholarship was the Great Library at Alexandria, which survived until AD 391 (although previous fires from 45 BC onwards, when Caesar's soldiers accidentally started one, had damaged the library). It would have provided a rich resource for Clement and the philosophic schools of Alexandria. When Clement arrived in Alexandria, he became the pupil of Pantaenus, who was in charge of the Catechetical School there.[408] Pantaenus showed his evangelistic zeal by going to India as a missionary and in time Clement took over the school with Origen as one of his pupils.

Clement was not simply an apologist in the strict sense of someone
defending the Christian faith to the civic powers, as Justin or Athenagoras,
with his "Plea Regarding the Christians" addressed to Marcus Aurelius in
AD 177, had been.[409] Clement's first book, one of a trilogy, was a powerful
refutation of pagan classical thought and an evangelistic defence of the
Christian faith. It was called *The Exhortation to the Greeks*.

Clement's work begins in a lyrical manner. Never short of a classical
allusion or reference, he sets the scene for his *Exhortation* by describing a
gathering of Greeks who come to pay their respects to a dead python. One
of their number, Eunomous, plays a lament for the snake on the Greek
lyre. As this day of lament progresses, the cicadas or grasshoppers begin
their song, not to a dead snake, but "to the all-wise God, a spontaneous
natural song, better than the measured strains of Eunomous".[410] In this
way Greek custom and thought is overtaken by a lyrical song which
elevated in its focus on the all-wise God, a God who is superior to the
Greek deities. In typical style, Clement then castigates what he considers
Greek deception by saying, "How in the world is it that you have given
credence to worthless legends, imagining brute beasts to be enchanted
by music, while the bright face of truth seems alone to strike you as
deceptive and is regarded with unbelieving eyes?"[411] With this excoriating
question, a prelude of much more to come, he begins a systematic *exposé*
of the deception of Greek myth and instead demonstrates the truth of
Christ. He is at pains to make this point: "For truth, like the bee, does no
harm to anything in the world, but takes delight only in the salvation of
men. You have taken God's promise; you have his love to man; partake
of his grace".[412]

Clement's method is to discredit and expose the fantasies and
deception of the Greek myths. Firstly, he shows that they are totally
immoral and unworthy of credence or respect. So knowledgeable is he
of Greek and Roman myths that he can delve into them, and expose
their corrupt entrails. He begins by describing the activities of the gods:
their lust for women and enjoyment of orgies;[413] their enjoyment of lewd
initiation ceremonies which are simply an initiation into promiscuity;[414]
their subjection to their own bodily needs;[415] and their appreciation of
human sacrifice, which was liturgical murder, as offered by the Lycatians,
the Lesbians and Phocaeans.[416] Clement writes: "This is how the daemons

love, they guide men to the fire".[417] The worship of gods was often simply a drug-inspired ecstasy.[418] Like Elijah on Mount Carmel taunting the prophets of Baal, Clement writes: "It is necessary, therefore, to supply the gods with attendance and nourishment, of which they are in need; so they have feasts, carousing, bursts of laughter and acts of sexual intercourse, whereas if they were immortal, and in need of nothing, and untouched by age, they would not partake of the pleasures of human love, nor beget children, nor even go to sleep".[419] For Clement, the Greeks are the true atheists. They have turned heaven into a drama, and divine nature into a subject for drama—a kind of heavenly soap opera.[420]

Having lambasted the antics of the gods as most un-godlike, Clement proceeds to expose the emptiness of statues and idols. He cites the example of Antinous, Hadrian's favourite and lover who died in Egypt. First, Antinous was given a mausoleum by the desolate Emperor, then a shrine and statue, until at last he was worshipped as a god. Such was the progress to deity, with éclat of imperial patronage. Clement reflects:

> So now we have a tomb of the boy who was loved, a temple and a city of Antinous: and it seems to me that tombs are objects of reverence in just the same way as temples are: in fact, pyramids, mausoleums and labyrinths are as it were temples of dead men, just as temples are tombs of the gods.[421]

Just as Isaiah inveighed against the nonsense of idols in Israel (Isaiah 44), so does Clement. The Romans, he says, ascribe their greatest successes to Fortuna, and believe her to be the greatest deity, even carrying her statue to the privy and erecting it there, thus assigning to her "a fit temple".[422] Statues are "motionless things incapable of action or sensation; they are bound and nailed and fastened, melted filed, sawn polished, carved", but their image is worshipped.[423] Smoke blackens them, swallows defile them and weather discolours them, but still they are worshipped. For Clement, all matter which is turned into statues comes from the earth; it is then fashioned by the artist, but the earth is to be walked on, not to be worshipped, "for I hold it a sin even to entrust the hopes of the soul to soulless things."[424] Art can be praised, but never should it persuade man it is the truth.

Next, Clement turns to the philosophers. Some, like Thales of Miletus, worship matter, saying the earth owes its origins to water. Others, like Anaximenes, say it is air. Empedocles says it came from love and strife and many, like the Persian Magi, say that earth owed its origin to fire.[425] Later, the Stoics will say the divine nature permeates all matter. Epicurus says that God has no care for the world—all is capricious and contingent. Aristotle's pupil, Theophrastus, suspects that God is spirit and in heaven.[426] The philosopher who comes closest to the truth is Plato, who says that God cannot be described at all.[427] He is a king of all things and from him comes good. The source of Plato's wisdom is both the Sibylline Oracles—a kind of anthology of Greek poetry and thought—and poetry such as that of Menander, Homer and Euripides,[428] as well as the Hebrew scriptures and in particular Moses.[429]

In the end, as with Justin, Clement arrives at the Hebrew prophets: the "all wise Jeremiah",[430] and the "Spirit-inspired Isaiah", and, perhaps above all, Moses. Through them God speaks as a Father to his children. Thus Clement eventually arrives at the teaching of the prophets, having shown the pitfalls of the gods, the deception of idols, the emptiness of statues and even the error of most philosophers. In the end, Clement pleads with evangelical fervour with his readers to be reconciled to the Father:

> O surpassing Love for man! He speaks not as a teacher to disciples, nor as a master to servants, or as God to men, but as a "tender father" admonishing his sons. Again, Moses confesses, "He exceedingly fears and quakes" when hearing the Word; do you not fear when you listen to the divine Word himself? Are you not troubled, are you not careful and at the same time eager to learn; that is to say, are you not eager for salvation, fearing God's wrath, loving his grace, striving after hope, in order that you may escape the judgement? Come ye, come ye, my little ones! For except you become once more as little children and "be born again", as the Scripture says, ye shall not receive the true Father, "nor shall ye ever enter into the kingdom of heaven".[431]

His readers are to recognise the authority and summons of the Word: "Let us ever listen to the voice of the divine Word"[432] and come "to a full knowledge of the truth".[433] With Pauline insight, Clement says, "When godliness sets out to make man as far as possible resemble God, it claims God as a suitable teacher; for he alone has the power to conform man to his likeness (see Ephesians 5:8–9 and 2 Corinthians 3:18).[434] In many ways, this summarises Clement's argument, but it was Augustine who would later add, in the face of the Pelagian controversy, that the divine spark alone gives humankind the desire for such godliness, and so make God their teacher. This desire comes entirely from his grace. Clement does admit that, "He [God] converts men when they draw nigh to him through fear".[435]

Having disowned the false ways of the Greeks and made clear the necessity of the Word, Clement urges the need for instruction in discipleship, which will be the main theme of his second main work, the *Pedagogue*, which we will come to. "Man, who was made for the contemplation of heaven, is in truth a heavenly plant".[436] First, disciples of Christ must eschew all the so-called teachers in temples, they are "ruffians with filthy hair, in squalid and tattered garments, complete strangers to the baths, with claws like wild beasts. Many are also deprived of their virility [i.e., castrated]. They are actual proof that the precincts of the idols are so many tombs or prisons."[437] The new convert is to cease from paying attention "to the godless devotees of daemon–worship"[438] and "having stripped before the eyes of all [perhaps an allusion to baptism], join in the real contest in the arena of truth, where the Holy Word is umpire, and the Master of the universe is president. For the prize set before us is no small one, but immortality".[439] This discipleship will mean turning one's back on customs, on reverencing creation or created objects, such as stones, stocks, snakes and birds,[440] and following his laws.[441]

Finally, in *Exhortation to the Greeks*, Clement returns to his first premise, the salvific power of the Word who:

> Clothing himself with the bonds of flesh (which is divine mystery), he subdued the serpent and enslaved the tyrant death; and, most wonderful of all, the very man who had erred through pleasure, and was bound by corruption, was shown to be free again, through his outstretched hands. O Amazing mystery! The Lord has sunk down, but man rose up; and he who was driven

from paradise gains a greater prize in heaven, on becoming
obedient. If our teacher is he who has filled the universe with holy
powers, creation, salvation, beneficence, lawgiving, prophecy,
teaching; this teacher now instructs us in all things, and the whole
world has by this time become an Athens and a Greece through
the Word.[442]

Faith in the Word is the essence of Clement's theology. "All these great
works of creation and gracious gifts he has let out to thee in return for
a little faith"[443] and with this promise: "The Word of God shall be thy
pilot and the Holy Spirit shall bring thee to anchor in the harbours of
heaven".[444]

The second of Clement's main works—in effect a trilogy—is the
Paedogogus or *The Instructor*, and is addressed to new Christians who
have come out of a pagan culture. In it, Clement is both the theologian
of the Word and the ethical philosopher. The first part is a description of
the Word, who is ultimately the Instructor; the second and third parts
concentrate on the outworking of this new life in Christ in a pagan world.
Clement says, "Let us designate this Word appropriately by the one name
Instructor or *Pedagogue*".[445]

For Clement, the eternal Word is the only true physician of the sick
soul. Men and women are both under the Instructor's charge. Their sexual
differences one day will disappear in heaven.[446] The Instructor is Christ:
"But our Instructor is the holy God Jesus, the Word, who is guide of all
humanity. The Loving God himself is our Instructor".[447] He will supply
the wisdom and redemption needed for our instruction. Thus, "with
all his power, the Instructor of humanity, the Divine Word, using all
the resources of wisdom, devotes himself to the saving of the children,
admonishing, upbraiding, blaming, chiding, reproving, threatening,
healing, promising, favouring; and as it were, by many reins, curbing
the irrational impulses of humanity".[448]

The means of receiving the healing offered by the Instructor is faith:
"Where faith is there is the promise; and the consummation of the
promise is rest. So that in illumination what we receive is knowledge,
and the end of knowledge is rest".[449] In this way we "put aside the old man,
and strip off the garment of wickedness, and put on the immortality of

Christ".[450] The means whereby we may grow up into maturity of faith is the milk of the Word.[451] Clement, ever the lover of a classical allusion or a biblical metaphor, now takes the metaphor of milk to its limits. A mother transforms her blood through her breasts to suckle her child (indicating Clement's physiological understanding), since "blood is the moister part of flesh, being a kind of liquid flesh; and milk is the sweeter and finer part of blood".[452] In the same way, the blood of Christ which saves is also the means of providing nourishment for the new-born Christian through its sweeter by-product milk.[453] Thus the Instructor saves and then feeds: "The same blood and milk of the Lord is therefore the symbol of the Lord's passion and teaching".[454] For Clement, the teaching of the Word needs to be made plain and further bolstered by instruction, so in the second and third parts, he gives further instruction about the kinds of lives Christians are to live in the fleshpots of the Empire.

The final two parts of *The Instructor* are more Clement and less the Word, although he would see the detailed advice he gives as springing from the instruction found in Old and New Testaments. The context of his instruction is the pagan world, for the wealthier classes in the cities of the Empire, and in his case Alexandria. There is much about the baths, how to conduct oneself at feasts, how to deal with luxury, drinking, sex, clothes, appearance, female attire, male appearance, hair, beards, shaving and even sleeping. This part of *The Instructor* is, Clement says, all about "how we ought to regulate ourselves".[455] It is the classical equivalent of contemporary instructions on how Christians should respond to parties, rock music, fashion, cookery, appearance, sex and drugs.

When it comes to "eating", Clement's rule is about simplicity and modesty. "Plainness of fare" is his watchword, for this is conducive to health, digestion and "lightness of body".[456] He is no advocate of gourmet cooking, writing, "we must therefore reject different varieties which engender various mischiefs, such as a depraved habit of body and disorders of the stomach, the taste being vitiated by an unhappy art—that of cookery—and the useless art of making pastry".[457] There were evidently few Christian "Bake-Offs" in Alexandria then! Clement was suspicious of imported foods, such as lampreys from the straits of Sicily, eels from the Maender, kid goats from Melos, mullet from Sciathus, mussels from

Pelorus, oysters from Abydos, thrushes from Daphnis and turbot from Attica.[458]

For Clement, "heavenly bread must rule the belly"[459] and "love is the celestial food, the banquet of reason".[460] The Christian is to demonstrate a restrained enjoyment: "We are to partake of what is set before us, as becomes a Christian, out of respect to him who has invited us, by a harmless and moderate participation in the social meeting; regarding the sumptuousness of what is put on the table as a matter of indifference, despising the dainties as they are, after a little, destined to perish".[461]

Few concessions are made by Clement towards drinking: "The natural temperate, and necessary beverage therefore, for the thirsty is water".[462] Wine on the other hand is full of danger: "Boys and girls should keep away from it", for through it "wild impulses and burning lusts and fiery habits are kindled; and young men inflamed from within become prone to indulgence of vicious propensities. The breasts and organs of generation, inflamed with wine, expand and swell in a shameful way, already exhibiting beforehand the image of fornication; and the body compels the wound of the soul to inflame, and shameless pulsations follow abundance, inciting the man of correct behaviour to transgressions; and hence the voluptuousness of youth overpasses the bounds of modesty".[463] In one concession, however, Clement says, "those who are advanced in life may partake more cheerfully of the draught … to warm, by the harmless medicine of the vine, the chill of age, which the decay of time has produced".[464] There were some benefits in old age!

Moving on from food and drink, he decries the use of costly drinking vessels made of gold or inlaid with jewels. Simple furniture or tableware that does the job is all that is needed.[465] Furthermore, feasts and nights of drinking are to be avoided. As far as laughter goes, a smile is fine, but giggling and continuous laughter are to be avoided, especially in front of elderly people.[466] All filthy speech is to be avoided and giving the *pudenda* unseemly names is also to be avoided.[467]

At feasts, modesty and restraint is to be the mark of the Christian: "Nor are you, in the midst of a feast, to exhibit yourselves hugging your food like wild beasts; nor helping yourselves to too much sauce, for man is not by nature a sauce-consumer, but a bread-eater".[468] Likewise, "frequent spitting too, and violent clearing of the throat, and wiping one's nose at an entertainment, are to be shunned".[469] Garlands of flowers on the head, called crowns, are also to be avoided. Flowers are to be admired and not used for adornment, since they are associated with offerings to the gods.[470] Tertullian warns of the same misuse of flowers. When sleep arrives, the bed must be simple, for Jacob slept on the ground and made a stone his pillow, with heaven his dream. If sleep is chased away by a surfeit of eating and drinking, then "the hiccupping of those who are loaded with wine, and the snortings of those stuffed with food, and the snoring rolled in the bed-clothes, and the rumblings of pained stomachs, cover over the clear-seeing eye of the soul, by filling the mind with ten thousand phantasies".[471] Lot is a clear example of such surfeit and as a result fell into "unhallowed intercourse".[472]

Finally, having provided a guide on how best to eat and drink and what to avoid in the excessive feasting of Alexandria's nightlife, Clement turns to clothes and make-up. As one might expect, Clement says: "Man requires clothes for nothing else than the covering of the body, for the defence against excess of cold and intensity of heat, lest the inclemency of the air injure us".[473] Fashion, dyes such as saffron and purple, are to be eschewed. Jeremiah, Elijah and John the Baptist are on Clement's catwalk of godly models.[474] Clothes should not be above the knee,[475] nor should any part of a woman be exposed. Sandals are to be simple. Jewellery is to be minimal, "for women ought to be adorned within, and show the woman beautiful".[476] As for make-up, the use of crocodile excrement (presumably plentiful by the Nile) or the "froth of putrid humours" or "soot to stain the eyebrows" or "cheeks rubbed with white lead", must all be rejected.[477] Likewise, men are not to be effeminate dressers, "cutting their hair in an ungentleman-like and meretricious way, clothed in fine and transparent garments, chewing mastic, smelling of perfume" and generally "inclining to voluptuousness".[478] Of such people Clement says, unless you saw them naked, you would suppose them to be women.[479] Showing his cultural limits, Clement goes on to write:

> The mark of the man is the beard by which he is seen to be a man and it is older than Eve, and is the token of the superior nature. In this God deemed it right that he should excel, and dispersed hair over the man's whole body. Whatever smoothness and softness

was in him, He abstracted from his side when He formed the woman Eve, physically receptive, his partner in parentage, his help in household management while he (for he was parted from all smoothness) remained a man, and shows himself man. And to him has been assigned action, as to her suffering [presumably in childbirth].[480]

Human trafficking of boys was very prevalent,[481] and homosexuality is thus condemned: "Men play the part of women, and women of men, contrary to nature; women are at once wives and husbands; no passage is closed against libidinousness; and their promiscuous lechery is a public institution and luxury is domesticated. O miserable spectacle! Horrible spectacle! A luxuriousness seeks everything, attempts everything, forces everything, and coerces nature".[482] The baths, often a place of sexual encounter, are to be circumspectly used, for it is known that potential mistresses are introduced to men while at the baths: men who advertise their status by sitting in gilded chairs attended by slaves who rub them down.[483] In all, Alexandria is a veritable fleshpot. Clement's guidance, though of its own day, is a chastening counterblast into the life of this opulent and frequently corrupt city.

Clement's third work in his trilogy is called *The Stromata* or *Miscellanies*. As its name suggests, it is a composite work of seven books (although Eusebius maintains there were eight books, so one is probably lost). In his introduction, Clement writes, "*The Stromata* will contain the truth mixed up in dogmas of philosophy, or rather covered over and hidden, as the edible part of truth be kept for husbandmen of faith, and no others".[484] The work exhibits Clement's great classical knowledge: of the Greek philosophers and of the Hebrew scriptures. Although in many ways eclectic in style and disparate in content, the material is grouped around seven books or themes. Clement is aware that he can be criticised for paying too much attention to the Greek classics and so pre-empts this by saying that it is necessary to track down truth, like hunting prey, and that the pursuit is a necessary part of the goal.[485] Another reason for this method is that those who are likely to object are forestalled in their opposition by Clement's knowledge of their philosophy, and are also made to work harder by evaluating the truth presented by degrees, and

not all at once.[486] Furthermore, for Clement, philosophy is a handmaid
to theology, and in that sense he is a precursor to Augustine and later
to Albert the Great, Thomas Aquinas and the schools in the European
universities, especially in Paris and Padua. For Clement, philosophy
is "preparatory training",[487] based on the supposition that the Word
may be found disseminated in philosophy, only to be revealed by the
superior illumination of the truth as found in the *Logos*. In these ways,
Clement can be said to be, in the widest sense, an apologist, not in terms
of writing to the Emperor, as Justin or others like him did, but because
he uses the common experience of Greek philosophy as a means of
defending Christianity. As Clement writes, "Philosophy, therefore, was a
preparation, paving the way for him who is perfected in Christ"[488] and "as
the encyclical branches of study contribute to philosophy, which is their
mistress; so also philosophy itself operates for the acquisition of wisdom.
For philosophy is the study of wisdom, and wisdom is the knowledge of
things divine and human in their causes. Wisdom is therefore queen of
philosophy, and philosophy is of preparatory culture".[489] This then is the
rationale for Clement's way of proceeding, and is to be the rationale for
much of the teaching of theology in the following centuries, probably up
to the Enlightenment.

The first four books of *The Stromata* cover the following subjects: Book
I is Clement's approach to theology; Book II is on the supremacy of faith;
Book III is on the reasons for marriage; and Book IV is on martyrdom. In
themselves, these subjects appear an eclectic mix and yet they cover issues
of immense significance to the church at the end of the third century AD.

Book I highlights the relationship of philosophy to theology, ending
with an overview of Jewish history and how Plato owes much of his insight
to the Hebrew prophets, and particularly Moses.[490] In this way, Clement
demonstrates the prevalent intellectual current in Alexandria of seeking
to reconcile Greek philosophy with the divine revelation in Christ, the
Logos, and also of showing the way the Hebrew story in general, and of
Moses in particular, influenced the Greek philosophers and especially
Plato. Alexandria was a melting pot of culture. Attempts had already been
made by the Jewish philosopher Philo to express Jewish thinking in Greek
concepts in the first century. Clement, and later Origen and Augustine,
would employ a similar method with Christianity, especially after the

arrival in Alexandria of Plotinus, the very influential neo-Platonist, in the third century.

If Book I demonstrates how Plato imitated Moses in the framing of laws,[491] and shows that Hebrew law is influential in Greek thought, Book II moves the argument forward to the importance of faith. The primacy of faith in apprehending the plan and purposes of God is something to which Clement frequently refers. For Clement, knowledge of God can only be attained through faith.[492] "For knowledge is a state of mind that results from demonstration; but faith is a grace from which what is indemonstrable conducts to what is universal and simple, what is neither with matter, nor matter, nor under matter".[493] In this way "knowledge is accordingly characterised by faith; and faith, by a kind of divine mutual and reciprocal correspondence, becomes characterised by knowledge".[494] Thus Clement embraces the Platonic concepts of knowledge, progress or contemplation, and perfection (not too dissimilar from Augustine and Gregory of Nyssa). For knowledge to bear fruit, it must be based in faith: faith in the truth of the *Logos* and submissive to the King who is the cornerstone of his thinking.[495] The outcome of this for Clement, notes Eric Osborn, is cheerfulness and coherence. Faith produces true knowledge. It also brings true repentance based on a healthy fear of God, along with patience and hope.[496] Faith-based knowledge of God brings a disciplined life: true manliness and not effeminacy;[497] resistance to being seduced as the Israelites were by the Midianites;[498] love through alms giving; and restitution and the protection of children.[499] The true Gnostics (and Clement uses the word "gnostic" without prejudice, seeking to redeem it for genuine faith) have illumination through faith, which leads to a disciplined life expressed in patience and perseverance.[500] This idea prompts Clement to write, "For peace and freedom are not otherwise won, except by ceaseless and unyielding struggles with our lusts".[501] It is not surprising that in Book III Clement's mind turns to the subject of marriage.[502]

Finding a healthy doctrine of marriage amidst all the currents concerning sexuality that were circulating in Alexandria in the late second century would always require considerable acumen and skill. Clement's view of marriage is essentially pragmatic and straightforward: if a man is attracted to a woman, they should marry. In saying this he has to face down all the various views about continence, abstinence, and the denigration of the body in ascetic Greek thought, along with a growing Christian asceticism, egged on by Gnostics in the Christian community. First of all, Clement dismisses the teaching of one Epiphanes, who is regarded by his followers as a god and worshipped in Cephallenia. Epiphanes is a Platonist who disregards monogamy and believes that human sexual desire is so strong that there should be no boundaries to sexual encounters. Epiphanes maintains that, "with a view to the permanence of the race, he has implanted in males a strong and ardent desire which neither law nor custom nor any other restraint is able to destroy. For it is God's decree".[503] The Gnostic Carpocratians indulge in love feasts and promiscuity.[504] Likewise, the Magi practise incest. The Marcionites and the philosopher Heraclitus regard birth as evil in some way, tainting the soul.[505] After a tour of several more heresies with their attendant sexual mores, Clement comes to a defence of marriage.

On the one hand, Clement upholds self-control on a rather Platonic basis, saying, "He who indulges his pleasures gratifies his body; but he who is controlled liberates from its passions his soul which is master of the body".[506] On the other hand, he staunchly defends marriage. To the person who argues that marriage and childbirth only prolong misery in the world and sustain the grip of death, he replies with the words of St John: "They went out from us, but were not with us. For, if they had been of us, they would have remained with us" (1 John 2:19). These opposing views are once again Gnostic in origin, in terms of which liberation from death can only come about by a prohibition on birth. One Gnostic gospel addressed to the Egyptians puts into Christ's mouth the words that he will destroy desire for the female and her works of birth and corruption.[507] For Clement, continence or abstinence is a discipline that can only be brought about by grace, and which should extend to things other than sex.

In the end, Clement commends marriage as a place of prayer, since the Lord says he will be present when two or three are gathered together in his name. "If a married couple agree to be continent it helps them to pray; if they agree with reverence to have sexual relations it leads them to beget children".[508] "All the Epistles of the Apostle [St Paul] teach self-control and continence and numerous instructions about marriage, begetting children, and domestic life. But they nowhere rule out self-controlled marriage".[509] Likewise, "any who dares to call marriage fornication, again falls into blasphemy against the Law and the Lord".[510] Self-controlled marriage admirably sums up Clement's view of the sexual side of marriage, which seems his main concern, given all the currents on sexuality present in his own day. It is a subject which is to further exercise the Fathers, and it is arguable that a healthy view of marriage does not fully arrive until modern times, and is still in progress.

The remaining books of *The Stromata* cover faith again, in Book V, true *gnosis* or knowledge, in Books VI and VII (both of which we will consider when looking at the church's response to Gnosticism in the next chapter), and in Book IV, martyrdom. Just as false asceticism mixed with Gnosticism can turn something good and a blessing, namely marriage, into a cause for reproach and possible shame, so a false asceticism can turn martyrdom into something to be sought rather than borne. For those who seek martyrdom, life is not a gift to be cherished, but a means of proving a kind of Stoic perfection;[511] a final act of self-denial, rather than the unwelcome loss of life in defence of God's truth and love. Once again, Clement lauds a life of self-denial and of the consciousness of heaven, both of which form a large part of the progress of the soul. "When, therefore, he who partakes gnostically [this is the true *gnosis* or knowledge of God] of this holy quality and devotes himself to contemplation, communing in purity with the divine, he enters more nearly into the state of impassable identity, so as no longer to have science and possess knowledge, but to be science and knowledge".[512] There is no doubt that martyrdom, rightly suffered, will be rewarded and will testify to the truth.

Throughout *The Stromata* the background noise of Gnosticism is present, breaking into the foreground on many occasions. Clement and Justin do much to refute its tenets, but it is time now to appreciate the threat of Gnosticism more clearly and show how Irenaeus in particular rebutted its appeal with the first full definition of the faith.

CHAPTER 5

Gnosticism and Irenaeus

On several occasions the Apostle Paul warned the first-century churches about the dangers of speculative theology. He might be talking about Gnosticism, for on one occasion he warns against "what is falsely called knowledge [*gnosis*]" (1 Timothy 6:20).

Elsewhere, Paul writes to Timothy that some "have wandered away from these [a good conscience and a sincere faith] and turned to meaningless talk" (1 Timothy 1:6). It seems that, among other things, they are guilty of misusing the Law (1 Timothy 1:7). Later in the epistle, he upbraids those who forbid marriage from a false view of asceticism and of marriage (1 Timothy 4:3). He warns against "godless myths" (1 Timothy 4:7). Paul also has a dislike of disputes about words, and arguments for argument's sake (1 Timothy 6:4). He considers such speculations unedifying and says they contribute only to confusion. They make for envy, strife, malicious talk, evil suspicions and constant friction between "men of corrupt mind" (1 Timothy 6:5). Timothy, by contrast, is to guard the sound doctrine entrusted to him and be faithful to what he has learned (1 Timothy 6:20; 2 Timothy 1:13; 2:14; 3:14–16).

This emphasis on "sound doctrine" came about because of false teaching that was circulating at the time about the Jewish Law, and the need to keep the Law in order to be justified (Galatians 2:16). Furthermore, there were certain myths and teachings circulating in Asia that lionised asceticism and taught there was need for mediators, such as angels, to reconcile humankind with God. This trend was evident in the heresy circulating around Colossae (Colossians 2:19), which argued the need for angelic orders to mediate, and put a special premium on ascetic disciplines with the appearance of religious merit.

If Paul was aware of these threats to the "sound doctrine" he was passing on to Timothy—threats based around myths, speculation and asceticism—so too was the Apostle John. For John, the threat was to the person and uniqueness of Christ. John's gospel, and especially its prologue, heralded the authority of Christ as the creator redeemer, the *Logos* made flesh. The attack on the person of Jesus was based on a philosophical presupposition about creation, widely held in the religions and philosophies of the ancient world, that the material world was corrupt, indeed evil—the result of a breach in the godhead. It was not something any self-respecting god would tangle with. Thus, to take on human flesh or bodily functions would have represented a travesty of true divinity. Jesus, being divine—so the argument went—could not have come in the flesh without compromising his divinity. It thus only *seemed* as though he took on flesh. This view came to be known as Docetism.

It was this false view of the evil nature of creation and of human flesh that drove the formulation of the doctrine of Christ. Either the *Logos* could mingle fully with human flesh, but not really be God (Arianism), or he could retain all the attributes of the godhead, but not fully take on human flesh (Docetism). The Christological controversies of the fourth and fifth centuries would be taken up with defining *how* Christ was both God and man, and *how* a unity of God and man could coexist within a single frame.

Before those controversies took centre stage, there was a preliminary struggle in the church with Gnosticism, a struggle which went on for well over a hundred years. The Gnostics sought to reframe the orthodox Christian narrative of salvation within a mythical explanation of creation that was part Jewish, part Christian, part Eastern and part a highly speculative form of Middle Platonism. The Gnostics' position threatened to suffocate biblical Christian faith by re-interpreting the Judeo-Christian salvation narrative within the context of a wider myth. Gnosticism can be likened to a cuckoo laying its theological eggs in another's nest, and raising its young at the cost of other healthy chicks. Or, to use a more sinister metaphor, it can be likened to a parasite that lays its eggs in a food source that it then gradually takes over. Justin Martyr and Irenaeus were aware of the threat of Gnosticism and its many offshoots, and for the first time began to define what heresy was and what orthodoxy was.

Gnosticism, as we shall see, was a many-headed hydra: slay one head and another would pop up. The full extent of the Gnostic phenomenon, which cannot be defined as a single doctrine sharing commonly held assumptions, was not fully revealed until 1945. It was then that an Egyptian farmer found a number of leather pouches containing Gnostic works in thirteen codices. These works included over fifty texts which had been read as sacred literature by a Gnostic community in Nag Hammadi, about 80 kilometres north of Luxor on the Nile.[513] The full range of Gnostic beliefs, together with the Gnostics' tendency to rewrite earlier Christian or Jewish works, such as the gospels of John, Mary, Thomas, or even Adam, in Gnosticism's own likeness, became clear with the discovery of the Nag Hammadi Gnostic treasure. There was no single movement that could be called Gnosticism, but rather a school of thought presenting itself in different guises.[514] The subsequent publication of these works, which were mostly translated from the original Greek into Coptic, is a story in itself.

It is hard to pinpoint exactly when Gnosticism emerged, but it was certainly present by the early second century and was to continue in its various forms into the fifth century and beyond. Although commonly thought to be derived from the mysticism of Simon Magus (see Acts 8:9ff), Gnosticism may well have originally sprung from a Jewish sect with an intense interest in Genesis. It may then have developed into a trans-religious movement affecting Christianity.[515] At any rate, it was a movement which shared common features among its sub-groups, yet had diversity as part of its essence.

In the seventeenth century, Henry More (1614–87) was the first to use the term "Gnosticism" for all the heresies that Irenaeus and his heresiological (heresy exposing) successors attacked.[516] The term Gnosticism was given meaning by those who opposed it, for *gnosis* simply means knowledge. At the heart of Gnosticism is a process of liberation or enlightenment of an elect or elite who are deemed to be trapped in an evil material world. *Gnosis* or knowledge offers the possibility of salvation or liberation from this condition. Gnosticism is thus dualistic, and distinguishes between the spiritual and the material, the soul and the body. The former is considered good; the latter is considered evil—something from which a person must escape.

If this seems simply a form of Platonism—and Gnosticism does share precepts and principles with Platonism—its wider narrative makes it both more distinct and more bizarre. It was a bold and highly speculative attempt to explain the origin and fate of the universe and to proclaim salvation "through a combination of Jewish scriptures, Platonist mythological speculation, and revelatory meditations on the structure of the human mind".[517] A further Gnostic narrative must be added, however, that suggests there is an unapproachable super-remote god or deity who gave rise to a number of emanations, one of which was responsible for creating the world.

This super-god, who is unknowable and unapproachable, sometimes called the "Father of Entirety" or the "Invisible Spirit", lies at the heart of Gnosticism. His characteristics are apophatic, i.e., unknowable, immeasurable, invisible, unlimited and so on. As the Gnostic text, the *Secret Book of John*, puts it, "The One is the immeasurable light, pure, holy immaculate. It is unutterable, and it is perfect in incorruptibility".[518]

Beneath the unknowable "Father of Entirety" are a number of "aeonic" emanations of the godhead. Essentially, these are powers that are less than the Father, but that nevertheless have divine roles. They come with names that are bewildering to the modern ear: Barbelo, Eleleth, Epesekh and others—there are six in all. These aeons are simultaneously actors, places, extents of time (our usual meaning for aeons) and modes of thought. Much like Plato's ideal forms or ideas, the aeons can be intelligence, truth, form, afterthought, forethought or wisdom—and to wisdom in particular we shall return.

Foremost among the aeons is the second principle, "the image of the perfect Invisible Virgin Spirit". In the *Secret Book of John*, she is described as emanating from the Father as the one who consents to give the "Invisible Spirit", Barbelo, her power: "Barbelo asked to be given *Life Eternal,* and the Invisible Spirit consented. When the Spirit consented, *Incorruptibility* appeared and stood by *Thought* and *Foreknowledge. Incorruptibility* glorified the invisible one and Barbelo. Because of her they had come into being".[519] It is Barbelo who begets a spark, which is the "Self-Originate" or Christ.[520] Unlike the other aeons, which emanate by being disclosed, Christ is the "Only Begotten" of the Father, and Barbelo is his father and mother.

"The Self-Originate or Christ serves as the transitional figure from the primal triad of the Invisible Spirit, the Barbelo and himself, to the numerous aeons that make up the entirety of the divine realm".[521] To further complicate matters, four luminaries attend the Self-Originate or Christ. They are Harmozel, Oroiael, Daueithia and Eleleth. These luminaries are in turn accompanied by others and provide dwelling places for the archetypes of ideal humanity, such as Adam, Seth, the primeval descendants of Seth, and the Gnostics themselves. Between them all there is a balance of masculine and feminine. The Barbelo is called "the mother-father", but is also thrice-made; with gender equality thus put at risk.[522]

If the foregoing description gives us a general view of the fantastic Gnostic godhead and its *modus operandi*, another important aspect of Gnosticism to consider, before we look at its method of salvation, is its doctrine of creation. The last of the 24 aeons or emanations from the "Invisible Spirit" is wisdom or Sophia, and she it is who, surprisingly, causes the breach in the godhead—i.e., a rift in the harmony of the aeons. This rift occurs when she has a thought of her own, without her divine male partner, resulting in a pseudo-aeon, the first divine being "that does not belong to the entirety of the immortals".[523]

This misshapen thinking is cast outside her being and is called Ialdabaoth, the misguided creator represented in Genesis, whose creation is flawed and corrupt. In other words, this is a fall before the Fall; it is not due to Adam, but takes place in a heavenly realm, and thus approximates the fall of Lucifer found in Jewish and Christian theology. It is the Gnostic answer to the question: why is the earth the way it is? The Christian and Jewish answer is that the world was created good, but was spoilt by Adam's fall. The Gnostic answer is that it was bad at the point of creation.

Thus "the transition from the spiritual entirety of blessed aeons to the material world of creatures appears to be a mistake, something that divine providence did not intend and, as we shall see, a problem that must be rectified".[524] This is the Gnostic answer to the Platonic question of how to understand the gap between the changing material existence of the world and the ideal of an unchanging, wholly spiritual existence, of which the One is the ultimate representative. The Gnostic answer is that the craftsman of the world was herself at fault. Sophia or wisdom formed Ialdabaoth.[525] In another Gnostic work, Zostrianos (later assimilated into Zoroaster), the legendary son of Yolaos, a Sethian visionary, encounters transcendental beings in a supra-celestial ascent.[526] Before his ascent, Zostrianos writes about his quest: "Abandoned in my inner corporeal darkness, psychical chaos, and dark lustful femininity with which I was unconcerned, and after I discovered the boundlessness of my materialism and reproved the dead creation within me as well as the perceptible divine world ruler, I powerfully proclaimed wholeness to those unrelated parts".[527]

This seems like the Gnostic equivalent of a Homeric Odyssey: the abandonment of warfare for a voyage of mystical contemplation to a distant homeland where harmony may be found. It demonstrates the notion of an evil creation resulting from the activity of a spurious god called Ialdabaoth, "who makes a highly imperfect copy of the spiritual entirety of which he had only a dim memory".[528] Having made the world and its creatures, Ialdabaoth creates Adam, making him upright in stature and with aspirations towards a higher reality.

Created first as a spiritual being, Adam is then given a material body and a partner in Eve; but Ialdabaoth muddies the waters further by enslaving them both. Originally, when Adam and Eve exist as "aspiritual androgynes",[529] the female revelatory principle is able to teach Adam as, "I (Adam) went about with her in a glory that she beheld in the eternal realm we had come from. She instructed me in the knowledge of the eternal God".[530]

Adam and Eve are then divided by an angry God, "the ruler of the realms and powers"[531] and the glory in their hearts departs and the previous knowledge of the spiritual rulers eludes them. Adam now no longer has acquaintance with these rulers, especially Ialdabaoth, who for his part attempts to rape Eve and her daughter Norea.[532] This rape is the origin of sexual intercourse: "For to this day sexual intercourse has persisted because of the first ruler. He planted sexual desire within the woman who belongs to Adam. Through intercourse the first ruler produced duplicate bodies (called Yahweh and Elohim). And he blew some of his false spirit into them".[533] Adam and his son Seth, together with

Eve, now look forward to a saviour referred to as "That Human Being".[534] From all this, Gnostic readers learn that sexual desire, anger, avarice and other passions have their origin in demonic interference.

If some of the events described in the preceding paragraphs provide an explanation for the existence of evil and flawed passion in the world, they also provide the context for salvation. If, instead of Ialdabaoth, we put the Devil, the Genesis account is not too dissimilar from this aspect of the Gnostic myth. Yet Gnosticism never really comes to terms with the original goodness of creation and the brilliance of the body and its life, albeit marred by sin. For Gnostics, the body remains the repository of unruly passions and messy experience. The central salvific motif is liberation through knowledge of the saviour, rather than redemption of our souls and bodies by a saviour, who became like us in every respect except for sin. Thus Docetism, the teaching that Jesus came in a way that *seemed* bodily (but was not actually flesh and blood) is very appealing. Humans must be awakened by knowledge (*gnosis*) and become recipients thereby of divine energy. Gnostic people form part of the tribe of Seth who, alone among Adam's descendants, will be saved.[535]

Inclusion into the elite Gnostic people comes from possessing true *gnosis*, which in turn comes from grasping the Gnostic literature, its myths, narrative and outlook. Jesus as Saviour is fitted into this narrative, but only within the construct of the Gnostic myth: he is not truly human. Gnostic literature is not always consistent, however. The writers of the different books compete with each other for effect, and no doubt for authority also. The way to salvation for a Gnostic disregards the Eucharist and instead provides liberation through *gnosis* and through an elaborate baptismal ritual, with which begins a mystical ascent to heaven. In the *Secret Book of John*, Forethought or Barbelo, one of the chief powers or aeons, describes how she has saved those who are in "the prison of the body" unaware of their divine origin and destiny.[536] The promise in the *Secret Book* is clear: "Those upon whom the spirit of life will descend and whom the spirit will empower will be saved, and will become perfect and worthy of greatness, and will be cleansed there from all evil and the anxieties of all wickedness, since they are no longer anxious for anything except the incorruptible alone, and concerned with that from this moment on, without anger, jealousy, envy, desire, or greed for anything".

The text continues: "They are affected by nothing but being in the flesh alone, and they wear the flesh as they look forward to a time when they will be met by those who receive them. Such people are worthy of the incorruptible, eternal life and calling. They endure everything and bear everything so as to finish the contest and receive eternal life".[537]

Salvation comes with illumination from Barbelo or Forethought, who says: "I am the Forethought of pure light, I am the thought of the Virgin Spirit, who raises you to a place of honour. Arise, remember that you have heard and trace your root, which is I, the compassionate. Guard yourself against the angels of misery, the demons of chaos, and all who entrap you. And beware of deep sleep and the trap in the bowels of the underworld. I raised and sealed the person in luminous water with Five Seals, that death might prevail over the person from that moment on".[538] The five seals are a distinctive part of Gnostic baptism, but we do not know exactly what they are or what truths they symbolise. They are the five steps of baptism: enrobing, washing, enthroning, glorifying and being caught up to luminous places. These five steps amount to five seals. Sealing may also refer to being anointed with oil or chrism. Whatever the rite of baptism signifies to the Gnostic, their rituals, more elaborate than those of Christians, serve as a solemn initiation into salvation. Baptism is the announcement to the candidate that they are liberated and set on a path or ascent to further liberation in the future. There is little understanding of the need for redemption from guilt, or of being baptised into the death of Christ[539] or of the remission of sins, or the substitutionary atonement of Christ's death on the cross. Baptism is therefore the start of a spiritual and intellectual ascent to increasingly abstract levels of existence,[540] not dissimilar from the ascent outlined in Plato's *Symposium* or in Jewish Apocalyptic as found in 2 Enoch. With the Gnostics, the ascent is increasingly abstract, has seemingly little practical outworking, does not involve intercession to change the world, and is not Christ-centred, as is the mystical tradition of the Desert Fathers or of mystics like Gregory Nyssen.

The Gnostic aspiration is to be gifted with knowledge of the Invisible Spirit following the example of Zostrianos, "who gains mystical contact with the divine through his own ascetic and intellectual efforts and through the revelation from divine beings, but falls short of ultimate *gnosis* with the Highest God".[541] The hero of a Gnostic work called *The Foreigner* provides a further example of mystic contact with the divine as the narrator contemplates his own intellect. *The Foreigner* recounts a mystical ascent to the Barbelo aeon and a series of revelatory discourses the narrator receives from the eternal being. In fact, he discovers the Barbelo as that which exists within him through contemplation.[542] Ritualised baptism and ascent are the means of gaining *gnosis*, the means of making contact with the divine, and the means of liberation from the corruption of earthly and bodily existence.

Gnosticism in Rome

At some point in the middle of the second century, Gnosticism arrived in Rome. As with all Judeo-Christian thought, it travelled from east to west from Palestine, Syria and Egypt to the Western Empire, and especially to Rome. Gnosticism would flourish in Egypt, as the Nag Hammadi collection of Gnostic scriptures demonstrates, but its reception in Rome was more complex. David Brakke likens the emergence of orthodoxy via a form of "proto-orthodoxy" to a horse race, with one eventual front-runner (proto-orthodoxy) coming to the fore out of a diverse group of runners and riders representing myriad Christian communities in the city of Rome.[543]

What this metaphor of a horse race gives us is the sense of a plethora of churches in Rome in the middle of the second century and no certainty which of them would become the front-runner. Many of these churches were home churches, presided over by an ill-defined episcopacy or groups of presbyters. These churches had an uneven attachment to orthodoxy, which at this stage did not really exist as such amidst the competing versions of Christianity. Nor, in AD 150, did the churches in Rome, or the "Great Church"—as they were sometimes collectively known—have a common procedure for identifying heresy and excommunicating errant followers. Justin Martyr and Irenaeus would take this process of identifying heterodoxy forward, but it would take shape over 20 years or more, from AD 150–180.

This process of defining orthodoxy was one of differentiation, in which Christianity firstly distinguished itself from Judaism,[544] then from Greco-Paganism, and lastly from Gnosticism. It was in reaction to each of these movements or religions that Christianity eventually defined itself and its own latent orthodoxy emerged. This process would take the best part of a century as each form of Christianity was evaluated, and either retained or discarded. Thus, "any model for Christian diversity in the pre-Constantinian era must recognise not only the hybridity and fluidity of early Christians and movements but also the unity of the bounded character of many of them". [545]

Numerous Christian communities came into view in the second century, but none had the power structure to enforce a single point of view or orthodoxy. By mid-century, such a power structure did appear, in the form of monarchical bishops in Rome and elsewhere. This episcopal model then spread. Nevertheless, the latent orthodoxy among the churches, which acknowledged, for instance, that the God of the Hebrews was also the God and Father of the Lord Jesus Christ, took time to emerge. In fact, it took the differing views of Marcion, and later the Gnostic Valentinus, both of whom refused to believe that the two Testaments of the Bible proceeded from the same God, to help the proto-orthodox define their views and lay down an orthodoxy which included both Old Testament and New Testament in a single Bible.

The unity of the Bible may seem obvious to us now, but the Bible only solidified as Old and New Testaments out of a debate with those such as Marcion, who believed scripture should contain only books on a list drawn up by him, i.e., mainly, and possibly only, St Luke's Gospel and Paul's letters. Alongside this process of defining orthodoxy, Justin Martyr, Irenaeus, and later Tertullian and Hippolytus, developed their notions of heresy as well.

Heresy did exist as a concept in the New Testament, but only came slowly to the fore in the second century. In his letter to the Corinthians, Paul writes: "There must be factions (or tendencies/*hairesis*) among you in order that those who are genuine among you may be recognised" (1 Corinthians 11:18–19). Paul originally considered these factions or heresies works of the flesh, but they soon came to be associated with false teaching.[546] Later, Ignatius of Antioch designated error, which accompanied schism or rupture from the bishop, as heresy. Thus Ignatius praised the Ephesians for their good order in God, since "all of you live according to the truth and no *hairesis* resides among you; rather you do not even listen to anyone unless he speaks about Jesus Christ in truth".[547]

For Ignatius, heresy was a "foreign plant" sown in the field of the true church. As Paul said, the way out of heresy is to guard the good deposit of the gospel and to be on guard against all false teachers (1 Timothy 6:20; 2 Timothy 1:14). In the middle of the second century, in Rome, there were many teachers of differing forms of Christianity with a swathe of seductive ideas. The question, which became most pressing, was which of them truly represented the Christian faith.

This process of differentiation, and the adoption of the idea that some forms of Christianity were heretical, developed in Rome as various teachers circulated in the city alongside and within the "Great Church".[548] By the second half of the second century, a number of forms of Christianity existed in Rome. The principal ones, and the ones which were to be labelled heretical, were those churches or Christians who followed Marcion, Valentinus, and their associates.

Marcion came to Rome from Sinope, a city on the Black Sea in the province of Pontus. He arrived in Rome during the oversight of Anicetus in the period AD 142–166.[549] He was a rich shipbuilder by background and when he arrived it is reported that he gave 200,000 sesterces to the Great Church, which was a very handsome gift. It soon became clear he had his own agenda. He worked for several years on a book he called the *Antitheses*, in which he recorded the differences between the God of the Law and the Gospel.

He argues, on the strength of this survey, that there are two Gods spoken of in the scriptures (including some New Testament scriptures, namely the letters of Paul and the Gospel of Luke, of which Marcion knew and approved). These Gods are the Creator and the Redeemer, the God of the Law and the God of the Gospel. This is straightforward ditheism. On top of this separation of the Old and New Testament, of Judaism and Christianity, of Law and Gospel, of violence and peace, Marcion reaches two practical conclusions. First, like the Gnostics, he has disdain for the material world, which he sees as part of the law-creation continuum, for which he has no time, and the second is his radical asceticism on the back of his Gnostic/Platonic view of the material world. This asceticism in turn includes both a proscription on marriage and a requirement for abstinence from all sexual activity.[550] According to Tertullian, Marcion introduced "his new god" in July AD 144, probably around the same time that he asked to meet with the presbyters of the churches in Rome to discuss the meaning of Christ's command not to put new wine into old wineskins.

It is possible that the presbyters took the first step in ejecting Marcion from the Christian community in Rome, by returning his money and proscribing his teaching. Apart from this, they had no formal means of excommunication besides a call to the faithful not to associate with him.[551] Once again, the "fractionated Christian communities of Rome" did not yet have the institutional authority and collective consciousness simply to exclude Marcion. Yet within a few years, with the coming of Justin Martyr, Irenaeus and a more authoritative See of Rome, an accepted proto-orthodoxy would emerge.[552]

Another contemporary teacher was Valentinus, the principal Gnostic spokesman in Rome during this period. Irenaeus writes that Valentinus came to Rome in the time of Bishop Hyginus (c. AD 136–140), flourished under Pius (c. AD 140–155), and remained until Anicetus (c. AD 155–166).[553] Hyginus was, according to Irenaeus, the ninth Bishop of Rome. He was widely regarded, even by opponents such as Tertullian, as brilliant and eloquent.[554] He most probably ran a school of theology and some of his pupils, for example Ptolemaeus and Heracleon, became influential in their own right.

What is clear is that Valentinus, Gnostic teacher though he was, clearly flourished in Rome, and it was only after he was passed over as bishop that his hidden agenda emerged, driven by strong personal ambition. His own work, *Gospel of Truth*, reveals the extent of his Gnosticism. Once again, Gnosticism is based on the precept that a true knowledge (*gnosis*) of the Father will produce unity. Valentinus writes: "It is within Unity that each one will attain himself; within knowledge he will purify himself from the multiplicity into Unity, consuming matter within himself like fire, and the darkness by light, death by light". There are strong Gnostic themes here: the acquisition of special knowledge that will bring enlightenment and experience of the unknowable Father; the implicit mistrust of matter which must be consumed by fire; and the openness to rituals and practices which help define the moment of *gnosis*. Valentinus's method of extending his influence was not like that of Marcion, who condemned those who disagreed with his ditheism. Instead, Valentinus divided the Christian community into two groups: an inner circle of "spirituals" and an outer circle of "psychics". His teaching was to move the "psychics" to be "spiritual" through *gnosis* precipitated by an elaborate form of baptism. One example of this method can be seen in a letter from Valentinus's protégé, Ptolemaeus, who counsels one Flora to a deeper understanding of the Mosaic Law. Ptolemaeus urges her to accept that there are several sources for the Mosaic Law, but in particular, "a demiurge and maker of the universe or world and of the things within it".[555] Ptolemaeus hopes to lead Flora from the simple view that the Law of the Old Testament came from the single understanding of God the Father to a deeper knowledge of its true origin.

Another example of how Gnosticism was at work in Rome at this time comes from an epigraph inscribed to one Flavia Sophie, located in a quiet suburb of Rome along the Via Latina, near where the Emperor Marcus Aurelius was born. The text on the gravestones contains these two epigrams:

> Longing for the fatherly light, O sister bride, my Sophie,
> In the ablutions of Christ anointed with
>   imperishable holy balsam
> You have hastened to gaze upon the divine
>   countenances of the Aeons,
> Upon the great angel of the great early counsel the true Son
> You have gone to the bridal chamber and
>   ascended to the . . . fatherly . . .
> This deceased did not have a usual ending of life
> She dies away and lives amid a truly imperishable light.
> She lives to the delight of the living, is really dead to the dead.
> O, earth, why are you astonished about this
>   type of corpse? Are you terrified?[556]

There are familiar themes here: gazing on the aeons, going to the bridal chamber to look upon the paternal light, receiving anointing through balsam, and the earth as the symbol of fallen matter created by the Demiurge. These epigrams demonstrate the attraction Gnosticism held for the aristocratic classes in Rome at the time. As Irenaeus recounts, the Valentinians devoted their attentions to those who were able "to pay a high price for an acquaintance with such profound mysteries".[557] It was especially upon women who were "well bred, elegantly attired and of great wealth" that the Gnostic Marcus, in particular, preyed.[558]

In the middle of the second century, Rome was full of diverse Christian and not-so-Christian teachings and teachers. Principal among the Gnostics and Ditheists were Valentinus, Cerdo and Marcion, who had followers such as Ptolomaeus, and the less scrupulous Marcus. On the side of the emerging proto-orthodoxy was Justin the Martyr, who came to Rome from Ephesus around AD 140 and remained there until his martyrdom under Iunius Rusticus around AD 165. He opened schools above the Baths of Myrtinus and wore the distinctive mantle of a philosopher. His approach was both refreshing and radical, suggesting as he did that the universal *Logos* had been present in parts of classical philosophy until fully appearing in the life and teaching of Christ.[559] As we have seen, he wrote extensively, including a work addressed, as Clement's was, "To the Hellenes", but which has since been lost.[560] His two Apologies, his *Dialogue with Trypho the Jew*, and his works *On the Sole Government of God* and *On the Resurrection*, demonstrate the scope of his endeavour, but it is Irenaeus who was to establish proto-orthodoxy in the late second century. And it is to Irenaeus's life and work, which was so seminal in the formation of Christianity, that we now turn.

Irenaeus

Irenaeus was another easterner who went west, in much the same way as Justin. In Irenaeus's case, it seems he was sent as a missionary from Smyrna to the church in Gaul at Lugdunum (Lyons). Possibly born around AD 130 or 135, he was most likely educated in Antioch.[561] He would have been around 20 years of age at the time of Polycarp's martyrdom in AD 155/156, which took place after Polycarp's visit to Rome the year before.

Irenaeus says he knew Polycarp when he was a boy, and that Polycarp was probably the most important influence on his life. Polycarp's influence is especially clear in Irenaeus's letter to Florinus, also a native of Smyrna, who had been inveigled into Gnosticism by Valentinus in Rome. In a piece entitled "To Florinus, On Sole Sovereignty, or God is not the Author of Evil", Irenaeus writes as follows: "When I was still a boy I saw you in Lower Asia in Polycarp's company [this was presumably at Antioch], when you were cutting a fine figure at the imperial court and wanted to be in favour with him". Irenaeus continues:

> I remember how he spoke of his intercourse with John [the Apostle] and with others who had seen the Lord; how he had repeated their words from memory; and how the things he had heard them say about the Lord, his miracles and his teaching, things that he had heard direct from the eye-witnesses of the Word of Life, were proclaimed by Polycarp in complete harmony with Scripture. [562]

Irenaeus then surmises that if Polycarp, whom he refers to as an Apostolic Presbyter, had heard any suggestion of Gnosticism he would have "fled from the very place where he had been sitting or standing when he heard such words" in much the same way that the Apostle John fled from the bath-house when he heard that the heretic Cerinthus was there.[563] Charles Hill, in his work on Polycarp, draws the conclusion that far from being a "rustic and unsophisticated writer of only one letter, Polycarp was a gifted orator and theologian, who had the distinction of being not only an Apostolic Father, but also an apologist, a heresiologist (an exposer of heresy) and a scriptural exegete".[564]

Irenaeus came to the Christian community in Lyons as a priest at some point during the AD 160s, during a persecution of Christians in the reign of Marcus Aurelius (AD 161–180). The region around the Roman city of Lugdunum, or present-day Lyons, had been inhabited by Celts from 750 BC. Around the same time, the coastal region, especially the mouth of the Rhone at Massalia (Marseilles), was colonised by Ionian Greeks from Phocaea, some 50 miles north-west of Smyrna.[565] In the following centuries, the Gauls spread across the region, followed by the Romans, who came to Narbonne in 121 BC. The height of this colonisation was under Julius Caesar and his successor, Augustus. Lugdunum became the Roman capital of Gaul and here the Emperor Claudius was born to Drusus, Augustus's adopted stepson (Livia's son by her first marriage).

By now Arles, Lyons, Orange and Avignon were all colonised, and with a mixture of Greco-Roman and barbarian culture, became centres of civic life in the region. The barbarians were themselves a mixture of Celts, Gauls and Aquitaini. The latter two groups had centres at Lyons and Bordeaux. It was at Lyons or Lugdunum that Irenaeus heard of the teaching of Valentinus, the seductive practices of Marcus in Rome, and the more exotic spirituality of the Montanists in Phyrgia. As a rising scholar-priest, he was sent by the church in Lyons to Bishop Eleutherus in Rome in AD 177 with a letter of censure concerning the Montanists. In Irenaeus's estimation, Eleutherus was the twelfth Bishop of Rome.[566] While he was away in Rome, a massacre of Christians occurred in Lyons, which included the godly Bishop Pothinus. On his return, Irenaeus was made the second Bishop of Lyons and remained so until his death, sometime near the end of the second century.

Irenaeus's Writings

It would not be an exaggeration to say that Irenaeus was the first great theologian of the post-Apostolic era. The Apostolic Fathers were more piecemeal or incidental in what they wrote. Irenaeus, by contrast, produced a response to Gnosticism as well as a comprehensive Christian theology. His work was like a cathedral: it had internal space, strong definition and a structure. It was solid and multi-faceted, compared with the higgledy-piggledy edifices of his opponents, and the smaller "parish church" contributions of his predecessors. His period as Bishop of Lyons spanned 20 years or more. He came from a tradition that encompassed both the confidence and sophistication of teaching from the east, but which was nonetheless firmly tethered to the Apostles, especially the Apostle John, whom his great mentor and father in God, Polycarp, had known personally. In terms of spiritual lineage, he was thus just one generation away from the Apostles. While aware of the church in the east and its language, thought-processes and inheritance, he was equally at home in Rome with the leaders of the church there. Finally, he was a bishop of a provincial capital and of a Christian community, which was open to various influences, both from Rome itself and from the barbarian tribes of the district. To a high degree, he combined in his person a range of influences, which were very unusual. Not even the great Augustine had such a head start when it came to instructing the church. Perhaps Irenaeus might be called the Athanasius of the west. Even if Irenaeus's life was not quite as tempestuous as Athanasius's, his writings were just as influential, and were produced at an early, yet critical, point for both doctrinal development and the stability of the church.

His writing appears to have been produced throughout most of the time he was Bishop of Lyons. His great work, divided into five books and written over a number of years, is *The Refutation and Overthrowal of Knowledge Falsely So-Called* or, as it is known by its more popular title, *Against the Heresies* (AH). The Greek text (Greek being the language in which it was first written) was consulted by Photius in Baghdad in the ninth century, but this version was most probably lost in the sacking of that city in 1258.[567] Only a Latin translation remained. Then, in 1904, in Yerevan, Armenia, Armenian versions of books four and five were found.

In 1930, Irenaeus was discounted by the German theologian Loofs when he applied the full panoply of source criticism to *Against Heresies*. Loofs did not consider him a theologian of the first rank. Since then, Loofs's seemingly impregnable case against the toleration and originality of Irenaeus has been deconstructed. As Behr now writes, "we will be able to appreciate, with greater sensitivity and accuracy, Irenaeus as

an advocate of toleration and diversity in contrast to those [in Rome]
who lacked his irenic quality".[568] Although criticised by many for using
his episcopal authority to limit Christian diversity, Irenaeus may be
seen more clearly as one who defended the Apostolic faith against the
mythologies of Gnosticism, and against Gnosticism's lopsided ethical
stance on humanity, sexuality and marriage, all ideas which were
dangerously circling the loosely-governed "Great Church" in Rome.

The first books of *Against Heresies* (I–III) came out when Eleutherus
was Bishop of Rome (AD 178–189), together with the "Letter to Florinus
on Sole Sovereignty", "On the Ogdoad" and "To Blastus on Schism". The
remaining two books of *Against Heresies* and the "Letter to Victor" came
out during Victor's episcopacy (AD 189–198).

Apart from other works referred to by Eusebius, such as a treatise
entitled *Concerning Knowledge* and some discourses on the Letter to the
Hebrews and the Wisdom of Solomon,[569] Irenaeus's other main work was
The Demonstration of the Apostolic Preaching, thought to be instruction
for new converts. It was likewise found as a manuscript in Yerevan in
1904.

Against Heresies

The first two books of *Against Heresies* were translated completely by the
Victorian Cleveland Cox and published in the Ante Nicene Fathers Series
in 1885. The text of *Against Heresies* that Cox translated is a hybrid of
Latin and Greek, consisting of a severely reduced Latin text of Book I,
supplemented by a Greek text from Hippolytus and Epiphanius.[570] Other
important translations and texts have come down to us from Erasmus
in 1526, the Benedictine Massuet in Paris in 1712, and then Harvey's
translation, made in Cambridge in 1857. New versions of the text were
made with new archaeological finds of Syriac fragments, as, for instance,
the Syriac manuscript from Nitria, now lodged in the British Museum.[571]

Whatever the vagaries of the textual transmission, the reader in
English is confronted in Books I and II with a hundred pages of twin

columns of Irenaeus's dense description of the Gnostic heresies that were confronting the church in Rome in AD 178, and of the growing Montanist movement. It is not easy reading, although Irenaeus sets to his task with gusto. He begins by warning his readers of the pitfalls that the Apostle Paul identified when it came to genealogies or speculative theology, or to giving teaching that has the appearance of knowledge, but which is specious, and which seems spiritual, but is in fact misleading.[572] "Error", Irenaeus writes, "is never set forth in its naked deformity, lest, being thus exposed, it should at once be detected".[573] Instead, the teaching set forth by Ptolemaeus and Valentinus, leading Gnostics, had first to be explained in order to be shown to be errant.

In Book I, Irenaeus addresses the friend to whom this work is dedicated, writing that he has made a study of the commentaries of Valentinus in order to explain their "portentous and profound mysteries", so that this friend might "avoid an abyss of madness and of blasphemy against Christ".[574] Irenaeus then puts in a disclaimer, saying that living among barbarous Celts (in Lyons) has done nothing for his classical skills of speech, and the recipient must make do with his homespun explanations.[575]

Explanation, which leads to exposure of falsehood, is Irenaeus's method, so he sets about describing the Gnostic system of aeons derived from the one incomprehensible and unapproachable aeon variously called Proarche, Propator and Bythus.[576] Further emanations (or beings) proceed from him. In these early chapters Irenaeus recounts what happened in the pleroma, and then, from chapter four of Book I, the focus shifts to what happens outside the pleroma—i.e., in the visible world or creation. Here, the different world of passions, of animals and humans, was said to be created by the combination of the Demiurge and Achamot or Sophia.

The Gnostics divide humanity into three types: the spiritual who have "knowledge" and who will pass into the pleroma or heavenly spheres, the animal-human who will pass into the place of the Demiurge, and the material who will be destroyed. Yet, according to their teachings, even the most "animal" among them may indulge their passions or lusts, so long as the spiritual part is nourished by the spiritual. Irenaeus writes, "Others of them yield themselves up to the lusts of the flesh with the utmost greediness, maintaining the carnal things should be allowed to the carnal nature, while spiritual things are provided for the spiritual".[577] At the other extreme, "spiritual" men must live in complete chastity.[578]

In Book I.8, Irenaeus charges that the Gnostic system is one which:

> Neither the prophets announced, nor the Lord taught, nor the Apostles delivered, but of which they boast that beyond all others they have a perfect knowledge. They gather their views from other sources than the scriptures; and, to use a common proverb, they strive to weave ropes of sand, while they endeavour to adapt with an air of probability to their peculiar assertions the parables of the Lord, the sayings of the prophets, and the words of the apostles, in order that their scheme may not seem altogether without support. In doing so, however, they disregard the order and the connection of the Scriptures, and so far as in them lies, dismember and destroy the truth.[579]

Irenaeus goes on in Book I.10 to present the rule of faith and a credal description of Christianity, in which he describes the single, universal faith of the church throughout the world as being Trinitarian, such that God's purpose is to "gather all things into one" (Ephesians 1:10), so that "to Christ Jesus, our Lord, and God, and Saviour, and King, according to the will of the invisible Father, every knee should bow, of things in heaven, and things on earth, and that every tongue confess", and that judgement will come on all "spiritual wickedness". [580]

From chapter 11 of Book I until chapter 21, Irenaeus gives further description of Valentinus's false teaching, as well as that of his followers or fellow Gnostics, especially Marcus, who used his Gnosticism as a means of seducing women.[581] Irenaeus describes the emanations of the beings below the pleroma until the arrival of the Ogdoad, one of the multiple emanations that exist there, having the number 888, which is Jesus.[582] (Eight is an important number in the Gnostic sequence.)

Furthermore, creation is the result of the Demiurge, a being inferior to the Supreme Being, who is responsible for the world and its corruption. Another name for the Demiurge, as we have previously seen, is Ialdabaoth, a corruption of the name Yahweh in the Bible. He it is who provoked the fall of Adam and Eve because he was unable to have children by Eve since Sophia prevented it. It is for this reason Ialdabaoth throws Adam and Eve out of paradise.

Adam and Eve then lose their light and are imprisoned in corrupted bodies governed by Ialdaboath's precepts, which are contained in the Jewish Law. Only by regaining the light that they have lost are they able to re-enter eternity and the pleroma. Seth becomes the line of hope for the future around which Gnostic aspirations settle. This is the Gnosticism described by Irenaeus and taught in its variant forms by the Gnostic teachers: the Ebionites, Cerinthusites, Nicolaitanes, Barbeliotes, Tatian, and others.[583] Irenaeus traces the genealogy of Gnosticism from Simon of Magus onwards in what is a comprehensive survey of their teaching and development, as he knows it.

Book II of *Against Heresies* is very much a sequel to Book I and was written at a similar time, probably around the time that Eleutherus was Bishop of Rome (AD 178–189).[584] Whereas in Book I the heresies of the Gnostics are broadly stated and described, in Book II they are rebutted and countered.

Irenaeus begins with a restatement of Gnostic beliefs, writing as follows: "I have also related how they think and teach that creation at large was formed after the image of the invisible *Pleroma*, and what they hold respecting the Demiurge, declaring at the same time the doctrine of Simon Magus of Samaria, their progenitor, and all of those who succeeded him".[585] At the outset, Irenaeus states that there is one God and that "he is the Creator, who made the heaven and the earth ... and to demonstrate that there is nothing either above Him or after Him ... He is the only God, the only Lord, the only Creator, the only Father, alone containing all things, and Himself commanding all things in existence".[586]

He needs nothing other than himself to create, certainly no intermediaries, whether angels or aeons; for God is pre-eminent and sufficient for all things. Nor is anything that was created made in the image of the aeons from the Gnostic pleroma. Rather, everything created bears the imprint of the Creator, and humans alone are made in his image.[587] Having demonstrated the singular power and capacity of God to create all things without any intermediaries, Irenaeus goes on to show that the work of Christ cannot be placed in any Gnostic system of interpretation either. The 30 aeons in the Gnostic system, for instance, are not symbolised by Jesus's baptism at the age of 30.[588]

Having argued that Jesus's ministry, parables, miracles and name are not window-dressing for Gnostic theory, but are instead the only true revelation of God the Father, Irenaeus ends his refutation by describing the destiny of man: humans may not be divided into those who are material and spiritual and are not destined to find an intermediate state in the afterlife in accordance with their level of *gnosis*. Rather, it is those who have received Christ's revelation of the Father that have eternal life.[589] Nor is there any truth in the idea of the transmigration of souls, in which souls body-hop from one existence to another. Souls are part of human bodies in this life and the next. They have a beginning, but are immortal, and their eternal destiny is dependent on God.[590]

The first two books of *Against Heresies* deal almost exclusively with the refutation of Gnosticism. The next three set out Irenaeus's mature theology, and as such are the first real attempt at a systematic theology in the early church. Not until Augustine in the west would such a task again be undertaken so systematically, while in the east theological writings were to be more occasional—responding especially to the Arian crisis—apart from Athanasius, who was a figure comparable to both Irenaeus and Augustine.

The next three books of *Against Heresies* present this mature theology and probably follow his shorter, more catechetical lectures to new converts, entitled *Demonstration of the Apostolic Preaching*. Irenaeus's theology is crafted around three central tenets: a presentation or *hypothesis*; an economy or *oikonomia*; and a recapitulation or *anakephalaiosis*. These are three tools of literary criticism which he may have learnt in the schools in Antioch during his education, and which would have given uncommon clarity to his understanding of New Testament theology and especially the writings of St Paul. Irenaeus's emphasis was on how the work of salvation, initiated and undertaken by God, Father, Son and Spirit, made man fully human.

In a parallelism learnt from Paul's own writings, Irenaeus states, "The glory of the human being is God",[591] and "the glory of God is a man fully alive and the life of man consists in beholding God".[592] These twin statements are in many ways the cornerstones of Irenaeus's theology.

Let us begin with the first tool of literary criticism ably wielded by Irenaeus, which is "hypothesis". Generally speaking, in English, hypothesis means a theory or thesis, often scientific, which can relate to any sphere of knowledge and which is ready to be tested in order to be proved true.

In classical criticism, hypothesis means an argument or plot in a narrative or play. So, for instance, the hypotheses of the plays by Euripides or Sophocles turn up in second-century Oxyrhynchus *papyri* in Egypt.[593] Likewise, the Genesis narrative of the creation of the world is described by the Christian writer Theophilus as being the first presentation (*hypothesis*) of the origin of the world.[594]

Irenaeus used the idea of *hypothesis* to show how the Gnostics distorted the narrative of the Bible and gospels in order to subvert the true *hypothesis* of the Bible and present quite another one from the same material. So Irenaeus says, as we have seen, the Gnostics "gather their views from other sources than the scriptures; and, to use a common proverb, they strive to weave ropes of sand".[595] He says in a metaphor it is like taking the sculpture of a king made of precious stones and gilded paint and re-arranging the stones to present quite a different image. That is what the Gnostics have done: they have taken the jewels of scripture that make up the portrait of Christ and have fabricated them into a totally different image, such as that of a dog or a fox.[596]

For instance, the Gnostics twist the prologue of John's Gospel so that it becomes an account of the aeons on the pleroma.[597] Yet the hypothesis given to us in scripture is the one taught by the Apostles themselves. They have given us the plot or teaching or hypothesis, which arises plainly from scripture. By contrast, Irenaeus gives us his own interpretation, which is that the correct hypothesis of the prologue is that there is one Lord Jesus Christ, the Word made flesh who gives life and light. All else is mere human fabrication.[598] The true handiwork of God is the coming of the Word made flesh who assumed the flesh of Adam to revivify humanity.[599]

The true hypothesis was gradually turning into a canon, not a creed yet, but a definitive hypothesis of the gospel. Tertullian and Clement of Alexandria were to do the same. Like the Hellenistic philosophers, they appealed to criteria in the infinite regressions of the sceptics or the ever-changing mutations of the Gnostics. In a situation where adversaries continually took on new shapes and forms, the necessity for such a canon became ever more urgent. Clement of Rome writes, "Let us put aside empty and vain cares, let us come to the glorious and venerable canon of our tradition … Let us fix our eyes on the blood of Christ, and let us know that it is precious to his Father because it was poured out for our salvation, and brought grace and repentance". [600]

For Clement of Alexandria, "The ecclesiastical canon is the concord and symphony of the Law and the Prophets in the covenant delivered at the coming of the lord".[601] The tradition is quite literally something which is handed down, like the tradition given by Jesus on the Road to Emmaus (Luke 24:25–31) or that referred to by Paul in 2 Timothy 1:13, 14, and in 1 Corinthians 11:23–27. The true tradition for Irenaeus is that which is predicted by the prophets, preached by the Apostles and practised in the early church.[602] Irenaeus revels in the variety of creation, comparing it to a melody in which we listen for the varied notes of the composer. "Those who listen to the melody ought to praise and extol the artist".[603] His opponents are guilty of fabrication (*plasma*), whereas he commends a hypothesis that is presented by scripture itself. His opponents' fabrication is synthetic: a rearrangement of truth according to their specious myths. Yet God has crafted with clay his own handiwork, like a potter, and his fabrication is genuine: "For flesh is the ancient handiwork (*plasis*) formed out of the dust by God for Adam, and John declares the Word of God truly took on this flesh.[604] The hypothesis, then, is that there is one God, the Father and Creator, who has revealed himself in his only Son, Jesus Christ, who was made known to his prophets and to the church by the Holy Spirit. The purpose of God was to "recapitulate" humankind.

In literary criticism, *anakephalaiôsis* or recapitulation tends to mean a concluding summary. In a legal setting, it is the summation of the facts and case by the advocate to the judge, so that a verdict may be given. Thus, a century before Irenaeus, the Roman rhetorician Quintilian writes, "The repetition and grouping of the facts, which the Greeks call *avakephalaiosis* and some of our writers call enumeration, serves both to refresh the memory of the judge and to place the whole case before his eyes, and, even though the facts may have made little impression on him in detail, their cumulative effect is considerable".[605] It would have been a device that Irenaeus would have known from his own rhetorical education.

When used theologically by Irenaeus it also had the wider meaning of fulfilment, a deeper meaning of reclamation and a fuller resonance of harmony than simply that of summary statement. Thus, typically for Clement of Alexandria, Christ's crown of thorns "recapitulated" Moses's vision of the *Logos* in the burning (thorn) bush.[606] It was a tool that lent itself, therefore, to the theology of integration, to demonstrating how Christ fulfilled what was promised in words, ceremonies and rituals in the Old Testament. But it was also a tool whereby Jesus restored human life, by taking on all its aspects in his own incarnate life. Irenaeus sometimes presses this doctrine to an unfortunate conclusion by saying that Jesus was 50 when he began his teaching ministry, thereby "recapitulating" older age. This was a case of making the facts fit the theory and was an unnecessary distortion of the gospel story.[607]

This scheme or tool of "recapitulation" was used by Irenaeus as a vehicle for showing Jesus's incarnation and life as the means of restoring the glory of God in a man or woman, thus making them fully alive. This could only come about by the action of Jesus entering the theatre of human flesh and taking on that flesh to revivify it by his life, death and resurrection. Irenaeus describes the process:

> Just as the first-fashioned Adam had his subsistence from untilled and yet virgin soil, "for God had not yet sent rain, and there was no human being to till the ground" (Genesis 2.5) and was fashioned by the hand of God, that is, by the Word of God, for "all things were made through him" (John 1.3), and the Lord took mud from the ground and fashioned the human being (Genesis 2.7) so also, when the Word himself recapitulated Adam in himself, he rightly received from Mary, who was yet a virgin, that generation which was the recapitulation of Adam. If then the first Adam had a man for his father, and was born to male seed, they would be right to say that the second Adam was begotten of Joseph. But if the former was taken from the mud, and fashioned by the Word of God, so the Word himself, when bringing about the recapitulation of Adam within himself, ought to have the likeness of generation itself. Why then did God not once again take mud, rather than work his fashioning from Mary? So that

> there should not be another fashioning, nor that it should be
> another fashioning which would be saved, but that same thing
> should be recapitulated, preserving the similitude.[608]

In other words, Christ, the Word of God, came to recapitulate or restore
what had been lost, by taking on human form in the incarnation. The
Word had first created or fashioned (*eplasmesen*) humanity in Adam from
the dust of the earth and the breath of God. Rather than start over again
in another creation after the Fall, and so "abhor the virgin's womb" (*Te
Deum*), the Word entered into human flesh to restore, by recapitulation,
the image that had been tarnished. Since Adam was made by the Word
(John 1.3) and was then recapitulated by the same Word—to become
again what had been lost in the Fall—Adam is, therefore, both a type of
the Word to come, as well as a display-case, although marred, of the image
of God (Genesis 1:27). Christ refashioned that image in man, through
the costly action of the Cross.

Further elements of recapitulation are added by the reversal of Adam's
disobedience through Christ's obedience. (This is similar to the Apostle
Paul's argument in Romans 5:12–21.) Thus Adam fails to obey the
commandment not to eat of the fruit of the tree of the knowledge of good
and evil, but Christ in the wilderness defeats the tempter and withstands
all temptations,[609] thereby recapitulating Adam's failure.[610] For unless "the
human being had been joined to God, he never could have become a
partaker of incorruptibility".[611] In summary, Irenaeus puts it as follows:

> For in times past it was said the human being was made in the
> image of God, but it was not shown to be so; for the Word was
> as yet invisible, after whose image the human was created; and
> because of this he easily lost the likeness. When, however, the
> Word of God became flesh, he confirmed both of these: for
> he both showed forth the image truly, himself becoming that
> which was his image, and he re-established the likeness in a sure
> manner, by co-assimilating the human being to the invisible
> Father through the Word becoming visible.[612]

The way humans enter into this re-vivified life or regeneration is by faith evidenced in baptism, and the way it is sustained is by being nourished on the scriptures and the Eucharist.

For Irenaeus, baptism is "the seal of eternal life and rebirth unto God, that we may no longer be sons of mortal men, but of the everlasting God".[613] The recapitulation of a human being is specifically for those who have died in baptism, sacramentally and spiritually. Thus, what Christ achieves in recapitulating human life by joining the Word of God to the humanity taken on in Mary's pure womb through virginal conception,[614] he then imparts to each believer in baptism.

In fact, in a piece of typical parallelism, Mary is able to do what Eve was not able to do, which is to bring about salvation for the whole human race by her submissive obedience to the Word.[615] The church now becomes the womb of new birth through the waters of baptism and is made such by the presence of the Spirit. For Irenaeus: "Where the church is, there is the Spirit of God, and where the Spirit of God is, there is the church, and every kind of grace, and the Spirit is truth".[616]

The Spirit also takes part in conveying the recapitulation to the believer, for "into this paradise the Lord has introduced those who obey his call, 'summing up in himself all things which are in heaven, and which are on earth' (Ephesians 1:10); but the things in heaven are spiritual, while those on earth constitute the dispensation in human nature. These things, therefore, he recapitulated in himself: by uniting man to the Spirit, and causing the Spirit to dwell in man, he is himself made the head of the Spirit. And gives the Spirit to be head of man: for through him [the Spirit] we see, and hear, and speak".[617] In the church there is spiritual food and nourishment, the scriptures and the Eucharist. "For just as the bread from earth when it has received the invocation of God, is no longer ordinary bread, but Eucharist, consisting of two things earthly and heavenly, so also our bodies, receiving the Eucharist, are no longer corruptible, having the hope of resurrection".[618] Recapitulation occurs through the assumption of human flesh by Jesus: prepared but then corrupted in Adam, and made new in the womb of Mary. Having assumed flesh, the Word hallowed all aspects of human life, bearing its shame and guilt on the Cross. And it is in the Cross that the supreme revelation of the nature and plan of God is made known. This emphasis—that it is through the Cross that the Word is revealed—means that the Word of God is always related to the Cross and is always, as it were, cruciform. Just as the scripture is permeated in this way by the figure of the Cross, following Justin, Irenaeus also points out that the Word of God who adorned and arranged the heavens and earth does so in a cruciform manner.[619]

The third principal building block of Irenaeus's theology is *oikonomia,* meaning economy or arrangement. Irenaeus's theology seems to be mostly shaped by the *logos* theology of St John, and the comprehensive overview provided in Ephesians by the Apostle Paul. In Ephesians, Paul speaks about the administration of this mystery of God's will (3:9–12) and likewise Irenaeus speaks of the economy of God's purpose or the arc of his salvation. God's saving plan began with the Patriarchs, especially Abraham; was established by Moses; foretold by the Prophets; and finally fulfilled in the Word made flesh. Recapitulation lies at the heart of this plan, but the arc of his work stretches from Adam to Christ, and the two are frequently contrasted by Irenaeus. Adam is in the first instance fashioned by the Word. Adam is a type of the true man to come. Although Adam admits sin and death into the Word's perfect creation, he is a type looking forward to the paradigm of the true man, the Word made flesh. He is never without hope, for the Word pre-exists the coming of Adam. Thus Irenaeus writes, "God having pre-determined the first, the animated human that is, so that he should be saved by the spiritual one; for, since the Saviour pre-exists, it was necessary that the one to be saved should also exist, so that the saviour should not be without purpose".[620]

Irenaeus's economy of salvation centres on Jesus Christ and consequently the fall of Adam is regarded by him as the *felix culpa,* not because the sin of Adam should be anything other than regretted, but because it necessitates the coming of Jesus Christ. So, for Ireneaus, "Starting from the completed and perfected work of Christ, we now understand the preliminary nature of what came before".[621] We start from the end, not from the beginning: from Christ's coming and not from Adam's fall. Adam is the type of the one-to-come, and the one-to-come recapitulates humankind and makes it fully alive. In Adam, a preliminary sketch is made of the full canvas, which is Christ. As Irenaeus says, "The Word of the Father and the Spirit of God, having become united with the ancient substance of the formation of Adam, rendered the human being living and perfect, bearing the perfect Father, in order that just as in the animated we all die, so also in the spiritual we may be all vivified".[622]

Adam is the animated human being saved by the spiritual one who revivifies the soul and body. Irenaeus is only interested in the soul as the seat of the intellect, and as a force that gives coherence to the body:

> Now the soul and the Spirit can be a part of the human being, but by no means a human being; the complete human being is the commingling and the union of the soul receiving the Spirit, begotten of the Father and joined to the flesh that was moulded after the image of God. When this Spirit, commingled with soul, is united to the handiwork, because of the outpouring of the Spirit the human being is rendered spiritual and complete and this is the one who was made in the image and likeness of God [623]

For Irenaeus, the glory of God is a human fully alive when the body, soul and the Spirit are commingled, and thus the human is perfected or completed.[624] The arc of God moves from the sketch (Adam) to the completed canvas (Christ); from the animated human being made alive by the breath to the revivified human made alive by the Spirit; from the dominion of death to the Kingdom of Life; from Jonah as good as dead in the belly of the fish to being on dry ground fulfilling God's purpose.

These three building blocks of theology: hypothesis, recapitulation and economy, become the mainstays of Ireneaus's work. *Against Heresies* is essentially a two-fold work. The first two books are a counterblast to Gnosticism, the remaining three lay out the first systematic theology of the early church until Athanasius in Egypt, Gregory Nazianzen in Constantinople, and finally Augustine in Hippo, take up the task of systematically explaining further aspects of the faith.

Irenaeus's theological vision is incarnational: the assumption of the flesh by the Word in order to heal and save. A human being for Irenaeus is "essentially and profoundly skilfully fashioned mud".[625] What the breath of God animates must be revivified by the Son of God, and by the power of the Spirit. If the so-called Great Church (i.e., a single catholic and orthodox church in Rome) barely exists before Irenaeus, it does exist after him. He elaborates upon orthodoxy, while at the same time identifying heresy. The orthodoxy he presents is of a symphony, or arc of salvation, in which a single overarching economy works for the revivification of human flesh until the point at which a man or woman becomes fully alive. Hence the work of God is a person fully alive.

By the time Irenaeus died at the end of the second century or the beginning of the third century (exact date unknown), he had outlived several Emperors, including Hadrian, Antoninus Pius, Marcus Aurelius, Lucius Verus and Commodus. Between them, these rulers covered a span of 80 years from AD 117 onwards. Four of them, until Commodus's dissolute reign, were the so-called "good Emperors", although that did not mean any abatement of persecution. Instead, the more traditional Roman rule of Antoninus Pius and Marcus Aurelius, re-enforced with strong doses of Stoicism, made for outbreaks of provincial persecution against Christians, especially in Vienne and Lyons in AD 177, just before Irenaeus was made Bishop, and after the martyrdom of his predecessor. The issues of persecution, the response of Christians, and how to deal with those who lapsed under its pressure, were to take centre stage, both in Rome and in North Africa. A new voice was to be heard in North Africa in the highly articulate Tertullian; and then a second voice in Rome in the tough-minded Hippolytus.

CHAPTER 6

North Africa: Tertullian and Cyprian

From the heartlands of Palestine, Greece, Egypt, Italy and Asia, Christianity spread to the Rhone Valley and across North Africa during the mid to late second century. The first written evidence of Christians in Punic North Africa comes from the Latin *Acts of the Scillitan Martyrs* who were located near Carthage (possibly in the province of Numidia)[626] in the year AD 180.[627] There is evidence, particularly in the writings of Tertullian, of vigorous Christian communities in Carthage, known to Rome as Africa *Proconsularis* (North Tunisia), as well as in Byzacena (South Tunisia), Numidia and Mauretania (Algeria), by AD 200.

By AD 200, the Christian population in Africa was significant. Tertullian writes, "We [that is, Christians] are but of yesterday and we have filled all you have—cities, islands, forts, towns, assembly halls, even military camps, tribes, town councils, the palace, the senate and forum. We have left you nothing but temples".[628] This passage is typical of Tertullian's breezy and zestful writing, and bears witness to the rapid expansion of the church in the area. Founded quite probably by Greek-speaking missionaries from the Levant, the church quickly grew.[629] These missionaries may well have translated the scriptures they brought with them into Latin, using "vulgar and colloquial" phrases,[630] hence the rudimentary nature of the first Latin translation of the scriptures. These Latin scriptures may have formed the earliest versions of the Latin Vulgate, which Jerome later came to refine and re-translate, at least in part.[631]

The growth of the church in the North African littoral came in the teeth of sustained opposition and persecution. Although there was no imperial policy of eradicating Christianity adopted by particular emperors, persecution rose and fell like a tide according to a combination of local feeling and the actions of local governors or prefects.

Carthage was the main centre for Christianity in the African province of Africa *Proconsularis*. It was one of the principal cities of the Empire, vying with its neighbour Alexandria. Following the Punic Wars and the defeat of Hannibal by Scipio Africanus at the Battle of Zama on 19 October 202 BC, Carthage became a vassal of Rome. Lingering resentment against Carthage, following its humiliation of Rome in the third century, flared up once more and the younger Scipio, Aemilianus, was sent to Africa by the Senate to punish the Carthaginians. He destroyed the great capital of Carthage in 146 BC. Yet despite being ploughed with salt as a sign of judgement, the city was later rebuilt under Julius Caesar and competed with Alexandria as the second city of the Empire until the emergence of Constantinople.

The city expanded steadily with the settlement of veteran soldiers from Julius Caesar and Octavian's armies.[632] Three thousand veterans were retired there with land. By 28 BC, Roman Carthage was well underway. Carthage had a substantial hinterland with as many as 83 "*castellas*"[633] and with the town of Thugga (present-day Dougga, in Tunisia) popular with Italian settlers. The Roman colony prospered, with its abundant natural resources of wine, grain and oil, and it soon became a breadbasket for the city of Rome, with its gargantuan need for bread. The port was rebuilt as a well-defended harbour, from which the grain ships would sail to Ostia, the port of Rome. Later, a Hadrianic aqueduct brought copious quantities of water from a source some 50 miles distant, and a fire during the reign of Antoninus Pius led to a substantial rebuilding of the city centre along gracious and elegant lines.

By the mid-second century, Carthage had become the boast of Africa: a seat of government and of the arts—where Apuleius (AD 124–170), the author of *The Golden Ass*, was educated, building on the much earlier inspiration of the popular North African playwright Terence (195–159 BC). In due course, Carthage became a centre for Christianity, boasting among its leaders Tertullian, Cyprian, and, finally, Augustine of Hippo.

When, in AD 197, news arrived in Carthage of the victories over the Parthians of the Emperor Septimius Severus, himself an African and a citizen of Leptis Magna in present-day Libya, the town went wild in celebration of their African commander's success. Not everyone celebrated with equal gusto, however. While in the streets of Carthage there was revelry, debauchery and drunkenness over the end of civil strife and threats to the Empire, as far as the Jews and Christians were concerned, these pagan celebrations were infected with idolatry and they could take no part in them.[634] To the average citizen the Christians would have seemed a strange and peculiar people. They had grown used to the Jews, but unlike them, Christians did not belong to a single ethnic group with its centre in Jerusalem. Christians were viewed with suspicion, a kind of fifth column in the mostly pagan Empire. They refused to worship the gods; they would not wear pagan insignia or garlands in the army; they spurned the gladiatorial combats and games; they threatened the social order by making little distinction between slaves and freedmen; and they did not resist punishment. Instead, they seemed to embrace death as a trophy of their faith. They worshipped on Sundays and their places of worship became known. Christians were often attacked on their way to worship and many rumours circulated about their practices.[635] They were said to kill children, drink blood and plot against the state. Furthermore, a new movement from Phyrgia in the east, called Montanism, had found ready followers in North Africa. Women were often the leaders and were ecstatically possessed, speaking words given to them directly or prophetically by God.[636] Whereas Jews had long been given protection under Roman law and by successive Emperors (although Claudius chose to eject them from Rome), Christians had no such support. They were more vulnerable to persecution, and their persecution in North Africa was to shape the church.

Persecution came to the province at the start of Commodus's reign, although not at the Emperor's behest. (This was because his favourite concubine was a Christian called Maria, who had saved several Christians in Rome from execution.) Persecution came instead through the local governor of the province, Vigellus Saturninus, who was proconsul in AD 180/181. Soon after his arrival in Carthage, this proconsul condemned to death some Christians from a small, obscure town near the provincial city. A transcript of the trial is found in the *Acts of the Scillitan Martyrs*, an important document about the treatment of Christians in North Africa in that period:

> In the consulship of Preasens (for the second time) and Condianus, on the 16th day before the Kalends of August, at Carthage in the secretarium:
>
> Speratus, Nartzalus, Cittinus, Donata, Secunda, and Vestia were brought in. Saturninus the proconsul said: You can earn pardon of our Lord the Emperor if you return to your senses.
>
> Speratus said: We have done nothing wrong, we have never turned our hands to wickedness; we have cursed no one, but return thanks when we are abused; and therefore we are loyal to our Emperor.
>
> Saturninus the proconsul said: We too are religious, and our religion is simple, and we swear by the genius of our Lord the Emperor, and we make offerings for his safety, which you ought to do too.
>
> Speratus said: If you will listen, I shall tell you a mystery of simplicity.
>
> Saturninus said: I shall not listen if you speak evil of what we hold sacred; please swear by the genius of our Lord the Emperor.
>
> Speratus said: I do not recognise the empire of this world; I serve instead the God whom no man has seen or can see with mortal eyes. I have committed no theft; but if I buy anything I pay the tax on it: for I recognise my Lord, the King of Kings and Emperor of all mankind.
>
> Saturninus the proconsul said to the rest: Stop being of this belief.
>
> Speratus said: An evil belief is to commit murder, to bear false witness.
>
> Saturninus the proconsul said: Don't be involved in this man's madness.
>
> Cittinus said: We do not fear anyone except the Lord our God who is in heaven.
>
> Donata said: Honour to Caesar as Caesar; but fear to God.
>
> Vestia said: I am a Christian.

Secunda said: What I am, I wish to remain.

Saturninus the proconsul said to Speratus: Do you persist in being a Christian?

Speratus said: I am a Christian; and they all shouted in agreement with him.

Saturninus the proconsul said: Do you not want an interval for reflection?

Speratus said: In a cause so just there is no deliberation.

Saturninus the proconsul said: What is in that satchel?

Speratus said: Books and Letters of Paul, a just man.

Saturninus the proconsul said: Have an adjournment of thirty days and reflect.

Speratus said: I am a Christian; and they all shouted together agreement with him.

Saturninus the proconsul read out his decision from a tablet: Speratus, Nartzalus, Cittinus, Donata, Vestia, Secunda, and the rest, having confessed that they live according to the Christian religion, since they obstinately persisted when give the opportunity of returning to Roman ways, are to be executed by the sword.

Speratus said: We give thanks to God.

Nartzalus said: Today as martyrs we shall be in heaven: thanks be to God.

Saturninus the proconsul ordered the herald to proclaim: Speratus, Nartzalus, Cittinus, Veturious, Felix, Aquilinus, Laetantius, Ianuaria, Generosa, Vestia, Donata, and Secunda I have ordered to be beheaded.

All said: Thanks be to God. And so they were all crowned with martyrdom together, and reign with the Father, the Son and the Holy Spirit forever and ever. Amen.

This account could not be more important. It shows the penetration of Christianity into the countryside around Carthage, but more than anything, it shows the uncompromising nature of African Christianity and its rejection of an alien pagan world.[637] There was little room for "discretion being the better part of valour" in North Africa. There was only valour, and the failure of all Christians to live up to this exacting standard of courage lay at the heart of a later controversy (the Donatist Controversy), which would remain at the centre of the North African church until the arrival of Islam in the seventh century. If the first evidence of Christianity in *Proconsularis* Africa was the testimony of the Scillitan martyrs around AD 181, its best-known martyr was Perpetua, who with her companion, Felicitas, was martyred in AD 202–203, also in the reign of Septimius Severus. The account, probably recorded by Tertullian, is remarkable for many things.

At the outset, the author, possibly Tertullian, is clear that the record of this martyrdom is for the honour of God, for the comfort of the church, which can draw strength from her example, and as a testimony to the power and presence of the Spirit.[638] It is highly probable that Perpetua, like Tertullian, was a member of the Montanist sect which was founded in Phyrgia, but which found its most ardent followers in North Africa. In the introduction to the account, Tertullian writes:

> Let those who restrict the power of the Spirit to times and seasons look to this: the more recent events should be considered the greater, being later than those of old, and this is a consequence of the extraordinary graces promised for the last stage of time. "For in the last days, God says I will pour out my Spirit upon all the flesh and their sons and their daughters will prophesy and on my manservants and my maidservants I will pour out my Spirit and the young men shall see visions and the old men dream dreams"
> *Acts 2:17–18*

He goes on to say:

> So too we hold in honour and acknowledge not only new prophecies but new visions as well, according to the promise. And we consider all other functions of the Holy Spirit as intended for the good of the church; for the same Spirit has been sent to distribute all his gifts to all, as the Lord apportions to everyone. For this reason we deem it imperative to set them forth and to make them known through the word for the glory of God. Thus

no one of weak and despairing faith may think that supernatural
grace was present only among men of ancient times, either in the
grace of martyrdom or of visions, for God always achieves what
he promises, as a witness to the non-believer and a blessing to
the faithful.[639]

Such an introduction seems to clearly endorse and validate the Montanist
movement, with its emphasis on prophecy, the Holy Spirit, the ministry
of women, and the gift of martyrdom. With this in mind, we approach
this extraordinary account.

At first, a number of young catechumens were arrested: Revocatus and
his fellow slave Felicitas, Saturninus and Secundulus, and with them Vibia
Perpetua. Perpetua was married and from a noble family. Her brother and
parents were alive. She was 22 years old and was still breast-feeding her
infant son. Her father was not a Christian and tried to dissuade Perpetua
from courting martyrdom by persisting in her Christian profession. But
Perpetua not only persisted in it, but also was baptised whilst under
arrest and before she was put in prison: a dark pit of a place in which she
feared for her infant son. For many days she endured further trials, but
she was able to move to a better part of the prison due to the intervention
of two deacons, Tertius and Pomponius. Her baby was then placed in
her family's care.

At the request of her brother, she prayed for a vision and was given one
in which an immense ladder reached up to heaven, with a dragon at the
bottom. Perpetua mounted the ladder, treading on the dragon's head, and
ascended until she reached paradise, in which a shepherd gave her ewe's
milk to drink. At this, she awoke with the taste of the sweet milk in her
mouth and the certainty that she would be martyred. Her father was now
beside himself with grief at her impending fate, as well as the distress and
danger it would bring to her whole family. He beseeched her to retract
and forgo her pride in her opinions, as he saw it, but Perpetua remained
steadfast. Later, at her trial in the Forum, with a great crowd watching,
he begged her while holding her son to "perform the sacrifice [to the
Emperor], and have pity on your baby".[640] Perpetua refused. Governor
Hilarianus threw her father out of court for contempt. Perpetua and her
companions were then condemned to the beasts. Her father refused to

hand back her baby, so breast-feeding was discontinued, but "as God willed, the baby had no further desire for the breast, nor did it suffer any inflammation".[641]

Perpetua had further dreams while waiting for the sentence to be carried out. She dreamt of her brother Dinocrates, who had died from cancer of the face when aged only seven and had been terribly disfigured by the tumour. In a vision, he appeared to be still suffering and unable to reach any water to drink. Her prayers brought him refreshment and well-being. A further dream showed Pomponius, the deacon, struggling alongside her in the amphitheatre. She prepared herself for combat with the beasts, found that she had the body of a man, and was fighting an Egyptian whom she discovered to be the devil.

Eventually, the day of her "victory" dawned. Felicitas, who had recently given birth, joined them in the arena: "Felicitas went from one blood bath to another, from the midwife to the gladiator, ready to wash after the childbirth in a second baptism".[642] Saturninus and Revocatus were matched to a leopard. Perpetua and Felicitas were stripped naked, placed in nets and dragged out to a heifer. The crowd was shocked at the sight of the two naked young women, one so recently having given birth "with milk dripping from her breasts". They were sent back to be properly clothed in loose, unbelted tunics. Perpetua was then thrown on the ground by the heifer. She re-arranged her tunic modestly and "asked for a pin to fasten her untidy hair, for it was not right that a martyr should die with her hair in disorder, lest she might seem to be mourning in her hour of triumph".[643] Meanwhile, Saturninus was thrown to a leopard. After one bite, he was suffused with blood. The crowd roared: "Well washed! Well washed!" as if it were another baptism.[644] He was thrown unconscious onto a heap with others to have his throat cut. Those able to stand and exchange a martyr's ritual kiss of peace did so. Perpetua, in full sight of the crowd, was brought out into the open and executed. "'She took the trembling hand of the gladiator and guided it to her throat'. It was as though so great a woman—feared as she was by the unclean spirit—could not be dispatched unless she herself was willing".[645]

Perpetua's death resonated throughout the North African church for years to come; it was a gold standard of Christian martyrdom in a church dominated by the virtue of martyrdom and the ignominy of the lapsed. Perpetua's sufferings were like a gem set in the ring of North African spirituality. We can see the Montanist leanings in the visions and prophecies, the sense that a martyr can, through intercession, release the departed from suffering, as in the case of the dream of Dinocrates, her younger brother. This was either a piece of psychoanalysis, or an example of someone actually being transferred from hell or purgatory to paradise. There is a note of anti-clericalism in the *Passion of Perpetua,* since Saturninus has a vision that the bishop and the priests are excluded from the presence of God until the martyrs plead for their inclusion.[646] The nobility of martyrs, the direct revelation of the Spirit, the embracing of suffering, the slight whiff of dissension from mere docile obedience to the bishop, are all characteristics of important characteristics of North African Christianity: independence from authority and vehement devotion. It was as if the fierce sun and heat of North Africa meant that Christians should be similarly uncompromising, fierce like the rays of the sun and hot in their passion to follow the Lord, without fear or favour. Gradually, a rift in spirituality emerged as the established institution of the church grew: a Latin church with strong connections to Rome and Italy. Alongside it was a church that yearned for the obvious manifestation of the *charismata* of the Spirit. It was to this church that Tertullian eventually went. He was "the first great teacher of unimpeachable doctrinal orthodoxy who dared to enunciate an unpalatable truth: the church is not a conclave of bishops, but the manifestation of the Holy Spirit".[647]

Tertullian

Tertullian was the foremost Latin theologian of the West writing at the beginning of the third entury AD. He was born in Carthage around AD 160 and was converted to Christianity at the end of the second century. Eusebius probably wrongly identifies Tertullian as a Roman jurist and as a priest, but Barnes makes a strong case against both these suppositions, which have nevertheless passed into the traditions of the church, aided by Jerome's scanty and misleading entry in his *Who's Who* of Christian writers and leaders, *De Viris Illustribus* (*Concerning Illustrious Men*). Jerome wrote this in Bethlehem in AD 392/3,[648] writing of Tertullian as follows:

"Tertullian, the next Latin writer after Victor and Apollonius, was a priest, a man of the province of Africa and the city of Carthage, and the son of a *centurio proconsularis*. He possessed a sharp and violent talent, and flourished in the reigns of Severus and Caracalla". He continues, "Tertullian was a priest of the church until middle age, but then because of the envy and insults of the clergy of the church of Rome, he lapsed into Montanism and refers to the New Prophecy in many treatises. In particular, he directed against the church discussions of modesty, of persecution, of fasting, of monogamy, and of divine possession in six books, with a seventh against Apollonius".[649]

Much more recent research has shown that Tertullian's father could not have been a *centurio proconsularis*, as no such office existed in the Roman military administration, and there is no evidence that Tertullian's father was a soldier.[650] Furthermore, Eusebius claimed that Tertullian was most likely the same person as Tertullianus, who was a published Roman lawyer writing mostly on family law in the late second century.[651] This is probably not the case because of the dating,[652] although this is not to say that Tertullian did not employ the rhetoric and devices of a lawyer. Eusebius thought that Tertullian presented his *Apologeticum* in the Senate personally, when he did no such thing. He was in fact addressing the magistrates of Carthage.[653] Furthermore, Eusebius had scanty knowledge of Tertullian and the western church, for he was writing in the different milieu of Caesarea in Palestine in the aftermath of Nicaea.

The picture of Tertullian is of a North African of considerable ability, educated in the schools of Carthage, in which there was at this time a burgeoning of intellectual confidence. The renaissance of the Greek East was proceeding apace. Emperors like Septimius Severus, himself a philhellene, stimulated the study of the Greek writers. Alexandria, as we shall see, flourished with the Neo-Platonism of Plotinus. Along the coast in present-day Libya, the Emperor Severus, whose hometown it was, rebuilt Leptis Magna as a town of extravagant magnificence. Philostratus declared the opening of the second Sophistic movement. These developments were slow to travel west to Carthage. In Carthage itself,

Tertullian, and later Cyprian, were well trained in the ways of rhetoric and philosophy, and were following in the rather raunchier and pagan footsteps of Apuleius, whose declamations in Carthage date from AD 160. Tertullian showed that he knew well the devices of rhetoric, such as *confirmatio, reprehensio* and *amplificatio,* and the great classics, as much as more recent literature. He deployed Herodotus, Pythagoras, Plato, the Cynics, Diogenes and Varro, Cornelius Tacitus, Menander of Ephesus, Empedocles, Cicero and Seneca, among others. He knew the scorn of a Juvenal and the steady knowledge of Pliny the Elder, and he would employ both styles in his polemical writings. Perhaps more than any other, he was to combine theology with deep knowledge of the Bible, philosophy and rhetoric. He was only surpassed in reflective theology, perceptive psychology and deep spirituality two centuries later by his fellow North African, Augustine. Until then, few touched him for blistering logic, powerful apology, passionate defence of a growing orthodoxy and an untamed spirit. All this took him outside the established church into the excesses of Montanism. If Augustine was to sow his spiritual wild oats in his association with Manichaeism before his conversion in Milan, Tertullian, by contrast, would in middle age join a Christian ecstatic movement called the New Prophecy, a movement which coincided with his restless spirit, and his search for truth and freedom.

Tertullian left behind a formidable legacy of teaching on a wide number of issues. Unlike Augustine and Origen, his works did not include scriptural homilies or commentaries, but his biblical knowledge was second to none. In one sense, all his writing was a defence or "apologetic" of Christianity and its proper practice in the public sphere.[654] The style of his writing was well suited to his purpose. His purpose was to defend, to instruct, to refute and to teach; hence his style was sarcastic, witty, ironic, erudite, dismissive and stern. His demands on the Christian community were great, his exposure of the pagan administration of the Empire and its "senseless" persecution of Christians was equally excoriating. So wide-ranging were his works that to get some sense of their scope, they can be divided into three main groups: his works of Apology; his ethical instruction to the Christian community; and his defence of orthodoxy with his refutation of the Gnostic Marcion and the Valentinians.

Tertullian is probably best known for his *Apologeticum,* written around AD 197, soon after his own conversion in the AD 190s.[655] It was written following a welter of tracts or pamphlets on the distinctiveness of the Christian community and the lifestyle of separateness from pagan culture it should follow (and to which we shall return). Although Eusebius thought it was a defence of Christianity offered by Tertullian to the Senate in Rome in person, it was probably offered instead to the magistrates and administrators of the Empire in Carthage. It is addressed:

> To the rulers of the Roman Empire, if seated for the administration
> of justice on your lofty tribunal, under the gaze of every eye, and
> occupying there all but the highest position in the start, that you
> may not openly inquire into and sift before the world the real
> truth in regard to the charges made against Christianity.[656]

It was to account for Christianity, defend its record of good citizenship in the Empire and expose the irrational persecution of Christians merely because of a name (Christian), that Tertullian wrote this philippic. He recognised that Christians were in a kind of exile in the Empire, so he wrote as follows: "She [the church] knows that she is but a sojourner on the earth, and that among strangers she naturally finds foes; and more than this, that her origin, her dwelling-place, her hope, her recompense, her honours, are above".[657] Though a sojourner, Tertullian defends Christianity and pleads, in a lawyerly way, for fair treatment of Christians in the courts.

The state was by now in fear of Christianity because of its very success and growth as a movement:

> The outcry is that the State is filled with Christians—that they are
> in the fields, in the citadels, in the islands; they [the State] make
> lamentations, as for some calamity, that both sexes, every age
> and condition, even high rank, are passing over to the profession
> of the Christian faith; and yet for all [that], their minds are not
> awakened to the thought of some good they have failed to notice
> in it.[658]

It is into this gap between the obvious appeal of Christianity to all walks of life and the irrational fear of the state at its success (because presumably Christianity threatened the pagan *status quo*) that Tertullian launches his appeal for reasonable and just treatment of Christians in the courts and public space of the Empire.

Tertullian makes the case that a Christian is a good citizen. He cites how, on the instructions of Trajan, the younger Pliny did not call for the hunting down of Christians by private informers, but only for them to be dealt with should they be brought before the courts on imperial charges. In other words, Trajan was not keen on a purge of Christians on the information of private informers, because he recognised their good citizenship.[659] Tertullian then points to the irony that torture was used against Christians to make them *deny* their faith, whereas with all other criminals, torture was used to make them *confess* their crimes. Thus in the former, torture was used to make people lie, whereas in the latter it was used to make people confess the truth.[660] The irony is part of Tertullian's case. He writes:

> Well, you think the Christian a man of every crime, an enemy
> of the gods, of the emperor, of the laws, of good morals, of all
> nature; yet you compel him to deny, that you may acquit him,
> which without his denial you cannot do. You play fast and loose
> with the laws. You wish him to deny his guilt that you might bring
> him out blameless and free from all guilt in reference to the past!
> Whence is this strange diversity on your part?[661]

He goes on to say that the name or term Christian had become a term of irrational abuse. So, for instance, one may say of a Christian, "A good man is Gaius Seius, only that he is a Christian".[662] The special ground of dislike of this sect is that it bears the name of its founder, nothing else. But also it may have been resented for its tone of moral superiority. In matters of sexual conduct, Tertullian wrote that:

> While Democritus, in putting out his eyes because he could not
> look on women without lusting after them, and was pained if
> his passion was not satisfied, owns plainly, by the punishment

he inflicts, his incontinence. But a Christian with grace-healed eyes is sightless in this matter; he is mentally blind against the assaults of passion.[663]

Tertullian's case was that the judgements against Christians were irrational and unjust, and the laws against them were like other laws which he calls unjust.[664] These laws against Christians, if they were indeed laws, must be repealed. Marcus Aurelius himself had cause to be grateful to Christians, whose prayers he recognised as ending a drought in Germany where he was fighting.[665] He sought also their protection from persecution, although many from Rome to Vienne were martyred on his imperial watch.

Having made the case that Christians were moral, good citizens and were even recognised as such by Emperors like Vespasian, Titus, Hadrian, Trajan, Marcus Aurelius and Pius, Tertullian wondered on what grounds they could be called traitors. Only, he concludes, because they do not worship the gods.[666] Yet these gods indulge in more vice, adultery, incest and pederasty than any of the Christians whom magistrates or governors punish for not worshipping pagan deities. Furthermore, worship in the pagan temples is mingled with deeds of licentiousness. Christians cannot be falsely accused in their devotion of worshipping an ass's head, a common slur on Christians, which had no basis in truth.[667] As Tertullian put it: "Our worship is of the One God" and "the crowning guilt of man is that they will not worship the one of whom they cannot be ignorant".[668]

Tertullian then gives a full account of the truth of the Christian faith. He recalls the scriptures of the Old Testament, faithfully translated in Alexandria into the Greek Septuagint. Christianity, he argues, was then, as in Tertullian's day, a written revelation[669] starting with Moses, "who antedates by a millennium the death of Priam",[670] and proceeding through the prophets until, finally and fully, with Christ. Christ is far more contemporary; indeed he is part of the Roman world, living in the reign of Tiberius. He was born of a virgin. He was the *Logos,* known as such to Greeks, and come in the flesh.[671]

This ray of God, then, as it was always foretold in ancient times, descending into a certain virgin, and made flesh in her womb is, in his birth, God and man united. The flesh formed by the Spirit is nourished, grows up to manhood, speaks, teaches, works, and is the Christ.[672]

He was the Logos of God, the primordial first-begotten Word, accompanied by power and reason, and based on the Spirit.[673]

Following Christ's death and resurrection, the disciples spread the word throughout the world, "suffering greatly themselves from the persecutions of the Jews, and with no unwilling heart, as having faith undoubting in the truth, at last by Nero's cruel sword sowed the seed of Christian blood at Rome ... We say, and before all men we say, torn and bleeding under your tortures, we cry out, 'we worship God through Christ'. Count Christ a man, if you please; by him and in him God would be known and adored".[674] These same disciples, he says, are fed by the affection of the "agape feast" and the teaching given there to go out into the world as both sojourners and martyrs. At these feasts "each is asked to stand forth and sing, as he can, a hymn to God, either one from the Holy Scriptures or one from his own composing. As the feast commenced with prayer, so with prayer it closed". Christians emerge into the world from prayer,

> Not like troops of mischief doers, nor bands of vagabonds, nor
> to break out into licentious acts, but to have as much care of
> our modesty and chastity as if we had been at a banquet. Give
> the congregation of the Christians its due, and hold it unlawful,
> if it is like assemblies of the illicit sort: by all means let it be
> condemned, if any complaint can be validly laid against it, such as
> lies against secret fashions. But who has suffered harm from our
> assemblies? We are in our congregations just what we are when
> separated from each other; we are as a community what we are
> as individuals; we injure nobody, we trouble nobody. When the
> upright, when the virtuous meet together, when the pious, when
> the pure assemble in congregation, you ought not to call that a
> faction, but a curia i.e. the court of God.[675]

Tertullian says that no matter what is conceived and deployed against Christians, nothing will change our confession: "With our hands stretched out and up to God, rend us with your iron claws, hang us up on crosses, wrap us in flames, take our heads from us with the sword. Let loose the wild beasts on us—[for] the very attitude of a Christian praying is one of preparation for all punishment".[676] No wonder he says at the end of this extraordinary Apology, so full of fire and confidence, that "the oftener we are mown down by you [pagans], the more in number we grow; the blood of Christians is the seed [of the church]".[677]

By any yardstick it is an extraordinary piece of writing, full of confidence and verve, certain that whatever is hurled against the Christians they will march on. Integrity and truth are on their side and cannot be suppressed; the gods are tin pot deities bent on immorality versus the majesty of Christ. They did not make Rome great, for many of these deities are recent inventions. The modest lives of the Christians speak for themselves, and they should not be dubbed criminals or traitors. Christians pray for the Emperors; they wrestle in their prayers,[678] which is the only violence they know, and they pay their taxes. Emperors are to be prayed for, but they are only men, not gods. "He [the Emperor] gets his sceptre where he first got his humanity; his power where he got his breath of life. Without ceasing for all our Emperors we offer prayer".[679] Emperors are human. Tertullian famously says: "If he is not a man, Emperor he cannot be. Even amid the honours of a triumph, he sits on that lofty chariot; he is reminded he is only human. A voice at his back keeps whispering in his ear, 'look behind thee, and remember thou art but a man'".[680]

Tertullian's *Apology* is backed up by a shorter piece written towards the end of his writing career in September AD 212, to the Proconsul of Carthage, Scapula, to whom he says, "a Christian is enemy to none, least of all the Emperor of Rome, whom he knows to be appointed by his God, and so cannot but love and honour".[681] Furthermore, in almost anachronistic language, Tertullian says:

> It is a fundamental human right, a privilege of nature, that every man should worship according to his own convictions: one man's religion neither harms nor helps another man. It is assuredly no part of religion to compel religion—to which free will and not force should lead us—the sacrificial victims even being required

are of a willing mind. You will render no real service to your gods
by compelling us to sacrifice.[682]

If a Christian refuses to sacrifice, then torture or death is "your cruelty,
but our glory".[683]

If Tertullian's most telling writing was the defence of Christians to the
imperial authorities, his longest writings were reserved for Christians in
defence of the orthodox or catholic faith. He explains how Christians
are to conduct themselves in the pagan world, what spirituality should
be theirs and lastly what they should believe against the heresies that
confront them, especially those of the Gnostics.

Tertullian was clear how Christians should conduct themselves in the
pagan world of ancient Rome. He wrote extensively about such matters.
His early writings, probably dated c.AD 196 or early 197, revolved around
these matters and while they may show the sharpness of a young convert,
such matters remained his concern throughout the fifteen years he was
writing.[684]

We may group together the following works, which demonstrate the
stern character of his ethical works: In *De Spectaculis* Tertullian forbids
Christians the "pleasures of the public shows".[685] Such shows included
gladiatorial combat, pagan events in celebration of the Emperor, games
and pageants. Too often they declare the glory of the god Bacchus or
other gods.[686] In fact, it is very hard to disassociate such events from the
pagan gods, he argues, and going to them could be as mistaken as giving
credence to their deities. For Tertullian, the sin of idolatry clings to the
shows and on this account alone they should be avoided. In them, "there
is a lust of money, or rank, or eating, or impure enjoyment, or glory—so
there is also a lust of pleasure".[687] Furthermore, Tertullian condemns the
change of behaviour that can occur at these shows:

> So that the same man who can scarcely in public lift up his tunic,
> even when the necessity of nature presses him, takes it off in
> the circus, as if bent on exposing himself before everybody; the
> father who carefully protects and guards his virgin daughter's
> ears from every polluting word, takes her to the theatre himself,
> exposing her to all its vile words and attitudes; he, again, who in

the streets lays hands on, or covers with reproaches, the brawling
pugilist, in the arena gives all encouragement to combats of a
much more serious kind; and he who looks with horror on the
corpse of one who has died under the common law of nature, in
the amphitheatre gazes down with most patient eyes on bodies
all mangled and torn and smeared with their own blood; nay the
very man who comes to the show, because he thinks murderers
ought to suffer for their crime, drives the unwilling gladiator to
the murderous deed with rods and scourges. [688]

For these and all the other reasons Christians were to avoid the games,
and in so doing they would surely be marked out from the general
community, giving opportunity thereby for further slander and
persecution. Furthermore, Tertullian wrote *De Idololatria*, warning
Christians not to be associated with traders who supported idolatry,
such as craftsmen who make charms, amulets, representations of gods
or images, or even schoolmasters who teach pagan myths, thereby
giving them credence among the young and impressionable. Nor should
Christians become embroiled with the feast days of the gods.[689] They
should not wear garlands or crowns of flowers or plants upon their heads
as honours, especially in the military, since these are often awarded in the
name of gods and devoted to pagan deities. Indeed, Tertullian wonders
whether Christians should be in the army at all: "Shall it be held lawful
to make an occupation of the sword, when the Lord proclaims that he
who uses the sword shall perish by the sword".[690]

In these ways, Christians are to be distinctive. In a society so long
used to pagan worship and myths, to a diet of theatre and spectacles
in the amphitheatre, to the carrying and use of arms, and to triumphs
conducted in the name of gods and for the honour, if not deification, of
the Emperor, Christians are disconcertingly different. It is as much the
general population as the administrators of the Empire who find Christian
non-compliance with pagan culture and Christianity's challenge to the
values that undergird it so provocative. Such provocation has to be set
alongside their commitment to pray for the Emperor, if not sacrifice to
him, their service to the poor, their cross-cultural inclusion of slaves and
owners in a common fellowship, and their insistence on virtues such as

love, patience, humility and kindness in their fellowship, which proved so attractive. Above all, it is their willingness to suffer rather than deny the name and authority of their founder, Christ. This is the final and incontrovertible testimony to the reality of the truth which they preach, and the hope which they have.

Tertullian not only instructs Christians to remain distinct from their pagan communities in these ways, but also enjoins on them a spirituality which will mark them out, and no more so than on the younger women or virgins in the Christian community. How they dress and conduct themselves is to be another distinguishing feature of the community.

Tertullian wrote two tracts on the dress or apparel of women in c. AD 197 and AD 205/6 (*De Cultu Feminarum*) and one on the veiling of virgins (*De Virginibus Velandis*) in AD 208/9.[691] It was a matter on which he and many of the Church Fathers wrote (Cyprian, Ambrose, Basil of Caesarea and Jerome, to name just a few). Tertullian is not afraid to be specific in his instruction. He calls it a "discussion", but he is quite clear about the outcome of his advice or instruction. He writes:

> Female habit carries with it a twofold idea—dress and ornament. By "dress" we mean what they call "womanly gracing"; by ornament what is suitable should be called "womanly disgracing". The former is accounted (to consist) in gold, and silver, and gems, and garments; the latter in care of the hair, and of the skin, and of those parts of the body which attract the eye. Against one we lay the charge of ambition, against the other of prostitution; so that even from this early stage (of our discussion) you may look forward and see what, out of all these, is suitable, handmaid of God, to your discipline, inasmuch as you are assessed on different principles (from other women)—those namely of humility and chastity.[692]

Arguments might be put forward by smart Carthaginians who are now Christians with such words as, "Let not the Name be blasphemed in us if we make any derogatory change from our old style of dress", but that finds short shrift with Tertullian, who sarcastically says, "Let us not abolish our old vices!" He goes on typically to riposte, "Will you fear to appear poorer, from the time you have been made more wealthy".[693]

Following the instruction of Peter, women are to nurture "the unfading beauty of a gentle and a quiet spirit" (1 Peter 3:4). For Tertullian, as for many, if not all, the Church Fathers, virgins should be veiled. In a separate tract, *On the Veiling of Virgins*, he makes this typical statement:

> Put on the panoply of modesty; surround yourself with the stockade of bashfulness; rear a rampart for your sex, which must neither allow your own eyes egress nor ingress to other people's. Wear the full garb of woman, to preserve the standing of virgin. Belie some of your inward consciousness, in order to exhibit the truth to God alone. And yet you do not belie yourself in appearing as a bride. For wedded you are to Christ: to him you have surrendered your flesh; to him you have espoused your maturity ... Walk in accordance with the will of your Espoused. Christ is he who bids the espoused and wives of others veil themselves (and) of course, much more his own (i.e. virgins).[694]

Tertullian advises all women to veil themselves, but especially so as to indicate that they are both unmarried, and married to Christ. It is worth remembering the veil was as common amongst women in second-century North Africa as it is today in Islam.

Besides his instruction to Christians to come out from among the pagans in the ways already described, and his sturdy defence of Christians to the magistrates of the Empire, Tertullian wrote brief tracts on what we might call the Christian life. These included tracts on prayer, baptism, repentance, patience and martyrdom. Writings on such themes were to become commonplace among the Church Fathers, but in many ways it was Tertullian who set the ball rolling. Repentance is especially concerned with what happens when sin occurs *after* baptism. Baptism was often deferred because of the expectation of a near sinless life thereafter. Hence, Tertullian writes, "We are not washed *in order that* we *may* cease sinning, but because we have ceased, since in *heart* we have been bathed already".[695] It was this expectation, that baptism was virtually a gateway to perfection and that mortal sin after baptism made repentance a second time a great difficulty—particularly because there may not be time for amendment of life—that led to baptism being deferred, sometimes until very close to death itself.

Tertullian's tract on prayer is based on the Lord's Prayer. For Tertullian, prayer involves "an epitome of the whole Gospel".[696] He gives a clause-by-clause exposition of the prayer and then a vivid *recapitulation* or summary thereof, which is typical of his compressed and energetic style:

> In summaries of so few words how many utterances of the prophets, the Gospels, the apostles—how many discourses, examples, parables of the Lord, are touched on! How many duties are simultaneously discharged! The honour of God in the "Father"; the testimony of faith in the "Name"; the offering of obedience in the "Will"; the commemoration of hope in the "Kingdom"; the petition of Life in the "Bread"; the full acknowledgement of debts in prayer for their "Forgiveness"; the anxious dread of temptation in the request for "Protection". What wonder? God alone could teach how he wished Himself prayed to. The religious rite of prayer therefore, ordained by himself, and animated even at the moment that it was issuing out of the divine mouth by his own Spirit, ascends by its prerogative into heaven, commending to the Father what the Son has taught.[697]

Typically, the longest part of Tertullian's commentary on the Lord's Prayer is not the content of the prayer itself, but the manner in which it should be prayed and especially, once again, by virgins. Because they had previously been a temptation to angels (Genesis 6:1–4), as well as to other men, they should be veiled when praying: "You are wedded to Christ: to him you have surrendered your body; act as becomes your husband's discipline".[698] Prayer was as much about *how* and *when* to pray as *what* to pray. Sometimes it seems that conventions surrounding prayer were in danger of taking over from its reality and power. In these ways Tertullian sought to give discipline to everyday Christian living, but his greatest contribution was undoubtedly in systematically dealing with opponents of Catholic Christianity. To these lengthy rebuttals we must turn.

For Tertullian, the existence of heresy was the flip side of orthodoxy. To have a Catholic or Orthodox faith almost inevitably meant there would be heresies too. He told his contemporaries that they should not be astonished at heresies. They surely exist as commonly as weeds in the flowerbed or as fevers in human life. A proof text for their existence was usually found among the Church Fathers in 1 Corinthians 11.19: "No doubt there have to be differences among you to show which of you have God's approval". Such heresies were to be expected and only the weak would succumb.[699]

Tertullian's longest work was against Marcion, who was hardly a Gnostic. He did not, like Valentinus, build a whole system of revelation around a theory of *gnosis*; nor did he classify humanity into three types of people: the material, psychical and spiritual, depending on the level of revelation or *gnosis* that each had received. Marcion essentially denied that the God of the Old Testament and the Father of Jesus were, or could be, the same deity. Initially, Apelles and Valentinus followed Marcion; but later they both deserted him in order to develop their own Gnostic and Docetic ideas.[700]

By the time Tertullian was writing against Valentinus's theories and heresy, Valentinus had died, and his followers were dispersed across the church in Rome and elsewhere. Valentinus had been spurred into heresy by his own thwarted ambition. He had hoped to become Bishop of Rome, as Tertullian tells us in *Against the Valentinians,* but he became "indignant that another had obtained the dignity (of office) by reason of a claim of confessor-ship (i.e., that man's arrest and imprisonment for his faith) and the office had been given to him". Consequently, Valentinus broke with the church and began establishing his own false teaching with eloquence and persuasiveness, as Tertullian recognised.[701]

By the time Tertullian wrote his longest defence of the gospel against the heresy of Marcion, in *Adversus Marcionem,* Marcion had been dead for over 40 years. That Marcionism should still merit such a lengthy response from Tertullian in AD 207/8 means that, as a heresy, it must have still been current and gathering followers. In the Ante Nicene Fathers' edition of *Adversus Marcionem,* the text fills 400 columns spread over five books.[702] It is therefore a very lengthy work—Tertullian's longest in fact.

The structure of the five books is straightforward. In Book I, Tertullian tackles Marcion's philosophical argument that there are two gods. In his second book, Tertullian identifies Marcion's creator god or demiurge as being the one, true, creator God who is good and has revealed himself in Christ. As the Manichees were later to do, Marcion attributed the origin of good and evil to two separate systems or gods, rather than a single creator from whom his creation was alienated through rebellion by humankind in general, and by Adam in particular.

Humanity's fall, Tertullian argues, does not show any failure in God, but rather resulted from the liberty of human beings, which was part of the glory of man's creation.[703] The liberty of man and the wilful rebellion of the Devil lie at the heart of the tragedy of the Fall and not any imperfection in God's plan, or the existence of two equal and opposite gods vying with each other over creation.[704]

Book III of this work disproves Marcion's Christology as Tertullian argues that Old Testament prophecies looked for their fulfilment in Christ, and therefore there is no disconnection between the Old and New Testaments. The latter fulfils the former, since the Old Testament prophets look to the coming of a divine Messiah.[705] Furthermore, Marcion's docetic view of the incarnation (i.e., that the pre-incarnate divine word only seemed to become human) was erroneous.

In Book IV, Tertullian uses the Gospel of Luke, the only gospel that Marcion accepted (although considering only part of it as accurate), for his refutation and to establish Christ as both Creator and Redeemer. This book by Tertullian is a full-scale commentary on St Luke's Gospel, written with the aim of showing that Christ fulfilled the prophecies of the Old Testament, especially those of Isaiah and Zechariah, and that he was "the Christ of the Creator", not a phantom, but flesh and blood who suffered in his body for the redemption of humankind.[706]

Finally, in Book V, there is a further study of Marcion's misuse of the Pauline Epistles, which he accepts, but nevertheless falsely interprets and twists to suit his meaning. As before, Tertullian maintains that Paul understood that the Old Testament prophets prophesied the Christ of the gospels. And furthermore, the Creator God planned this salvation since eternity, but only fully revealed his plan in Christ. So, Tertullian argues:

> This wisdom, he [Paul] says, once lay hidden in things that were
> foolish, weak and lacking in honour; once also was latent under
> figures, allegories and enigmatical types; but it was afterwards to
> be revealed in Christ, who was set "as a light to the Gentiles" by
> the Creator who promised through the mouth of Isaiah that he
> would discover "the hidden treasures, which eye had not seen"
> (1 Corinthians 2.18).[707]

Throughout his exegesis, Tertullian follows the hypothesis that God, who
is Creator, sent Christ in the flesh, who is also God, the Creator *Logos*.[708]
For his part, Marcion denied that Christ came in the flesh, was raised
in the flesh and, thus, was the substance of the shadow of that which
had come before. That shadow was the Law and the Prophets, while the
substance or body that casts that shadow, Tertullian argues, is the Christ
of God come in the flesh. Tertullian's five books work from this simple
and powerful hypothesis. He bases his argument, as ever, on detailed
exegesis of the scriptures and equally detailed knowledge of the heresy
which he sought to de-construct and destroy.

Two other works of Tertullian, entitled *De Carne Christi* (*On the Flesh
of Christ*) and *De Resurrectione Mortuorum* (*On the Resurrection of the
Flesh*), are his final answer to Marcionites, and to all those who devalue
the flesh to elevate the soul.

On the Flesh of Christ was written around AD 206, over ten years into
Tertullian's writing.[709] It was directed against the followers of Marcion
who were Docetic: that is, who believed that Christ did not really come in
the flesh.[710] Marcion was influenced by the Platonic view of the Godhead,
which said that what was truly divine was *not* capable of change. However,
although the substance of God did not change in the incarnation, the
Logos nevertheless took on flesh with all its attendant weakness, which
Marcion despised. What Tertullian calls the "reverend course of nature",
involving pregnancy and the mess of birth, was not abhorred by God
in the incarnation, far from it.[711] God embraced it in the incarnation.
Tertullian, through exegesis of the gospels, shows that Christ's flesh was
real and, in order to die, he had to be truly born. Whereas some say
that Christ's soul was in some sense corporeal, Tertullian maintains that
Christ was soul in body. "For while he saves our souls, which are not

only not of flesh, but are even distinct from flesh, how much more able was he to secure salvation to that soul which he took himself, when it was not also flesh".[712] Tertullian shows the symmetry of God's salvation in this way: sin entered the human family through Eve listening to Satan and believing him, while Mary, through believing the Angel Gabriel, gave birth to "our good brother", who would redeem humankind. A further symmetry is given to us by Tertullian, who records that "as, then, before his birth of the virgin, he was able to have God for his Father without a human mother, so likewise, after he was born of the virgin, he was able to have a woman for his mother without a human father".[713] It was this kind of symmetry that both Irenaeus and Tertullian enjoyed; but for Tertullian the main point was that Christ took on human flesh, which was like ours, only without sin.[714]

Tertullian's final blast against the Marcionites and their Docetic tendencies, in which the significance of flesh was denigrated, was his work *On the Resurrection of the Flesh*. Once again, Tertullian had to resist the Greek and ancient pagan culture of vilifying the flesh. The underlying philosophic position of middle Platonism, based on Plato's teaching in Timaeus, was that the demiurge was responsible for the creation of matter, and this was inferior to the life of the soul and its eternal destiny. This principle, which was then transferred both to full-scale Gnostic Christianity and to Marcion's teaching, resulted in their contempt for or denigration of the flesh as inferior to the soul. With regard to the Christian faith, this meant that they did not hold to the incarnation, since how could the *Logos* of God take on paltry human flesh? Nor did they hold to the resurrection of the body, since why would God seek to resurrect something which was as flawed as the body? In *On the Resurrection of the Flesh*, Tertullian seeks to uphold the full biblical teaching found principally in St Paul and John (e.g., 1 Corinthians 15 and John 5:24–30). He maintains that to be a Christian you must follow Christian teaching and not the ways of the heathen or the principles of Plato.[715]

The flesh has its existence from the Word of God. The Incarnate Christ was in the mind of the Creator from the first, even before he created human beings.[716] The body was a coat or tunic for the living soul. What happens to the body happens to the soul:

> The flesh indeed is washed in order that the soul may be cleansed;
> the flesh is anointed, that the soul may be consecrated; the flesh
> is signed (with the cross) that the soul may be fortified; the flesh
> is shadowed with the imposition of hands, that the soul may be
> illuminated by the Spirit; the flesh feeds on the body and blood
> of Christ that the soul likewise may fatten on its God.[717]

Furthermore, Christ died in his flesh to give salvation to body and soul:
for the body gives expression to the soul. Having established the principle
that our salvation affects both soul and body, and indeed that the body
is the entrance to the soul, Tertullian describes the biblical doctrine of
the resurrection from Paul and John's writings especially. The body to
be raised is not the "corporeality of the soul", but the flesh, as we know
it.[718] For just as we have borne the image of the earthly man, we shall
bear now the image of the heavenly man (1 Corinthians 15:41). Death
changes, without destroying, our mortal bodies—for now the corruptible
puts on the incorruptible (1 Corinthians 15:51–53). For, "if God raises
not men entire, he raises not the dead".[719] The heavenly session of Christ
(following his ascension) is a guarantee of the Christian's resurrection. [720]

Furthermore, the body in heaven cannot be guessed at, indeed "the
dispensation of the future state ought not to be compared with that of
the present world".[721] Tertullian says that much of the body, our bodily
equipment, will be redundant:

> There will be no meat because no more hunger; no more drink,
> because no more thirst; no more concubinage, because no more
> child-bearing; no more eating and drinking, because no more
> labour and toil. Death too will cease; so there will be no more
> need of the nutriment of food for the defence of life, nor will
> mother's limbs any longer have to be laden [pregnancy] for the
> replenishment of our race.[722]

So as one who would not guess at the future state, he could not resist
having a good shot at it!

In a little over 12 years, Tertullian had written prolifically and powerfully,
making an apology for Christianity in his famous *Apologeticum*, giving

instruction about Christian behaviour, rebutting the major heresies of the day, but by AD 210, when nearing 60, he appears to have joined the Montanist movement or movement of New Prophecy, about which he wrote in a lost work called *De Ectasi*, mentioned by Jerome in his list of Tertullian's works. The reason for this change is unknown: perhaps he had a growing frustration with the established and organised church, or perhaps he was simply attracted to Montanism's strict patterns of behaviour, or its uncompromising stance towards paganism and any collusion with the state. Or maybe his joining reflected his growing belief in the imminence of the second coming of Christ.

Whatever the reason, his works *On Fasting (De Jejunio)*, *On Monogamy (De Monogamia*—a development of his delightful earlier *Ad Uxorem)* and *On Modesty (De Pudicitia)*, which condemned second marriages and upheld the celibate state, denoted a more severe moral and spiritual stance. One further tract written at this time, *Adversus Praxean,* was to prove very influential. It entered a defence of the Trinity into the so-called Monarchian controversy in Rome, which we will study further in the next chapter dealing with the theological currents in the capital.

Tertullian's remaining years are shrouded in mystery. He may have lived to a great age. In Carthage, he would eventually be succeeded by Cyprian—a major influence on North African Christianity. More of a pastor, church leader and, in the end, a martyr, Cyprian's contribution would be different from Tertullian's, but the two of them laid the foundations of North African Latin Christianity and discipleship, upon which Augustine of Hippo would later build.

Cyprian of Carthage

Around AD 210, just when Tertullian's influential ministry was on the wane, and his writing career coming to an end, Cyprian was born in present-day Tunisia, either in or close by Carthage.[723] He came from an equestrian (patrician or aristocratic) family, with estates in the area which he was to give away, at least in part. He was born to pagan parents, was married, and trained as a jurist, orator and lawyer. He took the name Thascus Caelicius Cyprianus out of respect for a presbyter called Caecilianus, through whom he was converted and brought to baptism in c.AD 246, aged 35. It was quite probable they were relatives and both members of the powerful Roman family of Caecilii.

Cyprian gives an account of his earlier life in his letter *Ad Donatum*, in which he records, in general terms (with nothing like the mental analysis and reflection the church would later receive from Augustine of Hippo about his journey to conversion), his pursuit of a selfish life. In this letter he writes:

> While I was still lying in darkness and gloomy night, wavering hither and there, tossed about on the foam of this boastful age, and uncertain of my wandering steps … I used to regard it as a difficult matter, and especially as difficult in respect of my character at that time, that a man should be capable of being born again.[724]

Soon after his baptism, Cyprian decided on ordination, and while still very new to the presbyter's office was elected bishop by the people, as was the custom. His biographer recalls in glowing terms his humility and diffidence at so great an honour being given to one so young. Cyprian attempted to withdraw, but the crowd insisted.[725]

Cyprian was made Bishop of Carthage in AD 248/9 and was to remain thus for ten years. These were ten years which would come to be dominated by the persecution of the church on a scale previously unknown. Whereas the previous persecution had been at the whim of the local proconsul or governor, in the middle of the third century it became the wish of three successive Emperors—Decius, Gallus and Valerian—to persecute the church systematically as imperial policy. If Tertullian had seen persecution in his lifetime, sometimes of a particularly vehement nature—aided and abetted by the mob in the amphitheatre, as with Perpetua and her companions—now it was to have the full force of imperial policy. Persecution resulted in Cyprian's flight into self-imposed exile and then his martyrdom under Valerian. In Rome, it would account for the exile of Cornelius and the martyrdoms of Fabian and Stephen, all Bishops of Rome. This development of the persecution of the church may be accounted for by the weak state of the Empire in the middle of the third century: the continuing threat of the Parthians and Persians in the east, and the incursions of the Goths across the Danube.

As ever, when the Empire seemed vulnerable or worse, the Christians were considered to blame for stirring up the hatred and jealousy of the gods and provoking a resulting judgement. Only a sacrifice of Christians could appease the gods and turn the military losses. It was that unreasonable Roman logic Tertullian paraded in the *Apologeticum*: "If the Tiber rises as high as the city walls, if the Nile does not send its waters up over the fields, if the heavens give no rain, if there is an earthquake, if there is a famine or pestilence, straightway the cry is 'Away with the Christians to the lion!'". [726]

Cyprian's episcopacy was served in the teeth of this persecution. If his initial flight into hiding was controversial, he was later clothed with honour, dignity and authority in the church, both West and East, by his martyrdom. He was not a theologian in the style of Tertullian, more a church administrator and legalist, whose skills were pastoral in guiding the church through the storms of persecution and heresy. What he lacked in theological penetration and rhetorical élan compared with Tertullian, he more than compensated for with character and a deep care for the church.

He was a pastor-bishop rather than a wide-ranging theologian like Tertullian. He would write 12 tracts on church discipline, the longest being *Against the Jews*, and a further 82 letters. His main concerns were the treatment of the lapsed, the rehabilitation of apostates, the use of certificates called *libellacai*, the unity of the church and the necessity of re-baptism for those joining the true church from heretical communities.

Of his 12 tracts, we will look at two in particular: *On the Unity of the Church* and *On the Lapsed*. Cyprian sees the Devil as the one seeking to destroy the God-given unity of the church. He is the one who invents "heresies and schisms, whereby he might subvert the faith, might corrupt the truth, might divide unity." Darkness is his goal; deception is his way.[727] Cyprian acknowledges that primacy of authority belongs to Peter (although part of this text is disputed as to whether it was in fact written later to bolster the papacy) and that all true pastors are part of the one church. He asks, "He who deserts the chair of Peter, upon whom the church is founded, is he confident that he is in the church?"[728] Drawing on the Song of Songs, he emphasises the unity of the church: "My dove, my spotless one, is but one. She is the *only one of her mother*, elect of her that bore her" (Song of Songs 6:9). And then, in a telling one-liner, Cyprian says famously, "He can no longer have God for his Father, who has not the church for his mother".[729]

Like Jesus's robe, the church must be undivided and "there is one flock, one shepherd" (John 10:16). Indeed, there have to be differences of opinion in the church "to show which one has God's approval" (1 Corinthians 11:19). Although charismatic gifts like the new prophecy (Montanism) are impressive, observance of order is more necessary; and to cast out devils, and to do great acts upon the earth, is certainly a sublime and an admirable thing. But one does not attain the kingdom of heaven unless one walks in the observance of "the right and just way".[730] Rebellious leaders in the Old Testament met with severe punishment, for example Korah, Dathan and Abiram (see Numbers 16). In effect, Cyprian argues, given the unity of the church which is called and ordered by God, every effort must be made to protect and maintain this unity.

Another important and influential tract written by Cyprian was *On the Lapsed*. The tract begins with praise for those who resisted persecution without compromise: martyrs and confessors who were tortured and imprisoned, of whom Cyprian writes:

> How blissfully, how gladly does she open her gates, that in united bands you may enter, bearing the trophies from a prostrate enemy! With the triumphing men come women also, who, while contending with the word, have also overcome their sex; and virgins also come with double glory of warfare, and boys transcending their years with their virtues.[731]

But not all are so covered in glory; many are lapsed—that is, they have either burnt incense to an effigy of the Emperor or another god, or have denied their faith, or have bribed their way into receiving certificates called *libellatici,* which say they have complied with the magistrates and sacrificed, although they have not.

Some bishops had even "sacrificed".[732] Cyprian himself left the city of Carthage during the ten-month persecution under Decius (AD 250) and found a place of concealment from where he governed his diocese by writing many letters. For this action, Cyprian was accused of cowardice. In later persecutions some handed over scriptures or books of prayers to the authorities and so were called *traditores*. Later, in the English language, these *traditores* would assume the name traitors. But since large numbers of Christians found themselves in the category of the lapsed, how was the church to treat them?

Cyprian was moved with pastoral grief as he considered the lapsed. Some had complied too easily and burnt incense even before any pressure was applied. Some did so to hold on to their property, or even their lives. Others sought the "indulgence" of confessors, granting them a "*libelli pacis*", which meant that, if they were penitent, this was a plea for mercy and reconciliation both then and at the judgement seat of Christ. In other words, the merit of the martyr or confessor acted as an indulgence for the failure of the lapsed. Cyprian's response, both in *On the Lapsed* and his letters,[733] shows that he took a middle position when it came to the reconciliation of the lapsed to the church. He did not agree that, if penitent, the lapsed could never be reconciled to the church. Nor did he think that the indulgence of the confessors, together with penitence, was necessarily reconciliatory. But he did believe that, after a period of penance, a lapsed Christian could be reconciled; and, if gravely ill, a lapsed Christian might be reconciled sooner. He also told some bleak stories of those who took communion before a formal and proper reconciliation and thereupon grew gravely ill and died.[734]

Cyprian wrote tracts on many practical matters: *On Works and Alms*, *On the Vanity of Idols*, *On the Lord's Prayer* and *On the Dress of Virgins*, and his longest, *Three Books of Testimonies against the Jews*. These were becoming common topics for the early Pre-Nicene Fathers, whether Justin, Tertullian or Clement of Alexandria.

Cyprian's instructions might seem severe in our eyes. To the virgins, he says that in becoming objects of desire, "your shameful dress and immodest ornament accuse you: nor can you be counted now among Christ's maidens and virgins, since you live in such a manner as to make yourself an object of desire".[735] Furthermore, virgins are not to attend parties or even weddings, for "what place is there at weddings for her whose mind is not towards marriage", and there,

> In that freedom of lascivious discourse to mingle in unchaste conversation, to hear what is not becoming, to say what is not lawful, to expose themselves, to be present in the midst of disgraceful words and drunken banquets, by which the ardour of lust is kindled, and the bride is animated to bear (children), and the bridegroom to dare lewdness.[736]

It may well be that the well-bred Cyprian knew well the temptations of such occasions from his early manhood before his conversion.

During Cyprian's period of hiding in AD 250, he received support from Rome by letter. The Roman clergy, informed by the deacon Crementius of Cyprian's withdrawal, gave Cyprian their support: "In doing which [withdrawing] he acted rightly, because he is a person of eminence".[737] The same letter went on to say that deacons who visited martyrs in prison should swiftly bury their bodies. It was one of many letters in which the Roman church gave support to Cyprian and likewise Cyprian gave support to the Roman church and its leaders.

The link between Rome and Carthage was essential to both communities, not least in combating heresy or schism and the ordering of the church, but it was not automatic. In the case of Novatian, who became an anti-pope on the grounds of refusing to reconcile lapsed members to the church and setting up a rival church in Rome, Cyprian gave staunch support to Cornelius, the duly elected Bishop of Rome. But to Bishop Stephen of Rome, who admitted members who had been schismatic or in error to the church without further baptism (since their first baptism was invalid in Cyprian's eyes), Cyprian gave no support. Cyprian strongly believed in the necessity of re-baptism of schismatics or heretics who joined the true church and this was firmly endorsed by the seventh Council of Carthage (a local synod of the church in North Africa).[738]

Cyprian's view was to be overturned by Augustine, however, who held that baptism was an inviolable sacrament, offered by God himself, not dependent on either the morality or soundness of the one who presided over or performed it. Augustine thus gave the Catholic Church the tenet of *ex opera operato*, meaning that the sacraments are valid objectively, but their efficacy depends on being received by faith, *ex opera operantis*. Indeed, Augustine explicitly mentions Cyprian's Letter 73, written against Stephen in his work *On Baptism, Against the Donatists*, in which he says that if baptism depends on morality or catholicity, then many within the church are not validly baptised either.[739]

The seventh Synod or Council of Carthage was called in AD 256 to endorse Cyprian's view on baptism.[740] By 14 September AD 258, Cyprian would be martyred during the intense persecution of Emperor Valerian (AD 253–260). What Cyprian avoided in AD 250 under Decius's persecution, he now embraced, i.e., full martyrdom. And memorably, he prayed for the executioner who beheaded him in his garden and paid for his own costs. This made Cyprian a heroic figurehead of the church in North Africa, appealed to by subsequent Christians on both sides of the argument about reconciliation.

Division in the North African church in its response to lapsed Christians would not go away, however. Although for a time Cyprian's response to the lapsed held sway by virtue of its own good sense and his own reputation as a martyr bishop, it nevertheless occupied the middle ground. In Cyprian's teaching, Christians could be re-admitted to fellowship and communion following penance. But after the next great persecution of the church under the Emperor Diocletian, a split occurred which would not be healed. This was the Donatist schism (which we shall come to again in relation to Constantine in Chapter XI).

Diocletian proceeded to ask for the surrender of scriptures and liturgical books in the hope of disabling the leadership of the church. This time, the lapsed were not so much *libellicati* and *thurificati*—those who had certificates saying they had sacrificed or those who had actually sacrificed or burnt incense—but *traditores*, those who handed over the scriptures or liturgical books to the magistrates. Caecilian, the Bishop of Carthage, was accused of having compromised the faith by being consecrated by a bishop accused of being a *traditor*.[741]

At this point, a secessionist church formed around Donatus of Casae Nigrea. His teaching was that a *traditor*-infected Christian church could no longer be a true church and its sacraments, in terms of Cyprian's teaching, were thus invalid. Therefore, a separate Donatist church was set up, which thrived in the harsher climes of North African Christianity. It was a schism which would run and run, and not even Augustine's labours could reconcile them. In the end, only judicial force would compel the Donatists to come back into the Catholic Church, and then only a small proportion.[742] That is to run ahead, however. For the present, the middle and later years of the third century, especially those including Valerian, were to bring Rome to the brink of disaster.

CHAPTER 7

Meanwhile, in Rome

When the history of the church came to be written in the early fourth century, after the conversion of Constantine and the favourable settlement outlined in the Edict of Milan, the impression given by Eusebius was of the seamless emergence of the "Great Church" in Rome.[743] This was a triumphalist view that belied the long struggles of the church in the capital, where it faced many challenges, from persecution to false teaching. More recent scholarship, following W. Bauer's important and seminal work, *Orthodoxy and Heresy in Earliest Christianity*, shows that in the first half of the second century, there were several competing versions of Christianity in Rome. It was only after about AD 150 that an emerging and more assured orthodox Christianity became evident.

The difficulty of accurately reflecting the real picture of the church in Rome in the second century AD is heightened by present-day churches looking back to those early years in order to prove the longevity of their own traditions and, in so doing, muddying the evidence of what was *really* going on at the time. Thus, the Roman Catholic Church draws attention to the tradition of priesthood in which, it is argued, the sacrifice of the Eucharist was well established by the first century. Yet the truth is that the earliest Christians had "no special order of priests among their number, and ... the letter to the Hebrews regarded such an order as passé, belonging to the old covenant, now superseded".[744] For their part, the Reformers wanted to show that Apostolicity was firmly established as *the* principle determining the inclusion of writings in the scriptures. They wanted to demonstrate that authorship by an Apostle or one of their near companions (e.g., Mark and Luke) settled the issue of inclusion into the canon. It is true that Apostolicity was a vital principle, but the process of sifting through material such as *The Shepherd of Hermas*—which was very popular in Rome in the second century AD—to see if it could be accepted as canonical was a drawn-out one. And the *regula fidei* within the church (i.e., its own particular teachings about God, Christ and his work) was determinative in the formation of the canon.[745] In a word, it took time for this "Great Church" and its founding documents to emerge; indeed, it took most of the second century.

Furthermore, since "all roads lead to Rome", this teeming city of roughly a million people was to become a microcosm of all the many teachings that swirled around the Empire. Good teachers and dangerous teachers all found their way there. Ignatius came to Rome to die in about AD 108, writing to the churches along the way from Antioch that they must remain true. His teaching was then hallowed by his martyrdom. Justin likewise came from the eastern Mediterranean, from Ephesus. He literally set up shop in Rome near a bathhouse, wearing the philosopher's garb and teaching all who came to him. He too would be martyred for questioning the gods and refusing to sacrifice to them. Alongside these stalwarts of faith were other teachers in Rome, notably Marcion (*c.*AD 85–160) and Valentinus (*c.*AD 106–160), who between them had cash, which was beguiling, and heady intellectual resources: theories at once exciting and confusing. Marcion came with a gift of money for the Presbyterate of Rome, which they at first accepted. Such was the brilliance of Valentinus, according to Tertullian, that he was a candidate for becoming Bishop of Rome. But, having been passed over for that office, he became a full-blown teacher of Gnosticism instead.

Far from being outsiders of the church, these were *insiders* until their teaching exposed them. Few of these influential leaders were indigenous Romans. Marcion came from Sinope on the Black Sea, where his family were shipbuilders; Valentinus was educated and trained in Alexandria; Justin was originally from Nablus in Palestine and then Ephesus; and the two great advocates of what might be called Catholic orthodoxy, Irenaeus and Tertullian, were also from outside Rome. Irenaeus was a Greek missionary bishop at Lugdunum (Lyons) and came from Smyrna. Tertullian was a North African from Carthage. Thus none were Roman born and bred, but all were to have great influence, for good or ill, on the Roman church. The triumph of the "Great Church" was thus not so much a victory over external pressures (e.g., persecution or competing religious systems) "as a victory of one faction over another rival *within* the early churches".[746] Once again, the idea of "varieties of Christianity" existing in Rome and circulating in the first half of the second century is borne out by what we know. Yet the process of the bishops and presbyters of Rome sifting through these conflicting and competing elements in order to find orthodoxy is hard to fathom. Brakke speaks of "multiple Christian identities and communities which were continually created and transformed".[747] Catholicity or orthodoxy was established in response to the heresies that came to Rome or were generated there in the first half of the second century, especially in relation to Marcion and Valentinus. The two people who helped to give solidity to this Catholic teaching were, as far as we know, Irenaeus of Lyons (AD 130–202) and Tertullian of Carthage (AD 160–*c*.220), one following the other in quick succession. By the beginning of the third century, the church in Rome, although still fluid, was in a much stronger position in terms of discerning orthodoxy than had been the case a century earlier, but new challenges were to come.

Persecution and the Response of the Church

The Roman church existed under the shadow of civil, political and imperial power, and was therefore close to the political expediencies of Emperor and Senate alike. The end of the so-called "good Emperors" (named such by Gibbon) came about with the accession of Commodus, whose rule, as we have noted, was marked by all the worst excesses of the later Claudians, although his Christian mistress, Marcia, was an advocate for the causes of several high-ranking Christians. Commodus was murdered in AD 192 and Pertinax was proclaimed Emperor on 28 March AD 193, but he too was soon murdered. Julianus, who was put to death on 1 June of the same year, very briefly succeeded him.

At this point, the military commander from Leptis Magna, Septimius Severus, seized the imperial throne.[748] Having commanded legions in

Syria and then in Pannonia Superior from AD 191, he marched with his troops on Rome, and demanded the surrender of Pertinax's murderers. He won the backing of the Senate by refusing to execute any of them, and gained the support of the army and the plebs by distributing cash. He immediately began to shore up the Empire with admirable energy. His general, Tiberius Claudius Candidus, defeated a usurper in Byzantium called Pescennius Niger. He subdued Asia and Egypt and then, in AD 195, proceeded to invade Mesopotamia, taking Nisibis and defeating the Parthians. By AD 197 he was in Gaul, taking on the usurper Albinus, a North African who had been appointed Governor in Britain in AD 193, and now, having been declared Emperor, faced Severus at Lugdunum (Lyons) in Gaul. In AD 197, Severus decisively defeated Albinus before returning to Rome, where 29 of Albinus's supporters in the Senate were executed. The following year saw Severus back in Parthia, where Ctesiphon was sacked with great loss of life. A new Roman province of Mesopotamia was created, but Parthia, like the German tribes beyond the Rhine and Danube, was to remain a thorn in Rome's side for a century and more to come. It was during Severus's reign, although not at his instigation, that Christians in North Africa, notably Perpetua and her companions, suffered great persecution in AD 203, following the enforcement of the Senate's *New Regulations* against Christians.

Severus's son Caracalla returned Rome to ruthless and capricious government. Distinguished senators were humiliated or executed. While Caracalla was in the East, a fickle eunuch, better known for his juggling and sorcery than for judicious government, governed Rome. Caracalla wanted to be known as a soldier and gave himself the title Germanicus Maximus, but this after only slight victories against German tribes, a campaign in Asia, including Armenia, and a brief stay in Egypt which ended with him massacring the inhabitants of Alexandria. His own rule was brought to an abrupt end when he was murdered by a Praetorian Prefect called M. Opellius Macrinus.[749]

The period of imperial government which lasted a little over 60 years, from the death of Caracalla in AD 217 to the accession of Diocletian in AD 284, has often been called "the crisis of the Empire". In those years, there were no less than 18 emperors. The administration appeared to be unable to cope with the task of ruling an Empire that stretched from

Hadrian's Wall in the north to the deserts of the Sahara in the south, and from the Atlantic coast of Spain in the west to the Tigris in Mesopotamia in the east. If it is hard enough to unite an area like the present European Union, how much harder it must have been to unite the Roman Empire with only the communication systems of the third century to work with and most of the Middle East and North Africa too.

After the shortest of reigns, of just a few months, Macrinus, Caracalla's successor, was succeeded by Elagabalus. His reign was regarded by the historian Dio as an "appalling hiatus", encompassing the inclusion of eastern gods, rumours of sexual depravity and promiscuity, scant regard for the Senate and a political rift which brought the dynasty to its knees.[750] Elagabalus's 13-year-old cousin Alexander, who took the august name of Marcus Aurelius Severus Alexander Augustus, succeeded him. Much more deferential in his treatment of the Senate, he was nonetheless in the hands of his advisers, particularly his grandmother, Julia Maesa, and his mother, Julia Mamaea. The Emperor seemed "lethargic, feeble, and ineffective to the mutinous armies" who were themselves defeated by their old foes the Parthians in Mesopotamia.[751] The Emperor himself went to Antioch to help lead the campaign, but during a stalemate with the Parthian commander, Ardashir I, a new challenge arose from Germany, where the Alamanni had broken through the borders of the Empire near Mainz. The army sought a new champion and chose Julius Verus Maximinus: Alexander and his mother, Julia Mamaea, were summarily murdered in their tents.[752]

The years AD 235–260 were only to become worse and formed the heart of the so-called "crisis" of the Empire. Interestingly, this was the time in which the persecution against the church grew more acute, and was directed by Emperors in a way not seen since Nero. Maximinus was dragged into incessant campaigns against the German tribes. He did not go to Rome, but demanded increasing taxes to pay for the war. There was also disorder in Proconsularis Africa, and Ardashir I, a resurgent Persian leader in Mesopotamia, retook Nisibis.

When Africans refused to pay taxes to Rome, a regional governor was proclaimed Emperor. His name was Gordian, a member of the Gordiani family, which provided successive leaders. A senior official, with no military experience, Gordian was hardly the best usurper to take on Maximinus, but he had the support of the Senate, as had his son, Gordian II, who was simultaneously declared Emperor by the Senate in the Year of the Six Emperors. Maximinus then marched on Rome, but the combination of a winter's march through the Alps, his own severe style of leadership, harassment by skirmishers and loss of support from the local population around Aquileia, ran his campaign into the ground. Gordian I was murdered by his troops. Gordian II died in North Africa one month after his adoption as Emperor by the Senate. Whereupon the Senate chose Balbinus and Pupienus, who jointly and successfully took on Maximinus, but they were unpopular in Rome and were murdered by the Praetorian Guard. Finally, Gordian III, the grandson of Gordian I, was chosen, a boy of 13, in AD 238.[753] He was the youngest ever Roman Emperor and ruled for six years.

Gordian III was much more circumspect in winning the support of the Senate and presenting himself as a cultured philhellene. Nevertheless, this cultured young ruler came to be dominated by Timesitheus, an Anatolian army commander with a long and distinguished equestrian career. As the Emperor's chief adviser, Timesitheus faced further encroachment by the Parthians in AD 236–240. By AD 241, Ardashir had captured the client city of Hatra, making a full-scale conflict with Rome more likely. With his court and a massive army, Gordian III travelled to Antioch, reaching it in late AD 242. In AD 243, Gordian and Timesitheus crossed the Euphrates, marching on Ctesiphon, the Parthian capital on the east bank of the Tigris, opposite Seleuchia. Timesitheus died on the campaign and, in mid-February AD 244, Gordian III was defeated by Shapur, either killed in battle or murdered by his own men after defeat. (Shapur was the son of Ardashir, soon to be Shahanshah, who founded the Sassanian dynasty of the Parthian Empire, based in Persia or present-day Iran.) Philip, the Praetorian Prefect, replaced Gordian and was Emperor for the next four years.

From Trachonitis in southern Syria, Philip was in early middle age when he succeeded. He had the backing of the army and quickly negotiated a settlement with Shapur, leaving the Roman border well to the west. He was criticised for giving Armenia into the Persian sphere of influence and paying Shapur 500,000 gold dinars.[754] Shapur was to remain a constant thorn in the side of Rome till AD 270, however, and in future years would humiliate Rome in a way that had not happened since Hannibal.

Philip was Emperor from AD 244–249, a period troubled by further incursions in the middle Danube, raids by the Quadi and the Iazyges into Pannonia, and disturbances in Dacia—present-day Transylvania. By AD 248, large numbers of Goths had poured into Moesia Inferior. Roman armies under C. Messius Quintus Decius, a protégé of Maximinus and a distinguished senator, were so successful that Decius was proclaimed Emperor by the troops. Decius marched on Rome, where he met and defeated the Emperor's armies at Verona in September AD 249. Philip was killed and Decius became Emperor. It was to be a fateful outcome for the church.

Decius faced renewed fighting along the Danube, incursions by the Goths, attacks by the Carpi in Moesia Superior, and trouble in Rome. He sought to strengthen his public image by associating with other deified Emperors, but more particularly by beginning a controversial purge of the church, relieved only by his early death in a campaign against the Gothic host in AD 251. Decius's successor, Gallus (AD 251–253), continued the war against the Goths. Like his predecessor, the army chose him on the spot. He had been a Senatorial Governor of Moesia and was about 45 years old on becoming Emperor. He quickly made peace with the Goths, paying them a large subsidy, and returned to Rome to shore up his position as the new Emperor. He never left the city after that, a choice that earned him a reputation for indolence.

Elsewhere in the East, Shapur was once again on the move. He annexed Armenia and then moved up the Euphrates, taking Antioch to the east and sending an army into Cappadocia. Then he became bogged down in the area and, whilst withdrawing, was attacked by an army from Palmyra led by Odaenathus.[755] Further incursions by the Goths led by Cniva—responsible for the defeat and death of Decius—threatened Rome. Cniva led his troops as far as Macedonia, causing panic in Greece and leading to the hasty re-fortification of Athens. The army in Moesia, led by Aemilian, the governor of that province, declared him Emperor while Gallus languished in Rome. Once more an army marched on Rome to confront Gallus. This time, the armies met at Interamna, north of Rome, but before battle was joined, Gallus and his son were murdered by his troops. Aemilian's rule was brief. Valerian arrived with an army from the transalpine frontier to confront Aemilian, but once again, before the battle began, Aemilian was killed by his troops.

Valerian and his son Gallienus sought to reverse the recent defeats of Roman armies in Antioch and along the Danube. Valerian, now in his sixties, took the eastern front, proceeding to Antioch and Samosata on the Euphrates by AD 255. Valerian was to face a pincer movement: a Gothic or Borani force attacked down the western coast of the Black Sea and, sweeping all before them, took such important cities as Chalcedon and Nicomedia, while Shapur attacked from the south-east, taking advantage of Valerian's absence, and seized Dura and Circesium on the Euphrates. It was in the midst of this campaign, in the summer of AD 257, that both Valerian and Gallienus issued the first of their two orders of persecution against the Christians, the second following a year later.

The first order called on Christians to sacrifice to the gods or face execution, the second was an outright order to execute Christian leaders. It was this order that precipitated the martyrdom of Cyprian in Carthage and that of Sixtus II in Rome, together with six deacons, including St Lawrence. (Their tombs are in the San Callixtus Catacombs in Rome, near the Appian Way.)

It may not have come as a surprise to the Christians that Valerian was captured in AD 260 while negotiating with Shapur, the Sassanian king who was attacking Carrhae and Edessa on the Euphrates. To the Christians it would have seemed the providence of God. He was taken to Persia, where he died the same year. Gallienus, his son, would rule for a further eight years on his own, much of the time fighting the Goths on the Rhine and relying on Odaenathus of Palmyra to hold Shapur in check.

The sharp persecution of Christians, first by Decius and then by Valerian, brought fresh problems to the church. The issue revolved, as in Carthage, around how the lapsed should be treated. Two parties emerged in Rome, as they also would later in Africa. The latter was during the Great Persecution under Diocletian, which precipitated the Donatist controversy. The issue was over whether or not the lapsed could be received back into the church following penance. After the martyrdom of Bishop Fabian of Rome, two candidates emerged to succeed him:

Cornelius and Novatian, both chosen because of their ideas on how the lapsed should be treated.

Novatian was a learned presbyter of the church in Rome and would later write an early treatise on the Trinity.[756] According to Eusebius, Novatian concealed a burning desire to be Bishop of Rome which coloured his whole demeanour.[757] He contested Cornelius's candidacy because of Cornelius's more lenient treatment of the lapsed. Novatian held to the austere traditional view that those guilty of apostasy, murder or adultery could not be reconciled to the church. Cyprian of Carthage and Dionysius of Alexandria, both of whom had gone into hiding during the Decian persecution, so as better to rule their dioceses, supported the candidacy of Cornelius and his treatment of the lapsed.

Many mutually supportive letters passed between Cyprian and Cornelius. Letter 40 was sent to Cornelius about his refusal to acknowledge Novatian's election, and questioning the integrity of an attempt by Novatian to gain his support. Novatian had sent a delegation of deacons to Cyprian with news of his own consecration or ordination as bishop, asking for Cyprian's support. Cyprian refused, saying emphatically: "When in our solemn assembly they [Novatian's envoys] burst in with invidious abuse and turbulent clamour, demanding that the accusations, which they said they brought and would prove, should be publicly investigated by us and by the people; we said that it was not consistent with our gravity to suffer the honour of our colleague [Cornelius], who had already been chosen and ordained and approved by the laudable sentence of many, to be called into question any further by the abusive voice of rivals".[758]

In a further letter (No. 41), Cyprian affirmed his support for Cornelius. More correspondence was exchanged between Cornelius and Cyprian about some confessors who had been seduced into supporting Novatian's cause and had become important pawns in the struggle over Novatian's candidacy before Cornelius was able to win them back. Concerted support for Cornelius from Dionysius of Alexandria, Cyprian of Carthage, and Fabius of Antioch saw off the rival claims of Novatian *and* the church discipline he represented.

By AD 254, the supporters of Novatian had slipped away to Africa and Italy, although communities of Novatians would continue to exist and flourish in Asia Minor, especially in Constantinople. Canon 8 of the Council of Nicaea dealt with the fallout from the Novationists, recognising the ordination of priests in this breakaway church. But by the fifth century, these communities had either withered away or been repressed.[759]

Another schism over church discipline was looming. Once Novatian and his party had faded into the background, Cornelius became Bishop of Rome, although only for a short time. He was exiled by Decius's successor, Gallus, and died in exile, probably martyred, in AD 254. His successor, Lucius, was only Bishop of Rome for a year. Bishop Stephen, around whom the next controversy over church discipline revolved, then succeeded Lucius.

Stephen was a Greek by background who had become Archdeacon of Rome during Lucius's pontificate. During his brief episcopacy, Stephen pursued a policy of baptism that brought him into direct conflict with Cyprian and the church in Carthage and North Africa. The conflict arose because some converts were baptised in communities outside the official Catholic Church and Stephen was prepared to accept their baptism on the understanding that baptism in water in the name of the Trinity was acceptable throughout the church, wherever it was administered and by whomever. There was therefore no need to re-baptise people on entry into the Catholic Church.

Rather, as in the case of lapsed penitents, the laying on of hands should be sufficient for re-admittance.

According to Stephen, the sacraments do not belong to the church, but to Christ, so their efficacy does not depend upon the purity or soundness of the minister, but on the faith with which they are received. Furthermore, Stephen based his decision upon the Petrine authority given by Christ to Peter (and, he argued, to his successors as well, as in, "You are Peter . . . " (Matthew 16:18).

Stephen's position—although later supported by Augustine of Hippo—caused a storm with Cyprian, who insisted on re-baptism. Cyprian's doctrine was that there was only one true church, which existed under the authority of lawfully appointed bishops.[760] Although in one version of this document circulating in Rome, Cyprian acknowledged the supremacy of the Bishop of Rome,[761] in another version of *On the*

Unity of the Church, and in the heat of the controversy with Stephen, Cyprian did not assent to the primacy of Rome.[762] In fact, the primacy of Rome was not formally propagated until the time of Bishop Damasus (AD 366–384). Ambivalence in Cyprian's writings about the authority of the Bishop of Rome did not prevent him from strongly opposing Stephen over his policy of not re-baptising non-Catholic entrants to the church.

In a flurry of letters,[763] Cyprian made his position crystal clear:

> For I know not by what presumption some of our colleagues are led to think that they who have been dipped by heretics ought not to be baptized when they come to us, for the reason that they say that there is one baptism which indeed there is one, because the Church is one, and there cannot be any baptism out of the Church.[764]

The definition of the church raised by this controversy was to run and run through the ages. Since Cyprian considered a heretical church no church at all, when a candidate was baptised into the One Universal Church, then it was truly their first and only proper baptism. This fierce dispute only ended with Stephen's death. His successor, Sixtus, who like Cyprian would be martyred in Valerian's forthcoming persecution, took a more emollient line.

Dionysius, the Bishop of Alexandria, issued an *eirenicon* to try and bring the sides together, but Rome and Carthage agreed to differ. Fifty years later, with the outbreak of the Donatist controversy,[765] the Bishop of Rome had new grounds for making the church in Carthage abandon the sacramental theology of Cyprian. Before then, another theological controversy over the Trinity had blown up.

The Monarchist Controversy

During the late second and early part of the third centuries, a Christological controversy with deep Trinitarian repercussions took centre stage. It was a precursor to and forewarning of the much more divisive and long-lasting Arian controversy of the fourth century. It was a warning shot of what was to come. In short, the "Monarchians" were concerned with the problem of how to recognise the Son as God, along with the Father, without falling into the error of believing in two gods. They emphasised the *monarchy* of God, that is, that there can be only one God, just as there can only be one king in any state. Because of their belief in a single monarch in the Trinity they tried to solve the problem of Jesus's status in one of two ways. Either he was God the Father in the flesh, thereby impairing his true identity as Word made flesh, co-eternal and consubstantial with the Father—or they believed that Jesus was a normal human being who God the Father adopted at his baptism and endowed with a special outpouring of his Spirit for the task of mission. Somehow the church had to clarify the Johannine paradox of the Son's unity with, and yet distinction from, the Father.[766] Once again the origin of the controversy was to be found in Rome, but it quickly spread to Antioch, with repercussions for the churches in Carthage and Alexandria.

The controversy broke out during the episcopate of Victor in Rome, but it became full-blown during the time of his successor Zephyrinus (AD 199–217). It began as a revolt against the theology of Justin, who had spoken boldly of the *Logos* as another God beside the Father.[767] This overemphasis on the distinctiveness of the Son's godhead in relation to the Father seemed to promote the idea of two gods in the same way that Gregory of Nyssa would answer the Arian charge, late in the fourth century, by promoting three gods in his Nicene and Cappadocian doctrine of the Trinity. (Gregory's riposte to the charge of *tritheism* was dedicated to one Ablabius and entitled *Not Three Gods*.) For the present, Justin did justice to what would later be called the distinct *hypostasis* of each member of the godhead. He used the illustration of one torch being lit by another.[768] Although the eternal nature of the Son's divinity was not necessarily defended by this analogy, an overemphasis on the independence of each person of the godhead, especially the Father and

Son, ran the risk of the charge of ditheism (i.e., there being two gods), and this was the fear of the Monarchist movement.

The Monarchists, who came to the debate from a long and arduous battle with the Gnostics in the second century—as Irenaeus has made us aware—did not wish to concede the central point that there is one God who is both Creator and Redeemer. They therefore emphasised the unity of the Godhead and the monarchy of the Father. The very strength of their case against the Gnostics was a springboard for their defence of the *monarchy* of God. "The orthodox had insisted that there is no *first principle* other than God the Creator, no coequal devil, no coeternal matter, but a single *monarchia*."[769] Yet as so often happens in doctrinal argument, their compensating correction for the multi-emanations of Gnosticism resulted in an equally dangerous overemphasis on the *singleness* of the Father's divinity and status, at the expense of the standing of Christ as the divine *Logos*, the Word made flesh: fully God and fully man. The Monarchian critics of the *Logos* theology had, as we have noted,

> Two courses open to them. Either they could say that God who created the world was so incarnate in Jesus that there is no difference to be discerned between the "Son" and the "Father" (unless "Son" is a name for the physical body or humanity of Christ and "Father" a name for the divine Spirit within); or they could say that Jesus was a man like other men, but differentiated in being indwelt by the Spirit of God to an absolute and unique degree.[770]

In Rome, under the episcopacy of Zephyrinus (AD 198–217), the debate polarised around two individuals: Sabellius and Hippolytus (c.AD 170–235). Sabellius originated from the region of Pentapolis in Libya and was a presbyter in Rome. He believed that God was indivisible and the Son and the Spirit were modes of the single godhead. This led to the idea of modalism, in which the Father expressed himself in turn as both Son and Spirit. The Father therefore suffered in the Son (in the West this was called *Patripassianism*). Opposing Sabellius in Rome was the church's most significant theologian, Hippolytus, a follower of Irenaeus. He introduced the idea of *prosopa*, the Latin equivalent of the Greek *hypostasis,* through which he insisted on the differentiation of Father and Son as separate beings. He also wrote *The Apostolic Tradition,* a work that gives the earliest form of ordination of deacons and presbyters in the church (*c.*AD 200–220).

The waters of this incipient Trinitarian controversy were muddied further by a deacon called Callixtus, once a slave in the imperial household, who put forward a notion that the Father was the name for the divine Spirit indwelling the "Son", which is the human body of Jesus. Callixtus denounced Hippolytus as a ditheist (a believer in two gods) and, to Hippolytus's horror, Callixtus was elected Bishop of Rome in succession to Zephyrinus in AD 217.[771]

Hippolytus was shocked by Callixtus's actions. The slave turned pope who had been rescued from persecution some years earlier by Marcia, the Christian concubine of Commodus, now proceeded to loosen church discipline. He proclaimed that the church was to be like Noah's ark, in which there were clean and unclean beasts, and that the church should reconcile and reinstate any who had fallen into sin following baptism. He also recognised marriages between upper class women and men of inferior status, which was a scandal to Roman conventions. For Hippolytus, the author of *The Refutation of All Heresies*[772] and manuals on church order and discipline, this kind of church order and teaching proposed by Callixtus was anathema. Callixtus died in AD 222, by which time Tertullian had written his riposte to *Monarchianism,* called *Adversus Praxean,* in AD 208.[773]

Praxeas taught that "the Father himself came down into the virgin, was himself born of her, himself suffered, indeed was himself Jesus Christ",[774] and was, Tertullian says, the first to bring this monarchian theology from Asia to Rome. Worse than that—for Tertullian was by then a follower of Montanus and the New Prophecy movement from Phrygia—Praxeas turned Victor, the Bishop of Rome (AD 189–199), against Montanism, thereby in Tertullian's eyes diminishing the work of the Spirit. Tertullian states what he describes as his "rule of faith" on the Trinity in the following:

> We however as we indeed always have done and more especially
> since we have been better instructed by the Paraclete, who leads

men indeed into all the truth, believe that there is only one
God, but under the following dispensation, or oikonomia, as it
is called, that this one only God has also a Son, his Word, who
proceeded from himself, by whom all things were made, and
without nothing was made. Him we believe to have been sent by
the Father into the Virgin, and to have been born of her—being
both Man and God, the Son of Man and the Son of God—and
to have been called by the name of Jesus Christ; we believe him
to have suffered, died, and, after he had been raised again by the
Father and taken back to heaven, to be sitting at the right hand
of the Father, and that he will come to judge the quick and the
dead; he also sent from heaven from the Father, according to his
own promise, the Holy Spirit, the Paraclete, the sanctifier of the
faith of those who believe in the Father, and in the Son, and in
the Holy Spirit.[775]

Tertullian goes on to argue that monarchy does not preclude this
sovereignty being shared with other members of the Trinity, and nor does
such sharing of sovereignty affect the supremacy and sole government
of the divine being.[776] "Look to it", he says, "that it be not you rather who
are destroying the Monarchy, when you overthrow the arrangement and
dispensation of it, which had been constituted in just as many names as it
has pleased God to employ".[777] In other words, it is not for men to define
the sovereignty that God has ordered, but to recognise that in his very
eternal being there are three *persona* or *hypostases* who innately share this
sovereignty and monarchy. Furthermore, Tertullian shows both the Son
and the Spirit proceed from the Father, and that both share the Godhead
and its monarchy, but that both have distinct roles and beings.

For he argues:

Everything which proceeds from something else must needs be
second to that from which it proceeds, without being on that
account separated. Where, however, there is a second, there must
be two; and where there is a third, there must be three. Now the
Spirit indeed is third from God and the Son; just as the fruit of the
tree is third from the root, or as the stream out of the river is third

from the fountain (or spring), or as the apex of the ray is third
from the sun. Nothing is alien from that original source whence
it derives its own properties. In like manner the Trinity, flowing
down from the Father through the intertwined and connected
steps does not all disturb the Monarchy, while it at the same time
guards the state of the Economy.[778]

Such is Tertullian's fundamental answer to the monarchist argument of
Praxeas. Tertullian then embarks on *a tour d'horizon* of scriptures relating
to the Trinity.[779] He shows the distinctiveness of the Father, Son and
Spirit from scripture and the falseness of Praxeas's teaching on the Trinity,
which makes nonsense of the Cross from which Christ, as the eternal
Son of God, appealed to a Father who was distinct from him. If Praxeas's
monarchist doctrine was followed, the Father in the Son would be praying
to the Father in heaven.[780] If Praxeas's doctrine was followed, the essential
difference between Judaism and Christianity would collapse.[781] If there
was no difference, then what need would there be for the Gospel or the
New Covenant, for the redemption of Christ or the indwelling Spirit?
"For they deny the Father when they say he is the same (i.e., not distinct
from the Son) as the Son; and they deny the Son, when they suppose him
to be the same as the Father, by assigning to them things which are not
theirs, and taking away from them things which are theirs."[782]

In summary, Tertullian said that Praxeas "expelled the Paraclete and
crucified the Father". The definition of the Trinity had much further
to go, but Tertullian had set down a benchmark in the Monarchist
controversy. Further definition of words like *substantia* and *persona*
would be required, and in the east a whole new vocabulary of *homoousios*
and *hypostasis* was taking shape. The Monarchist controversy was an
opening theological salvo in the long drawn out theological war over the
Trinity that continued throughout the fourth century. The Monarchist
cause would be taken up by Paul of Samosata, the Bishop of Antioch, who
would be condemned as a heretic by a synod in AD 269.

In summary, the church in Rome during the third century was
buffeted by many storms, concluding with the Monarchist controversy.
Having thrown out the teaching of Marcion and Valentinus with the
help of Irenaeus and Tertullian, the church faced new issues of order

and discipline. There was the schism between Cornelius and Novatian about the right way to treat the lapsed. There were differences between Cyprian and Stephen on whether baptism outside the Catholic Church was valid. There was the fierce persecution of the church in the reigns of Severus, Maximian, Decius and Valerian, but despite all of this, the "Great Church" had by now clearly emerged.

Origen, who gave the church in Rome the name "Great Church", then went to the capital himself. He made a brief trip when Zephyrinus was Bishop of Rome (c. AD 199–217) because he "wanted to see the most ancient church of the Romans".[783] He met the *Logos* theologian Hippolytus, as well as Pope Zephyrinus and his successor Callixtus. But the visit permanently laid to rest the hope that he would find there the practice of Christianity "in its pristine apostolic purity".[784] The Monarchist controversy was raging, with Zephyrinus and Callixtus accepting a form of Monarchian theology which blurred the distinction between the Father and the Son, and to which Hippolytus was implacably opposed. Origen returned to Alexandria, and it may have been over this issue that he broke with Bishop Demetrius of Alexandria. He too, like Hippolytus, saw Father and Son as separate hypostases, but part of a single Godhead. A dispute over this with his bishop may have been a contributing factor to his leaving Alexandria and settling at Caesarea in Palestine. (He also accepted ordination by the Bishop of Caesarea without the prior consent of Demetrius.) The story of Origen is one of the most important and influential stories in the early church, and to this we now turn.

CHAPTER 8

Origen in Alexandria and Caesarea

Early in 332 BC, about five years after his succession and a year before his great military advance into Persia, Alexander the Great travelled to Egypt, subjugating the Levant in the process, in order to consult the oracle of Ammon at Siwah in the western desert about his future plans. On returning to the Nile, he took a ship from Memphis and sailed northwards down the river to make his most lasting contribution to civilization: the founding of Alexandria. At the river's mouth, he visited the Pharaoh's frontier fort of Rhacotis and explored the many outlets of the delta. He was much taken with the western edge of the site: "It seemed to him that the place was most beautiful for founding a city and that the city would be greatly favoured; he was seized by enthusiasm for the work and marked out the plan in person, showing where the gathering place should be built and which gods should have temples where, Greek gods being chosen along with the Egyptian Isis; he arranged where the perimeter wall should be built."[785]

Alexandria was to become one of the five great cities of the Roman Empire after Rome, Constantinople (not founded till AD 330), Antioch and Carthage. Close behind in significance were Corinth, Ephesus and Athens. Alexandria was to become an intellectual and commercial centre with its own distinctive style. It was also to become the seat of one of the most influential ancient families of the Greek world, the Ptolemies, one of three families to emerge from the shadow of Alexander's conquests. The Antigonids took over in Greece and Macedonia, the Seleucids in Syria, Mesopotamia and Asia Minor, and the Ptolemies in Egypt and Palestine, reaching as far north as Lebanon.

It was Ptolemy I Soter who built the city on the site chosen by Alexander. The village of Rakotis, with its old fort, was incorporated into the new city. A giant lighthouse was constructed on the island of Pharos, which became one of the wonders of the ancient world. It stood slightly higher than the American Statue of Liberty and at its base would have had two statues about 12 metres high: one of Ptolemy depicted as a Pharaoh, and the other of his wife portrayed as the goddess Isis.

Alexandria was planned by Rhodian Dinocrates and laid out as a grid with an east/west axis called the Canopic Way, intersected by a broad north/south axis stretching from Lake Mareotis in the south to the Great Harbour in the north. These boulevards were some 5 kilometres in length and were very impressive to visitors. Indeed, the whole city was overwhelming to new arrivals in terms of its situation, size, buildings and the opportunities it provided. The population—well fed by the grain from the delta—grew quickly to 300,000 in the late third century BC and by the Roman period may have increased to 400,000, just under half the size of Rome's population. The city was divided into five districts, with each designated by one of the first five letters of the Greek alphabet. The division was made in the third century BC, but was still in use in the fourth century AD.[786]

From the outset, Alexandria enjoyed synthesis in its architectural and cultural genes. It combined Egyptian and Greek culture and religion, Christian and Jewish faith, and Greek and Asian philosophy, with the many races living there side by side. From 319 BC, it was under Greek control, and then from 30 BC, after the suicide of Cleopatra and Mark Antony, Augustus took control. A large Roman garrison based at Nicopolis policed the city, soldiers were a common sight on the wide avenues, and a small Roman elite governed the city. It was a commercial centre that exported grain (later to Constantinople), along with the papyrus that grew so plentifully along the Nile, fine linen, glass and wine. These latter products were luxury articles in the Empire and their export made Alexandria rich.

The culture of the city was a heady mix of learning and entertainment, fuelled by strong commerce and the city's unrivalled position on the eastern Mediterranean. The early Ptolemies were responsible for two institutions which shaped the city's life. The first was the cult of

Serapis, and the construction of Alexandria's most significant temple, the Serapeon, where Serapis was worshipped. Serapis was part of a Greco-Egyptian cult in which the Egyptian gods of Osiris and Apis were deliberately combined, and symbolised by a bull. In Memphis, this god was worshipped in a more Egyptian manner, as a deity for the dead, but in Alexandria the cult was given a much more distinctively Greek flavour. Later, through the patronage of Roman Emperors, the Caesareum was built near to the Great Harbour, home to the Roman imperial cult and completed by Augustus. Nearby, a customs house called the Emporion stood, displaying the might of Rome resting on commercial power.[787]

The other noteworthy institution was the museum in the Brucheion, with its renowned library, reminding allcomers that, from the very beginning, this was a city of learning. The museum, which reflected the interests of the early Ptolemies especially, contained an unrivalled collection of ancient Greek and Egyptian texts. The purpose behind it was to gather as many corrected and well-attested Greek texts as possible. The inspiration for this came from Ptolemy II, who was a pupil of Zenodotus, and it was with this purpose in mind that Ptolemy had 72 Hebrew scholars, drawn from each tribe of Israel, translate the Hebrew scriptures into what became known as the Greek Septuagint. In displaying Greek works such as Homer's *Odyssey* and *Iliad*, Ptolemy hoped to prove the superiority of Greek culture over Egyptian.

The museum had its own staff, including an *epistates*—a priest or director. In the early days, scholars were lured to Alexandria by lucrative pay. Scholars of the museum had tax-free salaries, along with board and lodging in the precincts. Timon of Philus called these scholars "cloistered bookworms who argued in the chicken-coop of the Muses".[788] Although Greek texts were mostly collected by the museum, there were also works from Buddhist sources in the East and Jewish works, notably the Septuagint. The library grew over two centuries to around 400,000 volumes, with a further 90,000 volumes housed in a subsidiary library at the Serapeon. Both libraries were lost.

The museum was damaged or destroyed either during Julius Caesar's occupation of Alexandria in 48 BC, or much later during the Emperor Aurelian's suppression of the uprising of Queen Zenobia of Palmyra in AD

272. The library in the Serapeon was destroyed on the orders of Bishop Theophilus of Alexandria in the late fourth century.

In the meantime, these two libraries provided a stimulus and catalyst to scholarship: "One of the greatest contributions of the Museum and library to Alexandria was the trickle down effect they had on Alexandrian life. Numerous teachers and students were attracted to Alexandria from around the Mediterranean world. The city became known for its famous schools and teachers outside those officially connected with the Museum."[789] Among the significant influences on Origen in Alexandria before his move to Caesarea in AD 232 were the much earlier Hellenised Jewish thinker, Philo (25 BC–AD 50), who sought to synthesise Judaism with Greek philosophy, the neo-Platonist Plotinus (AD 205–270), and his teacher Ammonius Saccas (AD 204–270). All were to have an important influence on Origen (AD 184–254). The main spheres of influence in Alexandria during Origen's time were the Jews, the Gnostics and their writings, the Christian Apologist Clement of Alexandria (AD 150–215), the Platonic Schools overseen by Ammonius Saccas, and of course, the church. Given Alexandria's bent for scholarship and enquiry, it is not surprising that the city should have been the seedbed for the theological and philosophical radicalism and reaction which was to be both a blessing and a bane on the church in the third and fourth centuries and beyond.

It is generally thought that Christianity reached Egypt in a form strongly influenced by Judaism.[790] Some have said that the Christian community was strongly Jewish in tone and that no clear distinction was made between Christians and Jews. Barnard has suggested that the author of the *Epistle of Barnabas* was a converted rabbi from the Alexandrian synagogue.[791] In any event, at the outset, Christianity may have been seen in those early years in Alexandria, as elsewhere in the Empire, as simply another branch of Judaism.

In the New Testament, Apollos is identified as an Alexandrian Christian (Acts 18:24–28) who was "well versed in the Christian way". Whether he received his instruction in Alexandria around AD 52, we do not know. Eusebius gives us the well-received tradition that Mark preached the gospel in Alexandria, telling us that even when Mark arrived to preach there, there "was a large body of believers, men and women alike ... with an extremely severe way of life".[792] Another story of Christian origin is that it was Barnabas who preached in Alexandria.

Eusebius gives a list of seven men who allegedly led the Christian community, from Mark to Demetrius, who was bishop during the time of Origen. Of these, only Credo is referred to as bishop by Eusebius, strengthening the case that the earliest leaders of the church in Alexandria were most likely presbyters or elders.[793] Another suggestion, by Attila Jakab, is that Origen referred to such a structure at the beginning of his commentary on John, suggesting that the Christian community was divided into three parts: the common people, the priests (presbyters) and Levites (deacons).[794] In other words, for some time in Alexandria there were only two orders of ministry. In this quotation from his commentary on John, Origen may have been intimating that he was part of the common people and not a presbyter:

> Among us who follow the teachings of Christ, the majority who, for the most part, have no particular purpose in their lives and offer few activities specifically to God may, indeed, be the members of the tribes which have little in common with the priests and rarely cultivate the worship of God. But those who are really dedicated to the divine word and to their worship of God may, because of the excellence of their activities in this regard, be spoken of without absurdity as Levites and priests.[795]

It is possible that, although he was never formally ordained as a presbyter in the church in Alexandria, he regarded himself as a true Levite or deacon, but since, as he says, he dedicated himself to the divine Word and to the worship of God, he could be spoken of without absurdity as a Levite or priest.[796] Whether we see the beginnings of a split with the established hierarchy in Alexandria in this statement is uncertain, but considering his later break with Bishop Demetrius and his flight to Caesarea, it is possible that he was always an outsider to the hierarchy of the church. If not a presbyter or deacon in the established sense, what then was Origen's role in Alexandria when he was entering manhood at the end of the second century?

Origen's father was martyred in the persecution of Septimius Severus, so to provide for himself and his family, Origen began teaching as a *grammatikos* when only 18 years old.[797] He was a kind of secondary school teacher of grammar, a post inferior to that of the more advanced teachers of rhetoric, the sciences, music and mathematics. The *grammatikos* would teach the basic classical texts, especially Homer, Herodotus, Xenophon and Thucydides. What is important to realise is that it was essentially a textual discipline. Its four stages were: 1) criticism to establish what the ancient writer had actually written; 2) reading and reciting the text from memory; 3) explaining the text and what its true meaning was, including the meaning of any individual words and their etymology and use; and 4) judging the moral purpose of the text.[798] Earlier in second-century Alexandria, Apollonius Dyscolus, who lived in the Brucheion district, wrote his study of Greek syntax. Such textual criticism was similar in principle to biblical exegesis, and this would concern Origen all his later life. The disciplines gained would, on the whole but not entirely, stand him in good stead.

Origen began to gather a school around him, including some non-Christians wanting to hear him on the meaning of faith. Eusebius tells of two brothers, Heraclas and Plutarch, who became students. Others followed: Serenus, a woman called Herais, Basilides, Potamiaena and her mother Marcella.[799] The school grew. It became involved in preparing catechumenates for baptism. Origen then decided to give up the teaching of classics. He sold his classical scrolls and resolved to teach the faith only. And, for a while, he had the patronage of Bishop Demetrius.

Eusebius tells of many pupils coming to faith, so many that soldiers were placed on guard near Origen's house to prevent disturbances from pagans. In time, the establishment broke into two schools: one overseen by Origen's former pupil Heraclas, and a more advanced school led by Origen himself. At some point in this period, he began to learn Hebrew and began his great work of Old Testament textual criticism called the *Hexapla*. In what was surely one of the greatest works of ancient biblical studies, Origen gathered six texts of the Old Testament: the Hebrew text, a transcription of the Hebrew text in Greek, the translations of Aquila, Symmachus and Theodotion (all second-century Jews) and the Septuagint. It was, as you might imagine, a huge volume, perhaps one of the largest works in the ancient world, setting out these texts in six columns. Such an endeavour required considerable resources and it may have been at this time that Origen came under the patronage of a rich Christian called Ambrose, who had previously been a Gnostic, but who Origen brought to true faith.[800] Origen now worked for Ambrose, to whom he dedicated a number of his works. The provision of stenographers, copyists and secretaries would have made a work like the *Hexapla* possible.

From the age of 18 in AD 202 until AD 232, when Origen moved to Caesarea after a dispute with Bishop Demetrius,[801] he was busy at work as a teacher or *grammatikos*, then as an instructor of catechumens and more senior students, and, finally, as an author of many works for Ambrose and others. The works he produced during these 30 years were mostly commentaries on a number of biblical books, including Psalms 1–25, Lamentations, the earlier part of a commentary on Genesis, and John's Gospel. Alongside these biblical commentaries was his great systematic work *On First Principles,* and a lesser work *On the Resurrection.*[802]

Before appraising these works, it is worth remembering the major influences on Origen in Alexandria during these years. These influences comprised the Christian community and its early writings; the Jews and the learning of Hebrew; the Neo-Platonic schools which were reaching their heyday during Origen's life-time under Ammonius Saccas and Plotinus, the celebrated neo-Platonist; the Gnostics and in particular Valentinus; and finally the general syncretistic approach to religion and philosophy so prevalent in Alexandria and expressed both by Philo and the cult of Serapis. It was truly a heady intellectual mix, and all of it would influence Origen to some degree.

The Christian community in Alexandria in the second century was well endowed with examples of Christian thought and literature. A large number of post-Apostolic works were either produced in, or circulating around, Alexandria during the second century, beyond even the scriptures themselves, which were still in the process of being formalised. The Johannine corpus, and especially the Gospel of John, was revered in Alexandria, establishing the *Logos* theology of the incarnation which was to become central to Clement's and then Origen's thought; and later to that of Athanasius and Cyril.

Among writings from the post-Apostolic period circulating at the time were Gnostic writings such as *The Acts of Paul*, *The Gospel of the Hebrews*, *The Prayer of Joseph*, *The Preaching of Peter* and *The Shepherd of Hermas*, which was not Gnostic but for which Origen had a special regard. Origen quotes from several of these works in his writing, notably in his *Commentary on John*, which he began in Alexandria and finished in Caesarea.[803] A further influence on Origen was Clement of Alexandria (*c.*AD 150–215), who was in Alexandria during the early years of Origen's teaching before leaving for Antioch and Jerusalem in AD 212, towards the end of his life.

What appears to have happened in Alexandria was that a group of catechetical schools led by Christian teachers gained a reputation for textual scholarship. They were supported both by the church and by the Bishops of Alexandria. These schools tended to have small groups of disciples drawn by a magnetic personality or inspiring teacher, who would then lead them in both reading and interpreting the texts of scripture, as well as in a wider classical education.

One of the earliest such communities was led by Pantaenus, the teacher of Clement, who in turn taught Origen. Pantaenus was born in Sicily, converted to Christianity, and in about AD 180 was the first principal of the Catechetical School in Alexandria.[804] Eusebius describes Pantaenus as being "very distinguished in his education".[805] He was an ardent evangelist and had served as a missionary as far away as India. He became an effective leader of the exegetical school in Alexandria and among his pupils was Clement.

Clement became the principal of the school after Pantaenus and with the avowed aim of teaching his students to gain "gnosis"; that is, knowledge (which often meant knowledge both of the classics and the scriptures) to supplement faith. It seems that initially the schools focused on grammar for the younger pupils and then progressed to the *trivium* of classical education: the study of grammar, rhetoric and dialectic. After that, pupils moved on to the *quadrivium*, the four branches of mathematics: geometry, arithmetic, astronomy and the theory of music. Origen's teaching combined education in these disciplines with the textual exegesis of scripture, both the Old Testament (including Hebrew) and what would become the New Testament scriptures, especially John's Gospel.

When he moved to Caesarea, Origen continued this model of education and Gregory Thaumaturgus tells us that his teaching now involved physics, geometry, astronomy and ethics.[806] It transpires that Origen was a polymath, teaching across the curriculum, not neglecting classical education, but teaching the Bible and Christian faith as well. The apex of his teaching was the study of scripture with close attention to prayerful searching for the hidden meaning of the text.

His commentaries on John, Genesis and Matthew may have resulted from his lectures to his students. Their aim was to form a Christian person, rounded and balanced. The outcome was to produce a person full of virtue (that great classical word), practical wisdom, self-control, justice and courage—but now undergirded by mature Christian faith.[807] This was not done by teaching alone, but by continual exposure to Origen's personality and lifestyle. It was by a combination of teaching and seeing that a disciple would be formed. The Alexandrian tendency to synthesise knowledge, and Origen's own desire to integrate the biblical with the neo-Platonic, would lead him into controversy, however, brought about by his great systematic work, *First Principles*.

If the Christian milieu in Alexandria was well developed by AD 180, there were nonetheless three great challenges to producing mature Christian disciples in that city, quite apart from periodic bouts of persecution. These challenges came from the Gnostics, the Platonic schools of Alexandria and the large Jewish community. All three were strong intellectual and spiritual movements with which the church had to contend in order to emerge as an independent entity.

One of the most potent challenges to Christianity in Alexandria, as in Rome, where Irenaeus had refuted it, was Gnosticism. Valentinus taught in Alexandria for a time, probably from about AD 120–136, followed by his pupils Heracleon and Ptolomaeus—and from there Valentinus moved to Rome. It was these three in particular that Origen refuted in his commentary on the Gospel of John. Although Origen followed in the footsteps of Clement, who had commended *gnosis* as simply knowledge to be added to faith, Origen was no Gnostic himself. Rather, he needed to rebut the prevalent and widespread Gnostic teaching in Alexandria, both in his teaching and writing. This was personal as his patron Ambrose had been converted to orthodox Christianity from Gnosticism, and had asked to be rightly instructed.

There were three main points of conflict for Origen in countering the Gnosticism which was then rife in Egypt, where it was freely circulating in the form of the Gnostic Gospels and many other writings, as we have seen from the Nag Hammadi cache. These points of conflict were the doctrines of incarnation, free will and creation. Origen wrote extensively on all three. Firstly, he defends the uniqueness of the incarnation, which is described most profoundly in the Prologue of St John's Gospel. For Origen, the *Logos* sprang from the Wisdom of God from the beginning (*arche*), and this wisdom (another name for the *Logos*) was eternally hidden in God. "Wisdom is a more fundamental concept in Origen's Christology than logos".[808] But whereas for Ptolomaeus the *Logos* taking on flesh was seen as the origin of the Ogdoad, the first of eight deities in the Valentinian hierarchy of deities called the *Pleroma*, for Origen the incarnation was the making visible of the eternally begotten Son of God. Indeed, the foundational concept for Origen's Christology was God as Son; that is, he is Christ the *Son* of God. This assertion carried two necessary corollaries: the Son was both independent of the Father and yet of the same substance with him, being identical.[809] Origen therefore refuted Gnosticism and its interpretation of the incarnation, re-enforcing the unique event of the incarnation with the second person of the Trinity taking on flesh to reveal the Godhead and redeem humankind.[810]

The second main point of Gnostic theology he refuted was the doctrine of natures (i.e., that there are different types of humanity) and the consequent understanding of free will. His work, *On Natures*, was against Gnostic pre-determination: the idea that the three different natures were incapable of breaking out of their pre-determined path according to Gnostic teaching. These three natures were (i) a material nature which is doomed to perish; (ii) a spiritual nature which is associated with spiritual powers; and (iii) a psychic nature that is the intermediate between the other two, and which, with the help of *gnosis*, can be saved.[811] Gnostics believed that most people belonged to the material category and were therefore lost; with the fewest belonging to the spiritual category. In Book I of *First Principles*, Origen opposed the Gnostic idea of pre-determined natures. He believed created beings had a free choice of either obeying or rebelling. Thus, the Devil created by God rebelled of his own free choice and was determined to corrupt and destroy God's creation and lead humankind astray. Theoretically, at least, Origen left open the possibility that the Devil could change (exercise his free will) and so be redeemed. This outlook, as we shall see, was driven by his Neo-Platonic view of creation and the soul, and his desire to show the potentially omnipotent love of God to redeem all things. Origen was unwilling to say that God created the Devil as an angel with a natural pre-disposition towards evil, since this was prejudicial to the goodness of God, a cardinal point in Origen's theology. By contrast, the Valentinian Candidus proposed that the Devil was totally evil by nature and could only perish. Origen, on the other hand, maintained that the Devil was created good, rebelled, and was not pre-determined by his nature to be condemned. Candidus then maintained that Origen taught that the Devil could be saved.[812] Origen thought that to say that the Devil was predisposed to evil in the created order was unworthy, for although God foreknew, he did not foreordain, and this was a significant distinction.[813] To think anything other was unworthy of God. As an angel, the Devil, along with humans, had the ability to choose and so all were responsible for their actions, rather than simply predisposed by an unalterable nature. Augustine was later to question this teaching, of course, particularly in his dispute with Pelagius and the Pelagians.

The third point of dispute with the Gnostics was creation, although here the argument is even more opaque than Origen's dispute over free will and incarnation. This dispute involved a confused doctrine of creation, both in Gnostic teaching and also in Origen. By the late second century, the Gnostics had taken on the Neo-Platonic view of creation as resulting from the demiurge: a kind of secondary force. In the Platonic economy of godhead, this is *nous*, which accounts for the creation of the material world. In the Platonic system, *nous* (the intellect of God) is responsible for creation, but the Gnostics, seeking to account for a fallen or evil universe, gave the creation myth another twist. In their outworking, according to the Sethian system particularly, the demiurge acts as a craftsman blindly unable to see its progenitor Sophia, producing as a result a fallen or evil world over which one of the Archons, Ialdabaoth, holds sway.

Origen responded to this heterodox view by affirming the original goodness of creation according to the Genesis account. It is God and not an intermediary who creates the world. In this respect, he quotes *The Shepherd of Hermas,* saying, "Who created and ordered all things, and who, when nothing existed, made the universe to be".[814] The reason for the corruption in the world was not its faulty or evil origin, as the Gnostics maintained, but the waywardness and disobedience of its original human inhabitants. So, in *On First Principles,* he writes, "If our argument there is to be admitted to be sound, what other cause can we imagine to account for the great diversity of this world except the variety and diversity of the motions and declensions of those who fell away from that original unity and harmony in which they were at first created by God".[815] Even as he expresses this truth, we can sense that the Hebrew account of creation presented in Genesis is filtered through the Platonic concepts which now come to be re-expressed powerfully in Alexandria by Plotinus, a contemporary who, like Origen, had attended the schools run by Ammonius Saccas.

Having marked out the territory of disagreement with the Gnostics in the areas of incarnation, free will and the goodness of creation, Origen's predisposition towards a Platonic dualism of soul and body coloured his theology, fatally in the view of some, and gave a trajectory to his thought which many regarded as compromised.

Alongside the Gnostics and the Catholic Christian community led by Bishop Demetrius of Alexandria (soon to become Orthodox, following the advent of the Council of Nicaea) and the strong Jewish community in Alexandria, were the neo-Platonist schools. We know from Porphyry, Plotinus's biographer, that Origen attended, or knew of, Ammonius Saccas's schools in Alexandria. It was from Saccas that Origen received his superb education in philosophy. Indeed, Plotinus held Origen in high esteem; we are told by Porphyry that he knew of three (now lost) treatises on philosophy written by Origen.[816]

Origen was therefore trained in the philosophic schools and would use this training as an adjunct to a way of life recognisable as that of a philosopher in pursuit of truth, as well as an exegete in pursuit of revelation through the scriptures. He would be well versed in Middle Platonism—knowing Plato, Aristotle and the Stoic philosophers. None of these thinkers questioned the reality of God (or the *One* for a Platonic philosopher). What philosophy gave Origen was a way of understanding and using philosophic terminology and a way of withdrawal and contemplation common in the classical world and later embraced by Augustine, Basil and all the Cappadocian Fathers.

Philosophy led to an ascetic lifestyle and withdrawal to desert places, but it also planted in Origen's mind and heart the indelible notion of the supremacy of the soul and the spirit over the material. Origen found this as much in Platonism as he did in scripture; after all, the combining of the mud of the earth with the breath of God was the origin of human life. In the same way, in biblical interpretation, he constantly looked for *inner spiritual meaning* in outward literal, historical or philological expression. It was this dualism borne out of his philosophical approach that became the very air that he breathed and which powerfully informed both his general theology and his exegetical work. It would lead him to a doctrine of the final reconciliation of all rational creatures to God through a process of purging. There would be ultimate harmony in the end: a doctrine, with all its controversial implications, to which we must return. We will see the outworking of this doctrine as we survey his work both in Alexandria and then later in Caesarea.

The final piece of the jigsaw in terms of Origen's formation in Alexandria was his learning of Hebrew and his engagement with the Old Testament, which produced his great philological work known as the *Hexapla*. Origen clearly had a Hebrew teacher to whom he refers in *On First Principles* in the section on the Holy Spirit.[817] Armed with his knowledge of Hebrew, his exposure to the Platonic schools, and his position as the principal of the Catechumenate School in the city, he embarked on a period of teaching and writing in Alexandria which was to have a profound effect on the church and on the expression of the Christian faith, particularly in the East.

Origen's Alexandrian Writings

In approaching Origen's work, we must remember that much of his writing was destroyed in the sixth century over a controversy which came to a head in the fifth century. The controversy was partly due to his condemnation by the heresy-hunter Epiphanius of Salamis, but more generally it was because of the Platonic twist to his teaching, especially in relation to the pre-existent, immortal and eternal nature of the soul: a position which was unacceptable to the church. Thus, we have only a small proportion of his vast output available to us and then often only those writings which were more widely disseminated and translated into Latin by Rufinus in particular, or enclosed in other Greek works. One such work, the *Philocalia*, was edited and produced by Basil of Caesarea and Gregory Nazianzen, two of the Cappadocian Fathers or church leaders in Cappadocia. The first fourteen sections of the *Philocalia* are largely concerned with hermeneutics: what should we make of the text of scripture and how do we rightly wield the tools of exegesis? Origen's teaching on scripture and exegesis from Book IV of *On First Principles* is instructive in this regard and was reproduced by Basil and Gregory.[818] The following six sections of the *Philocalia* contain Origen's later work, *Contra Celsum*, which demonstrates how Christians can defend their faith in the light of pagan criticism. The final seven sections of *Philocalia* take up the theme of human freedom, another theme dear to Origen's heart, as he demonstrates in his argument on free will in Book III.1 of *On First Principles*.[819]

In the eastern part of the Empire, from the sixth century onwards, and following the anathematization of his teaching at the Second Council of Constantinople in AD 553, Origen's writings were for the most part destroyed because of Justinian's Imperial Edict. The reason for this treatment we will explore when we come to consider Origen's legacy, but as we turn to his Alexandrian writings, only a small proportion remain intact because of this controversy, and those that do survive are largely due to the Latin translations of Rufinus and the *Philocalia*.

The Bible from which Origen worked was still being formed in AD 220. The Old Testament had been standardised in the Septuagint translation and was widely accepted in the church as scripture, especially after the dispute with Marcion, who refused to believe that the God of the Old Testament was the God and Father of Jesus Christ. The works of Irenaeus and Tertullian had helped to unify the revelation of the one true God in the Old and New Testaments. Origen was to take the study of the Bible to a new level and his early years in Alexandria, before his move to Caesarea, demonstrated this.

The principal documents that have come down to us from this period are, firstly, his work of biblical textual analysis already mentioned, called the *Hexapla,* of which only small fragments remain. Then there are fragments of his work on Psalms 1–25, available because of their inclusion in the *Philocalia*, which provide an example of his hermeneutical principles in the early AD 220s.[820] Origen's commentary on Lamentations, which is a vivid example of his symbolic or spiritual interpretation of the Bible, written between AD 222 and AD 225, also survived.[821] His commentary on Genesis, of which we have only Book III, was also taken from the *Philocalia* and written around AD 229.[822] His most important work, which we would now call systematic theology, was *On First Principles* or *Peri Archon,* and was written around AD 230. Finally, his *Commentary on John,* which spans his later years in Alexandria and his years in Caesarea, has also come down to us. In AD 232, in the midst of all this industry, Origen moved to Caesarea, partly because of a dispute with his bishop.

As already noted, the production of the *Hexapla* was a prodigious task, one which Origen completed early on in his teaching career in Alexandria, and after he had mastered Hebrew. It was a word for word comparison of the Septuagint, the Greek translation of the Hebrew Bible, and three more or less literal translations of the Hebrew by Jewish scholars in Alexandria: Aquila, Symmachus and Theodotion. Alongside these three translations, Origen placed the Hebrew text, a Greek transliteration of the Hebrew, and the Septuagint. This six-column study was a huge reference work,[823] although only fragments remain. The motivation behind this great work of lexicography was establishing the true text of the Old Testament, which had now become an integral part of the Christian (rather than just the Jewish) Bible. In Alexandria and elsewhere, the Jewish community would not accept the veracity of the Septuagint. Furthermore, Christians suspected Jews of corrupting their own scriptures in order to refute

Christian apologetic arguments based on shared scriptures.[824] Origen, it seems, was preparing a recension of the Greek Old Testament:

> He used asterisks and obeli—critical signs developed by the Alexandrian grammarians—to mark those places where the Septuagint contained material absent from the Hebrew, and where Origen had supplied material lacking in the church's Bible from the Greek version of Theodotion, one of the recentiores.[825]

This detail may be baffling to us, but it shows the lengths to which Origen went as a biblical linguist.

The *Hexapla* was enormous, running into thousands of pages. The cost of its production would have been at least 155,000 denarii—two years' salary for a successful grammarian.[826] There is debate over whether the *Hexapla* was ever copied, such would have been the expense of doing so, with the French scholar Nautin arguing it wasn't, and others believing that some Old Testament books were reproduced at the very least, even if the entire work was not.[827] In any event, it resided in the library of Caesarea 150 years later, where it was consulted by Jerome as part of his own work of biblical scholarship; despite his recourse to this great work, Jerome, typically, had scarcely a good word to say of Origen.

Although only fragments remain because of the destruction of his work in the sixth century, especially in the East, we know Origen prepared, in addition to this prodigious effort of scholarship, commentaries on Genesis, Lamentations and Psalms 1–25. He also wrote on John's Gospel while in Alexandria, completing this commentary, as well as many others, when living in Caesarea.

The fragment on Genesis was composed around AD 229, shortly before his great work *Peri Archon* or *On First Principles*. The fragment we have was taken from the third of 14 books commenting on the first four chapters of Genesis. It was included in the *Philocalia* as an example of people's free will in choosing their destiny. In any age the Bible is studied in relation to the pressing issues of the day. Today, far more is written on sexuality and identity in relation to the Bible because these are the pressing issues in the contemporary church in the West. For Origen, one pressing issue the church faced, among others, was the influence of astrology, auguries or divination. Any reading of the lives of the Emperors invariably reveals speculation about the underlying influence of the gods. Auguries were recounted as if determinative of the Emperors' lives and it is about this mindset, so prevalent in the ancient world, that Origen writes, drawing insight from Genesis to do so.

Origen comments firstly on Genesis 1:14: "Let there be lights in the expanse of the sky to separate the day from the night, and let them serve as signs to mark seasons and days and years, and let them be lights in the expanse of the sky to give light on the earth" (NIV). While in our culture these verses would probably lead to a discussion about cosmology and the origins of the universe, in Origen's time they led to a discussion about free will and the limits of astrology. In general, Origen's argument is that if the stars determine our character, then moral responsibility is no longer within our power, and we can neither be praised for doing well nor blamed for doing badly.[828] If our destiny is determined by the conjunction of the stars, this can lead to a complete abandonment of responsibility. Origen argued, "Why also should we speak of what happens among men and of their sinful actions, multitudinous as they may be, when whoever holds such noble opinions has cleared them of all charges by ascribing to God responsibility for everything that is done maliciously and reprehensibly?"[829]

Origen goes on to consider whether prophecy likewise restricts free will, since if something is foreknown, does that mean that it is pre-destined? Do those included in a prophecy have their free will impaired or restricted? Origen's answer, considering the case of Judas, is that it is possible to foreknow something without pre-destining it: "One would comprehend that one who foreknows is not necessarily the cause of the things foreknown, and more than the texts that receive the imprints of the words of foreknowledge from him who foreknows".[830] Widening the discussion, Origen makes a number of further points: the Greek philosophers generally thought that foreknowledge meant pre-determination, something with which Origen does not agree, although Plotinus did argue for the freedom of the will.[831] Origen argues that the stars are not the *agents* of all that happens, but the *signs*; we cannot have a precise knowledge concerning these things, but the meaning of them is set forth in higher spiritual powers (e.g., angelic powers) who can interpret them rightly, and this was the purpose of the stars being signs. In fact, God "blinds us to the future", since knowledge of his plans "would release us from the struggle against evil" and would diminish our virtue by curtailing our ability to choose and struggle: "For to become a truly good person, beyond the measure of virtue we already have, requires a vigorous and sustained effort".[832] Origen summarises this debate by saying, "God's knowing what each person will do does not impair what is within our power. In the same way the signs which God has ordered simply as indications do not restrain what is within our power".[833] Origen does not deny the stars as signs, but he does deny their pre-determining capacities and that they are a restriction of our will.

Book III of Origen's commentary on Genesis was part of 14 books covering the creation narratives. These reflect the ancient world's fascination with origins and the advent of evil. Not only was this question of the origin of good and evil a vital aspect of pagan mythology, but it was also a powerful theme in Plato's writing and in the writing of Origen's contemporary, Plotinus. Origen's commentary on Genesis shows his proximity to Plotinus in maintaining the freedom of the human will, but his other Old Testament commentaries, which we have in fragmentary form, show different aspects of his methods of biblical interpretation.

Soon after his commentary on Genesis was completed in AD 229, Origen began his great work of systematising doctrine: *On First Principles* or *Peri Archon*. He may have felt the need to produce an overview of the Christian faith for his catechumenates before their baptism. The result, *On First Principles,* was the first handbook of Christian theology in the ancient world. Tertullian and Justin were essentially Apologists, while Irenaeus gave a wonderful recapitulation of Christian theology, namely, God in Christ making us once again fully human. Origen, however, gave the church the first handbook, which was systematic in scope. For many, it was fatally flawed by the incorporation of Plato's scheme of the immortality of the soul and the reconciliation of all things to God, i.e., the bedrock of universalism or the teaching that in the end—after purging— all will be saved. We shall return to Origen's teaching on creation, the Trinity and the consummation of all things later, but first we will look at his teaching on scripture and its interpretation as found in *On First Principles.*

The teaching on scripture and interpretation comes in Book IV of *On First Principles* (for the most part from Rufinus's Latin translation, which in some parts is suspect). Firstly, Origen suggests that the inspiration of scripture rests on the divine purpose of transforming the great mass of humanity. The very progress of the teaching of scripture throughout the world is an affirmation of its power and inspiration.[834] The second reason scripture is divinely inspired is the fulfilment of the prophecy it contains.[835] After the advent of Jesus, the true inspiration of the prophecies about him come to light and a trace of the divine presence is discerned as the hidden meaning of scripture wrapped in a humble style. Having established inspiration in both the Old and New Testament, Origen then gives his three-fold method of interpretation. First is a literal interpretation, which Origen calls the flesh or outward appearance of scripture. Second, a reader may progress further into the "soul" of scripture; and finally, he or she may discern the wisdom that God is revealing throughout scripture as a whole.[836] The method that Origen uses is to work through the literal meaning of scripture into its soul and spiritual meaning, that in so doing it may reveal the hidden wisdom of God, which is also the *logos,* to all.

Origen employs this method in his commentaries and in his preaching, stating his purpose in interpretation most vividly when he writes:

> The aim was not everyone who wished should have the mysteries laid before his feet to trample upon (Matt. 7.6), but that they should be for the man who had devoted himself to studies of this kind with the utmost purity and sobriety and through nights of watching, by which means perchance he might be able to trace out the deeply hidden meaning of the Spirit of God, concealed under the language of an ordinary narrative which points in a different direction and that might become a sharer of the Spirit's knowledge and a partaker of divine counsel.[837]

In his earlier recorded works in Alexandria, we can see Origen doing this both in his commentary on Psalms 1–25 and in his commentary on Lamentations. His commentary on the Psalms (1–25) was one of the earliest he produced. Written in the AD 220s, it was included in the

Philocalia by Basil the Great and Gregory Nazianzen to demonstrate Origen's biblical interpretation. What is clear in this fragment is that "the Wisdom of God has permeated the whole of scripture even to the individual letter".[838] Since for Origen the Wisdom of God was in essence the *Logos*, reading scripture was therefore *the way* of discovering Christ. Origen's commentary on Lamentations became part of a Byzantine anthology of scripture commentary (in *catenae*, meaning in chains) and so avoided destruction when Origen was anathematised in AD 553. Although there is a fair amount of philological and historical detail (in this case drawn from Josephus's description of the siege of Jerusalem in AD 70), the basic method of interpretation of Lamentations is spiritual. In other words, Origen looks for the inner spiritual or symbolic meaning of the text rather than its surface, literal meaning. The result is that in Origen's interpretation, Jerusalem in captivity, or under siege from the Babylonians, is like the soul of a Christian in captivity or under siege from demons. "The Gentile nations that loot the temple and even enter its holy of holies are a mob of vices that overcome the soul's governing-faculty (*hegemonikon*) and invade the sanctuary of reason (*logos*) where God can reside".[839]

Throughout his commentary on Lamentations, and despite the awful suffering of the population of Jerusalem, Origen maintains that God is acting mercifully, with no wrath or vindictiveness, in order to bring her back to himself. He writes, "Indeed the enemies also dared to perpetrate massacres in the Temple with God's permission. These very nations God everywhere prohibits from entering the congregation. For what else should we more properly consider to have been prohibited by God from entering the soul numbered in God's church than the works and intention of the flesh, since these are truly nations at enmity with God?"[840] "Like an enemy is well put," Origen goes on, "for God does not chastise out of enmity, but out of a desire to benefit either those who suffer or those who observe his chastisement".[841] Lamentations can therefore be read not so much as a lament arising from the historical suffering of the Jewish people, but as an illustration of God's love which wounds that it might heal, and as a metaphor of the soul's struggle with the flesh and demons which continually assault our souls.

On First Principles

Beyond his exegetical and linguistic work on the Old Testament text in the *Hexalpa*, in *On First Principles* Origen made the first attempt to write a systematic theology based on the barely formed Bible of Old and New Testaments. That this work was later anathematised and only existed, for the most part, in Rufinus's sometimes sanitised or misleading translation, was mostly because the objection to and anathematising of Origen's teaching centred on the *"end being like the beginning"*, by which he implied the reconciliation of all things. The difficulty with this particular teaching should not mask the brilliance of other parts of Origen's theology.

Origen flags his intention in the work with his opening sentence: "All who believe and are convinced that grace and truth came by Jesus Christ (John 1.17), and who know Christ to be the truth in accordance with his sayings, 'I am the truth' (John 14.6), derive the knowledge which calls men to lead a good and blessed life from no other source than the very words and teachings of Christ".[842] In his preface to *On First Principles,* Origen begins by saying his purpose is "to lay down a definite line and unmistakeable rule in regard to each of these [meaning members of the godhead]".[843] At the outset, Origen sets out to define "the nature of God and of the Lord Jesus Christ and the Holy Spirit and the nature of other created beings, the dominions and the holy powers".[844] In other words, his is the first comprehensive attempt at explaining the Godhead, creation and the nature of humanity. Tertullian was to follow Origen's lead shortly afterwards as both wrestled to explain the Trinity in the light of the Monarchian controversy.

An earlier visit to Rome at the height of the Monarchian controversy showed Origen the importance of defining the nature of the Trinity. The Monarchians, as we have seen, were concerned with the problem of how to recognise the Son as God, along with the Father, without falling into the error of believing in two gods. Origen's visit to Rome was around AD 215, when Zephyrinus was bishop there (*c.*AD 199–217). While there, Origen met the *Logos* theologian Hippolytus, heard the Monarchian views of Bishop Zephyrinus, and generally witnessed an uncertain and unconfident church, riven by factions and contrasting theologies about the Trinity.[845] As we know, all this was the prelude to the much greater controversy a century later. For his part, this immersion into expressing the relationship of Father and Son must have been the backdrop to Origen's own writing and reflection on the Trinity in *On First Principles*, and his commentary on John's Gospel, especially the Prologue. Origen begins to set this out in his preface to *First Principles*. "God", he writes, "is one, who created and set in order all things, and who, when nothing existed, caused the universe to be. He is God from the first creation and foundation of the world, the God of all righteous men".[846]

Christ was,

> Begotten of the Father before every created thing. And after he had ministered to the Father in the foundation of all things, "for all things were made through him", (John 1:13) in these last times he emptied himself and was made man, was made flesh, although he was God (cf. Hebrews 1:1; Philippians 2:7; John 1:14) and being made man, he still remained what he was, namely, God. He took to himself a body like our body, differing in this alone, that he was born of a virgin and of the Holy Spirit. And this Jesus Christ was born and suffered in truth and not merely in appearance, and truly died our common death. Moreover he truly rose from the dead, and after the resurrection companied with his disciples and was then taken up to heaven.[847]

Finally, of the Holy Spirit, Origen says that he "is united in honour and dignity with the Father and the Son", although he is less clear about whether he is begotten or unbegotten.[848]

Having introduced each member of the Trinity in the preface, Origen then proceeds in Book I to explain their existence, their being and their role. His opening description of the Father is polemical, for he says at the outset that the Father is not, as some say, corporeal. He is light and in his light (that is, in Christ's light) the Father's light will be seen.[849] God is Spirit rather than flesh (John 4.24). He has no material characteristics. He is incomprehensible and immeasurable.[850] In these assertions we see the beginnings of apophatic theology, which means describing God by saying what he is not. Therefore, our way of understanding him is by perception and reflection.[851] He is not a composite being of body and soul,[852] nor does reason dwell in a body.[853] So Origen asks the question, "Whence comes the power of memory, the contemplation of invisible things, yes, and the perception of incorporeal things reside in a body?"[854] For Origen, such faculties dwell in the soul, incorporated into the body. Likewise, God is spirit and we perceive and grasp him, in so far as we can, in the mind.[855]

The one who reveals the Father is the Son and in some way Origen anticipates the monophysite controversy[856] of the fifth century when he says, "For we must know this, that in Christ there is one nature, his deity, because he is the only begotten Son of the Father, and another human nature, which in very recent times he took upon him to fulfil the divine purpose".[857] Originally, the *Logos*, or the later-to-be-revealed Christ, existed as pure Wisdom, so "that wisdom must be believed to have begotten beyond the limits of any beginning that we can speak of or understand".[858] In other words, to contradict Arius's later saying that there was a time when the *Logos* did not exist, for Origen the pre-incarnate Christ existed as the wisdom of God, and since there was never a time in which God was not wise, there was never a time that the *Logos*, whose essence for Origen is wisdom, did not exist. Origen explains, "For Wisdom opens to all other beings, that is, to the whole creation, the meaning of mysteries and secrets which are contained within the wisdom of God, and so she is called the Word, because she is as it were an interpreter of the mind's secrets".[859] A little later, quoting Paul (Colossians 1:15) and Hebrews (Hebrews 1:3) in support of his argument, Origen cites the Wisdom of Solomon, for wisdom is the "breath of the power of God, and a pure effluence (that is emanation) of the glory of the Father. Nothing that is defiled can enter into her. For she is the brightness of the eternal light and an unspotted mirror of the working of God and an image of his goodness".[860]

Perhaps confusingly, Origen does go on to say that the existence of the *Logos* was an act of the Father's will,[861] which might have implied that there was a time before *that* decision that the *Logos* did not exist, so providing a window for Arius's doctrine that there was a time when the *Logos* was not and therefore the Son must be inferior to the Father because of not sharing the same substance or eternal nature. Origen wrote thus of the Son:

Whose birth from the Father is as it were an act of proceeding from the mind. And on this account my own opinion is that an act of the Father's will ought to be sufficient to ensure the existence of what he wills; for in willing he uses no other means than that which is produced by the deliberations of his will. It is in this way, then, that the existence of the Son also is begotten by him.[862]

There appears to be a tension in Origen's theology of the *Logos*. On the one hand the *Logos* is essentially wisdom, who like the rays from the sun is as eternal as the Father who is the source,[863] but on the other hand his existence is dependent on the decision of the Father's will, before which he is not begotten, thus implying that he is inferior. It is a tension that would be exploited in the Arian controversy and which requires further explanation to overcome it.

Next, Origen describes the person of the Holy Spirit.[864] He is the one who gives knowledge of the Father and Son through the inspiration of the scriptures:

We believe that there is no possible way of explaining and bringing to man's knowledge the higher and divine teaching about the Son of God except by means of those scriptures which were inspired by the Holy Spirit, namely the gospels and the writings of the apostles, to which we add, according to the declaration of Christ himself (cf Luke 24:25-27; John 5:39, 46), the law and the prophets.[865]

Origen is clear about the Spirit's divinity from Old Testament scriptures (Psalm 51:13; Daniel 4:6) and from the gospels and epistles (Matthew 3:16; John 20:22; Luke 1:35; 1 Corinthians 12:3; Acts 8:18). "From all of which", he says, "we learn that the person of the Holy Spirit is of great authority and dignity and saving baptism is not complete except when performed with the authority of the whole most excellent Trinity, that, by the naming of Father, Son, and Holy Spirit (Matthew 28:19); and the name of the Holy Spirit must be joined to that of the unbegotten God the Father and his only-begotten Son.[866]

In a simple but vital summary statement, Origen says, "For all knowledge of the Father, when the Son reveals him, is made known to us through the Holy Spirit".[867] Origen goes on to say that the Holy Spirit is to be found in those who are walking in the ways of Jesus Christ.[868] And again, with great clarity he says, "Thus therefore the working of the power of God the Father and God the Son is spread indiscriminately over all created beings, but a share in the Holy Spirit is possessed, we find, by the saints alone".[869] The Spirit sanctifies, but his greatest gift is to give knowledge and wisdom.[870] In a typical summary of the work of the Trinity in Christians, Origen says: "When therefore they obtain first of all their existence from God the Father, and secondly their rational nature from the Word, and thirdly their holiness from the Holy Spirit, they become capable of receiving Christ afresh in his character of the righteousness of God".[871]

If, along with Tertullian in the West, Origen made a major contribution to the development of the doctrine of the Trinity, he also made other significant contributions which were more controversial, about the nature of creation, the destiny of the soul, the operation of free will and the last things. We will now try and follow what Origen had to say about these.

For Origen, the cosmos may be a difficult place, but it is fundamentally beneficent.[872] He envisages a two-stage creation and, in Book III of *On First Principles,* writes: "God did not begin to work for the first time when he made this visible world, but that just as after the dissolution of this world there will be another one, so also we believe that there were others before this one existed".[873] A further twist in Origen's theology of creation was that an invisible, soul-only world preceded a corporeal one, the solid corporeal and visible world being created on account of "the excessive spiritual defects" which souls had suffered in the first pre-corporeal world.[874]

In other words, everything was originally in unity with God, but to some extent all fell, except for the human soul of the incarnate Christ. Some, like angels, did not fall as far, so did not have as far to return to a complete unity with the Godhead. Following this spiritual creation, God made a material universe in which he would bring fallen rational spirits back to himself. This material world then became a vale of tears and of soul-making; a place of struggle with the malevolent forces or adverse powers seeking to entrap them. But, in God's world, even the opposition of these malevolent powers is used to help the return of these souls. Here (on earth) God provides humans an opportunity for moral and intellectual purification that will ultimately restore them to unity with him, but only through obedience to Christ. Humanity was hurtling towards destruction and only the intervention of the Creator, sending "the only-begotten Son of God, who was the word and wisdom of the Father, when he lived with the Father in that glory which he had before the world was (cf. John 17:5), emptied himself, and taking the form of the servant became obedient unto death (cf. Philippians 2:7–8) in order to teach them obedience who in no other way could obtain salvation".[875] Response to this call to obedience depended on the operation of free will.

The exercise of free will is an important, indeed vital, part of Origen's theology, and he is at pains to defend both its existence and its free exercise with human responsibility. Not for him the Augustinian or Lutheran position of the "bondage or incapacity of the will", dependent for its operation on the grace of God. Rather, for Origen, it was an implicit moral choice to obey the revelation of God in Christ through the testimony of scripture. He could therefore be called an early Pelagian. Much of Book III of *On First Principles* is a discussion of free will, translated by Rufinus with some obvious interpolations and existing alongside a fragmentary Greek text of Basil's *Philocalia*, which had avoided destruction in the purge of his works.

Origen believed that free will is part of our human make-up. If he had known the word "genetics", he would have said this freedom of will was genetically driven. What Origen was especially reacting to was that human decision or external forces or agents drove human destiny. Thus he writes:

> To throw the blame for what happens to us on external things and to free ourselves from censure, declaring that we are like sticks and stones, which are dragged along by agents that move them from without, is neither true nor reasonable, but is the argument of a man who desires to contradict the idea of free will, for if we were to ask such a one what free will was, he would

say it consisted in this, that when I propose to do certain things
no external cause arose which incited me to do the opposite.[876]

Origen then proceeds, as so often with his work, to survey scripture in
order to prove his point, saying "there are in the scriptures ten thousand
passages which with the utmost clearness prove the existence of free
will."[877] He looks at the classic case of God's interaction with human will
in scripture of God hardening Pharaoh's heart so he would not release
the Israelites from Egypt until the final plague and killing of the first born
(Exodus 10:27). Here, Origen maintains that God's involvement did not
negate free will, for the possibility of obedience always remained open
to Pharaoh.[878] In any case, foreknowledge for Origen was never the same
as pre-determination.

Origen's teaching on free will was a response to the classical world's
commitment to the idea of fate, to the idea of different agencies
extraneously controlling human lives, to a myriad of superstitions
about the influence of stars and events in nature upon human beings.
Origen wanted to restore the dignity and responsibility of humanity by
saying man was *himself* responsible and free. That this teaching crossed
a border, later seen as Pelagianism, in which man *could* respond to God
out of volitional obedience rather than the grace of God alone, added
to suspicions about Origen in the fifth century, some 150 years after
his death. The expression of theology is often contextual however, and
Origen, as Irenaeus before him, was establishing the dignity and freedom
of humanity over the classical or Gnostic teaching of predetermination.
Irenaeus showed that the purpose of creation and redemption was to
demonstrate the glory of God in a human being fully alive. But what
was far more inflammatory for the likes of Epiphanius of Salamis, the
notorious heresy hunter of the late fourth century, was Origen's teaching
on the *last things,* the traditional expression for the theology of Christ's
return, judgement, heaven and hell.

As we have seen, Origen believed in the priority of the soul and a
non-corporeal creation in a previous creation in which perfect souls lived
in unity with God. Origen's main principle of interpretation was that,

> The end is always like the beginning; as therefore there is one end
> of all things, so we must understand that there is one beginning
> of all things, and there is one end of many things, so from one
> beginning arise many differences and varieties, which in their
> return are restored, through God's goodness, through their
> subjection to Christ and their unity with the Holy Spirit, to one
> end, which is like the beginning.[879]

For Origen, there would be an end of history marked by judgement, a
period of punishment and restoration, but one which, however long,
would lead in the end to unity with the Godhead. Whether the minions
of the Devil would be likewise reconciled after punishment and discipline
in the new age, the reader, Origen says, must judge.[880] There would be a
new heaven and a new earth and our corporeal existence would change
to a body more akin to ether, made up of heavenly purity and clearness.[881]
In other words, a spiritual body (see 1 Corinthians 2:9) will follow our
material bodies.[882] This teaching is invariably based on Paul's teaching
that God will be "all in all" (1 Corinthians 15:28). Everything will be
subject to him. All will bow the knee to Christ (Philippians 2:9–11).
However, the absence of eternal punishment for the Devil and all his
angels, the restoration of erring humans after a time of eradication or
purgatory and the possibility that even the Devil might be reconciled
were all causes, more or less, for Origen's later condemnation.

By AD 234, Origen was no longer on good terms with Demetrius,
Bishop of Alexandria, possibly because his teaching, either its content
or its brilliance, had made Demetrius jealous, or because Origen had
already been wooed by another bishop with the promise of ordination as
presbyter in Caesarea. For whatever reason, Origen sailed to Caesarea, in
Palestine, where he was welcomed by Bishop Theoctistus and ordained
presbyter. A new and very productive ministry was to open up until his
death in AD 249.

Caesarea

In some ways, Origen appeared more at home in Caesarea, the Roman city constructed by Herod the Great in honour of Augustus, than he had in Alexandria—at least latterly. Herod built Caesarea in the period between 22–10 BC, a seaside city of white stone that gleamed in the Mediterranean sun.[883] Like Carthage, it was built around a great harbour as one of the greatest building projects of Herod's career. It was a pagan city with a central temple for the worship of Caesar and many other temples besides. Alongside this strong pagan presence was a large Jewish community in whose country the city lay. A community of some 25,000 Jews resided there in the first century AD until the massacre of 20,000 during the Jewish rebellion of AD 66.[884] Despite this pogrom, the Jewish community grew in the second century and, by the end of it, well-known Rabbinic schools rivalled those in Tiberias and Sepphoris.[885] Under Rabbi Bar Qappara, a student of the great Rabbi Judah at Sepphoris, the school at Caesarea "became the most prominent of all the rabbinic centres in Palestine".[886] The great Rabbi Hishaya then established a school in Caesarea from AD 230 until his death in AD 250. For most of this time, Origen was himself in Caesarea and would no doubt have debated with the Jews, maybe even with Hishaya himself, although there is no historical evidence for this.[887] The discussions would have been in Greek, although it is clear that Origen had begun to learn Hebrew in Alexandria.

Origen may have felt at home in Caesarea for a number of reasons. He had visited the city once before in AD 215, when Emperor Caracalla mercilessly repressed a revolt in Alexandria, massacring many of her citizens. He had been warmly received then by the Bishop of Jerusalem, Alexander, and by Theoctistus, Bishop of Caesarea. He was ordained presbyter, either immediately after his arrival in AD 234, or possibly on a previous visit mentioned by Eusebius, and swiftly given a prominent teaching role in the diocese.

Philip, the evangelist and deacon (Acts 6:50), founded the church in Caesarea. It was here too that the centurion Cornelius, together with his household, became the first Gentile Christians and received the Holy Spirit (Acts 10:1–48). Philip lived there with his four unmarried, prophesying daughters (Acts 21:8–9) whom Paul visited on his way to

Jerusalem prior to being arrested. Paul was later imprisoned and tried in Caesarea, first by the provincial governor Felix, and two years later by his successor Festus (Acts 24:27). This background gave the church in Caesarea a primitive, historic and authentic tradition upon which it consciously drew. The church also appears to have had close links with the church in Jerusalem. After the grave disruption of the Jewish community during the Jewish Rebellion in Caesarea, in which Christians may well have been included as part of the Jewish community, some normality returned by the mid-second century. By AD 190, a council was held at Caesarea to decide when the passion of Christ and Easter should be celebrated, and this was recorded by Eusebius. Many Asian bishops thought that the fourteenth day of the lunar month Nisan should be the beginning of the Paschal festival, regardless of which day of the week it fell.[888] But the bishops of Jerusalem, Caesarea, Tyre, and Ptolemias appear to have acted in concert, siding with Rome, Gaul, and Pontus against the Asian and Phrygian churches, and argued that the crucifixion should always be celebrated on the Friday before Easter, and Easter should always be celebrated on a Sunday.

Origen found himself with warm support from the local bishops, who were well connected to the Jewish community in a city with obvious influence in the imperial Roman world and with a passion for education, as demonstrated by its great library. For the next 20 years, Origen would make his mark there: teaching and preaching regularly in the cathedral; working exegetically and sequentially through biblical books; giving us one of the earliest examples of expository preaching; writing important biblical commentaries on Matthew's Gospel, the Minor Prophets, the Song of Songs and many others, which were to become seminal in biblical studies; completing his *Hexapla,* which was eventually deposited in the library in the city; writing significant and influential pastoral works on prayer and martyrdom; producing his great apologetic work *Contra Celsum*; and founding a school that would form many future church leaders, including Gregory Thaumaturgus, who in turn inspired the mission of the church in Cappadocia and the Cappadocian Fathers. It was an astonishing legacy, and one we must explore further.

Like Hippolytus of Rome before him, and Chrysostom and Augustine after him, Origen began an extensive preaching ministry in Caesarea.

In his book, *Origen*, Pierre Nautin argues that the Caesarean church heard the whole Bible preached in a three-year lectionary cycle.[889] This would have included a daily morning, non-Eucharistic assembly from Monday to Saturday in which an Old Testament passage was read and a homily delivered. Both believers and catechumens attended these services. In addition, on Sunday, Wednesday and Friday evenings, there were Eucharistic services for believers only. Nautin argued that Origen began with the Psalms and the Wisdom literature, proceeded with the Prophets and ended with the Torah and historical books. Jerome gives a list of Origen's homilies, most of which would have been taken down in shorthand, and some of which he translated into Latin.[890]

Origen's preaching was therefore extensive, comprehensive and exacting. Eric Junod notes that Origen placed great intellectual, moral and spiritual demands on the church and he may well have tired of his congregation's lack of serious responsiveness.[891] Origen singled out avarice and lust for particular attention in his teaching, perhaps not surprisingly, given it was a busy city port. A frequent analogy that he used was that, like the Israelites departing Egypt, Christians were on a journey and needed to remove all carnal habits as they journeyed to the Promised Land:

> For what good is it for us to have gone forth from Egypt and yet carry around the reproaches of Egypt? What good is it to travel through the wilderness, that is, what does it help us to have renounced this age in baptism, but to retain the former filth of our behaviour and the impurities of carnal vices? Thus it is fitting, after the parting of the Red Sea, that is, after the grace of baptism, for the carnal vices of our old habits to be removed from us by means of Our Lord Jesus, so that we can be free from the Egyptian reproaches.[892]

It could have been the Apostle Paul speaking in one of his epistles. For Origen, biblical understanding should lead to moral change. His understanding of Paul centred on the fact that grace should lead to moral transformation.[893]

Origen's teaching was comprehensive and demanding. It was also extensive in range, and supported by commentaries. Much of it was lost in the interdict on Origen's work in Justinian's reign following his condemnation at the Second Council of Constantinople (the Fifth Ecumenical Council) in AD 553. Eusebius lists the commentaries written by Origen in Alexandria, including some not yet finished, e.g., the Gospel of John, Genesis, Psalms 1–25, Lamentations, Hebrews and the beginnings of a work on Matthew.[894] In Caesarea, this biblical work was greatly extended. Origen is thought to have preached 574 homilies, of which only 21 have survived in Greek, and no more than 90 in Latin. He was known to have preached a lengthy series on Luke, of which a few have survived.[895] However, the texts that did survive are sermons translated by Jerome into Latin and commentaries published by Rufinus, also in Latin. A small number of fragments, particularly from the Song of Songs, survived in Greek and were found in the *catena* (chain) commentaries of Procopius of Gaza.[896]

Of the many commentaries we know Origen completed in Caesarea— on Matthew, Romans, Ezekiel and the Minor Prophets—we will consider the commentary on the Song of Songs as a fine example of his work. According to Eusebius, the first five books of the commentary were begun in Athens during a visit in AD 229 to help the church there combat Gnosticism.[897] The work was completed in Caesarea. Once again, due to the purge of his works, we have only a fragment left of the commentary and a few of the related homilies Origen preached. Rufinus has given us, through his free Latin translation, the first four books of the commentary, which take us midway through chapter two of the Song. What we have in these four books, together with Jerome's translation of some of Origen's homilies on the Song, is a clear indication of Origen's love of the mystical meaning and truth of the book. In a preface to Pope Damasus's translation of Origen's homilies on the Song of Songs, Jerome wrote that Origen had surpassed himself. He had blazed a trail that was not to be extinguished in the early church. Athanasius, Gregory of Nyssa, Theodore of Mopsuestia, Theodoret of Cyrus and Maximus the Confessor all wrote commentaries on the Song of Songs with varying degrees of success.

For an interpreter like Origen, who looked almost intuitively and instinctively for the hidden meaning in the historical sweep of the Old

Testament, and in its rich and varied allegories, the Song of Songs—with its intimate language, passion and deeply personal perspective—was a golden repository of spiritual meaning about covenant love between the bridegroom *Logos* and the enamoured soul or bride. Origen would have known that the Jewish community in Caesarea used the Song of Songs in the celebration of Passover. But now, this testimony of personal love between Yahweh and Israel was added to the grandeur of the salvific acts of liberation recorded in Exodus. In other words, here was the intimate purpose of God behind the great acts of salvation and judgement enacted in Exodus made clear.

For Origen, all this was now to be transposed into the language of love, not only for Israel, but more so for the church and the individual soul. For Origen, the role of scripture itself was supremely demonstrated in the Song of Songs. For if, as Origen supposed, there are "hidden relations between the seen and the unseen, between earth and heaven, flesh and soul, body and spirit, and, if the world takes its origin from their uniting into one, then Sacred Scripture too has a visible and an invisible element. In the letter, visible to all, the Song has a body; in the hidden meaning in it, the Song has a soul".[898]

What Origen found in the Song of Songs was the culmination of God's love for the church and the individual soul. It forms the climax of seven songs in the Old Testament, from the Song of Moses at the deliverance of Israel to this one.[899] "Through his grace, Christ leads the church on and on, from a knowledge of self to the struggle against sin, to practices of asceticism, to the mystical ascent, until at last she is admitted to the *spiritalis amplexus* of mystical union with the *logos*".[900] Of this progress Origen says in the prologue, "The soul is moved by heavenly love and fairness of the Word of God, it falls deeply in love with his loveliness and receives from the Word himself a certain dart and wound of love".[901]

Here was the benchmark for all subsequent interpretation of the Song of Songs, especially that by Gregory of Nyssa. It was the culmination also of the Wisdom literature of Solomon, corresponding, as Origen says, to the Greek model of education. Just as Greek education revolved around the branches of learning of ethics, physics and enoptics (contemplation of the divine), Solomon arranged Proverbs, Ecclesiastes and the Song of Songs in a corresponding order of themes. Proverbs corresponds to ethics. Ecclesiastes corresponds to physics—deductions from the natural order—and the Song of Songs corresponds to the love of things both divine and heavenly. When followed together, these produce a mature and well-equipped disciple. This was both Solomon and Origen's path of development for the individual soul. Origen puts it thus:

> When the soul has completed these studies, by means of which it is cleansed in all its actions and habits and is led to discriminate between natural things, it is competent to proceed to dogmatic and mystical matters, and in this way advances to the contemplation of the Godhead with put spiritual love". [902]

The Song of Songs is therefore the culmination of the soul's development. It is the kiss of God upon the soul.[903] It is the consummation of love between the *Logos* and the beloved, when the soul is brought into the king's rich chamber, much as the Apostle Paul was taken into paradise.[904] It is the life-giving gift of love from the loving *Logos* to the Beloved. Considering this exposition of the Song of Songs in his commentary, no wonder Origen set a benchmark for the use of the book by later Church Fathers; although we only have a fragment (three books, of the entire ten) it is a tell-tale piece of deep understanding and appreciation of this most *enoptic* book. It is also not surprising, given the quality of Origen's devotional writing, that one of his greatest works is a small treatise on prayer.

Origen on Prayer

Origen wrote a number of pastoral works distinct from his commentaries, apologetic and dogmatic works such as *On First Principles* and *Dialogue with Heracelides*. (In the latter Origen defends the divinity of Christ, his pre-existent life and his full humanity after the incarnation and gives us his dictum, "The whole man would not have been saved unless he had assumed the whole man".)[905]

His more pastoral works were entitled *On the Passover, An Exhortation to Martyrdom* and *On Prayer*. This last work was in response to a request by a lady called Tatiana. Origen wrote *An Exhortation to Martyrdom* for his patron, Ambrose, who was facing arrest. With great nobility, Origen said, "If we wish to save our soul, so that we may receive it back as better than a soul, let us lose it to martyrdom. For if we lose it for Christ's sake, throwing it to him in dying for him, we purchase for it true salvation".[906] The short treatise on prayer was a companion volume to the *Exhortation to Martyrdom*.

The work *On Prayer* is undoubtedly a gem of early Christian literature. It begins with a survey of prayer in the Old Testament, and many examples of the efficacy of prayer from the life of Moses, also making the point that prayer was often accompanied with a vow—as when Hannah prayed for a son at the shrine in Shiloh and vowed to commit him to God as a lifelong servant. The treatise continues philosophically by facing the difficulty of *how* prayer can make a difference when God knows and determines the future anyway. Origen's answer to this conundrum is that:

> He has due regard to each movement of our free wills, prearranged what also is at once to occur in his providence and to take place according to the train of future events ... [but] He has on that account been careful to make due arrangements for each one and it is reasonable to believe that He also has precomprehended what a particular man is to pray in that faith, what his disposition, and what his desire.[907]

In other words, in the ordering of his will, God takes into account our prayers, together with his purpose, weaving them together in what becomes his providence. Using a vivid analogy, Origen says:

> Just as apart from woman and apart from the recourse to the function requisite for procreation, man cannot procreate, so one may not obtain certain things without prayer in a certain manner, with a certain disposition, with certain faith, after a certain antecedent mode of life.[908]

For Origen, prayer is a continuum of the believer's life. "He prays 'without ceasing' who combines prayer with right actions, and becoming actions with prayer. For the saying, 'pray without ceasing' can only be accepted by us as a possibility *if we may speak of the whole life of a saint as one great continuous prayer*".[909] Prayer as a discipline should be done three times a day, as Daniel did; in the morning as the Psalmist prayed; at the sixth hour as Peter prayed at Joppa; and in the evening. Further prayer may be offered at midnight. Prayer, Origen says, should entail four aspects: requests, prayers, intercessions and thanksgiving.[910] Prayer must be generous in scope, "Ask for great things and the little shall be added unto you: and ask for the heavenly things and the earth shall be added unto you".[911] For Origen, the great things are the gifts of God's grace and the shadow of these is the material blessings they may engender.[912] The former is the great thing, the material the little one. For Origen, the greatest gift of prayer is the effect it has on us, transforming us in the process.

Finally, Origen gives an exposition of the Lord's Prayer. We are to eschew the babbling of many words, play-acting in prayer like the hypocrites. We are to pray with confidence as adopted children.[913] Origen is helpful on "daily bread", translating it as "needful bread" or the food that abides unto eternal life. The word for *needful* in Greek, Origen points out, is *epiousion,* which is a compound of the word meaning essence. So this bread is essential and of substance. It is the Word himself. It is what we need. It corresponds to our inner rational and spiritual nature. It is wisdom. And as Abraham fed the angels at Mamre with the bread made from fine flour, so we too may impart "spiritual and rational nourishment not only to men but also to divine powers", meaning the angels.[914] The other meaning or allusion in *epiousion* is *epienai,* meaning to go on, so this bread is also sustenance for the coming age. It thus has eschatological significance. It is bread given today, but for tomorrow. On forgiveness, or forgiving our debts, Origen firstly focuses on what these debts might be. He says we have debts in the sense of obligations: to a widow to care for her, to a bishop to obey him, to our husband or wife, if married, not to deprive them, to our own personal angel who cares for us, to be grateful to the Holy Spirit that we bear his fruits.[915] He then goes on to say that we are to forgive those who have offended us, on condition of their penitence.

Origen writes a helpful section on the last petition in the Lord's Prayer, which is, "Deliver us from temptation". He begins by saying that all who seek to follow the Lord will face trials and difficulties in their lives. The Psalmist says so, and the Apostle Paul amply demonstrates this in his own life of suffering—for it is through many afflictions that we must enter the Kingdom of God (see Acts 14:22). The Lord's Prayer cannot therefore suppose that we will avoid such trials or that the Lord will prevent them, rather "it is when a man succumbs in the moment of tempting that he enters into temptation, being held in its nets".[916] He goes on, "We ought therefore to pray, not that we be not tempted—that is impossible—but that we be not encompassed by temptation"[917] and the reason for not being encompassed by temptation is that "we make a manful stand against contingencies and are victorious"[918], exercising our free will and receiving strength through prayer.

Finally, Origen gives practical suggestions for praying: to lift our hands when praying, to stand unless prevented by infirmity of foot disease, for "standing is preferred", to pause before praying and empty the mind of distraction, to kneel if confessing sins, to look for the most solemn spot in the house to pray in, to pray looking east for that is "the dawn of the true light".[919] He recapitulates the progress of prayer: first ascribe glory to God, he says, then proceed to thanksgiving, then confession, then ask for great and heavenly things for one's nearest and dearest, and lastly, give glory to God through the Holy Spirit, as in Psalm 103.

In conclusion, in a moving and touching way, Origen addresses both Ambrose and Tatiana and ends with humility:

> I have struggled through my treatment of the subject of prayer and of the prayer in the Gospels together with its preface in Matthew. But if you press on to the things in front and forget those behind and pray for me in my undertaking, I do not despair of being enabled to receive from God the Giver a fuller and more divine capacity for all these matters, and with it to discuss the same subject again in a nobler, loftier, and a clearer way. Meanwhile, however, you will peruse this with indulgence.

If it is true to say that what we are in prayer before God is truly what we are, then Origen was a true shepherd of his flock and a model of pastoral care. His pastoral writings reveal his genuine care.

Origen's final genre of writing or teaching, alongside his commentaries and homilies, his dogmatic writings—*On First Principles* (*Peri Archon*)—and his pastoral papers for patrons or followers, was his great apologetic work *Contra Celsum*, in which he demonstrated the full panoply of his learning. As a piece of apologetic writing it is the Greek equivalent of Augustine's *City of God. Contra Celsum* is focussed on the writing of a man called Celsus, who wrote an indictment of Christianity in a book suggestively titled *True Doctrine*. Origen was invited to reply to this critique of Christians and the church. While *City of God* presents the weaknesses, failures and fantasies of the pagan world as typified by Rome, against the majesty, permanence and truth of the City of God, Origen's work is an answer to a single sceptic who represents the views of many.[920]

Contra Celsum, like *City of God* some 165 years later, is the culmination of the whole apologetic movement.[921] Here Origen is indebted to Clement, Justin, Tatian, Theophilus and Athenagoras. Their contention was that Moses preceded the Greek philosophical schools and was the true source of all wisdom. The Apologists joined forces with the critique led by the Academy and its second-century BC debater, Carneades, against the anthropomorphic goings-on of the gods as depicted by Homer, which were equivalent to a modern television soap opera. Like many apologists in the broadest sense—including Augustine—Origen combined Platonism of an eclectic kind with the insights of the Stoics on ethics and free will. The Stoics believed in a *pronoia* (the opposite of paranoia) or providence at work in the world, with which they believed man might be associated through an ethical use of free will. This intellectual stance, combined with his commitment to the Bible, became the bedrock of Origen's rebuttal of Celsus.

Eusebius tells us that Origen wrote *Contra Celsum* during the reign of Philip the Arab, when he was more than 60 years old and at the height of his powers and reputation.[922] He also tells us that Origen wrote the eight books in response to "the attack made on us by Celsus the Epicurean in his *True Doctrine*".[923] The identity of Celsus is uncertain, however. Almost certainly he had died some years before. He may have lived during Hadrian's reign or been a friend of Lucian of Samosata in the second half of the second century AD, but there is no certainty: the only things we know about Celsus are gleaned from the text itself.[924]

Origen's patron, Ambrose, sent him Celsus's work and asked for a response. In reply, Origen wrote his eight-book treatise, numbering some 500 pages. The manuscript tradition of *Contra Celsum*, as with other of Origen's works, is complex. There are some extracts from Books I–VIII in the *Philocalia*, the anthology of Origen's works put together by Basil and Gregory Nazianzen, and a further complete Greek manuscript, *Vat. Gr. 386*, from which all subsequent texts are derived, is held in the Vatican Library. From both of these, Paul Koetschau has compiled the standard text for the Berlin Academy corpus. We do not have Celsus's original work, *True Doctrine*, only those passages quoted in Origen's reply. These are enough to give us a flavour of the original; and since Origen's method was to quote *True Doctrine* a fair amount, a significant amount of it may thus be found.

Celsus's theology or philosophy was not untypical of second-century Roman thinking. He represented an ancient tradition that combined the notion of monotheism with a multiform polytheistic expression, similar to that of Hinduism today. The Platonic tradition from the fourth century BC thought of the popular gods as intermediaries between the supreme God and human society. They were classified as *daemons* and known as such both in Paul's writings (1 Corinthians 8:5) and in Augustine's *City of God*. Celsus was committed to this easy and accommodating view, and his main criticism of Christians was that they had abandoned it, or had never subscribed to it. For Celsus, to worship a local deity was simply to worship the local representative of the supreme Lord. Celsus had great respect for ancient customs and one of his main criticisms was that Christians did not respect tradition; indeed, Christianity was a *parvenu* religion to him, not worthy of respect. Again, for Celsus, Christians were taking others away from their old traditional customs, their traditional worship and their gods, and, if left unchecked, would corrupt the whole structure and stability of society. It was not an uncommon objection to true Christianity both then and since.

In other words, Christianity was too dangerous, too uncompromising, too exclusive of other ways and not willing to accommodate the ancient ways of religion. Instead it sought to overthrow them, like Paul in Ephesus bringing the worship of Diana to an end and threatening the economy and structure of the city (see Acts 19). For Celsus, Christianity was a closed and secret society with strange customs proclaiming a false *logos*, thereby requisitioning the Greek philosophical word *logos*, which implied reason, and applying it to Jesus. Celsus thus provided a brief or cause for persecution. Origen responded at length, like Clement of Alexandria before him, showing that Christ was the fulfilment of that which was promised in Plato, but not realised in pagan worship.

The point is clearly made by Origen in Book 7.42. In *Timaeus* (28 BC), Plato writes: "To find the Maker and Father of this universe is difficult, and after finding him, it is impossible to declare him to all men". Origen says that if Plato had truly found the divine *logos*, then he would "not have reverenced anything else and called it God and worshipped it", but we affirm, says Origen, "that human nature is not sufficient in any way to seek for God and to find him in his pure nature, unless it is helped by the God who is the object of the search".[925] Earlier in his work, Origen says that Christ did not come down to see what was going on, but that anyone "who has received the coming of the Word of God into his soul changes from bad to good, from licentiousness to self-control, from superstition to piety".[926]

Origen rebuts Celsus on many points. He describes the true resurrection as not the re-animation of a dead body, but a completely new spiritual body.[927] He defends the authenticity of Moses against Celsus's attack on him as a corrupt, wonder-working Egyptian who misled his people from their ancestral gods.[928] He decries the words Celsus puts into the mouth of an imagined Jew as being false, since he could not believe that Jesus was the expected Christ. Celsus said that Jesus employed magic arts and was not filled with the Spirit of God at baptism. The Jews' rejection of Christ as the divine *Logos* commended them to Celsus.[929] Furthermore, Christians themselves were barbarians, ignorant of philosophy and learning, suspicious of knowledge, who traded their beliefs in a secret society. Origen was happy to agree that Christians were often ill-educated, but demonstrated that he could not be included among them, as he had ample opportunity to show his learning in the writing of *Contra Celsum*.

What Celsus could not come to terms with, as Arius later would not be able to either, was the idea that Christ was truly God and as such involved in the creation of matter (which had the potential for evil), and yet that as God he would inhabit weak human flesh and be incarnate; that he would become immanent and not remain transcendent; that he would reveal himself to unlettered and ignorant people; and that he would transform our bodies at the resurrection. Origen answers point by point, remaining true to the incarnation at the heart of his theology. He is sure that God created the material world. He is sure that God in Christ took on human flesh. By doing so, Christ overcame evil and enabled human free will to become what humanity was intended to be.[930]

At much greater length and covering far more ground, Origen also answers Celsus's *True Logos or Justice* in his *Contra Celsum*. This is one aspect of his many-sided work in Caesarea: his preaching, his commentaries, his devotional works, this great apologetic masterpiece, and his guidance and teaching at the theological school of which he was the principal. Gregory Thaumaturgus tells us of this school in glowing terms. There Origen taught philosophy, theology, mathematics, homiletics and rhetoric. The school was to have lasting influence on Gregory the Miracle Worker, as he indicated in his panegyric to Origen,[931] in which he praised his style and knowledge, attributing to him his own understanding of philosophy and theology. Perhaps Gregory's greatest tribute to Origen was his statement that "he incited us much more to the practice of virtue, and stimulated us by the deeds he did more than by the doctrines he taught".[932] Gregory went on to have a profound influence in Cappadocia and Caesarea, where he became bishop, not least on the families of the Cappadocian Fathers themselves.

Origen himself was to face the Decian persecution of AD 249 onwards at the end of his days. Eusebius tells of Origen's arrest and the torture to which he was subjected:

> "As for Origen", he writes, "the terrible suffering that befell him
> in the persecution, and how they ended, when the evil demon
> (Decius) bent on his destruction, brought all the weapons in his
> armoury to bear and fought him with every device and expedient,
> attacking him with more determination than anyone he was

fighting at that time—the dreadful cruelties he endured for the word of Christ, chains and bodily torments, agony in iron and the darkness of his prison; how for days on end his legs were pulled four paces apart in the torturers' stocks—the courage with which he bore threats of fire and every torture devised by his enemies" and through it all "he left messages full of help for those in need of comfort".[933]

Although the persecution, like Decius's rule, was short-lived, Origen died within a year of his release, a physically broken, elderly man. He left a legacy which was both brilliant and controversial.

Origen's theology was both orthodox in the essentials and heterodox (arguably) at the margins of the faith; too influenced, many supposed, by Platonic dualism and by the allegorical interpretation of the Bible. For every positive affirmation of his theology there appeared a caveat. He was committed to the doctrines of the Trinity and incarnation. He believed in the divinity of Father, Son, and Holy Spirit, but later came to be accused of opening the door to Arianism through some of his vocabulary. Although he affirmed the supreme agency of the *Logos* in creation as expressed in John's Gospel (see John 1:3), he nonetheless had an unusual doctrine of creation, believing that the first creation was of souls and the second of a material universe to which these fallen souls became attached. Although no one was more committed to understanding the Bible and its philology than he, he opened the door to wholesale allegorisation of the Old Testament. Above all, his eschatology was found to be at fault, believing from his neo-Platonic background the immortality of the soul and the reconciliation of all things to God. Not only did he believe in the pre-existence of the soul before its material incarnation (albeit in a fallen state), but he believed that at the end of time everything would be restored to how it was in the beginning. In other words, there would be no everlasting punishment or final exclusion from the all-encompassing presence of God, but through a form of purgatory, lasting if necessary for aeons, everything would be reconciled and restored, even the Devil. It was these ideas, possibly still in gestation at the time of his death, as Heine makes out, which become a focus for his rejection by Epiphanius of Salamis, Augustine, and lastly and crucially, by the Emperor Justinian.

For Augustine, Origen's doctrines of creation and fall were too unfocussed; his emphasis on the power of the human will too strong; and his emphasis on the ability to act freely without the aid of prevenient grace too overstated. In the western tradition, Jerome also took against Origen, apart from his commentaries. Rufinus, his interpreter in the West, was accused of watering down Origen's theology in his translations and not representing him properly. The verdict of time on his extraordinary work and life was that he was brilliant yet flawed; but there is no doubting the influence he had in the centuries that followed, especially with regard to the interpretation of the Bible.

Part Three: Reform and Revolution

Diocletian: Reform and Persecution

The persecution of Christians under Decius was to last the whole three years of his reign and the period after his death was marked by almost perpetual instability. Over the next 30 years, until the arrival of Diocletian, there would be ten emperors. Most of their reigns would be, on average, three years. Some, like Aurelian, would manage five eventful years; many would be murdered within a single year (e.g., Aemilianus in AD 253, Tacitus in AD 275–276, and Florianus in AD 276). This 30-year period was thus one of acute vulnerability for the Empire, threatening its very existence. The period reached its nadir in AD 260 when Sapor, the Emperor of Persia, used the back of Valerian, the former Emperor of Rome, as a mounting block for his horse. Valerian had been defeated and captured by the Persian king in an ignominious defeat and would later die in captivity. Although his reign was one of the longer ones in the period, running from AD 253–260, it ended in ignominy and in the humiliation of the Roman Empire. His capture was symptomatic of a deep malaise in the Empire that was in need of careful and prolonged treatment. It was not until AD 284, and the advent of Diocletian as Emperor, that this treatment would finally begin, although Diocletian's rule was also a period of acute danger for the church.

Problems for the Empire almost always came from one of two directions: either from across the Rhine or the Danube in the north of the Empire, or from Persia in the south-east. When attacks from these places occurred at the same time, the resources of the Empire would be stretched to breaking point. Threats from the east came from the ambitious Empire of Persia, which was located on the great rivers of the Tigris and Euphrates, on the other side of a Roman buffer client state ruled from Palmyra in present-day Syria. In the north, the threat was from migrations of tribes from eastern Germany, the Caucasus, the Caspian Sea and even from as far away as China. Such tribes included the Alans, the Huns and the Sarmatians. From yet further north, other tribes invaded the Empire from Scandinavia and the north German plain that stretched up to Russia. These were the Ostrogoths, the Visigoths, the Franks, and the Saxons from the Elbe area. Together, these tribes, although in no way united in any strategy except that of coincidence, placed incessant pressure on the borders of this vast Empire, an area comparable, in present-day terms, to Europe, the Middle East and North Africa. The tribes that pressed the Empire's borders were not highly organised nations, but simply loose tribal associations in which all adult males bore arms and followed a dynamic leader. By the mid-third century, wars along the Rhine, the Danube and the Euphrates were almost unceasing.[934]

During the early part of the third century, the old Persian Empire, now under Sassanid leadership, grew fast. The Sassanids originally came from the Iranian plateau, claiming descent from the Achaemenid Empire of Darius and Xerxes. Ardashir, their leader, was crowned King of Kings in Cetisiphon, near modern Baghdad, in AD 226. Zoroastrianism was the official religion of the state, although it later mingled with Gnosticism to form a new religion led by Mani called Manichaeism, which became popular by the end of the third century.

The Empire under Ardashir expanded as far east as the Punjab and as far west as the Roman Empire. Ardashir's son Sapor I continued this rapid and aggressive expansion. He conquered Armenia and Georgia in his first Roman War, but this advance was eventually checked by Emperor Gordian III in AD 242. Gordian successfully captured the cities of Carrhae, where Crassus and his legions had met with disaster in 33 BC, and Nisibis on the Tigris. He defeated Sapor at Resaena, but in a later campaign died in battle and was succeeded by Philip the Arab, who concluded a treaty with Sapor in which Sapor relinquished rights over Armenia and was paid a large indemnity in lieu. Philip could not linger in the east for long as he needed to return to Rome to shore up his support as Emperor.

Sapor began a new Roman War in AD 250, during Decius's rule as Emperor. For his part, Decius was entirely occupied taking on the Goths in the Balkans, where he campaigned for the full three years of his reign, until he was killed in the Battle of Dobrudja.[935] Meanwhile, in the east, the Romans suffered a catastrophic defeat at the hands of Sapor in the Battle of Barbalissos, where a Roman army of some 60,000 was overcome at a site east of Aleppo on the Euphrates in present-day northern Syria. Then Antioch, the chief city of the eastern Empire, fell to Sapor and the eastern Empire appeared disastrously fragmented.

The new Emperor, Valerian, set about reclaiming Roman territory in Syria, which he did by retaking Antioch. In pursuing the Sassanids back into Mesopotomia, Valerian was captured at Edessa (modern-day Irfa, in Turkey) and was held until his death in captivity. It was Valerian who Sapor humiliated by using him as a mounting block when getting on his horse. A vivid stone relief of this event was carved at *Naqsh-e Dustam*, a Persian necropolis about 12 miles from Persepolis, where the tombs of Xerxes, Darius I and Arta-Xerxes may be found. This was the nadir of the Roman Empire in the third century.

At the time of Valerian's capture, the Empire had split three ways. Gaul, southern Germany and Britain had sworn allegiance to the Roman commander on the Rhine, operating out of Trier. Gallienus, Valerian's son, retained power, despite opposition from some of his father's general staff, and ruled Italy, North Africa and the Illyricum as best he could from Rome. In the east, a new military star had risen in Palmyra.[936] This was Odaenathus, the ruler of Palmyra, who would be called the *corrector totius orientis*. His task would be to defend the eastern borders of the Empire against the Persians, but he grew powerful and became too strong at the expense of Rome.

In a way, this division of the Empire into different areas of jurisdiction recognised informally what would be formalised under Diocletian, namely, that no one person could rule an empire so vast and complex as the Roman Empire, and that its government would have to be divided up. The years between the demise of Valerian in AD 260 and the emergence of Aurelian in AD 270 were ones of confusion in which Gallienus and then Claudius II were the successive Emperors.

Claudius, another Emperor chosen by the army, spent most of his time campaigning in the Balkans against the Goths, winning one notable victory over them in *c.*AD 268 at Naissus (present-day Nis, in Serbia). Yet by the end of his reign, both Gaul and Palmyra were presenting fierce challenges to his government. When Claudius died in AD 270, the by now upstart regime in Palmyra, under its redoubtable Queen Zenobia, invaded Egypt. On Claudius's death, another general, Aurelian, took charge. He faced trouble in Gaul, Egypt and the Balkans, but his rule of five years was to be unusually influential for the future direction of the Empire.

Aurelian was not simply a superb general, but also a man with a shrewd understanding of the psychological, religious and political implications of warfare. Wherever possible he favoured diplomacy over warfare.[937] His task was to defend Italy against attack, check once and for all the rising power of Palmyra, and subjugate insurgency in the northern and western parts of the Empire, consisting of Gaul, Britain and Spain. Having seen off an early threat to Italy and Rome, he turned his attention to Zenobia and Palmyra before finally subduing Gaul. Of the three campaigns he conducted, the most interesting and influential was his campaign against Palmyra.

Palmyra was a case of a client state which had become too arrogant, challenging the hand that gave her power. Aurelian was to humble her ambitions. Advancing through Asia Minor, Aurelian retook Egypt and then turned on the Palmyrenes at Emesa, present-day Homs, and defeated them. On the day of the battle, when the Roman line seemed about to give way, Aurelian had a revelation or apparition of a god whom he named *Sol Invictus*—a more palatable Romanised version of the local cult of Elagabal in Syria. The revelation of this apparition by the Emperor to his troops and later to Rome (where the cult of *Sol Invictus* was then set up) was a lesson in warfare not lost on Constantius, Constantine's father, who was serving as an officer in Aurelian's army. Forty years later, at another critical battle, Constantine would himself have a revelation, and one which would change the world.

Aurelian now set about restoring the Empire with unambiguous purpose and intent. He made a generous peace with Palmyra, took its Queen Zenobia as a captive to Rome, and hoped that his eastern borders would be peaceful from then on. However, the peace was so generous that once Aurelian had returned to Rome the Palmyrenes rebelled again. This time, Palmyra was destroyed by Rome's harsh response. Aurelian installed the new deity of *Sol Invictus* as a new cult in Rome. He built new walls round Rome that are still clearly visible today, in order to improve its security. He allowed the church to govern itself, refusing to intervene in the case of Paul of Samosata,[938] and he did not impose any harsh sanctions against it. He subdued Gaul and let go of the region of Dacia (present-day Hungary) north of the Danube, which could not be defended.[939] He attempted to renew the currency, but his measures did not restore confidence in the coinage. Despite all these actions, undertaken with great energy, he did not command the support of his general staff in the army and in AD 275 a cabal of officers murdered him.

A further period of instability ensued, and for the next ten years a series of Emperors grappled with the old problems, but without lasting success. Emperors Tacitus (AD 275–276), Florianus (AD 276), Probus (AD 276–282), Carus (AD 282–283), Numerian (AD 283–284) and Carinus (AD 282–285)—the last two were co-emperors—swiftly followed each other and all of them, except for Carus, who was possibly struck by lightning in his tent, were murdered by the army.[940]

In AD 284, the army chose yet another of its general staff to become Emperor. This time it was a relatively junior officer, although commander of the household troops, one Gaius Valerius Diocles (Diocletian). Standing on a rostrum and facing the legions, he asked if it was their will for him to become Emperor. They cried, "Augustus" and draped the purple cloak across his shoulders, amidst the deafening clash of weapons beating their shields. His first action was to deny that he had had any part in the recent murder of the last Emperor, Numerian, and then, while still on the rostrum, he ran his sword through the Prefect Aper, who was suspected of capturing Numerian and killing him secretly in a closed litter. On hearing of Diocletian's appointment, Numerian's Co-Emperor Carinus fled to the west, where he too was murdered.

Diocletian took sole charge of the Empire against a background of eight murdered predecessors, continuing invasions of the Balkans and Rhine, an ever-present threat from Persia and an Empire that had lost confidence and cohesion and was buckling at the knees. No recent Emperor had ruled long enough to make a difference. No plan was forthcoming to rule this vast and disparate territory. But Diocles, later Diocletian, was conservative in outlook, the last great preserver of the *ancien regime* and its panoply of pagan gods, a superb organiser and a willing delegator of power, and he ruled long enough to reform and stabilise the Empire. His fatal blemish in the eyes of Lactantius, a contemporary Christian apologist, rhetorician and historian, however, was his hatred for, and persecution of, the church.

The challenges facing the Empire were almost insuperable and can be grouped into six broad areas: the overall governance of a vast area under continual pressure from outside; military defence of the same; problems with the currency and lack of confidence therein; the economy, taxation, and in particular the control of prices; the administration and communication of government policies across the Empire; and the treatment of religious minorities, especially Christians. These are, of course, the kinds of challenges that any Empire or conglomeration of nations might face. Diocletian almost succeeded in meeting them, except that in persecuting the church he alienated one of the most influential minorities in the Empire and made his government seem anachronistic by holding on to a pagan culture that was fast being superseded.

What Diocletian knew, and what he had observed as he took up the mantle of Augustus, was that no one man could rule this Empire. The threats to Roman hegemony were too many for a single commander to deal with. Aurelian could not have been more energetic in pursuit of this goal, but he had barely succeeded. As soon as one military threat was squashed, another arose. In an Empire where distances were so great that it took weeks to assemble and march an army from one part to another, there needed to be a more devolved authority and command. Gaul would take years to subjugate, Britain was on the brink of rebellion under Carausius, and Persia and the Germans were an ever-present threat. Diocletian needed to appoint a co-regent who would have equal powers to himself and be his heir.

He chose Maximian, several years his junior, a fellow general who had served with him under Aurelian, Probus and Carus.[941] Maximian came from obscure peasant stock, from the region of Sirmium (Sremska Mitrovica). He was an implacable enemy, but a fierce friend. He was a man of great energy; ruthless if need be, but straightforward and without intrigue. Diocletian appointed him Co-Emperor or Augustus in AD 285 in Milan in order to concentrate his energies on Gaul and the Rhine, restore order, improve defences, clear up any Germanic invasion and deploy the military. It was to be a five-year project in itself. "Maximian was to be the great Illyrian soldier-Emperor, conquering enemies and covering himself with glory, while Diocletian was to be the supreme paternal governor, carefully directing the restoration of the state".[942] Diocletian still possessed the recognised *auctoritas,* only now it was shared. He focused his energies on securing the Danube against the Goths and the Orient against renewed Persian attack. Having campaigned effectively in Syria, Diocletian brought the King of Persia, Vahram, to a new peace treaty favourable to Rome in AD 287. He settled his main centre of administration at Nicomedia (Izmit) at the south-eastern end of the Sea of Marmara.

The two Augusti were soon to be expanded into a tetrarchy. Despite the treaty with Persia and the subjugation of Gaul, Britain under Carausius remained in defiance of Rome. Carausius's rule was stable, well founded, set to last and well defended by the Channel. To combat this state of affairs and prepare for another drawn out campaign, each Augustus appointed a Caesar or Junior Emperor. There would now be four commanders in the Empire. On 1 March AD 293, Maximian duly bestowed the purple on his Praetorian Prefect, Marcus Flavius Constantius, the father of Constantine. Constantius married Maximian's daughter, Theodora, and divorced Constantine's mother, Helena, who was of humbler stock. Likewise, Diocletian gave the same title of Caesar to Gaius Galerius, an experienced general in his army. Gaius Galerius married Diocletian's daughter Valeria. Thus the tetrarchy was cemented together by family ties. Ruling became a family business.

In this way the Augusti became a tetrarchy, a sculpture of which may be seen in St Mark's Square, Venice. Diocletian had divided the Empire into four: Constantius taking Britain, Gaul and Spain; Maximian, Italy and North Africa; Galerius, the Illyrian provinces; and Diocletian, Asia and Syria. The idea was that, in due time, the Augusti would resign in favour of their Caesars and their rule would continue. Diocletian even built his vast retirement home in Split in preparation for that event; but much was to occur before then.

The tetrarchy now set to work. Constantius was given the task of bringing Britain, under its usurper leader, back into line. He soon gained the support and use of the continental coast so as to mount an invasion from a secure base. He took Boulogne (Gesoriacum) and built two new fleets. By AD 296, he was ready to invade.[943] At the same time, Carausius had been murdered by Allectus, a senior member of the government who succeeded him. Constantius eventually managed to land his troops at Dover and successfully marched on London, overcoming all opposition. Britain was thus restored to the Empire.

Elsewhere in the Empire, Maximian led troops against rebellious tribes in North Africa, securing Carthage in March AD 298. Diocletian gave himself to securing the lower Danube and pacifying the Sarmatians, while Galerius gave himself to the defence of the Empire in the east in the wake of a resurgent Persia under a new King Narses, who was determined to make his mark and who invaded Armenia. At first, Galerius suffered defeat, but then Diocletian himself re-established his authority, which had been overtaken by a revolt in Egypt. Alexandria was taken back in AD 298, along with the Theabaid and Fayum regions of the Nile.[944] In the end, Galerius had success in Erzerum, retaking Armenia, also taking Nisibis near the Tigris, and finally capturing the Persian capital of Ctesiphon on the east bank of the Tigris, north of present-day Baghdad. A treaty was struck with the defeated Persians, which was not ungenerous, and this peace was to last for 40 years.[945]

The result of these campaigns over the five years from the inception of the tetrarchy was a measure of peace on all fronts: Britain, the Rhine, the Lower Danube in Pannonia, Egypt and the East were all stabilised. The year AD 298 was indeed an *annus mirabilis*. Triumphant buildings, including a great arch, were erected in Thessalonica, recording Galerius's victories.[946] It was a brilliant result for the policy instigated by Diocletian. But what had been conquered or pacified must now be ruled. The business of governing effectively, fairly and equitably was, as ever, harder to achieve. One ambitious teenager who experienced these heady days in the court of Diocletian, and possibly in the army of Galerius also, was the young Constantine.[947] He learnt lessons there for his own government in the years to come.

Administrative Reforms under Diocletian

If the establishment of the tetrarchy was the single largest departure in the government of the Empire, it was by no means the only one. In addition to the tetrarchy, Diocletian further reformed the army and border controls, strengthened the currency and attempted to fix prices across the Empire. He re-organised the administration of the Empire, greatly increasing the size of the civil service.

Ensuring the safety of the Empire was paramount, hence the reform of the army. Walls like those of Hadrian in Britain, or ditches and obstacles elsewhere, were not enough to hold off invasions, especially at times of mass migrations of people—just as we are experiencing in the twenty-first century. These barriers were good for surveillance, but they could not deter.[948] Large parts of the Empire had become destabilised by recurrent incursions of peoples from the East, especially across the Rhine and Danube into the regions of Gaul and Illyricum. The result of this was that populations fled, the land became vulnerable to further attack, proper administration ceased, and neither income nor taxes were produced. In response to these incessant dangers, Diocletian and his generals came up with a new and primarily defensive system. The borders of the Empire were long since fixed, and no further invasions or annexations were envisaged, unless temporarily necessary in order to repel an invader, as with Persia in the east.

The principle around which Diocletian's military reforms was based was strength in depth. The two elements of the defence forces were mobile field forces (*comitatenses*) and stationary frontier forces (*riparenses*).[949] With the inception of the tetrarchy, there was much less risk of civil war and so less need for very large standing armies. What was required was highly mobile, smaller forces that could reinforce strategic garrisons at the frontier. This strategy involved enlarging the size of the army overall. Diocletian created a 53-legion fighting force, raising 14 new legions.[950] When legions were at full strength of 5,000 troops, it meant an army of some 265,000. In addition to this, there were large numbers of cavalry and the *limitanei*, a kind of reservist corps, taking the total size to nearer half a million soldiers. Recruitment for such an army, especially when engaged in arduous campaigns, ran to about 90,000 men a year.

There were incentives. Whereas in the early stages of the Empire, after 25 years' service, retired soldiers were given land grants, now, under Diocletian, there were tax exemptions for the soldiers themselves and for their immediate families of wives and parents. With such a need for fresh recruits, it is not surprising that Rome frequently resorted to recruiting barbarians who had settled within the Empire to fill the ranks. Involvement in the army by such barbarians often resulted in them becoming the most senior officials in the Empire.

The hard-point defences at the frontiers included walled towns, large or smaller forts and well-fortified villas or farmhouses capable of re-enforcement. Food and equipment were also located at strategic points to resource mobile units. In Britain, sea defences were provided by a series of coastal forts from the Wash to the Isle of Wight. These included Brancaster, Burgh Castle, Walton Castle, Bradwell, Reculver, Richborough, Dover, Lympne, Pevensey and Portchester. Seventeen centuries later, these great coastal forts still convey a sense of purpose and determination typical of Diocletian's time.

To sustain a fighting force and defences across such a vast Empire required a strong economy, with the army being the single-most expensive part of the budget. Knowing this, Diocletian implemented reforms both to the currency and to the economy itself. The soaring cost of the army, the reduction of agricultural land because of instability, invasion and endemic inflation in the third century, all contributed to a weak economy. The tax system was inefficient and those who ranked in the middle strata of society were overwhelmed with the expectations of the *munera*, which were civic duties for the running of towns, like roads, public buildings, sewage and water supply.

Aurelian had begun the process of improving the coinage. He replaced devalued coinage with two new stable denominations: one set at 20 sesterces or five denarii, the other a smaller denomination of two denarii (in effect "printing" money).[951] Diocletian brought out a gold *aureus*, which was so valuable and prestigious that it was only used as a donative to troops or as payment to very senior officers. A new silver coin was introduced with the value of twenty to one *aureus*. Yet the scarcity of silver was such that it was hard to hold its value.

Alongside efforts, however faltering, to strengthen the currency, Diocletian sought to make taxation more effective. The taxation system involved a land tax, a poll tax on every adult head of population, and an army tax called the *annona militaris,* which essentially imposed compulsory provision for the army when they were stationed in a given neighbourhood. Alongside these taxes, there were trade taxes (at customs), sales taxes and various taxes on manufacturing. In other words, the forms of taxation from that day to this are very similar. In AD 296, a new census began, not dissimilar to the Domesday Book in England, which took eight years and catalogued both people and wealth. Every field, orchard, vineyard, olive grove, labourer, slave, child, horse, ox and pig was catalogued. A classification system called *iugum* was used to quantify the amount of land needed to grow a certain amount of barley or wheat. People were counted for the poll tax or *caput* tax, with women counted as half a *caput* and adult males between the ages of 14 and 65 assessed as a single *caput.* What was clear, as Mark Twain once said, was that death and taxes were indeed inescapable. Failure to pay taxes resulted in floggings and death. All in all, Diocletian made a new concerted effort to collect taxes across the Empire from Egypt to Gaul, and none would escape either assessment for, or payment of, taxes.

Diocletian's economic reforms were even more ambitious. He firmly believed in the benefits of control and the fruits of firm administration across the Empire and thus sought to impose a command economy and fixed prices. In early AD 301, having settled the borders and repelled invaders, he tried to establish economic uniformity through an imperial rescript or edict entitled *De Pretiis* (Concerning Prices). It was a leap in the dark. Economic policy was hitherto more a question of balancing income (taxation and the income from imperial estates) against expenditure—the cost of the court, the army and the administration. Beyond a balanced budget, careful accounting, and sound husbandry or estate management, there were few other economic measures open to the government, apart from controlling wheat prices. Now Diocletian sought to extend control far beyond wheat.

In early AD 301, Diocletian published the enormous *De Pretiis,* which laid down compulsory maximum prices for over a thousand goods or services. Set out in 32 sections, it had an imposing preamble following citation of the names of the four rulers in the tetrarchy, their titles and military victories. The preamble continued:

> As we recall the wars we have successfully fought, we must be grateful for a tranquil world, reclining in the embrace of the most profound calm, and for the blessings of a peace won with great effort. It is demanded, both by right thinking public opinion and by the dignity and majesty of Rome, that this fortune of our state, second only to the immortal gods be faithfully established and suitably adorned. Therefore we, who by the gracious favour of the gods, stemmed the former ravaging tide of the barbarians by destroying them, must guard this peace, established for eternity, with due defences of justice.[952]

Part of "guarding the peace" for Diocletian was preventing the inflation of prices by unscrupulous businessmen. He thus proposed not fixed prices, but maximum prices across the Empire. The main categories were foodstuffs, raw materials, clothing, transport, wages and various service charges. All prices were denominated in *denarii communis*. The average wage was 2.25 denarii a day (in Jesus's day, *c.*AD 30, it was one denarius a day). Thus prices were set for wheat at 100 denarii per *modius* or 8 litres, barley at 60, kidney beans at 100 denarii, spelt at 200 denarii, while cloaks (from Africa) were anything from 1,500 to 10,000 denarii.[953]

Although the motivation behind the edict was laudable, in that it sought to prevent extortion and unscrupulous business practices, it was unenforceable and too crude for the economic needs of so vast an Empire. Some withdrew goods or services from the marketplace out of fear, wary of prosecution; others sold their goods on the quiet out of sight of government officials. Within a few years, the system of price fixing was a dead letter, but it was indicative of Diocletian's confidence in strong central government that he even brought it forward in the first place. Alongside these economic reforms, Diocletian re-organised the administration of the Empire as a whole.

A renewed currency, a larger standing army, a revised taxation system, including greater rigour in collections, and a new pricing policy all required a strong administration. Diocletian, the great administrator, accordingly also reformed the administration of the Empire. In AD 293, soon after the creation of the tetrarchy, he began a root and branch reform of imperial administration, including boundaries and governorships. He created a hundred provinces, nearly double the previous number. These provinces were grouped together in regions or dioceses, of which there were 12 in all, which were in turn placed under four Praetorian Prefects in Trier, Milan, Nicomedia and Antioch. Rome had its own City Prefect. Frontier provinces were armed; interior provinces were no longer militarised. Likewise, civil and military administration was kept separate. Africa was split into three new provinces, and Asia into six. Governors were now more like civil servants rather than members of the patrician and senatorial classes as before, except in Italy, where governors had the traditional title of "correctors" and were drawn from the old senatorial class. Their responsibilities were more clearly defined and they became more accountable to the tetrarchy for the discharge of their duties.

The Senate was replaced by the new imperial administration, with prefects set over all the vicars or governors of the provinces. The Praetorian Prefect was in effect the Prime Minister of the Emperor. The Consistory Court enforced all imperial legislation. The Emperor governed by rescripts or edicts, which were enforced by the court. Now living in his palace at Nicomedia, Diocletian took on the appearance of an ever more god-like figure. Yet for Diocletian there was one more area to bolster, the very heart of paganism, which, as a conservative, he believed should be upheld at all costs. Its main antagonist he saw as the dangerously socially subversive Christian Church, which should thus be eradicated through persecution. Like all totalitarians, Diocletian brooked no ideological opposition, and late in his reign he attempted to force the church into line.

The Great Persecution

It was probably in March AD 302 that Diocletian wrote as follows from Alexandria: "The Immortal Gods in their providence have so designed things that good and true principles have been established by the wisdom and deliberations of eminent, wise, and upright men. It is wrong to oppose these principles, or desert the ancient religion for some new one, for it is the height of criminality to try and revise doctrines that were settled once and for all by the ancients, and whose position is fixed and acknowledged".[954]

Diocletian was writing to the Proconsul of Africa, Julianius, about the Manichees, but it could very well have been, as it was a year later, about the Christians. Both movements were seen by Diocletian as an affront to the ancient pagan deities which had been part of Rome for a thousand years, and before Rome, deities of the Greeks, whose cult Diocletian was now assiduously promoting. Indeed, as part of his re-invigoration of Empire he was fervently reviving ancient Roman cults both locally and across the Empire. It was because of this policy that the Empire and the continuing spread of Christianity were on a collision course. It took only a spark of anger in Diocletian to activate one of the worst persecutions of the church in its history.

By AD 298, there were already signs of trouble in the army when a centurion by the name of Marcellus suddenly publicly renounced his oath of allegiance to the Emperor during a public festival in Tangier. He exclaimed that he obeyed only Christ as Lord and would have no part in the weapons of this world or the service of idolatrous rulers. The transcript of his trial was as follows:

> Agricolanus (the Magistrate): Did you say what appears in the official records of the Governor?
>
> Marcellus: I did.
>
> Agricolanus: Were you in service with the rank of centurion of the first class?
>
> Marcellus: I was.
>
> Agricolanus: What madness possessed you to renounce your oath and speak as you did?

Marcellus: There is no madness in those who fear God.

Agricolanus: Did you say all those things which appear in the official records of the Governor?

Marcellus: I did.

Agricolanus: Did you throw away your arms?

Marcellus: I did. A Christian who is in the service of the Lord Christ should not serve the affairs of this world.

Agricolanus: The acts of Marcellus are such as to merit disciplinary punishment. Accordingly, Marcellus formerly in service and having the rank of Centurion of the first class, having declared that he had degraded himself by publicly renouncing his oath of allegiance, and having moreover put on record insane statements, it is my pleasure that he be put to death by the sword.

As he was being led away to execution, Marcellus said: "Agricolanus, may God be kind to you!" And after he had said this he was slain with sword, and so obtained the martyrdom he desired.[955]

In AD 298 or 299, a military order concerning religious observance was passed which required *adoratio* of the Emperor's image, together with sacrifice. It appears to have been initiated by Galerius's Danube armies, but may have spread further. Christians who refused to comply were stripped of their rank and Eusebius tells us that a great many Christians were thus treated.[956] But a worse and more extensive persecution was to follow outside the army. The trigger was a sacrifice at Apollo's shrine at Didyma. The Christian historian Lactantius, sometimes called the Christian Cicero, who had been appointed Professor of Rhetoric at Nicomedia by Diocletian and later adviser to Constantine, gives an account of this moment:

While in the East Diocletian, always fearfully anxious to know the future, sacrificed victims and sought to read events in their livers. And some of the servants who knew the Lord were present at the sacrifice, and put the immortal sign (of the Cross) on the pieces. The demons therefore fled and the sacrifice was spoiled. The Haruspices were filled with fear when they saw no signs in the entrails at all, for it seemed as if their sacrifices were unacceptable. They offered fresh victims but again saw nothing.

Finally, the Chief Haruspex, Tagris, whether out of suspicion or because of something he had seen, declared the sacrifices were producing no response because sacrilegious men were participating in sacred things.

Diocletian became so furiously angry at this, that he ordered not only those who attended the sacrifice, but everyone else in that palace, to offer sacrifices themselves; and those who hung back should be beaten with rods. He also had orders sent out to all army commands, that the soldiers should sacrifice, or face dismissal.[957]

Soon afterwards, on 23 February AD 303, the day of an ancient Roman festival (for the god Terminus, ironically), the Emperor posted the first edict of persecution at his imperial capital, Nicomedia. Churches were to be destroyed, the scriptures were to be burned and all services banned. Christians lost all privileges of rank and were excluded from all courts of law. The edict excited the mob, and, with no protection from the army, the Christian building (surely one of the earliest churches) was burnt down. It was the beginning of the Great Persecution. What *kristallnacht* was for Jews in Germany in 1938, this edict was for Christians in the Empire, although the scale of slaughter never reached the levels of the Holocaust. The Empire fortunately lacked the organisation to carry out such a full-scale, comprehensive persecution, so the effect of the edict or rescript was patchy and haphazard from the start.[958] Indeed in the eastern part of the Empire in Armenia, after ten years of imprisonment by his own king, Gregory the Illuminator gained acceptance for Christianity having brought healing to his monarch. Whereas a fire in the palace in Nicomedia, which Diocletian had built when making the city his capital in the East, gave added impetus to the purge of Christians in the civil service. As with the fire in Rome during Nero's rule, this fire too was blamed on the Christians.

The question that has puzzled historians is why, after 18 years of rule, did Diocletian, so late in the day, begin this sudden and wholesale persecution of Christians? Although his anger could be fierce and brutal,

that alone surely could not have accounted for this policy? Some say that
members of his family, namely his wife Prisca and daughter Valeria—who
was married to his Caesar, Galerius—were Christians and had been able
to restrain him before. Others contend that it was Galerius who had
wanted the persecution all along, but for years Diocletian had been able
to resist persecution as an impractical policy. Or it may have been that
a tipping point in strategy occurred at Didyma, or at least around that
time, at which Diocletian's desire for a settled, ordered and prosperous
Empire was overturned by his conservative desire to keep the culture and
religion of Empire the same. Religious conservatism and a yearning for
traditional culture overcame the desire for settled public order. Because
of its increasing influence, the need to rein back the church became more
pressing, which in turn became a matter for imperial action. Diocletian
must have been persuaded that the persecution was a practical possibility
as well as a religious necessity. Maybe it was for these reasons that there
began the fiercest persecution of Christians, certainly since Decius, and
probably since the more limited persecution of Christians under Nero.

The persecution began with the destruction of the Great Church in
Nicomedia. The church stood in full view of the Imperial Palace. Soldiers
led by the prefect and other officials surrounded it. The doors were beaten
down; church furniture was removed; the scriptures and liturgical books
were burnt; siege engines were put into position and the walls reduced
to rubble. Diocletian and Galerius watched from the palace. What began
in Nicomedia now spread across the Empire: churches were demolished,
scriptures burnt, sacred vessels confiscated. Christians who refused to
sacrifice were driven from office, losing their jobs in imperial service.
Diocletian was not going to create a new raft of martyrs, so there were few
arrests and very few executions. One exception was Euethius, who had
torn down the official notice of the edict that was put up in the central
square of the city.[959] The effect of the initial persecution was mixed. Some
Christians compromised and sacrificed; others laid low. As a whole, the
church stood firm. In North Africa, there emerged a split in the practice
of the church in response to the demands of local magistrates to hand
over the scriptures. Some made little resistance and handed over, if not
scriptures, liturgical books; others believed any compliance was wrong,
and gave those who acquiesced the name *traditors* (traitors) since

they handed over books to the authorities. Mensurius, the Bishop of Carthage, handed books over to the authorities, fuelling the great division in the North African Church between the Donatists (who refused to compromise) and the Catholic Church (which sometimes did).

The persecution intensified. The palace fire in Nicomedia was then blamed on the Christians and used as a pretext for fiercer persecution. Members of the imperial family, Prisca and Valeria—Diocletian's wife and daughter—were ordered to sacrifice. Imperial officials were likewise ordered to sacrifice and, if they refused, tortured. One Peter, an official, was stripped naked, lacerated with whips, had salt and vinegar rubbed into his wounds, and was then slowly burnt.[960] A further turn of the screw followed: another edict was issued in the summer of AD 303, and all clergy were imprisoned. The leader of the church of Nicomedia was beheaded; gaols were filled with clergy. As Eusebius wrote:

> The spectacle of what happened beggars description: in every town great numbers were locked up, and everywhere the gaols built long before for homicides and grave robbers were crowded with bishops, presbyters and deacons, readers and exorcists, so that now there was no room in them for those convicted of crimes.[961]

Eusebius went on to describe the heroic courage of martyrs in Phoenicia, Egypt, Alexandria, Phrygia and Antioch, where girls took their own lives rather than be raped, and others suffered fearful torture: reeds driven under the fingernails, melted lead poured on their backs, private parts and bowels eviscerated.[962]

The persecution spread, but was patchy. The second, more intense, edict of the summer of AD 303 was not implemented in the West. Constantius (the father of Constantine), based at Trier in Gaul, hardly complied with the first edict, let alone the second. He had no antipathy towards Christians, so took only a few nominal measures against them. In the East, under Galerius in particular, the persecution raged. Lactantius saw it as the essential precursor to the return of Christ: the Armageddon before Christ's victorious millennial reign on earth. Far from cowing the church, the persecution openly prepared it for the eventual outcome of victory foretold in Revelation.[963]

By AD 304, Diocletian was in ill health, giving Galerius further opportunity to take his policy of persecution to ultimate and extreme lengths. A fourth edict was issued, which virtually passed a death sentence on all Christians who would not sacrifice. Christianity was proscribed and became a *religio illicita* in the eastern part of the Empire, although the persecution in the East was being overtaken by other more significant political events. Whatever the reason for the persecution, it remains an awful and cruel indictment of Diocletian's otherwise generally effective rule. Galerius was to continue his campaign, long after Diocletian, right up to a year before his death in AD 311. The persecution resulted in hundreds of martyrs rather than thousands, and compared with the purges against Jews or Christians in Europe, Russia and China in the twentieth century, the numbers put to death were relatively few. The pressure exerted on the church was immense. The perennial question in times of persecution, whether to resist or comply, produced as much fallout, especially in North Africa, as the persecution itself. The physical pain brought lasting psychological and spiritual pressure. Yet Diocletian's role in this short but very sharp purge was swiftly brought to an end.

As the twentieth anniversary of his assumption of power as Emperor came around, together with the anniversary of the creation in AD 285 of the tetrarchy, when Maximian was created joint Augustus in the West, Diocletian contemplated the unthinkable. He would resign the office of Augustus, held for life by every previous Emperor, and retire instead to his palace, which was being built near Split on the Adriatic. The internal logic of the tetrarchy was that the two Caesars—the deputies of the Augusti—would then take over, having been groomed for office for years. Maximian, Diocletian's faithful Augustus in the West would resign and make way for Constantius, his Caesar, and likewise Diocletian for Galerius. Preparations were well advanced in Rome for this extraordinary event of triumph and abdication. Rome, the ancient capital of the Empire, would celebrate the years of Diocletian and Maximian, and in so doing prepare for their abdication.

The day for the celebration of both Diocletian and Maximian's rule was set for the *vicennalia*, 20 November AD 303: signalling 20 years since

Diocles was proclaimed Emperor by the Roman army. The celebrations in Rome were followed by a return to Nicomedia and Milan, where the agreed abdications were to take place some 18 months later on 1 May AD 305. Diocletian's journey back to Nicomedia via Ravenna was interrupted by a serious illness. He recovered, but was much weaker, although not weak enough to prevent him from taking command with Galerius of a campaign against Germanic tribes along the Danube.[964] By 28 August, he had reached the vicinity of Nicomedia.

On 1 May AD 305, the unprecedented happened. Accompanied by Galerius, Diocletian mounted a high platform where, 21 years earlier, he had been proclaimed Emperor by the troops. Resplendent in purple robe and covered in jewels, and surrounded by his court, Diocletian explained he was tired and ready to lay down the responsibility of office. Galerius was to succeed him, with Maximinus appointed Caesar. Diocletian took off his purple cloak and placed it on Maximinus. In Milan, Maximian did the same, bestowing his cloak on Severus as Caesar, with Constantius—the father of Constantine, who was then in Diocletian's court at Nicomedia—becoming the Augustus in the West. It was, on the face of it, a peaceful transfer of power, which brought Constantine closer to the imperial throne, but the succession sought by Diocletian would not be so long lasting or secure. When the time came, Constantine would be ready to seize power himself. He would never retire like Diocletian, who he watched relinquish the purple that day. Furthermore, there is no doubt that his reign, the result of careful observation of Diocletian, would change the world.

CHAPTER 10

Constantine and the Roman Revolution

Constantine was born on 27 February AD 282 at Naissus (Nis, in modern-day Serbia), where his father, Constantius Chlorus, was serving as Governor of Dalmatia. Constantine's mother, Helena, was a local woman, not a highborn Roman aristocrat, who, after seeing little of her son in his teenage years, came to figure greatly in his later life. She was thought to be either a Turk from Drepanum, in Bithynia—later renamed Helenopolis in her honour after her son became the ruler of the Roman Empire[965]—or the daughter of a British king. The former is considered much more likely and she is, in fact, often described as a tavern keeper, or even a barmaid.

Constantius Chlorus, Constantine's father, sided with Diocletian after the murder of the Emperor Carinus and was rapidly promoted. When Diocletian divided the Empire into the tetrarchy in March AD 293, Constantius became Caesar or Deputy Emperor in the West under Maximian. Such an office necessitated him giving up his "common law" wife Helena and making a dynastic marriage with Theodora, the daughter of Augustus Maximian. He also had to give up his son Constantine, who then spent the best part of ten years as a virtual hostage in Diocletian's court in Nicomedia, thus ensuring his father's loyalty.

Constantine was educated in Nicomedia and rose to become a tribune in Diocletian's legions. He saw the workings of the imperial court at first hand and witnessed the manner in which Diocletian ruled. He was to remain there until Diocletian abdicated in AD 306 and then he would serve the irascible Galerius, an even greater scourge of Christians. On being sent a summons by his dying father to return to Britain,[966] Constantine (or Constantius as he was originally called) managed to flee the court at Nicomedia after a heavy drinking session with Galerius, who was at that point the Augustus in the East. In his stupor, Galerius gave Constantine an opportunity to leave.[967] Constantine rode poste-haste from Nicomedia to Boulogne—and then on to England by boat—taking with him his three-year-old son Crispus, whose mother Minervina had previously died. When he next returned to the continent, Constantine would be the self-proclaimed Emperor or Augustus.

By AD 306, following the abdication of Maximian, his father Constantius had become Augustus of the West. He was rewarded, in part, for the successful campaign he had earlier fought against the usurper Carausius in Britain, and against Carausius's murderer and successor, the sallow and less flamboyant financier Allectus, whom Constantius had defeated in September AD 296. Early in 306 Constantius initiated a new campaign against the Picts, yet only a few months later, on 25 July AD 306, Constantius died in York, much like a previous Emperor, Septimius Severus, who, though conqueror in the East, died in York following a campaign against the Picts. Constantine had barely arrived from Nicomedia when he was proclaimed Augustus by the legions in York. He was another usurper, as Constantius Chlorus already had a Caesar who was supposed to succeed him: Flavius Valerius Severus. Before his death, Chlorus and his officers in Gaul and Britain had prepared the way for his son. Unlike previous usurpers proclaimed Emperor in Britain, Constantine was to succeed and become sole ruler of the Empire, so what happened in York that day would literally change the course of history.

Although Galerius initially received news of Constantine's acclamation by the troops as Caesar with fury, Constantine soon consolidated his position. Having settled the outstanding rebellion in the north of England, he moved rapidly to Trier, which he made his headquarters, and greatly expanded the city, building a basilica and very spacious and impressive baths. Like his father before him, he also proclaimed an edict of toleration towards Christians and Jews.[968] From Trier, Constantine conducted campaigns against the Franks, showing the implacable side of his nature by having two of their kings who had been captured thrown to the wild beasts.[969]

Meanwhile, Severus remained Augustus in Milan, but Maxentius, the former Emperor Maximian's son, could not bear to see Constantius's son seize power, so he took to the field himself. Diocletian's carefully crafted plans of succession were in danger of collapse. The Praetorian Guard now deserted Severus and acclaimed Maxentius Augustus instead. Maxentius then firmly established his rule in Rome.

Diocletian was wheeled out of retirement, where he was growing cabbages, to settle the issue of who should govern, but events now had a momentum all of their own. The old Emperor in the West, Maximian, sought an alliance with Constantine, who was given Fausta, Maximian's youngest daughter, in marriage. They were married in September AD 307 and a panegyric was given on the occasion of their marriage, extolling Constantius and saying that the unconquered sun god, *Sol Invictus*, had himself carried Constantius up to the heavens. This was an early indication of Constantine's already-established fascination with a divinity associated with light. Constantine was praised, but for his part was extremely cautious of committing himself unreservedly to Maximian and his ambitions.

Diocletian was once again consulted and, at a council at Carnuntum, Galerius replaced Severus with Licinius as Augustus, Constantine was made Caesar in the West, and in the East, Galerius appointed Maximinus.[970] It was one thing to elect Licinius as Emperor, however, but quite another to successfully impose him on the West. In fact, neither Maximian nor Maxentius, his son, had given up hope of ruling. Maxentius was the self-proclaimed Emperor in Rome, and the old Emperor, Maximian, made a final bid for power, appearing in the purple in Arles just five years after he had abdicated. Constantine took this bid for power seriously, and marched on Marseilles, whence Maximian had retreated, but Maximian committed suicide rather than face his son-in-law.

Constantine had shown himself a bold strategist and tireless organiser. He had his father's abilities as a soldier: he knew how to prepare an army for battle, and was also unwilling to commit himself to others until he was sure of their genuine support. He was tall for a Roman, approximately 5ft 9in, with a strong aquiline nose, cleft chin, powerful forehead and steady, searching eyes.[971] He had also shown himself to be sympathetic towards Christians. He knew the Bishop of Cordoba, Ossius, personally, as well as the Bishops of Trier and Cologne.[972] In his panegyric, written after Constantine's death in AD 337, Eusebius wrote:

> No one was comparable to him for grace and beauty of person, or height of stature; and he so far surpassed his peers in personal strength as to be a terror to them. He was however even more conspicuous for the excellence of his mental qualities than for his superior physical endowments; being gifted in the first place with a sound judgement, and having also reaped the advantages of a liberal education. He was also distinguished in no ordinary degree both by natural intelligence and divinely imparted wisdom. [973]

What can be said of Constantine was that he was ambitious and had great confidence in his own ability, trained at the court in the service of Diocletian, and, increasingly as we shall see, had a strong belief in his personal destiny. It seems that he knew what he wanted to become, as well as where he would part company with his predecessors, especially in their senseless persecution of Christians. In AD 310, having seen off Maximian, he was ready to make the ultimate bid for power in the West and considered marching on Rome and wresting power from Maxentius, the self-proclaimed Augustus in the West. He was just waiting for the right moment.

The March on Rome

Events were gathering momentum. After his return to Trier from Marseilles, and before taking on the Franks again in present-day Lorraine, Constantine had some sort of religious experience at Grand, in Gaul, at the Temple of Apollo. A panegyrist, who spoke about Constantine in his newly built basilica in Trier in AD 310, said of that experience:

> I believe Constantine, that you saw Apollo accompanied by Victory offering you laurel crowns each of which forecast thirty years. This is the number of years that ought to be owed to you beyond Pylian old age [a reference to Nestor the aged hero in Homer's *Illiad*]. You saw yourself and recognized yourself in the

appearance of him to whom the divine songs of the Bard [Homer] granted the rule of the whole world.[974]

At the very least it was a kind of divine beckoning to reach for the highest prize, and a precursor to another vision from a greater messenger to vanquish in quite a different name: Jewish rather than Greek. A year later, Galerius was dead. If Lactantius is to be believed, Galerius died like Herod the Tetrarch (Acts 12:23), eaten by worms and polluting the air with pungent fumes from his decaying and suppurating body. For Lactantius, it was less than just deserts for the onslaught Galerius had unleashed, with Diocletian, against Christians in the Great Persecution. For Constantine, Galerius's death represented another move on the chessboard of his ambition. Licinius now succeeded Galerius in the East, with his Caesar Maximinus, whom he loathed, as his deputy. Licinius and Constantine came to an arrangement whereby Licinius would tie down some of Maxentius's forces in northern Italy, while Constantine invaded from Gaul. This was in return for Constantine's support for Licinius's struggle with his own deputy, Maximinus.[975]

Maxentius was no pushover, however much Eusebius blackened his reputation in his *Life of Constantine*. For Eusebius, Maxentius was a serial adulterer with other men's wives (except in the case of one Christian wife who took her own life rather than suffer his advances), was addicted to sorcery and was no friend of the church.[976] In fact, the truth was a little different. Maxentius had made peace with the church in Rome, not carrying out either Diocletian or Galerius's persecution, and was an able military commander who had already seen off Severus and quelled an insurrection in North Africa. With the death of Galerius, the support of Licinius, and relative peace in Gaul and on the Rhine, now was the time for Constantine to seize the crown. Constantine was received in Autun in present-day Burgundy in AD 311 with another panegyric extolling his pedigree and his gifts, declaring that he worshipped none of Diocletian's pantheon of gods, but only one, a god named by the speaker as the *Mens Divina*—the Divine Mind. This deity, who was neither *Sol Invictus* nor Apollo, would soon be more fully revealed to Constantine and his followers.[977]

The campaign to invade Italy and take Rome would not be easy. It required planning as well as skill and good fortune. Of the different routes across the Alps, including Petit St Bernard by way of modern Ivrea, Constantine chose the relatively high pass of Mt Cenis. Having taken the Alpine town of Segusio, he marched towards Turin. Under the command of Rauricius Pompeianus, Maxentius's forces marched from their garrison town of Milan to meet Constantine. Constantine's forces won the day; his superior infantry, which had been trained in combat on the Rhine, proved irresistible. Soon the road to Milan lay unprotected and other cities, seeing the way the wind was blowing, came over to Constantine, who then occupied Aquileia on the Adriatic, making almost all of northern Italy his. The road to Rome now lay open.

Having lost his northern army, and with no more soldiers than Constantine, Maxentius faced constant desertion, as subordinates, guessing the future, took evasive action. Having appointed Anullinus, the Prefect of Rome, Maxentius rode out to war, although apparently with little confidence as he stowed away his personal symbols of authority in wooden boxes under a shrine near the Palatine, where they lay hidden until finally unearthed in 2006. These boxes contained three lances, four javelins, three glass and chalcedony spheres and a sceptre, all wrapped in deteriorated silk. Maxentius would never use them again.

Maxentius drew his troops up outside the walls of Rome. They had their backs to the River Tiber, close to the Milvian Bridge. Constantine's soldiers were as numerous as Maxentius's army, but more confident in the wake of their successful campaign in the north of Italy. Constantine's men also appeared to have a new symbol that combined the Greek letter *chi* (pronounced "ch") with the letter *rho* (pronounced "r"): this could be interpreted either as a reference to Christ or to the Greek word *chrestos*, meaning good luck or blessed.[978] However, for Eusebius and Lactantius, there was no doubt what it meant. Eusebius tells how Constantine received a vision of the Cross of Light in the heavens at midday with an instruction to conquer by that symbol.[979]

To underline this daytime vision, Christ also appeared to Constantine in a dream or vision at night and commanded him to use a standard made in the shape of a cross in his battles. The standard was made with the letter P intersecting with an X (the *chi rho* symbol). The upright javelin and cross bar was then covered with a banner attached to the transverse bar, on which were embroidered precious stones interlaced with gold. Below the banner was an image of the Emperor. This standard came to be known by Roman soldiers as the *labarum* and was always carried in battle thereafter. Eusebius writes: "The Emperor constantly made use of this sign of salvation as a safeguard against every adverse and hostile power, and commended that others similar to it should be carried at the head of all armies".[980]

Throughout Eusebius's description of Constantine, there is more than just a hint of Constantine as a new Moses. Indeed, there is a strong and conscious comparison of Constantine with Moses. Like Moses, Constantine was God's chosen instrument to bring freedom to his people after long years of servitude. Like Moses, Constantine fought against his people's enemies and prevailed. Like Moses, Constantine formed a tabernacle, denoted by the presence of the *labarum*, where he went to pray before instructing his army. Constantine was the new liberator, in effect. Eusebius says of him in this panegyric, or threnody, written after Constantine's death:

> So dear was he to God, and so blessed; so pious and so fortunate in all he undertook, that with the greatest facility he obtained the authority over more nations, than any who had preceded him, and yet retained his power, undisturbed, to the very end of his life. [981]

The defeat of Maxentius was not in itself the pivotal moment which brought about the end of pagan Rome, but it was more than the first significant step in that direction. Twelve years later, in AD 324, when Constantine finally defeated the Eastern Emperor, Licinius, a revolution took place in the Roman Empire which would not be reversed except for a few brief years under the apostate Emperor Julian, who sought to put the clock back to paganism. The revolution was in the end irreversible, only temporarily overthrown in the West by the barbarian Goths in AD 410, and by Islam in the East a thousand years later in 1453 with the fall of Constantinople. The barbarians in the West, under their leader Alaric, were Christian in the main, although Arian, while Byzantium did not succumb to Islam for another thousand years. The revolution that Constantine began in AD 313, following the defeat of Maxentius at Milvian Bridge, was sudden: it was a seismic cultural and religious shift that literally changed the world forever. But the revolution was also gradual. For instance, there was no wholesale destruction of pagan temples, although some attacks were made against Christian shrines, as in Jerusalem or Mamre. There was no punishment of pagans *per se*, as there had been of Christians by pagan Emperors such as Diocletian, Galerius and many others before them. There was no immediate change to the social order in terms of slavery or marriage. There was little or no change to the administration or the legal system.

In Constantine's assumption of power there was, therefore, both continuity and change. When Constantine entered Rome after his victory, he did not sacrifice to Capitoline Jupiter, as his predecessors would have done. He kept in place several of Maxentius's senior officials, such as Anullinus, who was prefect of the city. But he clearly signalled a new direction of policy under his government by returning to the church all the property that had been confiscated. Maxentius had himself ended the persecution of Christians in the West, but he had not gone so far as reversing all legislation prejudicial to Christians.[982]

The event that was to be most influential in determining the future of the church took place between Licinius and Constantine at Milan late in AD 312. This came to be known as the Edict of Milan, granting toleration of worship to all in the Empire, not just to Christians. "It is this document [a letter from Licinius to the governors of the eastern provinces], repetitive and enormously long, that stands in the Christian tradition as the official beginning of the new era in the relationship between Church and state".[983] What the edict did was grant toleration to all religious worship, both pagan and Christian. It was a remarkable assertion by the Emperor that freedom of thought and religious variety was to be permitted; but it was an ideal, which was not to be fully realised either in the short or the long term.

When Constantine became the undisputed Emperor in the West after the battle of Milvian Bridge, he was 31. It was just six years since the death of his father and his own proclamation as Emperor by his troops in York in AD 306. He was to rule for 30 years from his proclamation in York:

an astonishingly long time for a ruler in those days and a full ten years longer than Diocletian. For ten of those years Constantine ruled as sole Emperor of East and West, something that Diocletian had worked hard *not* to do. Until his decision to attack Licinius in AD 317, and Licinius's eventual defeat and deposition by Constantine in AD 324, Constantine consolidated his power base in the West. In the end, he was to be the first Roman Emperor ruling from Byzantium, or Constantinople as it became, but in these early years of his reign Constantine was very much centred on the West.

The first two years of Constantine's reign were spent in Gaul, and in particular at Trier, but this did not prevent him from beginning an ambitious building programme in Rome. Rome would forever reflect Constantine's hand, not only in the building of his Victory Arch, placed near the Coliseum, but also the Church of Santa Croce in Gerusalemme and the Basilica Constantiniana, which became the Church of St John in Lateran and the Cathedral of Rome. Figures of Constantine were everywhere to be seen. On the top of the Arch of Constantine the figure of the Emperor drove a four-horse chariot. Looming above the Arch itself was a colossal statue of Constantine. The inscription on the Arch read:

> The Senate and the people of Rome dedicated this arch, decorated with images of his triumph, to the Emperor Caesar Flavius Constantine Greatest Augustus, pious and fortunate, because, at the prompting of the divinity, by the greatness of his mind, he, with his army, avenged the State upon the tyrant and his whole faction at the same instant with just arms.[984]

The arch itself exemplified continuity and change, as it was made up of friezes taken from earlier monuments dedicated to Hadrian, Marcus Aurelius and Trajan. It also heralded, or at least intimated, the new divinity in whose name Constantine fought. The arch was a sculptural cut-and-paste; applying the great names of the past to Constantine's victory, which was itself dedicated to a new, unnamed, divinity. These images, together with the new churches in Rome, made any visitor or citizen aware that the city was now under new Christian management, and a combination of military victory with a new piety.

If continuity and change were evident in the physical environment, they were also evident in the legal and administrative changes in the Empire.[985] The principles that guided Constantine's government were justice for the weak in the face of more powerful adversaries; support for the stability of the family unit; a conservative attitude to the institution of slavery; the continuing use of traditional punishments as practised by previous emperors; and banishment of divination and private consultation with a *haruspex*. (This last change was typical of Constantine's reforms, limiting the use of a *haruspex* to the public sphere of pagan temples, and prohibiting their use in a private house.)

Constantine showed himself both traditional and innovative when it came to legislation on marriage. Since the time of Augustus, and the *lex Julia*, marriage laws had been designed to promote marriage as the basic unit of society, especially in its upper echelons; to encourage the birth of children and heirs; and to punish adultery with exile of the guilty parties or worse. Constantine repealed some of the more onerous and unfair provisions of the previous legislation in AD 320. For instance, he relaxed penalties on freeborn women who married "fiscal slaves" (higher-class slaves, often bureaucrats) and on those who remained celibate after a previous marriage with less than three children. However, he did keep in place fines for those who did not have children, as Constantine believed this was the result of wives practising a rudimentary form of contraception.[986] Once again, there was continuity of marriage legislation with a modicum of reform around the margins.

As with the administration of the law, most of the punishments remained the same, although there were signs of a more humane attitude towards the vulnerable, such as minors, slaves and widows. From AD 318, bishops were included as judges and were permitted to administer justice in civil cases within their flocks, thereby beginning the tradition of church courts, which were to become such a bone of contention in medieval Europe. The point of this change was to provide an alternative to civil and criminal courts, which were congested and subject to endless cycles of appeals.[987] A rescript of AD 321 was granted to Bishop Ossius of Cordoba, one of the clerics closest to Constantine, that people of "religious mind" could free their slaves "in the bosom of the church".[988] On 18 March AD 318, Constantine ordered that judges should give sufficient reasons and explanations for their verdicts when issuing decisions in important cases. In cases where one litigant had died and a will or estate was contested, Constantine ordered a time limit so that the bereaved family was not left in suspense over its future. Similarly, time limits were given in cases where people might have lands or assets returned to them which had been taken when they were minors. Once again, reforms were being made on the margins that show Constantine's great interest in the working of the law, his determination to involve the church as an agent of justice, and his desire to defend the vulnerable in the judicial process.

All these judicial and administrative changes were marks of Constantine's new style of government, but by AD 317 his sights were on the extension of his administration, initially in the Balkans, but then into the whole eastern region of the Empire. In AD 316, Constantine made slow progress from Trier to Arles, down the Rhone Valley, celebrating on 7 August the birth of his and Fausta's first son, who was also called Constantine. This movement was to signal a new departure in his administration, which would see him permanently leaving the western and northern parts of the Empire for a new power base in the East. (Some make the case for an earlier return to Britain, because *adventus* coins were minted in Britain with Constantine's image in AD 314.)[989] In fact, he would only return to Rome twice more, in AD 318 and AD 326.[990] From Arles, Constantine went on to Verona, Serdica and then Sirmium, which became his centre of operations until he defeated Licinius. It seems that, from this period, Constantine increasingly harboured the thought of becoming the single Augustus for the whole Empire.

The Road to Constantinople

Issues of succession now drove Constantine to look eastwards and wonder whether the Empire could once again be under the charge of a single Emperor. Licinius was married to Constantine's half-sister, Constantia, and both Constantine and Licinius had sons within a year of each other. Constantine tried to exclude his nephew from succession as Caesar, putting forward Bassianus, his brother-in-law, instead, and granting him authority over Italy.[991] Constantine was later to accuse Bassianus of conspiracy and have him executed during a time of tension among the leading figures of the Senate in Rome. Constantine's attribution of victory at Milvian Bridge to Christ did not prevent him from jockeying for greater imperial power, and, it seems, sacrificing Bassianus to those ends. When it came to the ways of imperial power, *plus ça change plus c'est la même chose*. By October AD 316, relations between Licinius and Constantine had deteriorated further. Licinius ordered the statues of Constantine taken down in Emona, which amounted to a declaration of war, and a military campaign ensued.[992]

On 8 October AD 316, the forces of Licinius and Constantine engaged in a full-scale dawn to dusk battle at Cibalae (modern-day Vinkovci, in Croatia, not far from Sirmium), in which both Emperors were fully involved. Constantine was visibly in charge of the right wing of his army, which finally drove back Licinius's left wing after fierce hand-to-hand fighting. Licinius left the field having suffered worse casualties and retreated east to Thrace, pursued by Constantine. There came a further battle at Adrianople (modern-day Erdine, which was the scene of many battles as it commanded the east/west, north/south roads between the Balkans and the East).

Once again, Constantine had the better of the battle, but Licinius was no slouch at military strategy and, having disengaged his troops successfully, managed to place his army to the west of Constantine, thereby cutting his lines of communication and supply. Despite his strong position, and maybe because of Constantine's aggressive tactics, Licinius preferred to sue for peace. A treaty was made at Serdica on 1 March AD 317, in which Licinius ceded all his European territories except for Thrace to Constantine and agreed to execute his recently-appointed army commander, Valens, whom he had made Caesar, thereby opening the way for Crispus, Constantine's eldest son from his first marriage, and his infant son Constantine II, to be proclaimed Caesars, along with Licinius's infant son. Whatever happened in the future, Constantius Chlorus's descendants (that is, the father of both Constantine and Licinius's wife, Constantia) would dominate the future succession of the Empire.

For Eusebius, looking on as a Christian and churchman, it was clear that the providence of God had arranged all this, and that both Licinius, and before him Maxentius, were only getting their just deserts. In his *Life of Constantine (Vita Constantini)*, Eusebius portrays the division of the Empire under the two Augusti as being like day and night: Constantine's rule in the West was all light and fragrance, while Licinius's rule in the East was all darkness and stench. According to Eusebius, Licinius added moral degradation to his intemperate treatment of Christians (although Licinius had been a co-signatory of the Edict of Milan, granting freedom of worship to Christians throughout the Empire).

Eusebius wrote of Licinius as follows:

> Moreover, being himself of a nature hopelessly debased by sensuality, and degraded by the continual practice of adultery and other shameless vices, he assumed his own worthless character as a specimen of human nature generally, and denied that the virtue of chastity and continence existed among men.[993]

For the next seven years there would be an uneasy truce between Constantine and Licinius. At the Treaty of Serdica, Constantine was at the height of his powers. He was 45, Fausta had given birth to their second son on 7 August AD 317, and a third son would follow five years later in AD 323. Constantine's family seemed stable and assured. He continued to reside at Sirmium and ruled an Empire from Hadrian's Wall in Britain to Africa, from the tip of Spain in the west to Thrace in the east. Only the eastern provinces, governed from Nicomedia and Antioch, were outside his sway. Yet Constantine wanted to be sole ruler of the whole Empire, founding a new family dynasty, and he believed this was his destiny. Eusebius also believed that God was calling Constantine to be Emperor of the entire Roman Empire.

Eusebius considered Constantine the new Moses, leading his people from servitude to liberation, from persecution to freedom. Eusebius's account or chronology is somewhat patchy and makes the case that church leaders in the East were suffering estrangement from the state, and that congregations were being forced out into the countryside, because they were not allowed to worship in town churches. In fact, the truth was more that there were early signs of division in the church hierarchy as a result of the Arian controversy, and a rift in Alexandria over the treatment of Christians who had compromised their faith. (We will hear more about both issues in the next chapter.)

Constantine's new campaign against Licinius began in the summer of AD 324. A fleet had been prepared to attack Byzantium and Constantine's army marched east.[994] Once again, the two Augusti met at Adrianople on July 3, and once again Constantine prevailed. Once more Constantine fought under the standard of the *labarum*, first envisaged at the Battle of Milvian Bridge, a standard, it was believed, which afforded miraculous protection to its bearer and victory to the army. Constantine appears to have led the decisive attack himself and was wounded in the leg. Licinius fled the battlefield for the city of Byzantium, and appointed an army commander, one Martianus, to command his troops west of the Bosporus, while he himself raised a new army to fight at Chalcedon. The campaign was now determined by sea. Licinius's navy was no match for the newly-prepared western fleet. Byzantium was soon taken and a field army under Constantine landed at a place called Chysopolis. Licinius was once again out-matched and he fled to Nicomedia, where the bishop, another Eusebius, together with Constantia, Constantine's half sister and Licinius's wife, negotiated terms of surrender. Licinius was sent into exile in Thessalonica, where he was executed on charges of conspiracy.

Constantine was now ruler of the whole Empire, extending east to the Tigris and Euphrates, and including present-day Syria, Alexandria, Jerusalem and the holy places of the Bible. He would rarely leave the East again. Only in AD 326, when he celebrated the twentieth anniversary of his accession, would he return to Rome. In style he was the new Christian Augustus: long-lived, bold and aggressive as an adversary, but cautious and thoughtful as a ruler. He had a streak of ruthlessness, was beholden to no aristocratic faction—indeed he was isolated from the great families of Rome. He was a friend of the church, and devoted to the God with whom he made common cause. He would live for another 13 years. There was time enough to consolidate his power, found a new eastern capital bearing his name, make provision for the future, be a friend of the church and a mediator in its troubles—but not, it seems, enjoy the reciprocal affection of his family. Two years later, his eldest son Crispus was executed in mysterious circumstances, and Fausta, to whom he had been so obviously devoted in the past, was removed from public life. Zosimus said that Fausta was killed by immersion in a boiling bath, either for her liaison with Crispus or for falsely accusing him and thus causing his execution. Whatever happened, Constantine did not marry again and his relationship with his mother, Helena, now appeared to give him the support and affection which had sadly become so absent from his own immediate family.

Constantine and Fausta had had five children between AD 316 and AD 323, three sons and two daughters in swift succession. Fausta was widely celebrated by Constantine on new issues of coins, where she was depicted as the fecund and pious Empress. All this came to an abrupt end in AD 326 when she disappeared from public view at the very time the imperial family would normally have been at the centre of a renewed and triumphant life in the Empire. We know that, in AD 326, Crispus, Constantine's oldest son by his first marriage, was executed in Pola in modern-day Croatia on the instructions of his father.[995] For stepmother and stepson, Empress and Caesar, to disappear simultaneously from public life, with no mention made by contemporary sources, has generated more than a whiff of scandal—some supposing that an incestuous relationship developed between the two, for which Fausta was exiled and Crispus executed. It is not until AD 369, well after Constantine's death, that Eutropius writes:

> Constantine, through insolence born of success, changed
> somewhat from his pleasant mildness of spirit. First he assailed
> his relatives, killing his son, an excellent man, and then the son
> of his sister (Licinius's heir and Constantia his sister's son), a
> youth of agreeable nature, and after that, his wife, and then many
> friends.[996]

Whatever the cause of Crispus's execution or Fausta's exile and fall from grace and death, in his final years Constantine was isolated and remote. Whether a change in Constantine's character precipitated these events or whether the change sprang from them is a judgement for which we have too little evidence, but what we do know is that his mother, Helena, figured a great deal in his later life until her death in AD 328, just nine years before his own.

Having defeated Licinius in AD 324, Constantine was caught up with the affairs of the church and, in particular, in summoning the Council of Nicaea in AD 325, at which he played a leading part. We shall trace its course and significance in the next chapter. Then, in AD 330, Constantine made one of his most historic moves in founding the city of Constantinople as the New Rome. Rome itself would never recover its significance after the defeat of Maxentius. Spurned by the Emperors who preferred the newer cities of Trier, Milan, and Sirmium, Rome would, bit by bit, become a backwater of ancient privilege and past glory. It looked increasingly like a city of the past as imperial administration moved elsewhere, but it clung tenaciously to its pagan traditions, which, as the years went by, seemed more and more outmoded. Rome now had a new rival in Constantinople, and, although it was never surpassed in size or population by Constantinople, it became like an overripe plum that lazily fell into the lap of the barbarians; while Constantinople continued for another thousand years as the focus of Roman power, inextricably intertwined with the eastern, Orthodox expression of faith rather than Roman Catholicism.

It is said that Constantine had a divine vision to build his new capital at and around Byzantium. The powerful Emperor Septimius Severus, who had punished the city for its opposition by burning it to the ground and then rebuilding it in Roman style, had captured and rebuilt Byzantium in AD 193. Severus's new city boasted colonnaded streets, a basilica, a new bathhouse and circus.[997] A dual axis of roads was laid out: one running north to a building called the *Strategeion*, and another running west called the *Mese*, which connected the Forum with the city walls in the west.

Constantine now decided to build his new capital here, not to replace Rome, but to be its equal in the East. He set about expanding its size by setting out new city limits (the *limitatio*) in which a priest would walk the new boundaries, ploughing a furrow. When the city was ready for this new beginning, it was formally inaugurated in a ceremony (the *inauguration*). Constantine funded this great project by releasing funds from Licinius's treasury and went about building a city that reflected his newly formed faith. Thus he used a Christian variation of the ancient Roman tradition of city building, incorporating within the new build both churches and temples. This was typical of Constantine's usual style of embracing both continuity and change.

Constantine's plan was to expand the city greatly, so as to cover the whole peninsula from the Gold Horn in the north to the Sea of Marmara in the south, and to move its walls to the west, enclosing much more of it. A further extension of the walls was undertaken by Theodosius II to give us walls still plainly visible in present-day Istanbul. The Mese, the great highway going west from the city, was also extended by at least two miles to a new Golden Gate linked to the Egnatian Way, which then traced its way west to Rome. At one intersection of the Mese, a huge new statue of Constantine was erected, or rather, his head was grafted onto an existing statue of Apollo (the column still stands today on Istanbul's *Yeniceriler Caddesi*). The result was a symbol of what Constantine was prepared to sanction: a cut and paste solution to the need for erecting a new victory monument—the new on top of the old, the Christian Emperor on top of the popular pagan deity, with economy triumphing over unrestrained extravagance. A great palace was built behind the circus, which later became a full-scale hippodrome. So vast was the palace that some 6,500 people were employed within its walls. It was the administrative centre, court and home to the Emperor. Within its precincts was a further palace called the House of Hormisdas, where a Persian prince to whom Constantine had given sanctuary resided. Later in the sixth century, Justinian and Theodora would live there before their succession as Emperor and Empress.[998] It was a sort of Clarence House to the monarchs' Buckingham Palace.

What made the new city distinct and unique was the presence of churches right from its inception. The first churches to be built were *Hagia Eirene* (Holy Peace), and then later *Hagia Sophia* (Holy Wisdom) and the Church of the Apostles, next to which was Constantine's own mausoleum. To have churches designed into the cityscape of a normally standard pattern of design for a Roman city was novel and indicates the new set of values and convictions that governed Constantine's thinking. It was not that churches were the only places of worship in the city, for there remained also pagan temples. In building Constantinople, Constantine did not erase Byzantium and her temples. There was now a mix of temples and churches.[999] Pagan temples were found both outside and inside the new city walls, while churches were mostly within, although not exclusively so, as St Mocius's Church was just outside the new city wall.[1000] Constantine indicated that he served only the one God and Father of the Lord Jesus Christ, but he nevertheless allowed other deities' shrines in New Rome. Thus the mother of Zeus, Magna Mater, and Rhea, all had shrines in the new city, and so did Tyche (Fortune), in the form of a new goddess, Anthousia, who Constantine brought in to replace the ancient Byzantium goddess Keroe.[1001] In terms of places of worship, Constantinople had a mixed spiritual economy, but nonetheless the presence of churches placed so close to the administration of imperial power in the city was both novel and striking. Constantine made *Hagia Sophia* his own imperial church. It was to remain so for successive emperors, although rebuilt after the great fire caused by riots in Justinian's reign in AD 532. Despite this mixed economy of worship in the city, there was no doubt about Constantine's own preference for worship, and his own commitment to Christianity.

Constantinople was to be the centre for the administration of the Empire for both West and East. His edicts would run throughout the Empire, even if there were other centres of authority, such as the Senate in Rome. The Empire had been governed for the past 300 years by a mixture of aristocratic senatorial power and imperial sovereignty, with its own officials guaranteed by the army. Past officers of state, such as consuls, existed still, but these ancient offices were now melded into a combination of regional and imperial government that emanated from the court and its governing body, the *Consistory*—literally those who stood to advise the Emperor. From this court, edicts or rescripts would come which were executed by various officials across the Empire.

Constantinople, like all principal cities or capitals, needed to be able to provide the administration of government. A Whitehall must be provided so that the state could function. At court, the Praetorian Prefects retained the rank of most eminent men (*vir eminentissimus*). Below them were the most famous men, *vir clarissimus*, among whom were numbered senators based either in Rome or in the new Senate in Constantinople. Finally, there was a third grade called "most perfect men" or *vir perfectissimus*, among whom were provincial military commanders, and diocesan and provincial officials. (That is, it was a Roman civil diocese, the form of which the church then followed when creating ecclesiastical dioceses.) At the same time, the *comes* or counts were regularised as imperial appointments based in the Court, and often with military responsibilities, rather than *magisters*, the former title approved by the Senate.[1002] In other words, the administration became increasingly court-based and revolved around meetings of the Consistory, rather than the Senate. In Constantinople, the Senate was aristocratic too, generously patronised by the Emperor with houses and rewards, and largely concerned with the administration of the city. The whole system was a complex amalgam of old and new, but in general the power inevitably shifted more and more to the imperial court, and its own administration.

Constantine, in a short space of time, reunited the Empire under a single ruler, himself; prepared for the founding of a dynasty based on his family; by and large settled the Empire peaceably with few wars on its eastern (Persian) and northern (German) borders and began a new capital and administration in the East at his newly founded city of Constantinople. But a new united Empire was hard to achieve and would not outlive Constantine. Diocletian had been right in that respect. He also granted freedom of worship to Christians and pagans alike. It was a mixture of continuity and change, a revolution, but one whose consequences would only gradually emerge. The organs of government remained the same. Public buildings may have had different values, but their outward appearance still seemed familiar. Nor did Constantine bring great social change. Virtue, rather than a profession of Christianity, was still sufficient for inclusion in public administration. The existence of slavery was still respected in law. If a woman secretly married a slave, both would be executed according to a law Constantine passed, as late as AD 329.[1003] Nevertheless, he did not want children to be sold into slavery by reason of poverty, so the state should provide food, shelter and clothing.[1004] However, children born to relationships between upper class men and slaves could never be legitimate. Contrastingly, some of Constantine's policies supported the "worthy weak".[1005] Marriage and family life were likewise strengthened. In a word, Constantine sought to provide a stable framework in society, so that government could continue unfettered. He advocated a change of worship, but not yet a revolutionary change of direction. He sought stability in society in the terms of his age, and likewise he sought stability in the church, which he generously upheld, but which he discovered all too soon could be surprisingly factious. Dealing with those factions was to draw Constantine into the heart of church administration, doctrine and politics. This is the next part of the story.

CHAPTER 11

The Road to Nicaea

There is little doubt that Constantine was a visionary in both the narrow and the broad sense of that word. He was given to visions, having had some kind of epiphany linked to Apollo when still in France. According to a panegyrist in Autun in AD 310, Apollo offered Constantine a laurel crown of victory.[1006] Whether Constantine himself claimed he was a visionary, or whether this was just part of a public orator's hyperbole, we cannot be sure. We can be more certain, however, that by AD 312 Constantine had had some kind of conversion to Christ, following in the footsteps of his father Constantius, who had a real sympathy for Christians demonstrated in his unwillingness to carry out the persecution of the church initiated by Diocletian and Galerius. His half-sister Constantia's profession of Christianity also influenced Constantine. Then, in AD 312, the night before his victory at Milvian Bridge, and according to the Christian authors Lactantius and Eusebius of Caesarea, Constantine had a vision that his soldiers should fight under the *chi-rho* symbol denoting Christ, and thus fight for the "Highest God" as Lactantius put it. Constantine was also convinced in a dream that he should do this. It is not surprising then, given the resulting victory over Maxentius, that Constantine made good his new-found following of Christ, and his incipient membership of the church, by quickly rewarding the church with a new settlement made at the beginning of his reign.

Constantine gave land and wealth to the church straight away. He gave territory to build new churches in Rome, as with St John's Lateran. He also gave many privileges to church leaders, investing bishops with civil powers of jurisdiction and exempting clergy from taxation and the onerous burdens of *munera* (civic responsibilities for roads, drains and public buildings etc.). He altered this later, however, because many became priests simply to avoid these expenses.[1007] He also allowed people of "religious mind" to free their slaves in the "bosom of the church". These measures, together with the Edict of Milan, issued by both Augusti, Constantine and Licinius, afforded freedom of worship, thereby changing at a stroke the standing of Christians and the church in the Empire. Intervening on behalf of the church so publicly gave a new responsibility to an Emperor who was now avowedly Christian. Whereas in pagan Rome the Emperor was bound to consult the *haruspices* and make sacrifices to the gods, seeking their guidance and favour, now Constantine had himself become a kind of king-priest. He made it his business to bring both worldly status and organisational unity to a church which was facing, or about to face, some of its most intractable doctrinal problems.

The first great ecclesiastical crisis facing Constantine on becoming Emperor in the West was the Donatist controversy. This controversy, which was to dog the church in North Africa until the arrival of Islam, had its roots in the conduct of Christians during times of persecution. Some Christians, like Perpetua, who in AD 207 embraced martyrdom despite being the mother of a new infant, were bold martyrs; others, like Bishop Cyprian of Carthage, at first evaded execution. (Cyprian at first went into hiding during Decius's persecution of AD 250, but was later executed under Valerian.) Cyprian's view, as we have seen, was that if the "lapsed" showed adequate penance they could be re-admitted to fellowship in the church. The trigger for a deepening dispute occurred when Caecilian was consecrated Bishop of Carthage by Mensurius. Caecilian was regarded by his opponents as "lapsed", having bowed to imperial pressure, and was also seen as an opponent of some confessors and the Abitinian Martyrs. Both Caecilian and Mensurius approved of Cyprian's view that the "lapsed" should be re-admitted to fellowship, and that if they were priests, should also be re-admitted to their ministry after due penance. A more hardline group, led by Donatus and Majorinus, felt that Caecilian was a *traditor* (literally, one who handed over sacred books to the authorities during the reign of Diocletian—and hence a traitor), but more especially that his predecessor Mensurius had done abominable things during the Great Persecution of Diocletian.

The dispute was further complicated by secondary matters, such as the legality of Caecilian's election, which added fuel to the fire. The upshot was that there was a deep rift between the church that had undergone persecution without compromise (such as the Abitinian Martyrs), and those *traditors* who had handed over scriptures or religious texts to the persecuting authorities. In the midst of this enmity between church members, Constantine had to find a way for peace and, if possible, reconciliation.

Constantine's first move was to restore what had been taken from the persecuted Christians in North Africa, as elsewhere. He wrote to Anullinus, possibly the son of the Anullinus who had persecuted the Abitinian Martyrs, the urban Prefect of Rome, asking for the restoration of lands and property taken from Christians.[1008] Next, Caecilian, who was a friend of Ossius of Cordoba, who in turn was a close confidant of Constantine and a member of his court, stole a march on other church leaders in North Africa by persuading Constantine to order the *Rationalis*—the chief financial officer of Africa—to give money only to priests loyal to Caecilian.[1009] Soon Majorinus, the leader of what would become the Donatist Church, heard of Constantine's support for Caecilian and strongly objected to his being singled out for such favour. A petition was made to Constantine that their case be heard before a council of bishops. Following the precedent of Aurelian, who had chosen a council to hear a case in his reign, Miltiades, Bishop of Rome, was chosen to hear the case and to adjudicate.

The council was a disaster. Shortly beforehand, Majorinus died. Donatus presented the case but was scarcely heard, as Miltiades used the council as an opportunity not only to hear this case, but to extend the influence of the papacy over all of North Africa. He gave Donatus no encouragement that he had been heard and understood, and Donatus, in turn, accused Miltiades of being a *traditor*.

The Gallic bishops on the council questioned the integrity of Constantine's episcopal confidant, Ossius. Donatus demanded that Caecilian recognise all Donatist bishops in Africa, and finally, on the council's advice, Donatus was forbidden by the Emperor to return to Carthage. None of this was conducive to a compromise, and Constantine realised as much. A second petition was made to the Emperor, and this time the case was heard at Arles in Provence.

The Council of Arles opened on 1 August AD 314 with Constantine present as a layman, very aware how badly the council had gone in Rome and wanting Arles to be more effective. The council heard evidence about the Donatist controversy and also about the issue of the date Easter should be celebrated. With regard to Donatism, three main canons or rules were passed. Those who could be shown through documentary proof to have handed scriptures, liturgies, communion vessels or the names of fellow Christians over to the persecuting authorities were to be removed from office, but any ordinations they had undertaken were not invalid. Secondly, action could only be taken against someone if there was clear documentary proof, since the atmosphere had become so embittered that witnesses were bribed to speak against suspects. Thirdly, those who falsely accused their brethren should be excommunicated. Donatus was not permitted to set up an alternative ecclesiastical structure from which all trace of compromise was purged. Rather, those who were proven to have "lapsed", in the sense of being *traditors,* would be removed from office only on the production of proper written evidence, with their official actions respected and not overturned. This may not have been all that Donatus wanted, but it was a fair way of proceeding, allowing bygones to be bygones, seeking clear evidence where it was needed, and upholding the actions of ministry when it came to ordinations. Sadly, these decisions were not enough, for Donatism was too extreme to accept such a settlement and so the Donatists only provoked exasperation.

As the most powerful man in the western world, it must have been salutary for Constantine to sit as a layman in the council chamber and not intervene. He effectively curtailed his own powers so as to allow a compromise or settlement to emerge, but no such result was forthcoming. For the future, he may have noted that a softly-softly approach would not work in the face of such intransigence. He respected the independence of the church; yet he saw from the rebarbative behaviour of some participants that gaining a settlement would frequently be difficult. It was clear where Constantine's sympathies lay. In an exchange with council delegates following the conclusion of the council, he castigated the Donatists for their stubborn and arrogant attitude, and their unwillingness to reach a settlement along fair and judicial lines. In a letter following the council, he wrote as follows:

> In very truth it was not without good cause that the mercy of Christ withdrew from these [the Donatists], in whom it is as clear as day that their madness is of such a kind that we find them abhorrent even to the heavenly dispensations; so great a madness persists in them when, with incredible arrogance, they persuade themselves of things that it is not right either to say or hear, repudiating the equitable judgement that had been given by the will of heaven ... They demand my judgement, when I myself await the judgement of heaven.[1010]

The Council of Arles did not end the complaints of the Donatists; it only fuelled them further, such was their stubborn mindset. In AD 315, they came forward with fresh complaints, bringing to light documents to prove that Felix of Abthugni, who had ordained Caecilian, was in fact himself a *traditor*—although Felix had already been previously acquitted in Rome in AD 313. It seemed they were pursuing a witch-hunt rather than promoting the good order of the church, and when it came to it, their evidence was found to be a forgery. After protracted hearings of the Donatists' case in Arles, and then in the autumn in Milan, Constantine dismissed the council, once more coming down in favour of Caecilian.

On 10 November AD 316, Constantine appears to have lost patience with the Donatists and ordered the *vicarious* of Africa to consider confiscating their churches.[1011] By AD 317, the controversy was no longer considered purely religious, but had become a civil dispute. Tragically, on 12 March AD 317, imperial troops burst into a Donatist church in Carthage and slaughtered the congregation. This only fed the mentality of martyrdom, but for Constantine and the Empire it marked a *rubicon* that was crossed when religious disputes were settled (or rather prolonged) by the sword. The assault on the Donatists continued as part of imperial policy until AD 321, when Constantine decided to restore the exiled Donatist bishops.

In fact, imperial policy had not worked in North Africa. The Donatist Church grew in size and significance. At a synod in AD 337, the Donatists were able to assemble 270 bishops in Carthage: "The foundational tale of the Donatist movement, one of courage in the face of oppression, murder and persecution, was a far more compelling tale than the Caecilianist story of theft and corruption".[1012] The whole Donatist controversy was for Constantine an object lesson in the limits of imperial power. He could defeat an opponent on the battlefield and thereby secure a victory, heralding new possibilities, but to defeat an entire religious movement that appealed to the perspective of the North Africans was an entirely different matter.

Perhaps it was this lesson, drawn from a protracted dispute, that prepared Constantine for a potentially even more significant controversy, this time brewing in Alexandria and whipped up by a popular priest named Arius, who published his credal statement of faith in AD 320. In it he supposed that there was a time when Christ (as the pre-incarnate Word) *was not*—that is, did not exist, and equally, therefore, there was a time when God was not a Father, for, "it is God alone (who is) monad and first principle of all things, who exists in this way before all things. That is why he exists before the Son (*pro tou huiou*)".[1013] So what were the origins of this most pernicious of heresies?

The Origins of Arianism

The background to the intellectual and philosophical expressions of Arianism is a combination of Middle Platonism and Stoicism. As we know, the ancient world was suffused with Platonism and its tenets, including the notions of a single remote absolute monad, the supremacy of the soul, and the existence of ideal forms to which we may aspire through contemplation, suppression of the flesh and the ascent of the soul. Many of these concepts would mingle with Christian teaching, not least in Origen, Gregory of Nyssa and later Augustine, although in different ways (which we cannot explore here). Neo-Platonism and Middle Platonism, so influential in Alexandria and the East, only fuelled the fire of Platonic thinking, giving rise to Gnosticism, whose massive influence we have noted, and then, indirectly, to the teaching of Arius and Arianism.

Arius sought to resolve the tension in much of this Middle Platonic teaching, which had taken such a grip on Christianity in Egypt and Syria and from there also in Rome, by denying the New Testament witness to Christ as uniquely God and Man. How Christ was God and Man together in a single person was a controversy which would be fought out between Nestorius and Cyril in the fifth century. "Arius resolves the tensions in Christian thinking by a simple assimilation of God the Father to the remote and isolated absolute of Middle Platonism and of the Son to the creative demiurge".[1014] This struck at the very heart of the Christian faith as expressed in the Bible. It put Christianity within the framework of Middle and Neo-Platonism as a further polytheistic expression of the one almighty God. It made Jesus a creature rather than the Creator; it denied his consubstantial existence with the Father and the Spirit; and it denied and broke his own saving identification as God with humankind that was made through the incarnation. As a teaching, Arianism appealed to Middle Platonism and also to the Germanic tribes, with their liking for polytheism. It also gave plenty of scope for human effort in salvation. For, if Christ is adopted by the Father on account of his moral advancement, then he becomes a pattern for us: "His obedience is the prototype for our own, the disposition that leads to adoption as children of God".[1015]

If the deep background to Arianism was Middle Platonism mingled with Stoic ideas, the more recent past of Arianism was the teaching of Origen. Because of the complexity and sheer range of Origen's writings and biblical exegesis, it is possible to make the case for a direct link from Origen to Arius, although that would be a disservice to Origen and would read back into his work the errors of Arius. What we see instead is that those areas of Trinitarian theology, which were as yet undefined, or not defined and confirmed by the mind of the church, created opportunities for extrapolation by a teacher like Arius who sought to over-define or wrongly define what was previously left unstated, and in the process leave biblical Christianity behind.

Perhaps there are three points worth making in relation to Origen and the subsequent teaching of Arius. Firstly, much of Origen's understanding of Christ's relationship to God is modelled on the teaching about Wisdom in the Book of Proverbs. For Origen, Christ was the Wisdom and Power of God from the beginning.[1016] As such, Origen thinks of the Son as mirroring the Father's existence and as "intrinsic to the nature of God".[1017] Secondly, the Son's existence is essential to God's being and what God from all eternity wills to be. After all, the Son is the Wisdom and the Power of the Father. They are inseparable and yet distinct. The Son is the image and revealer of the Father as "light from light". Like brightness from the sun, you cannot have one without the other. Such metaphors were to become favourite vehicles of explanation of the Trinity for the writers of the Creeds, as at Constantinople in AD 381, where Christ was described as "light from light" and "true God from true God", and by Augustine in *De Trinitate*. Origen, although showing the closest possible indwelling of the Son in the Father, is nevertheless not yet ready to employ the *ousia* language which will become the touchstone of Nicene Trinitarianism (*ousia* meaning substance). For Origen, the use of *ousia* language, and of the Son being of the same substance as the Father, may have strengthened the notion of the full divinity of the Son, but at the expense of considering a material separation of the Son from the Father.[1018] He preferred the biblical notion of the Son as the Wisdom and Power of God.

Nevertheless, and paradoxically, if Origen was shy about using *ousia* language, he was not shy about using the term *hypostasis*, which in his vocabulary meant separate existence. From this we may deduce that Origen was happy to define the distinct individuated beings of the Godhead, but not how they came to be distinct while still all being united. Given this kind of Trinitarian thinking in Origen's *On First Principles*, Arius stressed that Father and Son were not of the same substance and were very much distinct beings.

It is now time to see the development of the controversy from its beginning to the calling of the first great ecumenical council at Nicaea by Constantine.

Arius, his Teaching, and Nicaea

Little is known about Arius's background. He came from Upper Libya and the region of Cyrene. In a letter to one of his circle, Eusebius of Nicomedia, he describes himself as a fellow *sulloukianista*, which is generally taken to mean that they were both followers of a teacher or theologian from Antioch called Lucian, a biblical scholar and founder of the School of Antioch and influential in the later theology of Diodorus of Tarsus and Theodore of Mopsuestia. Lucian was an influential subordinationist theologian, believing in the subordination of the Son to the Father. This view had been heretically expressed by Paul of Samosata (c.AD 200–275), a former Bishop of Antioch, and subsequently condemned by the church. It was nonetheless still an influential line of thinking in Antioch. It is also possible that Arius was taught by a neo-Platonist, Iamblichus of Apamea, a Syrian who taught Neo-Platonic philosophy near Antioch from AD 304. Arius then had strong Platonic leanings and had been exposed to the Monarchian controversy in relation to the Trinity, in which the Son was subordinated to the monarchy of the Father.

If Arius spent time in the region of Antioch being exposed to the philosophical and theological teaching described above, he then returned to North Africa and Egypt and was ordained by Bishop Peter of Alexandria in AD 312. He must have come swiftly to prominence and was a skilful debater, being persuasive and ascetic, and seems to have appealed both to the Alexandrian dockers as well as to the 700 holy virgins he supervised.[1019]

At this time the Meletian controversy was tearing the church in Alexandria apart. Meletius was the Bishop of Lycopolis in the Nile Delta who had been imprisoned during the Diocletian persecution. He took a hard line against those who had lapsed during that persecution, refusing to re-admit them to communion, much like the later Donatists. As such, he was at odds with his provincial bishop, Peter of Alexandria. Arius, together with twenty-eight other bishops, sided with Meletius and the Donatists around Carthage. Arius presented himself as both ascetic and hard-line and as such was part of a large constituency. In AD 321, he threw down a theological gauntlet in a credal letter to the new Bishop of Alexandria, Alexander, whose secretary was the young Athanasius. In it, and among other things, he wrote, "The Son who is tempted, suffers, and dies, however exalted he may be, is not to be equal to the immutable Father beyond pain and death".[1020] Such a saying sounded a death knell to Christianity.

Arius's theology affirmed the absolute uniqueness and transcendence of God as the unoriginate source (*agennetos arche*) of all reality. Because of this, Arius began his uncompromising letter to Alexander in these terms: "We acknowledge one God, who is alone ingenerate [self-existent], alone eternal, alone without beginning, alone true, alone possessing immortality, alone wise, alone good, alone sovereign". He went on to say that there were "three hypostases", but that the Son was not coeternal with the Father.[1021] What flows from this is that, firstly, the Word must be a creature that the Father has formed by his own fiat and who is not self-existent. Secondly, since Arius argues this is the case, the Word must have a beginning, or in his words, there was a time when the Word did not exist, and thus he is not eternally part of the Godhead. The Arian slogan was that "there was when he was not". For Arius, the Son could not be co-existent with the Father, since this would be the end of monotheism. Thirdly, the Son could have no communion with, or direct knowledge of, the Father. "Although He is God's Word and Wisdom, he is distinct from that Word and that Wisdom which belong to God's very essence".[1022] The Son is therefore creature pure and simple. And, as with all other creatures, the Son is of a different substance from the Father's essence. In an epistle to Athanasius, Arius said that "He (Christ) is not God truly, but by participation in grace ... He too is called God in name only".[1023] Much of this teaching is found in piecemeal form in the fragmentary quotations of Arius's *Thalia*, which was later used for his condemnation by Bishop Epiphanius of Salamis in Cyprus.

The result of this teaching, which Arius began to publish from AD 318, was a great assault on biblical Christianity. In no time, the full import of what Arius was proposing became clear—an attenuation of the Son's divinity. The initial debate occurred between Arius and Alexander, the Bishop of Alexandria, as demonstrated by a credal letter dated as AD 320 by the German scholar Opitz in his *Urkunde*. Alexander formally excommunicated Arius following this letter. A synod of 100 bishops met in Bithynia to condemn Arius and his followers, whereupon Arius sought support from Eusebius of Nicomedia and Eusebius of Caesarea.[1024] In AD 324, Bishop Alexander wrote an immensely long letter called *the philarchos* to his namesake, who was then Bishop of Constantinople, in which he complained about the activities of Arius and Achillas, and also about Arius's formation of heretical churches in Alexandria, which had received support from around three unnamed bishops and had set off riots there. A further letter, *henos somatos* ("of one body"), possibly drafted by Alexander's young secretary, Athanasius, complained of the influence of Eusebius of Nicomedia and the teaching of Arius, and was signed by many of the Alexandrian clergy. In this letter, Alexander recorded the errors of Arius: saying that there was a time when the Father was not yet a Father (i.e., the Son had not been generated); that the Father made the Son out of nothing, so the Son was a creature not sharing in the essence (*ousia*) of the Father.[1025] After this clear rejection by Alexander, Arius moved from Alexandria to Palestine, where amazingly, despite his deposition in Alexandria, his congregation was given permission to meet.

In AD 323, as well as embarking on a war with Licinius to win the Eastern Empire, Constantine sent his envoy, Ossius, Bishop of Cordoba, to Egypt to try and reconcile Alexander and Arius. After becoming aware through the failure of this mission of the deep rift between Arius and the Alexandrian church, and also of the danger of Arius's teaching to the church, Constantine began, with the support of Pope Silvester of Rome, to plan for a council for most of the Eastern bishops and some representatives from the West. The Council of Nicaea was in the making. Initially, Constantine thought that Antioch should be the venue, but for reasons of convenience, and after his defeat of Licinius, he chose Nicaea. Situated alongside a pleasant lake south of Nicomedia, and next to the imperial summer palace, it seemed a suitable location for a great assembly of bishops.

The Council of Nicaea was not the first church council. In the Acts of the Apostles (Acts 15), and under the leadership of James, the Lord's brother, the early church came to a decision about including the Gentile Christians in what was then a largely Jewish church, and about various obligations to the Law. Other councils followed. The Council of Elvira in Spain in AD 306 excommunicated prostitutes, actors and gladiators, and forbade the use of pictures in churches. In AD 314, Constantine

summoned a council in the West at Arles, as we have seen, to deal with
the issues raised by Donatism.[1026] As he had done in the West, now
Constantine did in the East. He assembled a council which he would
attend and which would iron out the differences between the various
parties and set down a statement of faith to which they could agree.
Already, the bishops Narcissus of Neronias and Constantine's biographer,
the church historian Eusebius of Caesarea, had been disciplined for
holding that there was more than one *ousia*. Eusebius never retracted
his conviction that the Son and the Father were two distinct *ouisiai*.[1027]
Constantine himself may not have grasped the deep Christological and
salvific issues at stake in the Arian controversy, but he had an innate
understanding of the damage this controversy could do to the unity and
mission of the church. Indeed, he criticised both Arius and Alexander,
saying it was "wrong in the first instance to propose such questions as
these, or to reply to them, when propounded".[1028] Constantine would
have preferred no public discussion of these matters, to avoid a rift in the
church. But now that there was a rift and a potential schism, he regarded
it his duty to restore unity to the church.

In June AD 325, the council opened with an address by the Emperor
himself. Eusebius records the opening moments of the council as follows:

> Now when the appointed day arrived on which the council met
> for the final solution of the questions in dispute, each member
> was present for this in the central building of the palace, which
> appeared to exceed the rest in magnitude. On each side of the
> interior of this were many seats disposed in order, which were
> occupied by those who had been invited to attend, according
> to their rank. As soon, then, as the whole assembly had seated
> themselves with becoming orderliness, a general silence
> prevailed, in expectation of the emperor's arrival. First of all, three
> of his immediate family entered in succession, then others also
> preceded his approach, not of the soldiers or guards who usually
> accompanied him, but only friends in the faith. And now, all rising
> at the signal which indicated the emperor's entrance, at last he
> himself proceeded through the midst of the assembly, like some
> heavenly messenger of God, clothed in raiment which glittered

as it were with rays of light, reflecting the glowing radiance of a purple robe, and adorned with the brilliant splendour of gold and precious stones. Such was the external appearance of his person; and with regard to his mind, it was evident that he was distinguished by piety and godly fear. This was indicated by his downcast eyes, the blush of his countenance, and his gait. For the rest of his personal excellences, he surpassed all present in height of stature and beauty of form, as well as in majesty, dignity of mien, and invincible strength and vigour. All these graces, united in suavity of manner, and a serenity becoming his imperial station, declared the excellence of his mental qualities to be above all praise. As soon as he advanced to the upper end of the seats, at the first he remained standing, and when a low chair of wrought gold had been set for him, he waited until the bishops had beckoned to him, and then sat down, and after him the whole assembly did the same.[1029]

It was, quite apart from its business, an enthralling event and a never-to-be-forgotten occasion of imperial dignity and ecclesiastical confirmation. Only 12 years previously it would have been undreamed of that a Roman Emperor should sit down in conference with the bishops.

Constantine then addressed the council, saying that in his judgement "internecine strife within the church of God is far more evil and dangerous than any kind of war or conflict". He went on:

I feel my desires will be most completely fulfilled when I can see you all united in one judgement, and that there is a common spirit of peace and concord prevailing among you all, which it becomes you, as consecrated to the service of God, to commend to others. Delay not dear friends: delay not, you ministers of God, and faithful servants of him who is our common Lord and Saviour: begin from this moment to discard the causes of that disunion which has existed among you, and remove the perplexities of controversy by embracing principles of peace.[1030]

After Constantine's address, delivered in Latin, but with simultaneous translation into Greek, Eusebius of Caesarea, one of the pro-Arian bishops, and under threat of excommunication, stepped forward with a statement of faith, which Constantine declared to be exactly like his own. It did not contain the key word *homoousios*, but it was sufficiently orthodox to gather some support. Next to speak up was Eustathius of Antioch, who read a piece written by Eusebius of Nicomedia, another Arian-leaning bishop. It was clearly heretical. In the light of this, Constantine produced his pre-prepared statement of faith which we have come to know as the Nicene Creed, composed, it is said, by a Cappadocian priest named Hermogenes.[1031] It was a statement which not only declared the truth about the Father and Son, but incorporated anathemas against the doctrines of Arianism. It read as follows:

> We believe in one God, The Father Almighty, Maker of all things visible and invisible—and in one Lord Jesus Christ, the Son of God, the only begotten of the father, who is of the same substance of the Father; God of God, Light of Light, true God of true God; begotten not made, consubstantial with the Father; by whom all things were made, both which are in heaven and on earth; who for the sake of us men, and on account of our salvation, descended, became incarnate, was made man, suffered, and rose again on the third day; he ascended into the heavens, and will come to judge the living and the dead. We also believe in the Holy Ghost. But those who say, "there was a time when he was not" and "before his generation he was not", and "he came to be from nothing", or those who pretend that the Son of God is "of other hypostasis or substance", or "created" or "alterable or mutable", the universal and apostolic Church anathematizes.[1032]

It was the first universal creed to be promulgated.[1033] On 19 June AD 325, the bishops formally adopted the Creed, which was later attached to canons promulgated at a council at Antioch around AD 341. Although it was the most momentous decree of the council, there were many other canons besides on church discipline and practice. *Canon 1* excluded eunuchs from the clergy, unless they had suffered involuntary castration at the hands of doctors or barbarians; *Canon 2* prohibited the ordination of neophytes (recent converts) and *Canon 3* the harbouring of women in a household of a priest who was not a member of the family. *Canon 4* required that all other bishops of a province consecrate a bishop, if possible. *Canon 5* required that an excommunication imposed by one bishop should be honoured by all. *Canon 6* affirmed the pre-eminence of Alexandria and Antioch in the East, effectively downgrading Constantinople, which was a relatively new arrival. *Canon 7* provided for the special importance of the See of Jerusalem, but not at the cost of the See of Caesarea: presumably resolving a local dispute of seniority in Palestine. *Canon 8* provided that clergy, ordained in Rome by the schismatic Novatian, should have their ordinations universally recognised. *Canons 9* and *10* allowed for the revocation of the ordination of criminals. *Canons 11–14* dealt with terms of penance for the inclusion of the "lapsed". *Canon 15* forbade the translation of a bishop from one see to another, and would catch out Gregory Nazianzen in AD 381, preventing him from being transferred from the drab See of Sasima to the new capital of Constantinople.[1034] The same restriction was placed on presbyters and deacons. *Canon 17* forbade usury, the lending of money at interest. *Canon 18* forbade deacons giving presbyters (their seniors) the Eucharist. *Canon 19* required those who had followed the heretic Paul of Samosata, Bishop of Antioch from AD 260–268 and a Monarchist in Trinitarian theology—who believed that God adopted the human Jesus as his son—to be re-baptised into the one universal church. *Canon 20* forbade kneeling in prayer during worship and on the feast days of the church, requiring people to stand to pray.[1035]

A quick glance at these canons shows them to be a mixed bag, reflecting the culture and authoritarian structures of the day. A greater degree of control was to be exercised by Emperor and bishops. Issues of hierarchy were addressed, both in terms of episcopal sees and the status of the clergy. Practices were standardised in relation to penance, and even the physical mode of praying was laid down. The church was nothing if not prescriptive. Uniformity of practice was the aim, with the strongly authoritarian structure of society in the late Roman Empire shining through and understandably affecting the church.

The question of the celebration of Easter was not especially dealt with at Nicaea, although there was an anathema against those who celebrated it on any date other than one fixed by "the Great and Holy Council".[1036] In his address to the bishops at Nicomedia, Constantine had stressed that, in his understanding of Christianity, great significance must be given to the resurrection; and celebrating it uniformly across the church was very important to him. At the time, one group in the church held that Easter should be celebrated on the Sunday following the first full moon after the spring equinox; another held that it should be celebrated on the date in the Greco-Roman calendar that corresponded to Nisan 14, or on the nearest Sunday to it.

The Council of Nicaea was undoubtedly a benchmark in church discipline and doctrine, as we can see from the canons, but it also outlined in its "Creed" an orthodox theology of the Trinity. It would not be firmly embedded or widely published until the Council of Constantinople in AD 381, but it would provide both a vocabulary and a rule against which other descriptions of the Trinity could be tested. The dispute would continue to run, not least because Constantine's heirs, Constantius II and Valens, would themselves adopt and support Arian theology. Unprepared to say that the Son was of the same substance as the Father (*homoousios*), they preferred the term *homoios kat' ousian* (like in essence), against which Athanasius, Bishop of Alexandria, and the Cappadocian Fathers fought.

In the immediate aftermath of Nicaea, Constantine seemed to have brought peace to the church, but it was short-lived. Eusebius of Nicomedia and Arius quickly resiled from the Creed and were disciplined. Eusebius was relieved of his see and Arius and two Libyan bishops were exiled. Eusebius of Caesarea, no advocate of the Nicene Creed, preferred his own baptismal creed of Caesarea. In AD 328, Arius and his companion, Euzoius, were reinstated after their willingness to sign their own home-made, rather "non-committal creed",[1037] as also were the exiled bishops Eusebius of Nicomedia and Theognis of Nicaea, after only three years of exile.[1038]

After the death of Alexander, Bishop of Alexandria, and the succession of Athanasius in the summer of AD 328, ecclesiastical civil war broke out between Eusebius of Nicomedia and Athanasius. At the same time, once the majority of bishops saw that the term *homoousios* was being seriously challenged by the *homoios kat' ousian* party, or even worse, the later *homoian* party (who implied the Son is like in will, but not in substance, to the Father), they rallied to defend the term *homoousios* as the quickest and simplest way of defending the Nicene Creed.[1039]

The controversy continued, fragmented and splintered into different groups—each with more refined interpretations, and in some cases what was essentially a theological dispute widened into a jealous dispute about relations between sees, or between bishops over their obedience to the Emperor. In AD 335, Arius was once again upheld by a synod of sixty bishops meeting in Jerusalem, provoking the ire of Athanasius, now the main protagonist of the Nicene cause, who demanded a further synod to re-examine Arius. The new synod met in Constantinople in AD 336. During this synod, Arius fell ill and died of an internal rupture while in a public lavatory.[1040] The following year Constantine died, but the dispute continued throughout the Empire to the end of the century and beyond. By AD 381, the Council of Constantinople under Theodosius I re-affirmed the Nicene Creed, so that by then the church, both Catholic and Orthodox, knew its own mind, even if unreconciled Arian sections of the church were to exist for many years to come. Constantine had sought the peace and the unity of the church as it faced the most critical and protracted theological crisis of its existence. Although Constantine could not settle it, he provided a way by which orthodoxy would eventually triumph.

Constantine's commitment to the church, his devotion to Christ and his hope of resurrection should not be in doubt. His profession of faith was neither pragmatic nor a matter of convenience. It was deeply personal, and at the same time revolutionary for the Empire and for the future of Christianity. His own creed and statement of faith are not only demonstrated in his numerous attempts to ensure the unity of the church, whether at Arles or Nicaea, but more personally in his address, called *Oration to the Saints,* given either in AD 315 or AD 325 (the scholars are divided) and recorded by Eusebius. It is a lengthy address, would have taken almost two hours to deliver, and was given either at Nicomedia[1041] or at Rome.[1042] It is a truly astonishing piece of reflection and proclamation by Constantine about his understanding of his Christian faith.

The address is divided into 26 sections, or chapters, in the style of the age. It is therefore carefully conceived and presumably intended as a personal definition of the Emperor's faith. The first ten chapters mark a definite break with paganism in the statement that there is one God who is creator of all. In chapter three, Constantine states, "God, who is ever above all existence, and the good which all things desire, has no origin, and therefore no beginning, being himself the originator of all things which receive existence".[1043] Constantine argues that because there is one Creator God, a united harmony in all things is possible; prayer is efficacious and there is opportunity for mercy in providence to proceed. It is a well-constructed and thought-out argument in contradistinction to the myriad of gods existing for all eventualities in paganism. In chapter five, he goes on to glorify Christ as "the foundation of the Universe", who has himself "created the race of men" and placed animals and vegetation in his care. Creation could not have happened by chance (chapter seven) as "a mighty and benevolent creator would be needed to appease the eternal conflicts of the elements".[1044] Constantine applauds Plato, as Origen did before him, and Augustine did later, but "no philosopher has understood how the sum of things is governed by the Father through the offices of the Son".[1045]

In the next section, chapters 11–19, Constantine focuses on the salvation offered by the Son. In chapter eleven, he writes that Christ was not overcome by the violence of men, but rather yielded to the "love alone he bore the human race".[1046] This in itself demonstrates that Constantine understood the heart of the gospel (see John 3:16). More than that, in this section on the incarnation, he says pithily, "an eternal nature received the beginning of a temporal existence", and then, in a passage of rich allusion and oratory, proceeds to what is quite possibly the heart of this address:

> But how do we explain his descent to this earth, and to men?
> His motive in this, as the prophets had foretold, originated in his
> watchful care for the interests of all; for it needs must be that the
> Creator should care for his own works. But when the time came
> for him to assume a terrestrial body, and to sojourn on this earth,
> the need requiring, he devised for himself a new mode of birth.
> Conception was there, but apart from marriage: childbirth, yet
> pure virginity: and a maiden became the mother of God![1047] Thus
> an eternal nature received a beginning of temporal existence:
> a sensible form of a spiritual essence, a material manifestation

of incorporeal brightness appeared. Alike wondrous were the circumstances, which attended this great event. A radiant dove, like that which flew from the ark of Noah, alighted on the Virgin's bosom: and accordant with this impalpable union, purer than chastity, more guileless than innocence itself, were the results, which followed. From infancy possessing the wisdom of God, received with reverential awe by the Jordan, in whose waters he was baptized, gifted with that royal unction, the spirit of universal intelligence; with knowledge and power to perform miracles, and to heal diseases beyond the reach of human art; he yielded a swift and unhindered assent to the prayers of men, to whose welfare, indeed, his whole life was devoted without reserve.[1048]

The incarnation and the hope of resurrection are the two aspects of Christ's life which especially gripped Constantine. That the creator of the world should become human and blast a way through death, providing hope of resurrection, was something that no previous deity, imagined and/or worshipped, could provide. Christ and his coming had been predicted by the Jewish prophets, and more interestingly for a pagan audience, by the Erythraean Sybill, who in an acrostic recorded and translated from Greek by Cicero, predicted the coming of Christ and the Day of Judgement, as did Virgil, according to Constantine.[1049]

Finally, in chapters 20–26, Constantine gives contemporary meaning to his faith. He condemns three previous Emperors for their persecution of the church: Decius, Valerian, and Aurelian, saying their early and premature demise or humiliation was due to their persecution of Christians. He says that lightning terrified Diocletian, as his palace in Nicomedia had once been struck and burnt. And he ascribes his own success as a military commander to God, saying, "To thee, Piety, I ascribe the cause of my own prosperity, and all that I now possess".[1050] For Constantine, God is "the invincible ally and protector of the righteous; he is the Supreme Judge of all things, the prince of immortality, the Giver of everlasting life".[1051]

Constantine combined continuity and revolutionary change: the beginning of the end of paganism and the start of what would become Christendom. He combined the social mores of the past and a traditional view of the order of society, while at the same time giving a new direction to law, worship and culture; a trajectory which he began and which would be taken forward, especially in the East, by Theodosius, a distant descendant, and his family.

The final years of Constantine's reign, from the aftermath of Nicaea to his death in AD 337, built on what had gone before, but there was also a sense of sadness or loss in amongst his many achievements. In AD 326, his son Crispus was executed and his wife Fausta died under suspicious circumstances. This was a far cry from earlier years and the depiction of Constantine in his chariot drawn by two centaurs, holding Fausta, his young wife, amorously, and with a childlike Crispus next to them.[1052] Nicaea brought peace to the church immediately after the council, but then the great protagonist of orthodoxy, Athanasius, challenged the imperial settlement with his treatment of Meletius of Lycopolis and the Arians in Alexandria. He had been asked to seek reconciliation, yet he threatened to stop the grain supply to Constantinople unless they were disciplined. The tables were turned on Athanasius at the Council of Tyre in AD 335, where Eusebius of Nicomedia opposed him, and it was Athanasius who was sent into exile to Trier in Gaul. This was the first of five exiles in Athanasius's long-running battle with Constantine and Constantine's more Arian successors for the establishment of orthodoxy and the *homoousios* declaration of Nicaea. Peace in the church would be a long time coming.

In the absence of an Empress, Constantine's mother Helena became the main female Christian icon of the Empire. A devout Christian herself, she began pilgrimages to the Holy Land from AD 327, with the full and enthusiastic support of Constantine. In AD 332, the Church of the Holy Sepulchre, which covered the place where Christ had been buried, was dedicated. Eusebius tells us of its gilded ceiling and its polished marble floor, its exquisite craftsmanship and unutterable beauty.[1053] The building of basilicas followed in Bethlehem and at Mamre, where the three angels had appeared to Abraham.

Constantine's legacy in construction is truly astonishing: the city of Constantinople was dedicated in AD 330 with a new hippodrome, palace and walls, and with the radiate naked statue of Constantine placed on top of a huge porphyry column 37 metres high.[1054] There were churches scattered around the periphery of Rome, transforming the city from a pagan centre to a Christian one, as well as great churches in Palestine and Constantinople. Finally, there were colossal statues of Constantine in Rome, one seated in the Basilica of Maxentius, and the other a free-standing colossus somewhere on the Capitoline Hill, with its gigantic surviving face some 2 metres high, and hands with closed fingers, except for the index finger, which was pointing to heaven.[1055] Both colossal statues were awe-inspiring, for Constantine projected his image and power in a way not seen since Augustus, who in representation he resembled.

This legacy was itself a powerful projection of his power, if not his Christian humility. Reconciling his imperial power and Christian humility constituted a difficulty for an Emperor. The dilemma for Constantine was how to depict his sense of divine calling as Emperor with his servant-hearted faith in a supreme God revealed in Christ. There was no previous model in the history of Rome. Eusebius recalls how a bishop flattered Constantine after the dedication of the Church of the Holy Sepulchre, by saying that he would rule alongside the Son of God. Eusebius writes: "He was annoyed on hearing these words, and told [the bishop] he should not say such rash things, but should rather pray for him, that in both this life and the next he might be found worthy to be God's slave".[1056]

A paradox therefore lies at the heart of Constantine's kingship: on the one hand he projects enormous power and sovereignty as the sole Emperor of a vast Empire—perhaps even surpassing the Jin Dynasty of the same period in China—but in his heart he cherishes the role of Christ's servant or slave. It must have been an uneasy alliance of the worldly and the spiritual, especially in an Empire which needed a powerful central character if it was to survive.

By AD 337, the year of Constantine's death, and after 30 years of his reign as Caesar, Augustus, and finally sole Emperor, the Empire appeared to have peace at its borders. In AD 332, the Goths had been defeated again and the Sarmatians, an Iranian tribe, were checked in AD 334, although they would settle in the Western Empire. Persia was momentarily militarily dormant, although a new war was planned against them by Constantine before he was overtaken by illness.[1057] Persia's King Sapor II had previously been encouraged in a letter from Constantine to treat his

Christian subjects justly.[1058] Armenia had become a Christian kingdom. The city of Constantinople had been dedicated and was growing quickly. In the sphere of faith, Constantine sought a degree of toleration which would not be continued: Jews were not harassed provided they did not persecute those who became Christians,[1059] and while Constantine did not encourage paganism, its sacrifices or the building of pagan temples, practising pagans were not persecuted. In the Post Nicene period, Constantine sought compromises with quarrelling parties for the peace of the church: Eusebius of Nicomedia was reinstated and Athanasius was exiled for his intransigence towards followers of Arius and the hard-line followers of Meletius in their treatment of the lapsed.

When death came, it came quickly. No transfer of power was possible before Constantine's death. His sons were spread throughout the Empire. Constantine II, his eldest son, was in Trier; Constans was in Milan or Rome and Constantius, his second son, was in Antioch. Constantine was taken ill at Easter AD 337. For healing, he visited the hot baths of Constantinople. Knowing that the sickness was dangerous, he asked the bishops that he be baptised. (In keeping with the practice of the time, this rite was often deferred to the end of life in order to prevent the damnation that might come from committing mortal sin after baptism.)

Constantine said: "The hour has come in which I too may have the blessing of that seal which confers immortality".[1060] He was dressed in the white robe of the neophyte and baptised in Nicomedia.

Eusebius wrote:

> Thus was Constantine the first of all sovereigns who was regenerated and perfected in a church dedicated to the martyrs of Christ gifted with the Divine seal of baptism, he rejoiced in spirit, was renewed, and filled with heavenly light; his soul was gladdened by reason of the fervency of his faith, and astonished at the manifestation of the power of God. At the conclusion of the ceremony he arrayed himself in shining imperial vestments, brilliant as the light, and reclined on a couch of purest white, refusing to clothe himself with purple any more.[1061]

On Pentecost, 22 May AD 337, Constantine died. The guards tore their clothes and wept. People ran wildly through the city. His corpse was placed in a golden coffin. He lay in state surrounded by candles and on an elevated bier in the palace in Nicomedia, wearing the diadem and purple robe and encircled by attendants. His coffin was then removed to Constantinople, where he was buried in the Church of the Holy Apostles in his new capital, and not in Rome, where his sister and mother had been buried (in Sts Marcellinus and Peter, off the Via Labicana, outside the Aurelian city walls).

Constantine was initially buried in a porphyry sarcophagus and placed in a mausoleum close to the Church of the Holy Apostles.[1062] Later, in AD 359, his tomb was moved at the behest of his son, Constantius, to the Church of St Acacius by the Patriarch Macedonius. His first resting place near the Apostles was more telling, however. He was to be included with relics of the Apostles in a church designed in their memory. Constantine was to be thought of as a final apostle. After all, he symbolised the advent of Christian faith to the heart of a previously pagan Empire, however problematic this became in the future. After 250 years of witness to Christ and persecution by the Empire, the church now lay at the heart of imperial institutions. The forthcoming years would show how well it fared as it moved from being victim to master.

CHAPTER 12

Conclusion

The story of how the faith of a small Jewish sect, following a little-known Palestinian rabbi, became the faith of the Emperor of the Roman Empire, and of the Empire itself, and a faith that was freely practised by hundreds of thousands from AD 313 onwards, is extraordinary by any stretch of the imagination. Yet for Christians who know Jesus to be the Son of God, raised from the dead, it is unsurprising. For as the great Jewish rabbi and teacher Gamaliel said to the Sanhedrin in Jerusalem when asked whether Peter should be punished further for preaching Jesus: "If their purpose or activity is of human origin, it will fail. But if it is from God, you will not be able to stop these men, you will only find yourselves fighting God" (Acts 5:38–39).

The fact that God was working in and through his church did not spare it, however. For 200 years and more—from the age of the Apostles till the Edict of Milan, when religious toleration was granted in the Empire—the church was characterized by pain, death, struggle, and confusion. While Islam swept all before it, with Arab victories under Khalid ibn al-Walid at Gaza, Yarmuk and Jerusalem, advancing through the Levant, North Africa and Spain, bringing Islam in their wake, Christianity spread through the blood of its martyrs, and for most of this period was despised by pagans and Jews alike. Later on, when the church was given a taste of temporal power, it too resorted to coercion of its opponents and those whose theologies it deemed faulty.

The question we must try and answer is how the generally small Christian communities in Jerusalem, Antioch (where they were probably much larger), Corinth, Rome, Ephesus and later Alexandria, as well as those in the lesser cities and towns of Asia and Europe, managed to sustain their spiritual life and even grow in the face of persistent opposition. Part of the answer must be that they were prepared by their founder for a struggle that would come both from within the church and from without. When Paul knelt on the beach in Miletus and said farewell to the Ephesian elders, he warned them that "savage wolves will come in among you and will not spare the flock. Even from your own number men will arise and distort the truth in order to draw away disciples after them. So be on your guard" (Acts 20:29–31a). The warning could not have been more prescient.

Firstly, there were "savage wolves" from outside the church: the authorities, the power-wielders, and the Jewish and Roman governments. The church was born into persecution. Peter and John were hauled up before the Sanhedrin and punished; Stephen was stoned; James the Apostle was beheaded in Jerusalem. Persecution followed the church wherever it went: first in the form of Jewish antipathy in the towns of Asia and then Europe, and then in the form of more incidental opposition from pagans in Philippi and Ephesus, where Paul challenged pagan norms and even the working of the local economies. But this internecine, mainly Jewish conflict between church and Judaism spread to become one between church and the pagan, Roman and Hellenised Empire. This conflict led to the savage persecution of the church, which initially lasted for nearly 250 years.

The reasons why there was such antipathy between Christians and the Empire are complex, and no one rehearses them more exhaustively than Augustine in *The City of God*. Rome, viewed as an Empire and not just as a city, was built on the back of a host of deities. These deities formed the backbone of religious and social life. There was a god to be remembered, appeased or sacrificed to for almost every eventuality. Christians would have nothing to do with pagan worship, and, in many cases, would not even eat the meat offered in sacrifice to these deities. They did not approve of the games or of the gladiatorial combat which was often linked to pagan worship, preferring to boycott these activities. They found it hard to serve in the army because too often the army was seen as the avenging force of the gods against the barbarians. The way of life of Rome was built upon success and ambition. The *cursus honorum* (the Roman career

path for the ambitious) was too self-regarding for Christians, and too
dependent on praise, whether it was praise of a general for victory over
Rome's enemies in a Triumph, of a senator for his eloquence, or of a young
man for his skill in combat. Praise was the oil that greased the engine
room of power. By contrast, Christians exalted humility, patience, peace
and self-giving love. There was some overlap between the value systems
of Rome and the church, such as the characteristic which Rome called
stoicism, but for the Christian, fortitude was merely the testing of their
following of Christ and a way of maintaining hope.

As a community, Christians looked un-Roman, marching as they did
to the drum of a different value system. Their kingdom was indeed not
of this world; their patriotism was questionable; they followed another
Caesar or Lord; they did not enjoy what Rome enjoyed: blood, human
success, combat, violence, and the gods. They did approve of virtue and
some classical writers, such as Plato and Cicero, who were generally
applauded (see especially Origen, Augustine and Clement). All of this
made them an easy target, indeed a scapegoat for the ills of Rome.
Christians even became part of the games themselves. This was bullying
or persecution on a grand scale.

When Nero needed a scapegoat for the great fire of Rome in AD
64, he quickly made Christians bear the brunt of popular fury for the
devastation. Christians were burnt as torches in his palace gardens and
there began a persecution of peaks and troughs that ran for the next
250 years. If the Roman hierarchy, from Emperor down to Governor,
saw Christians as subversive of the state—neither serving the gods nor
sacrificing to the Emperor—they were also seen as convenient scapegoats
when anything went wrong. As Tertullian famously made clear in his
powerful invective: "If the Tiber rises too high, or the Nile too low, the
remedy is always feeding the Christians to the lions".[1063] If Roman armies
were lost in battle, if fire or earthquake destroyed cities, if the rivers rose
and flooded crops, or if the harvests failed through drought or disease,
then Christians were fair game. Rome saw their slaughter as a panacea
for pagan ills, but the slaughter neither extinguished nor cowed the
Christians' faith. As soon as one fell, another rose; as soon as one was
buried, others congregated to sing and worship.

The reason for Christian resilience was that, whereas the Roman authorities thought to stamp out Christians by state violence, the Christians saw death and torture as the ultimate test of their discipleship. Persecution, and the expectation of persecution, had been writ large throughout the teaching of Jesus and the Apostles. "Blessed are those who are persecuted because of righteousness, for theirs is the kingdom of heaven", said Jesus in the Sermon on the Mount (Matthew 5:10). For many, if not all, this was a blessing they were prepared to embrace. Unjust suffering, nobly borne for God, followed in the footsteps of Christ. Jesus himself suffered unjustly, as Peter made abundantly clear in his epistle (1 Peter 2:20–25). Many of the Apostles, from Peter and Paul onwards, were executed; others, like John the Apostle, suffered exile. (Even as an old man John was put to forced labour in the stone quarries on Patmos.) After the Apostles, many others continued to suffer. Polycarp, by then an old man, was burnt to death in Smyrna with gracious words on his lips. Ignatius, the Bishop of Antioch, was escorted under guard to Rome, where he looked forward to embracing the lions and martyrdom. Much later, in North Africa, Perpetua, a scantily-clad breast-feeding young mother, was led out to die in the arena of Carthage, rejoicing in the privilege of martyrdom. Cyprian, having previously avoided execution, was beheaded in his own garden, even paying the expenses of his executioner. These were just the well-known few among countless others. Thousands died or were tortured as persecution rose and fell under different Emperors. Under Nero, Marcus Aurelius, Septimius Severus, Decius, Valerian and then finally under Diocletian and Galerius, persecution rose to reach a crescendo. Apart from great suffering and extraordinary courage, persecution gave rise to two further by-products for the church: the Apologists and the lapsed.

Apologists were those who were prepared to argue the case for Christianity in the public forum, and to do so knowing they might lose their lives. Theirs was an appeal to right reasoning, to natural justice and to good government. It was directed ultimately at the Emperor himself, and in the meantime at all the magistrates and office-holders beneath him. In a society where Emperor-worship was common and given automatically to the Augustus or Princeps, an Apologist's argument, although reasonable, was nevertheless seen as subversive of the Roman worldview. Christians argued that they were good, both in lifestyle and in intention; indeed they were more moral than many of those who did not oppose paganism—it was just that they could not burn incense to the Emperor as though he was a god or lord. Unafraid to argue their point, they demonstrated that Christianity was not only a fulfilment of Judaism, in that the Old Testament prophets predicted the Messiah's death and resurrection, but that Christ's teaching was infinitely superior to the goings on of the gods, who in moral terms displayed the significant human failings of sexual exploitation and violence, writ even larger. Only Plato, who they believed was heavily influenced by Moses, came close to Christ in terms of teaching, wisdom and insight. While they were busy debunking, the Apologists assured the Emperor of their prayers and their loyalty as citizens. In the end they recognised he was only a man. They, like the slave posted in the chariot of a general in a Roman Triumph, were there to say to the Emperor that he was only mortal. As T. S. Eliot wrote in "Burnt Norton", humans can only bear so much reality, and however reasonable the Apologists' arguments were, and however laden with classical learning and allusion, they did not change the way officials or the Emperor treated Christians. For the officials, it was not worth bucking the system and agreeing with the good sense of the Apologists' arguments. Thus many, like Justin Martyr, were killed, while others, like Tertullian and Clement, escaped. The cumulative effect of their arguments did gradually weaken the intellectual case for persecution, and, out of the glare of public conflict, must have given reason for doubting the correctness of public policy. Nevertheless, that policy of insisting on worship being given to the Emperor persisted until a sudden change took place at the very top. What the Apologists did was to show that Christians were no intellectual slouches. Many were deeply acquainted with the classics, with philosophy, and with the Hebrew writers. In a society where the teaching of grammar and rhetoric encompassed such authors and held them up for study and emulation, their learning was impressive and their arguments could not easily be brushed away or hushed up with persecution.

If persecution stimulated the work of the Apologists, it also brought to the fore the issue of the lapsed. The reality of many *lapsi*, or lapsed Christians—those who agreed to burn incense to the Emperor or who had a certificate that they had done so, even if they had not—became a huge issue for the church, splitting it in many places. As we have seen, this lay at the root of the breakaway Donatist Church in North Africa, as Christians there sought to establish a pure church in which leaders had not compromised their faith. The intransigence of the Donatists frustrated Emperor Constantine at the Council of Arles, as we have seen, as indeed Athanasius's intransigence would later frustrate him in the aftermath of Nicaea. In Rome, as in North Africa, a similar split occurred for the same reason, leading to a division between Novatian (a hard-liner when it came to welcoming the lapsed) and Cornelius. These two became rival bishops of Rome, with different conditions for the re-admission of the lapsed after penance. For those who took the hard line that the lapsed could not be re-admitted to fellowship, nor participate in the Eucharist, not even Cyprian's sensible model of inclusion following penance was acceptable. The controversy exposed a perennial problem for the church in the face of persecution, which was that those who acted with *valour* in the face of persecution found it hard to accept with grace the seeming and often real compromises of *discretion* or weakness by the lapsed. The valorous believed that the church should be an army of saints rather than a hospital for sinners.

Not only did the issue of the lapsed provoke a split in the church, which in North Africa was long lasting (indeed it lasted until the arrival of Islam in the seventh century), the controversy also had side effects, which were in themselves contentious. The question was whether sacraments performed outside the universal Catholic Church were valid, or whether those re-joining the Catholic Church (not just the Roman Catholic Church, but the universal Catholic Church of East and West) needed to be re-baptised, or if priests needed to be re-ordained, because their original baptism or ordination was not valid. Cyprian, whose view was that salvation could only be obtained within the true Catholic Church and that baptism was only valid within the true church and the Spirit-filled community, disagreed with Stephen, Bishop of Rome (AD 254–256), who took the view that baptism in water in the name of the Trinity was valid *wherever it was given*, and that those baptised outside the church should not be re-baptised, but reconciled like penitents with the laying on of hands. For the sacrament was not the church's, but Christ's; and its validity depended on faith, and the form in which it was given, not the correctness or purity of the minister. This sharp dissension only ended when Stephen died and Cyprian was martyred. Then, 150 years later, Augustine would find himself echoing Stephen's teaching in relation to the Donatist Controversy.

If the "savage wolves" of persecution circled the church from its very beginning until Constantine and beyond, other wolves, that is, those wearing sheep's clothing, also troubled the church from the Apostolic era, and likewise far beyond Constantine's reign. These were the false teachers of whom both Jesus and the Apostles spoke in their teaching and letters. Paul warned the church, as did other Apostolic writers such as Peter, John, James and the writer to the Hebrews, to expect false teachers. These were not slow in coming forward. Indeed, during Paul, Peter and John's lives, false teachers were already evident: sometimes as Judaizers insisting on circumcision and the observance of Jewish Law; sometimes as antinomians, encouraging licence in discipleship on the grounds that where sin is, grace abounds. Sometimes they took the form of Gnostic or Docetic disciples, putting the Christian faith within an overarching Gnostic worldview, or saying that Jesus had not really come in the flesh (see 1 John 4:2). Finally, sometimes they appeared promoting false asceticism, speculative thought based on genealogies, or the worship of angels (Colossians 2:16–18; 1 Timothy 5:3–5). All these false teachers were around during Apostolic times, and the early church had to contend almost continuously with a stream of false teaching like the above. This was especially the case in Rome and Alexandria in the second century.

The discovery of the Nag Hammadi cache of Gnostic texts in Egypt gives some idea of the extent of Gnosticism in the second-century Roman world. A development of Middle Platonism, Gnosticism sought to include Christianity in its overall system. It is not until one sees the many Gnostic gospels in circulation that one realises the full scale of this assault on biblical Christianity. It was powerful in Alexandria and then in Rome. When Valentinus failed in his attempt to become Bishop of Rome (c.AD 150), he revealed instead a full-scale system of Gnosticism, likened to the *Gospel of Truth* found in the Nag Hammadi cache. It took Irenaeus and his careful rebuttal of Gnostic teaching to show how far Gnosticism in general, and Valentinus in particular, had strayed from the faith of the scriptures. If Irenaeus was the first theologian and church leader to expose fully the error of Gnosticism, he did so with the very positive theology that the glory of God was shown in a man fully alive, recapitulating the purpose and manner of Christ's coming. Christ came as the incarnate Lord to redeem fallen humans into the creation, as they were intended to be. In this way, Christ restored their glory and in so doing demonstrated his own unfathomable grace and condescension. He, Christ, became as we are that we might become as he is. This is not far from Gregory Nazianzen's dictum of two centuries later that "Christ assumed what he came to heal".

If Irenaeus was the first authoritative bishop-theologian to provide an orthodoxy for the church at a time of great doctrinal ferment, his lay contemporary, Tertullian, provided a substantial rebuttal of Marcion's heresy that there were two gods, the one of the Old Testament who was bellicose and belligerent, and the one of the New Testament who was peace-loving and tolerant. More than anyone else, Irenaeus and Tertullian provided benchmarks for Christian theology in the second century and resisted both the savage wolves of the persecutors and those wolves in sheep's clothing who sought so disastrously to distort the faith. By so doing, they established a canon of teaching for the church, when for a moment it seemed like any one of these extraneous theologies might supplant a truly biblical faith. Later, it would be the turn of Athanasius and the Cappadocians to answer the false teaching of Arius and to secure the divinity of Christ as *homoousios* with the Father and a full member of the Trinity with the Spirit. This struggle would continue for a hundred years. Then, at the end of this period, there would be the struggle to adequately define the divinity and humanity of Christ.

The underlying question was and is: what was it about the church which made it at once so appealing to its contemporaries and so enduring, assailed as it was by the savage wolves of persecution and the false wolves in sheep clothing? For over two centuries the church survived and grew in conditions of great pressure and complexity, from the time of the Apostles to Constantine. It would be easy and true to say that God himself preserved a witness in the church over this period, but beyond God's overruling providence, what were the features that attracted so many to a community despised by the Roman authorities and society? What were the characteristics that helped it survive, and more than that, grow?

Christian communities in the second and third centuries had a uniqueness that was not found elsewhere. In the midst of a militaristic society, they exhibited qualities of love, compassion and peace alien to the Roman values of power, praise and conquest. In a society which lauded the strongest and bravest, which are praiseworthy characteristics, Christians exalted strength-in-humility and power constrained by purity. In a society which was stratified into clear social groups, in which the greatest divide was between slave and free, the Christian community sought to dissolve these differences over time, not by rebellion or antipathy, but by fellowship together, of slave and free, and indeed of male and female in Christ (see Galatians 3:28). In a culture where the weakest were sometimes left out to die, not least unwanted infants, in the church, care of the poor, widows, foundlings and the elderly was evident, as was sharing of food, shelter and clothing. Tending the sick, visiting the prisoner, clothing the naked, feeding the hungry, caring for the widow and the orphan were the care of the whole church community, and in doing these things disciples followed the dominical command.

If these were some of the social outworkings of the Christian faith, which made the church visible and different from surrounding society, at the heart of the community was the worship of, and hope in, Christ the Lord. Records of his life and teaching had become available in many churches by the mid-second century. The Synoptic Gospels were well known, and John's Gospel was becoming so. Paul's letters were collected and circulated *en bloc*. There was a corpus of scripture to inspire and direct the community. Beyond that, there was an existential knowledge of Christ himself in the fellowship of the community and in the presence of the Spirit. A study of the graffiti, or the murals, in the catacombs in Rome shows the hopes of ordinary Christians who were buried there in their hundreds of thousands (there are 600,000 burials in St Callixtus Catacombs alone, spread over three centuries, including large numbers of infants and children). Murals on the walls of these catacombs include several of groups of Christians celebrating the Eucharist or the Lord's Supper, anchors signifying the surety of faith. They reveal people standing in prayer to receive from God, and from Christ himself, who is especially loved and depicted as the Good Shepherd who guides his followers through life and also beyond death.

The Crucifixion of Christ was despised by some Romans as an exhibition of weakness. Around AD 200, one Roman famously depicted a Christian, Alexamenos, worshipping his God, by drawing in a house on the Palatine Hill a man worshipping someone with a donkey's head dying on a cross. It was a straight piece of mockery. As Paul warned, the Cross would be "a stumbling block to the Jews and folly to the Gentiles, but to those whom God has called, both Jews and Greeks, Christ is the power of God and the Wisdom of God" (1 Corinthians 1:23–24). If Christ provided a model of unjust suffering as well as redemptive love from the Cross, it was the hope of resurrection and eternity which especially attracted followers in an age when neither pagan gods nor Platonic philosophy held out any certainty about life beyond the grave. Forgiveness, hope, resurrection, eternal life and a fellowship of love on earth across social boundaries, made the Christian church at its best a fit response to a world too often marred by cruelty and injustice.

When Ignatius travelled to Rome under guard to await his martyrdom from wild beasts, he praised the unity of several of the congregations he visited on the way. When bishop and flock were at one, the resulting unity and witness, he said, was glorious. He wrote to the Roman Church ahead of his arrival there, bearing his testimony. He said:

> I am writing to all the churches and giving instruction to all that
> I am willingly dying for God, unless you hinder me. I urge you,
> do not become an untimely kindness to me. Allow me to be bread
> for the wild beasts; that through them I am able to attain to God.
> I am the wheat of God and am ground by the teeth of the wild
> beasts, that I may be the pure bread of Christ.[1064]

His suffering would be to God's glory. Ignatius, like the anonymous writer of the Epistle to Diognetus, took the view that, "they live on earth but participate in the life of heaven".[1065]

It was such a mentality and hope that armed the church against the "ravenous wolves" and turned her sufferings into her and her master's glory. For the Christians, knowing the truth and grace that is in Christ, it was only a matter of time before they would be vindicated: their sufferings would be their glory.

Chronology

44 BC: Assassination of Julius Caesar.

27 BC: Octavian, Caesar's heir, becomes Caesar Augustus.

4 BC: Death of Herod the Great.

***c*.4 BC:** Birth of Jesus in Bethlehem.

AD 14: Death of Augustus, Tiberius becomes Emperor.

***c*.30:** Crucifixion and Resurrection of Jesus Christ.

***c*.34:** Conversion of Saul (Paul).

37: Caligula becomes Emperor.

41: Claudius becomes Emperor.

***c*.43:** Paul's First Missionary Journey.

46: Paul's Second Missionary Journey, including Philippi, Thessalonica, Athens, Corinth.

***c*.49:** Expulsion of Christians and Jews from Rome by Claudius.

***c*.53–57:** Paul's Third Missionary Journey, Ephesian Ministry.

54: Nero becomes Emperor.

***c*.57:** Arrest of Paul in Jerusalem, followed by trial in Caesarea.

***c*.60:** Paul in Rome, Prison Letters, Philippians, Ephesians, Timothy I & II.

***c*.64:** Peter and Paul's execution in Rome.

***c*.64:** Publication of Mark's Gospel in Rome.

64: Great Fire of Rome.

66: Jewish Revolt.

68: Assassination of Nero.

68/69: Year of the Four Emperors, Vespasian becomes Emperor.

70: Destruction of the Temple in Jerusalem by Titus's army.

***c*.70s:** Publication of Matthew's and Luke's Gospels.

***c*.90:** Publication of John's Gospel.

*c.*100: Justin Martyr born in Nablus.

*c.*107: Martyrdom of Ignatius, Bishop of Antioch.

112: Pliny's letter to Trajan about dealing with Christians.

117–138: Reign of the Emperor Hadrian.

130: Foundation of Aelia Capitolina on site of Jerusalem: Jews banished from Jerusalem.

136–165: Valentinus, Gnostic leader in Rome.

155: Justin publishes his First Apology in Rome.

*c.*156/7: Polycarp's martyrdom in Smyrna.

*c.*160–225: Tertullian.

161–180: Marcus Aurelius, Emperor.

*c.*170: Irenaeus, Bishop of Lyons, writes *Against Heresies.*

177: Martyrs in Lyons and Vienne.

*c.*185–231: Origen in Alexandria, writes *Hexapla,* critical edition of the Hebrew Bible.

*c.*190: Clement succeeds Pantaenus as Principal of the Philosophical School in Alexandria.

193–211: Septimius Severus, from Leptis Magna.

*c.*197: Tertullian's *Apologeticum.*

199–217: Outbreak of the Monarchist Controversy over the Trinity.

203: Martrydom of Perpetua, 22, and Felix in Carthage.

231: Origen moves from Alexandria to Caesarea, Palestine.

249–251: Decius's persecution of Christians.

251–258: Novatian, anti-pope; schism over treatment of the lapsed.

253–260: Valerian, who was captured and humiliated by the Persians.

258: Martrydom of Cyprian of Carthage.

270–275: Aurelian restores the integrity and borders of the Empire.

284–305: Diocletian, who reorganises the Empire into East and West with an Augustus and Caesar for each part.

303: The Great Persecution begins in Nicomedia, and spreads throughout the Empire.

306: Constantius Chlorus dies in York. Constantine declared Caesar by the Praetorian Guard, aged 36.

312: Battle of Milvian Bridge, Maxentius defeated. Constantine's conversion to Christianity.

313: Edict of Milan. Constantine and Licinius, Emperor in the East, guarantee toleration for Christians.

319: The heresiarch Arius comes forward with his teaching in Alexandria that Christ was not an eternal, divine being.

324: Constantine defeats Licinius and selects Byzantium as site of a new Capital in the East, Constantinople.

325: Council of Nicaea.

327: Helena, Constantine's mother, founds Church of Nativity in Bethlehem and Church of the Holy Sepulchre in Jerusalem.

328: Athanasius (296–373) becomes Bishop of Alexandria.

336: Athanasius's first of four exiles.

337: Death of Constantine, his three sons succeed.

Dramatis Personae

Arius (*c.*AD 250–336): Heresiarch from Libya. He believed and taught in Alexandria that Jesus was not fully God and that "there was a time when he was not". This concurred with some Greek philosophical thought that could not mix the divine and the human, but it challenged Christianity to its core. He was banished, but supported by some bishops like Eusebius of Nicomedia. The Council of Nicaea (AD 325) was called by Constantine and established in the Nicene Creed that the Son was of the same substance (*homoousios*) as the Father.

Athanasius (*c.*AD 296–373): Resolute Bishop of Alexandria (AD 328–373) and Arius's main theological opponent. He succeeded Alexander of Alexandria as bishop and attended the Council of Nicaea as his secretary. Often outspoken, he stirred opposition against himself in Constantine's and his successors' court. He was exiled to Trier in AD 336, returning in AD 337. He was exiled a further four times: spending time with St Antony in the desert, and in Rome. He wrote *De Incarnatione*, a classic on the Incarnation: "God became like us that we might become like him."

Augustus (Emperor): Known as Octavian, he was the great nephew and heir to Julius Caesar. He defeated the assassins of Caesar at Philippi and then Mark Antony and Cleopatra at Actium in 31 BC. He ruled as Augustus from 27 BC and died in AD 14. He ruled arguably the greatest Empire for the longest time, ensuring *Pax Romana*.

Aurelian (Emperor AD 270–275): He restored the fortunes of Rome, following Valerian, against the Goths, and took over Palmyra— defeating Queen Zenobia—Egypt and Gaul. Orleans was named after him. He advanced the worship of *Sol Invictus*.

Claudius, the younger brother of the popular Germanicus: He succeeded Caligula in AD 41 and reigned until AD 54. Physically weak: a man of letters not war. He invaded Britain in AD 43 and expelled the Jews from Rome after disturbances.

Clement of Alexandria (*c.*AD 150–215): Taught theology and philosophy in Alexandria, where he headed the Catechetical School. Wrote extensively on Christian living and manners, e.g. the *Paedagogus*. He wrestled with Gnosticism, but less comprehensively than Irenaeus.

Constantine (*c.*AD 272–337; Emperor AD 306–337): Succeeded his father as Augustus in the West in AD 306 at York, when acclaimed by the army. Defeated Maxentius, his rival in the West, at the Battle of Milvian Bridge, Rome, in AD 312. He had a vision of Christ before the battle, and his troops adopted the *Labarum* XP. Proclaimed the Edict of Milan in AD 313, giving religious toleration to Christians in the Empire. He favoured the church, intervening in its disputes to bring peace. He defeated Licinius, Augustus in the East, to rule the whole Roman Empire, East and West. He founded Constantinople and called the Council of Nicaea. Succeeded by three sons who fought with each other.

Cyprian of Carthage (AD 210–258): Bishop of Carthage who came from a rich Berber family. Used his wealth to counteract the effects of the plague. As Bishop of Carthage, he supported Pope Cornelius in the Novationist crisis. He went into hiding during the Decian persecution, but was executed during the Valerian persecution in AD 258. He wrote on the church and the treatment of the lapsed.

Decius (Emperor AD 249–251): Began a severe persecution of the church in Rome, Carthage and Alexandria. Many Christians killed for refusing to sacrifice, including Pope Fabian. A *libellus* had to be obtained from a magistrate certifying that a Christian had sacrificed or he would be punished. Decius died on campaign in the Balkans.

Diocletian (Emperor AD 284–305): Born Diocles, from Split in
Dalmatia. A successful general, he went on to reorganise the
Empire, dividing it into four commands: an Augustus and Caesar
in both East and West. Henceforth, Emperors could retire and
promote their Caesar as the Emperor or Augustus. A traditionalist,
he unleashed a fierce persecution of the Christians called the Great
Persecution.

Hadrian (Emperor AD 117–138): One of the most influential
emperors. General and politician who fixed the borders of the
Empire, e.g. Hadrian's Wall in Britain. Lover of all things Greek.
He finally supressed the Jewish Bar Kochba revolt and re-named
Jerusalem *Aelia Capitolina*, banishing Jews from the city, except for
once a year. Established his succession through Antoninus Pius and
his heirs Marcus Aurelius (AD 161–180) and Lucius Verus.

Herod the Great (Ruled Palestine from 37–4 BC): Ruthless and
cunning, he massacred the innocents in Bethlehem after hearing of
the birth of Christ. Palestine was divided into three territories and
ruled by his sons.

Ignatius (c.AD 35–c.107): Bishop of Antioch, successor to St Peter. An
Apostolic Father. Martyred in Rome c.AD 107. Influential writer
and leader.

Irenaeus (c.AD 130–200): Bishop of Lyons from either Syria or
Smyrna. Greek-speaking. Wrote *Against Heresies*, defending
Christianity against Gnosticism. He was the first systematic
theologian: biblical and insightful in arguing for Christ's restoration
of humanity.

Jesus Christ (c.4 BC–c.AD 30): Jewish Messiah, Son of God. Crucified
under Pontius Pilate and rose again from the dead. His followers
were first called Christians in Antioch.

Josephus (c.AD 37–c.100): Jewish historian of the Jewish Rebellion, in
which he took part. He was captured by Vespasian and spared. He
described the destruction of Jerusalem by Titus, whose personal
adviser he became. He settled in Rome, wrote *The Jewish War* in AD
78 and was granted Roman citizenship. In AD 94, he published *The
Jewish Antiquities*.

Julius Caesar (100–44 BC): General, consul and dictator. He subjugated Gaul with great loss of life, a brilliant general. Shared power in Rome with Pompey and Crassus. Marched on Rome, famously crossing the Rubicon, seized power as dictator and was assassinated by Brutus and others for betraying the values of the Republic.

Justin Martyr (*c.*AD 100–*c.*165): An Apologist, i.e. one who makes a defence. Came from Nablus in Palestine. Converted to Christianity from Greek philosophy. Taught in Rome, appealed to the Emperor Antoninus Pius to be accepted as a Christian philosopher, but was rejected and martyred.

Marcion (*c.*AD 85–160): Heresiarch who came from Sinope on the Black Sea, linked with Gnostic movement but chiefly maintained that the God of the OT and NT were different. He was condemned by Tertullian in his lengthy *Adversus Marcionem* in *c.*210. The church in Rome eventually rejected Marcion.

Nero: Emperor from AD 54–68, succeeding Claudius. Unstable and tyrannical, he murdered his mother. He blamed the great fire of Rome in July AD 64 on the Christians.

Novatian (*c.*AD 200–258): A rigorist Roman presbyter who, during the time of the Decian persecution, took a strong line towards the lapsed (those who sacrificed in front of the magistrate). He led a breakaway group from Rome, and was elected an anti-pope. He may have been martyred under Valerian.

Origen (*c.*AD 185–254): Brilliant linguist, philosopher and theologian from Alexandria. Head of the Catechetical School. Studied under neo-Platonist Ammonius Saccas. Prolific writer and linguist. Works include *On First Principles*, *Against Celsum* and a biblical commentary on the Old Testament, the *Hexapla* (six parallel texts of the Old Testament). Moved to Caesarea in AD 231, where he began a new training school and wrote commentaries. Disowned by the church in the fifth century for his Platonic views on creation, the soul and judgement.

Paul the Apostle (*c.*AD 5–*c.*65): Converted Pharisee and persecutor of the church. Baptised in Damascus. Spent some years in Arabia and then 14 years elsewhere before he was called to Antioch by Barnabas and then to his missionary work. He planted churches throughout Asia and Europe. Arrested in Jerusalem, imprisoned in Rome and executed. He wrote most of the New Testament.

Pliny the Younger (AD 61–*c.*113): Roman Governor of Bithynia, who sought advice from the Emperor Trajan about how to deal with Christians in his province.

Polycarp (*c.*AD 69–*c.*155): Bishop of Smyrna, who knew the Apostle John and Irenaeus. Martyred in Smyrna after serving Christ for 86 years. His martyrdom is included in the writings of the Apostolic Fathers.

Tertullian (*c.*AD 155–240): Prolific, brilliant author, wordsmith and theologian from Roman North Africa, not a member of the church hierarchy or teacher in a theology school. Rapier-like prose. Famous for his Apologetics, especially the *Apologeticum*, and his polemics on church discipline, morals, Marcion (a Gnostic) and church polity. Crafted an early Latin definition of the Trinity. Allied himself latterly with Montanists, a charismatic ascetic sect from Phrygia.

Tiberius: Succeeded Augustus in AD 14. He reigned until AD 37. A great general, but after the death of his son Drusus became reclusive, living a degenerate life on Capri. Caligula succeeded Tiberius and may have murdered him. The Sea of Galilee is sometimes called the Sea of Tiberius. He was Emperor for most of Jesus's life.

Titus: Vespasian's son, Emperor from AD 79–81. General who defeated the Jewish Revolt of AD 66. Besieged Jerusalem, 40,000 killed. He sought to prevent the destruction of the Temple, but the Jews made their final stand in it. In Rome, completed the Coliseum and commemorated by the Titus Arch.

Valentinus (AD 100–160): Leader of the Gnostic sect in Rome. Taught that there were three types of people: spiritual, psychical and material. Only the spiritual have received light or gnosis. His cosmology: supreme being called Bythos, earth formed through Sophia. Christ an *aeon* sent to save humankind. Brilliant but deviant, he was passed over as Bishop of Rome.

Valerian (Emperor AD 253–260): He renewed the Decian persecution against Christians. Many distinguished martyrs died: St Cyprian, St Lawrence, Novatian, St Denis in Paris and Patroclus at Troyes. He renewed the campaign in the East, but was crushingly defeated at Edessa, and humiliated by Shapur, King of Persia. He died in captivity, a nadir of Roman fortunes.

Vespasian (Emperor AD 69–79): Became Emperor after the hiatus following Nero's death, called the Year of the Four Emperors. He was a successful general serving in Britain and Syria. He took on the Jewish Revolt in Palestine from AD 66. Made Emperor by the army and began the Flavian Dynasty.

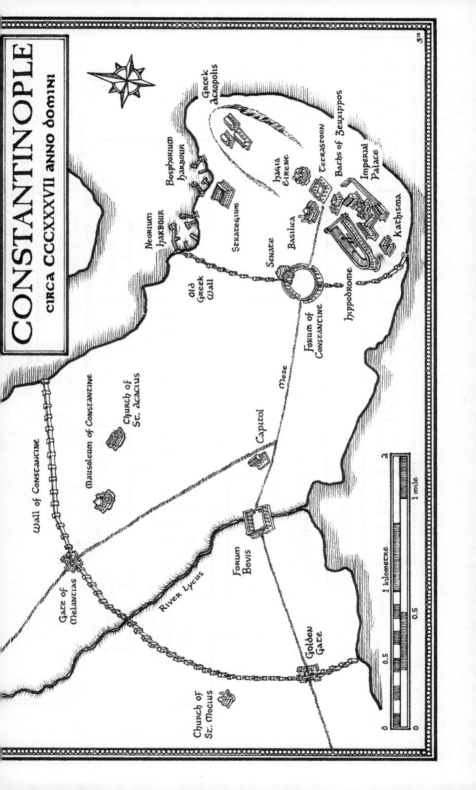

CONSTANTINOPLE

CIRCA CCCXXXVII ANNO DOMINI

Greek Acropolis

Bosphorium Harbour

Neorium Harbour

Strategium

Hagia Eirene

Senate

Basilica

Terrastoon

Baths of Zeuxippos

Old Greek Wall

Imperial Palace

Kathisma

Hippodrome

Forum of Constantine

Mese

Capitol

Wall of Constantine

Mausoleum of Constantine

Church of St. Acacius

Forum Bovis

River Lycus

Gate of Melantias

Golden Gate

Church of St. Mocus

0   0.5   1 kilometre
0   0.5   1 mile

THE JULIAN-CLAUDIAN DYNASTY

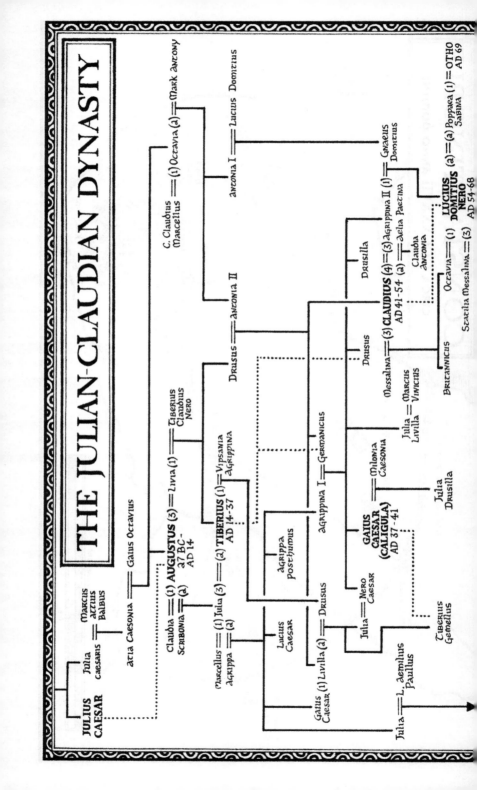

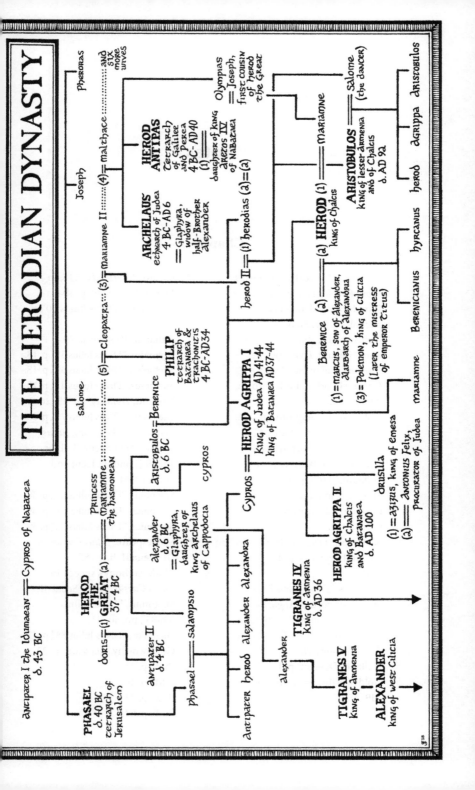

THE HERODIAN DYNASTY

Notes

Chapter 1

1 Adrian Goldsworthy, *Augustus: From Revolutionary to Emperor* (London: Weidenfeld & Nicholson, 2015), p. 488.
2 Goldsworthy, *Augustus*, p. 489.
3 Tom Holland, *Dynasty: The Rise and Fall of the House of Caesar* (London: Little, Brown, 2015), p. 6.
4 Goldsworthy, *Augustus*, p. 236.
5 Suetonius, "Divus Julius 4", in *The Twelve Caesars,* trans. R. Graves and J. B. Rives (London: Penguin, 2007), p. 2.
6 Tom Holland, *Rubicon* (London: Little, Brown, 2003), p. 111, 274.
7 Suetonius, "Divus Julius 13", p. 5.
8 Holland, *Dynasty,* p. 16.
9 Ibid.
10 Suetonius, "Divus Julius 25", p. 11.
11 See Goldsworthy, *Augustus,* Appendix I, pp. 483–486, for a description of the offices in the *Cursus honorum.*
12 Holland, *Dynasty,* p. 17.
13 Goldsworthy, *Augustus,* pp. 449–450.
14 Cicero, *To Friends, 2.15,* in Holland, *Rubicon,* p. 304.
15 Suetonius, "Divus Julius 30", p. 17.
16 Plutarch, *Pompey,* p. 79.
17 Suetonius, "Divus Julius 38", p. 18.
18 Suetonius, "Divus Julius 39", p. 18.
19 Suetonius, "Divus Julius 42", p. 20.
20 Holland, *Dynasty,* pp. 25–26.
21 Suetonius, "Divus Julius 79", p. 36.
22 William Shakespeare, *Julius Caesar,* Act I Scene II, lines 135–9 (London: Dent and Sons, 1935).
23 Suetonius, "Divus Julius 81", p. 38.
24 Suetonius, "Divus Julius 81", p. 39.
25 Suetonius, "Divus Julius 82", p. 39.
26 Shakespeare, *Julius Caesar,* Act III Scene II, line 185.
27 Mark Anthony's speech in *Julius Caesar,* Act II Scene II.
28 Suetonius, "Divus Julius 83–85", pp. 40–41.
29 Suetonius, "Divus Julius 88", p. 42.
30 Goldsworthy, *Augustus,* p. 22.
31 Ibid., p. 31.
32 Ibid., p. 46.
33 Ibid., p. 73.
34 Ibid., p. 84.

35 Ibid., p. 95.
36 Ibid., p. 107.
37 Ibid., p. 131.
38 Suetonius, "Divus Augustus
    27", p. 57.
39 Goldsworthy, Augustus, p. 151.
40 Ibid., p. 161.
41 Ibid., p. 179, 180.
42 Ibid., p.193.
43 Suetonius, "Divus Augustus
    10", p. 47.
44 Goldsworthy, Augustus, p. 198.
45 Cassius Dio, 51.21.5, quoted
    in Ibid., p. 209, and see also p.
    247.
46 Ibid., p. 248.
47 Ibid., p. 217.
48 Ibid., p. 250.
49 Suetonius, "Divus Augustus
    46", p. 71.
50 Ibid., p. 72.
51 Goldsworthy, Augustus, p. 220.
52 Ibid., p. 234.
53 Ibid., p. 255.
54 Ibid., p. 304.
55 Augustine, Confessions Bk
    3.7, tr. H. Chadwick (London:
    Oxford University Press, 2008),
    p. 38.
56 Goldsworthy, Augustus, pp.
    315–316.
57 Ibid., p. 311, citing Donatus,
    Life of Virgil, and Galinsky,
    Augustan Culture (Princeton
    University Press, 1996), pp.
    20–24.
58 Suetonius, "Divus Julius 83", p. 40.
59 Suetonius, "Divus Augustus
    62", p. 78.
60 Holland, Dynasty, p. 122.
61 Ibid., p. 123.
62 Ibid., p. 135.

63 Ibid., p. 136.
64 See Cassius Dio, 56.31, on the
    death of Augustus; Suetonius,
    "Tiberius 21", p. 116.
65 Cassius Dio, The Roman History:
    The Reign of Augustus 56.30,
    tr. Ian Scott-Kilvert (Penguin,
    London, 1987), p. 245.
66 Holland, Dynasty, pp. 174–6.
67 See Josephus, Antiquities,
    XI.8.4–6; Simon Sebag
    Montefiore, Jerusalem:
    The Biography, (London:
    Weidenfeld & Nicholson,
    2011), p. 53.
68 Montefiore, Jerusalem, p. 55.
69 Ibid., p. 56.
70 Ibid., p. 61.
71 Ibid., p. 68.
72 Ibid., p. 80.
73 Ibid., p. 82.
74 Goldsworthy, Augustus, p.
    295; see also M. Speidel, The
    Roman Army in Judea under
    the Procurators, Roman Army
    Studies, vol. 2 (Leuven: Mavors,
    1992), pp. 224–232.
75 Montefiore, Jerusalem, p. 85.
76 Ibid., p. 87.
77 Goldsworthy, Augustus, p. 293.
78 Montefiore, Jerusalem, p. 90.
79 Holland, Dynasty, p. 182.
80 Suetonius, "Divus Augustus", p.
    100.
81 Holland, Dynasty, p. 184.
82 Tacitus, The Annals, Book II, p.
    37, first published 1886, First
    Rate Edition, Amazon ISBN
    978151228 72189.
83 Ibid., p. 79.
84 Ibid. 4:38, quoted in Holland,
    Dynasty, p. 202.

85 Holland, *Dynasty*, p. 197.

86 Suetonius, "Tiberius 43", p. 127.

87 Suetonius, "Tiberius 46", p. 128.

88 Holland, *Dynasty*, p. 240.

89 Ibid., p. 243.

90 Ibid., pp. 244–246.

91 Tacitus, *The Annals*, Book VI, p. 151.

92 Pilate was Prefect from AD 26–36.

93 Herod Agrippa was the grandson of Herod the Great and his bewitching wife, Mariamme. Both his grandmother and his father, Aristolobus, had been executed by his father. His mother Salome was a friend of Mark Antony's daughter Antonia—she was the niece of Augustus, that is Augustus's sister Octavia's daughter by Mark Antony—before he took up with Cleopatra. In time Herod Agrippa was made client King of Judea, AD41–44. (See Montefiore, *Jerusalem*, p. 111.)

94 See Tacitus, *The Annals*, Book IV, p. 113.

95 Both were ascetic Jewish communities centred on the strict observance of the Law, and waiting for the Messiah and the re-establishment of the Jewish Kingdom, see F. F. Bruce, *New Testament History* (London: Oliphant, 1971), p. 65ff.

96 F. F. Bruce, *NewTestament History* (London: Oliphant, 1971), p. 153.

Chapter 2

97 See story of the Tower of Babel in Genesis 11:1–7.

98 F. F. Bruce, *New Testament History* (London: Oliphant, 1971), p. 202.

99 Romans 7:15, but see the whole section of Romans 7:7–25, which shows Paul's self-analysis of his and all humans' weakness.

100 This was a concession from the Romans to allow the High Priests to order their own faith.

101 See F. F. Bruce, *Paul, Apostle of the Free Spirit* (Exeter: Paternoster, 1977), p. 81.

102 See Galatians 2:2 and 2 Corinthians 12:2 where Paul says he went to Jerusalem taking Titus, who was already an associate, to meet with the Apostles and leaders there.

103 Saul took the governor's name, Paul, and so identified himself personally, or in name, with the Gentile mission.

104 Porphyr was an expensive and highly regarded cloth used by

the elite, and eventually used in the Byzantine Empire to denote imperial rule. To be in the purple was to be born to imperial rule. Among the Roman elite purple was the colour that bordered their togas to denote the senatorial class. Purple dye was taken from a sea urchin and its trade was under imperial control.

105 Bruce, *Paul: Apostle of the Free Spirit*, p. 242.

106 Augustine, *City of God,* Bk IV.32, tr. H. Bettenson (London: Penguin, 2003), p. 176.

107 Miriam T. Griffin, *Nero: The End of a Dynasty* (London: Routledge, 1987), p. 70.

108 See Robert Jewett, *A Chronology of Paul's Life* (Philadelphia: Fortress Press, 1979), Appendix p. 161.

109 Suetonius, "Gaius Caligula 11", in *The Twelve Caesars,* tr. Robert Graves (London: Penguin, 2007), p. 145ff.

110 Holland, *Dynasty,* p. 258.

111 Ibid., p. 277.

112 Cassius Dio, 59.29.9. cited by Holland, *Dynasty,* p. 289.

113 Suetonius, "Gaius Caligula 36", Penguin tr. Robert Graves 2007, p. 164.

114 Ibid., p. 15.

115 Suetonius, "Gaius Caligula 37", Penguin tr. Robert Graves 2007 p. 165.

116 Holland, *Dynasty,* p. 298.

117 Ibid., p. 311.

118 Suetonius, "Divus Claudius 20", Penguin tr. Robert Graves 2007, p. 190.

119 Suetonius, "Divus Claudius 27", p. 196.

120 Suetonius, "Divus Claudius", Penguin tr. Robert Graves 2007, p. 195.

121 Romans 16:1–16: "among whom are Priscilla and Aquila" (16:3).

122 Bruce, *Paul: Apostle of the Free Spirit,* p. 475.

123 See his first book to Theophilus: Luke 1:3 and then Acts 1:1.

124 See Appendix, Herod the Great's family.

125 Granted under the *lex Iulia de ui publica c*.23 BC by Augustus. See Bruce, *Paul: Apostle of the Free Spirit,* p. 38.

126 Bruce, *Paul: Apostle of the Free Spirit,* p. 364.

127 Ibid., p. 475, Chronology of Paul's Life.

128 Suetonius, "Nero", p. 209.

129 Ibid., p. 209.

130 Miriam T. Griffin, *Nero: The End of a Dynasty* (London: Routledge, 2000), p. 45.

131 Suetonius, "Nero 9", p. 211.

132 Griffin, Nero, p. 51ff.

133 Ibid., p 60.

134 Holland, *Dynasty,* p. 351.

135 For a full description of how the murder was carried out, see Tacitus, *The Annals,* Book XIII, Reprint of 1876 translation (The Perfect Library), p. 227.

136 Suetonius, "Nero 11", p. 213.

137 Holland, *Dynasty,* p. 357.

138 Ibid., p. 358.

[139] Cassius Dio, *Histories* 61.2.2; Holland, *Dynasty*, p. 360.

[140] Tacitus, *The Annals*, Book XIV, 8, p. 253. Republished by The Perfect Library, Amazon ISBN 9781512287189.

[141] Holland, *Dynasty*, pp. 368–72.

[142] Eusebius, *The History of the Church (HE)*, tr. G. A. Williamson (London: Penguin, 1989) p. 57.

[143] Holland, *Dynasty*, p. 376.

[144] Ibid., p. 380.

[145] Tacitus, *The Annals*, Book XV, p. 294.

[146] Ibid., Book XV, p. 294.

[147] Holland, *Dynasty*, p. 393.

[148] Tacitus, *The Annals*, Book XV, p. 295.

[149] Suetonius, "Nero 31", p. 224; Holland, *Dynasty*, p. 389.

[150] Suetonius, "Nero 35", p. 228.

[151] Holland, *Dynasty*, p. 394.

[152] Ibid., p. 159.

[153] Goldsworthy, *Augustus*, p. 58.

[154] Josephus, *The Jewish War*, tr. G. A. Williamson (London: Penguin, 1969), p. 146.

[155] For a full text of Agrippa's speech in Jerusalem, read Josephus, *The Jewish War*, pp. 148–154.

[156] Ibid., Bk III, p. 180.

[157] Ibid., Bk III, p. 181.

[158] Ibid., Bk III, p. 185.

[159] Ibid., Bk III, p. 212.

[160] Ibid., Bk IV, p. 229, 231.

[161] Ibid., Bk IV, p. 242ff.

[162] Ibid., Bk IV, p. 248.

[163] Montefiore, *Jerusalem*, p. 125.

[164] Suetonius, *The Twelve Caesars*, pp. 242–273.

[165] Ibid., p. 279.

[166] Suetonius, "Vitellus 17", p. 273.

[167] Josephus, *The Jewish War*, Bk V, p. 315.

[168] Ibid., Bk V, p. 460.

[169] Ibid., Bk VI, 90 ff. pp. 332–333.

[170] Ibid., Bk VI, 277, p. 347.

[171] Ibid., Bk VI, p. 360.

[172] Josephus, *Jewish Antiquities*, XX.9.1, quoted in *A New Eusebius* (London: SPCK, 1975), p. 1.

[173] Eusebius, *HE*, p. 60.

[174] Ibid., Bk III, 5.3, p. 68.

[175] Suetonius, "Divus Vespasian", p. 281.

[176] Ibid., p. 282.

[177] Suetonius, "Domitian 10", p. 302.

Chapter 3

[178] See Eusebius, *The History of the Church (HE)*, Bk. III, tr. G. A. Williamson (London: Penguin, 1989) p. 83.

[179] Ibid., Bk V.8, p. 154.

[180] Ibid., Bk III, p. 83.

[181] Ibid., Bk III, p. 80.

182 Morwenna Ludlow, *The Early Church*, (London: I. B. Tauris, 2009) p. 75.

183 Eusebius, *HE*, Bk II.17, p. 52.

184 Ibid., Bk II.17, p. 53.

185 Bart D. Ehrman, *The Apostolic Fathers*, Loeb Classical Library (Boston, MA: Harvard University Press, 2003), p. 3.

186 Ehrman, *The Apostolic Fathers*, p. 6.

187 Eusebius, *HE*, Bk III.37, p. 100.

188 See Ehrman, *The Apostolic Fathers*, p. 23, and on this subject, see especially James S. Jeffers, *Conflict at Rome: Social Order and Hierarchy in Early Christianity* (Grand Rapids, MI: Fortress Press, 1991).

189 Bruce Metzger, *The Canon of the New Testament: Its Origin, Development and Significance* (London: Oxford University Press, 1997) p. 40.

190 Ehrman, *Apostolic Fathers*, p. 35.

191 Ibid., pp. 36–37.

192 Ibid., 1 Clement 3, p. 39, quoting Deuteronomy 32:15.

193 Ibid., 1 Clement 3, pp. 39–40.

194 Ibid., 1 Clement 5, pp. 43–44.

195 Ibid., 1 Clement 17, p. 67.

196 Ibid., 1 Clement 10, 12, p. 53, 55.

197 Ibid., 1 Clement 13, pp. 58–59, quoting Matthew 5:7; 6:14–15; 7:1–2, 12; Luke 6:31, 36–38.

198 Ibid., 1 Clement 16, p. 63.

199 Ibid., 1 Clement 16, p. 63.

200 Ibid., 1 Clement 47, p. 119.

201 Ibid., 1 Clement 9, 11, p. 51, 53.

202 Ibid., 1 Clement 10, p. 53.

203 Ibid., 1 Clement 44, pp. 114–115.

204 Ibid., 1 Clement 19, p. 71.

205 Ibid., 1 Clement 21, p. 77.

206 Ibid., 1 Clement 21, p. 75.

207 Ibid., 1 Clement 48, p. 123.

208 Ibid., 1 Clement 47, p. 121.

209 Ibid., 1 Clement 59, p. 143.

210 Ibid., p. 161.

211 Ibid., 2 Clement 1, p. 165.

212 Ibid., 2 Clement 3, p. 169.

213 Ibid., 2 Clement 4, quoting Matthew 7:21.

214 Ibid., 2 Clement 5, p. 171.

215 Ibid., 2 Clement 5, p.171.

216 Ibid., 2 Clement 12, pp. 183–184.

217 Origen, *Homily 6*, in Luke.

218 Eusebius, *HE* 3:22, p. 83.

219 Ehrman, *Apostolic Fathers*, Ignatius, Romans 5:1, p. 275.

220 Ibid., Ignatius, Romans 5:2, p. 277.

221 Ibid., Ephesians, p. 219.

222 Ibid., Ephesians 2, p. 221.

223 Ibid., Ephesians 5:1, p. 225.

224 Ibid., Ephesians 5:6, p. 225.

225 Ibid., Ephesians 7:1, 9:1, p. 227, 229.

226 Ibid., Ephesians 7:2, p. 227.

227 Ibid., Ephesians 9:1, 2, p. 229.

228 Ibid., Ephesians, p. 219.

229 Ibid., Magnesians 3:1, p. 254.

230 Ibid., Magnesians 10:3, p. 251.

231 Ibid., Magnesians 11, p. 253.

232 Ibid., Trallians 1, p. 257.

233 Ibid., Trallians 3:1, p. 259.

234 Ibid., Trallians 7, p. 263.

235 Ibid., Philadelphians 1, p. 285.

236 Ibid., Philadelphians 4, p. 287.

237 Ibid., Philadelphians 5:2.

238 Ibid., Philadelphians 6, p. 289.

[239] Ibid., Philadelphians 7:1, p. 291.
[240] Ibid., Philadelphians 7:2, p. 291.
[241] Ibid., Smyrneans 1, p. 295, Polycarp, pp. 311ff.
[242] Ibid., Smyrneans 7:2, p. 303.
[243] Ibid., Smyrneans 4, pp. 300–301.
[244] Ibid., Smyrneans 6, p. 303.
[245] Ibid., Polycarp 2–7, pp. 313–321.
[246] Ibid., Polycarp 3:2, p. 313, 315.
[247] Ibid., Romans 13, p. 269.
[248] Ibid., Romans 2, p. 273.
[249] Ibid., Romans 4:2, p. 275.
[250] Ibid., Romans 3:3, p. 273.
[251] Ibid., Romans 5.3, p. 277.
[252] Irenaeus, *Against Heresies*, v.33:4; Eusebius, *HE* 3:39, p. 101.
[253] Ehrman, *Apostolic Fathers*, Papias 3, Fragment, p. 99, and Papias 5, Fragment, from St Jerome, *Lives of Illustrious Men*, 18, p. 107.
[254] Eusebius, *HE* 3:39, p. 102.
[255] Ehrman, *Apostolic Fathers*, Papias 3, Fragment, p. 101, and Papias 8, Fragment, pp. 109–110.
[256] Eusebius, *History of the Church* 3:39, p. 103.
[257] Irenaeus, *Against Heresies*, Book III.3, TANF Vol. I, p. 415 (Eerdmans, 1975).
[258] Ehrman, *Apostolic Fathers*, Polycarp, Philippians 1.3, p. 335.
[259] Ibid., Philippians 7, p. 343.
[260] Ibid., Philippians 5:2, 3, pp. 340–341.
[261] Ibid., Philippians 6, p. 341.
[262] Ibid., Philippians 7, p. 343.
[263] Ibid., Philippians 11, pp. 347–348.
[264] Ibid., Philippians 11, p. 373.
[265] Ibid., Martyrdom of Polycarp, pp. 362–363.
[266] Ibid., p. 369.
[267] Ibid., p. 371.
[268] Ibid., p. 371.
[269] Ibid., p. 373.
[270] Ibid., p. 377.
[271] Ibid., p. 379.
[272] Ibid., pp. 385, 387.
[273] Ibid., p. 387.
[274] Ibid., p. 389.
[275] Ibid., p. 393.
[276] Ibid., p. 397.
[277] Ibid., p. 395.
[278] Harry Y. Gamble, *The New Testament Canon: Its Making and Meaning* (Oregon: Wipf and Stock, 1985), p. 12.
[279] Ehrman, *Apostolic Fathers*, 1 Clement 13, p. 57, 59.
[280] Eusebius, *HE* 5.8.
[281] Ehrman, *Apostolic Fathers*, 1 Clement 15, quoting Mark 7:6, p. 61.
[282] Ibid., Vol I, p. 24.
[283] Gamble, *The New Testament Canon*, p. 35.
[284] Bruce M. Metzger, *The Canon of the New Testament* (London: Oxford University Press, 1997), p. 76.
[285] Metzger, *The Canon*, pp. 84–86.
[286] Irenaeus, *Against Heresies*, 3.11:8–9, quoted by Gamble, *The New Testament Canon*, p. 31.
[287] Gamble, *The New Testament Canon*, p. 43.
[288] Ibid., p. 46.

289 Metzger, *The Canon of the New Testament*, p. 192.

290 Ibid., pp. 191–201, and for the Muratorian Fragment, Gamble, *The New Testament Canon*, pp. 93–95.

291 Gamble, *The New Testament Canon*, p. 95.

292 Ehrman, *Apostolic Fathers*, Shepherd of Hermas, p. 162.

293 Ibid., Shepherd of Hermas 2:1, p. 179.

294 Ibid., Visions, 13:1, p. 205.

295 Ibid., Commandments, 31:6, p. 251.

296 Ibid., Visions, 23, p. 229.

297 Ibid., Visions, 25:1, p. 235.

298 Ibid., Commandments, 29:1, p. 245.

299 Ibid., Commandments, 36, p. 263.

300 Ibid., Commandments, 39, p. 275.

301 Ibid., Commandments, 42, p. 283.

302 Ibid., Commandments, 43, p. 287.

303 Ibid., Commandments, 45, p. 293, 295.

304 Ibid., Commandments, 46, p. 297.

305 Ibid., Parables, 50, p. 309.

306 Ibid., Parables, 51, pp. 310–315.

307 Ibid., Parables, 90:1, p. 421 and Parables 92:2, p. 427.

308 Ibid., Parables, 80, p. 393.

309 Ibid., Parables, 88, p. 415.

310 Ibid., Parables, 90:8, p. 423.

311 Ibid., p. 412.

312 Ibid., Didache, 7–10.

313 Ibid., 11–13.

314 Ibid., 15.

315 Ibid., Didache, 16.

316 Ibid., Shepherd of Hermas, pp. 6–8.

317 Ibid., Barnabas, 2:7, p. 17.

318 Ibid., pp. 25–29.

319 Ibid., 19:4, p. 77.

320 Ibid., 19:10, and 9, p. 79.

321 Ibid., 21:1, p. 81.

322 Ibid., Vol II, p. 122.

323 Ibid., Vol II, p. 128.

324 Ibid., Vol II, Ep. to Diognetus, 2, p. 133.

325 Ibid., 4:1, p. 137.

326 Ibid., 5:9, p. 141.

327 Ibid., 7:2, p. 145.

328 Ibid., 8:9, p. 151.

329 Ibid., 9:2–5, p. 151.

330 Ibid., 11, pp. 155, 157.

331 Hans von Campenhausen, *Ecclesiastical Authority and Spiritual Power in the Church of the First Three Centuries* (London: A & C Black, 1969), pp. 55ff.

332 Von Campenhausen, *Ecclesiastical Authority*, p. 85.

333 Ehrman, *Apostolic Fathers*, 1 Clement, 17, p. 76.

334 Ibid., 1 Clement, 30, p. 89.

335 Ibid., 1 Clement, 45.4, p. 115.

336 For Clement's great prayer, see Ibid., 1 Clement, 59, 61, pp. 141, 142 and 145.

337 Ehrman, *Apostolic Fathers*, Ephesians, 5.3, p. 225.

338 Ibid., Magnesians, 6.2, p. 247.

339 Ibid., Trallians, 3.1, p. 259.

340 Ibid., Philadelphians, 7.2, p. 291.

341 Ibid., Smyrneans, 8.2, p. 305.

342 Ibid., Didache, 15.1, p. 441.

343 Ibid., 11–12, pp. 435, 437.

Chapter 4

[344] Edward Gibbon, *The History of the Decline and Fall of the Roman Empire*, ch. 3, quoted in *The Letters of the Younger Pliny*, tr. Betty Radice (London: Penguin, 1969), p. 26.

[345] Anthony Birley, "Nerva" in *The Lives of the Later Caesars* (London: Penguin, 1976), p. 34. This publication is based on the so-called *Augustan History*, now thought to have been written by a single author in the late fourth century, who was concealing his identity as several authors.

[346] Miriam Griffin, "Nerva to Hadrian," in *The High Empire*, The Cambridge Ancient History, Vol XI (Cambridge University Press, 2005), p. 126.

[347] Birley, *Lives of the Later Caesars*, p. 40.

[348] Ibid., *Lives of the Later Caesars*, p. 41.

[349] *The Letters of the Younger Pliny*, 10.11, p. 264.

[350] *Ibid.*, 10.14, p. 265.

[351] Ibid., 10.17b.

[352] Ibid., 10.33, p. 271.

[353] Ibid., 10.39, p. 273.

[354] Ibid., 10.37, p. 272.

[355] Ibid., 10.96, p. 293.

[356] Ibid., 10.96, p. 293.

[357] Ibid., 10.96, p. 294.

[358] Ibid., 10.96, p. 294.

[359] Ibid., 10.96, p. 295.

[360] Ibid., 10.97, p. 295.

[361] Griffin, "Nerva to Hadrian", p. 125.

[362] Birley, *Lives of the Later Caesars*, p. 52.

[363] Ibid., p. 61.

[364] Ibid., p. 67.

[365] Ibid., p. 68.

[366] Ibid., p. 71.

[367] Anthony Birley, "Hadrian to the Antonines," in *The High Empire*, The Cambridge Ancient History, Vol XI, 2005, pp. 135–137.

[368] Birley, *Lives of the Later Caesars*, p. 71.

[369] Birley, "Hadrian to the Antonines", TCAH, Vol XI, p. 138.

[370] Birley, *Lives of the Later Caesars*, p. 82.

[371] Birley, "Hadrian to the Antonines", TCAH, Vol XI, p. 145.

[372] Birley, *Lives of the Later Caesars*, p. 72.

[373] Birley, "Hadrian to the Antonines", TCAH, Vol XI, p. 146.

[374] Birley, *Lives of the Later Caesars*, p. 72.

[375] Ibid., p. 85.

[376] Birley, "Hadrian to the Antonines," TCAH, Vol XI, p. 149.

[377] Birley, *Lives of the Later Caesars*, p. 101.

[378] Ludlow, *The Early Church*, p. 34.

[379] Ibid., p. 34.

380 See Xystus in Justin, *Dialogue with Trypho the Jew* 1, TANF, Vol I (Grand Rapids, MI: Eerdmans, 1975), p. 194.

381 Justin, *Dialogue with Trypho*, p. 195.

382 Ibid., p. 195.

383 Ibid., p. 196.

384 Ibid., p. 197.

385 Ibid., p. 198.

386 Ibid., p. 198.

387 Ibid., p. 198.

388 Ibid., p. 200.

389 Ibid., p. 202.

390 Ibid., p. 208.

391 Ibid., p. 225.

392 Ibid., p. 245.

393 Ibid., p. 258.

394 Ibid., p. 262.

395 Plato, *Republic* 18, quoted by Justin in *The First Apology*, TANF, Vol I, iii, p. 163.

396 Justin, *The First Apology* viii, TANF, Vol I, p. 164.

397 Ibid. xiii, p. 166.

398 Ibid. xiv, p. 167.

399 Ibid. xx, p. 170.

400 Ibid. lx, p. 183.

401 Ibid. lx, p. 138.

402 Ibid. lxi, p. 183.

403 Ibid. clxvi, p. 185.

404 Ibid. lxvii, p. 186.

405 Justin, *The Second Apology* iii, p. 189.

406 Ibid. v, p. 190.

407 Ibid. viii, p. 191.

408 Eusebius, *HE* 5.10, p. 156.

409 Athenagoras, "Plea Regarding Christians" in *After the New Testament*, ed. Bart D. Ehrman (London: Oxford University Press, 2015), p. 82.

410 Clement of Alexandria, *Exhortation to the Greeks*, tr. G. W. Butterworth (Loeb Classical Library, Boston, MA: Harvard University Press, 1960), p 5.

411 Ibid., p. 5.

412 Ibid., p. 15.

413 Ibid., p. 31.

414 Ibid., p. 33 and pp. 66–67.

415 Ibid., p. 77.

416 Ibid., p. 93.

417 Ibid., p. 95.

418 Ibid., p. 31.

419 Ibid., p. 77.

420 Ibid., p. 135.

421 Ibid., pp. 112–113.

422 Ibid., p. 115.

423 Ibid., p. 117.

424 Ibid., p. 131.

425 Ibid., pp. 146–147.

426 Ibid., p. 151.

427 Ibid., p. 155.

428 Ibid., pp. 169, 171.

429 Ibid., pp. 159, 173.

430 Ibid., p. 175.

431 Ibid., pp. 183, 185.

432 Ibid., p. 189.

433 Ibid., p. 191.

434 Ibid., p. 193.

435 Ibid., p. 193.

436 Ibid., p. 217.

437 Ibid., p. 201.

438 Ibid., p. 211.

439 Ibid., p. 211.

440 Ibid., pp. 223, 225.

441 Ibid., p. 238.

442 Ibid., p. 239.

443 Ibid., p. 245.

444 Ibid., p. 253.

445 Clement of Alexandria, *The Instructor* (Savage,

MN: Lighthouse Christian
Publishing), p. 11.
446 Ibid., p. 17.
447 Ibid., p. 17.
448 Ibid., p. 57.
449 Ibid., p. 29.
450 Ibid., p. 31.
451 Ibid., p. 33.
452 Ibid., p. 35.
453 Ibid., pp. 35, 41.
454 Ibid., p. 41.
455 Ibid., p. 5.
456 Ibid., p. 76.
457 Ibid., p. 76.
458 Ibid., p. 76.
459 Ibid., p. 77.
460 Ibid., p. 78.
461 Ibid., p. 81.
462 Ibid., p. 88.
463 Ibid., p. 89.
464 Ibid., p. 90.
465 Ibid., p. 100.
466 Ibid., p. 106.
467 Ibid., p. 109.
468 Ibid., p. 111.
469 Ibid., p. 113.
470 Ibid., p. 120.
471 Ibid., p. 127.
472 Genesis 19:30–38; Clement,
The Instructor, p. 127.
473 Clement, The Instructor, p. 133.
474 Ibid., p. 137.
475 Ibid., p. 138.
476 Ibid., p. 142.
477 Ibid., p. 151.
478 Ibid., p. 157.
479 Ibid., p. 159.
480 Ibid., p. 159.
481 Ibid., p. 161.
482 Ibid., p. 161.
483 Ibid., p. 169.

484 Clement of Alexandria,
Stromata I (USA: Beloved
Publishing, 2013), p. 9.
485 Clement, Stromata I.ii, p. 10.
486 Ibid. I.ii, p. 10.
487 Ibid. I.ii, p. 13.
488 Ibid. I.v, p. 13.
489 Ibid. I.v, p. 16.
490 Ibid. I.xxi–xxix, pp. 48–82.
491 Ibid. I.xxv, p. 75.
492 Ibid. II.ii, p. 84.
493 Ibid. II.iv, p. 89.
494 Ibid. II.iv, p. 89.
495 Eric Osborn, Clement of
Alexandria, pp. 269–276, and
Clement, Stromata II.iv, p. 91.
496 Ibid. II.vi, pp. 97–100.
497 Ibid. II.xvii, pp. 116–117.
498 Ibid. II.xviii, p. 118.
499 Ibid. II.xviii, p. 122.
500 Ibid. II.xx, pp. 126–127.
501 Ibid. II.xx, p. 133.
502 Ibid. II.xxiii, pp. 140ff.
503 Ibid. III.ii, p. 148.
504 Ibid. III.ii, p. 149.
505 Ibid. III.iii, p. 150.
506 Ibid. III.v, p. 161.
507 Ibid. III.ix, p.170.
508 Ibid. III.xii, p. 177.
509 Ibid. III.xii, p. 180.
510 Ibid. III.xii, p. 181.
511 Ibid. IV.v, p. 198.
512 Clement, Stromata IV.v, p. 205.

Chapter 5

[513] Nag Hammadi means geese grazing grounds.

[514] David Brakke, *The Gnostics* (Boston, MA: Harvard University Press, 2012), p. 90.

[515] Brakke, *The Gnostics*, pp. 84–85.

[516] Ibid., p. 19.

[517] Ibid., p. 52.

[518] "The Secret Book of John", 2.25–4.19, in *The Nag Hammadi Scriptures*, ed. Melvin Meyer (New York: HarperOne, 2007), p. 109.

[519] "The Secret Book of John", in *The Nag Hammadi Scriptures*, p. 111.

[520] Brakke, *The Gnostics*, p. 55.

[521] Ibid., p. 55.

[522] Ibid., p. 57.

[523] Ibid., p. 58.

[524] Ibid., p. 58.

[525] The name Ialdabaoth is probably a mixture of Aramaic and Hebrew: a corruption of the Greek form of Yahweh or Iao (in Greek), but the whole word in Aramaic may mean "child of chaos", see footnotes 53–56 in "The Secret Book of John", *The Nag Hammadi Scriptures*, p. 118.

[526] John D. Turner, "Introduction to Zostrianos", *The Nag Hammadi Scriptures*, p. 537.

[527] "Zostrianos", tr. John D. Turner, in *The Nag Hammadi Scriptures*, p. 545.

[528] Brakke, *The Gnostics*, p. 63.

[529] Ibid., p. 66.

[530] "The Revelation of Adam", tr. Madeleine Scopello and Marvin Meyer, in *The Nag Hammadi Scriptures*, p. 347.

[531] "The Revelation of Adam", p. 347.

[532] Brakke, *The Gnostics*, p. 67, and "The Secret Book of John", in *The Nag Hammadi Scriptures*, p. 127.

[533] "The Secret Book of John", in *The Nag Hammadi Scriptures*, p. 128.

[534] Brakke, *The Gnostics*, p. 66.

[535] Ibid., p. 69.

[536] Ibid., p. 54.

[537] "The Secret Book of John", 25, 26, in *The Nag Hammadi Scriptures*, p. 128.

[538] "The Secret Book of John", 31, 8–17, in *The Nag Hammadi Scriptures*, pp. 131–132.

[539] The "Holy Book of the Great Invisible Spirit" posits the myth that the Great Seth was the incarnate body of Jesus and in his death he "nailed down the powers of the thirteen realms". See *The Nag Hammadi Scriptures*, p. 265.

[540] Brakke, *The Gnostics*, p. 78.

[541] Ibid., p. 80.

[542] Ibid., p. 81; and see also "Marsanes", tr. John D. Turner, in *The Nag Hammadi Scriptures*, pp. 629ff.

[543] Brakke, *The Gnostics*, p. 9.

[544] See Galatians, especially 3:10–14, and The Council of Jerusalem as described in Acts 15:22–29.

[545] Brakke, *The Gnostics*, p. 5.

[546] See 2 Peter 2:1; and John Behr, *Irenaeus of Lyons: Identifying Christianity* (London: Oxford University Press, 2015), pp. 38–39.

[547] Ignatius, "Ephesians 6", tr. Bart D. Ehrman, Loeb Classical Library (Boston, MA: Harvard University Press), p. 225.

[548] The term Great Church (a term originated by Origen) designated house fellowships—there being no church buildings as yet—whose presbyters were banded together in a loose association under a bishop with a certain loose authority in the city as a whole.

[549] See Irenaeus, *Against Heresies* (*AH*), III.4.3b, TANF, tr. M. Dodds (Grand Rapids, MI: Eerdmans, 1975), and Behr, *Irenaeus of Lyons*, p. 25.

[550] Behr, *Irenaeus of Lyons*, p. 26.

[551] See Titus 3:10; 2 John 10; see also Tertullian, *Praescr. 30*; Behr, *Irenaeus of Lyons*, p. 26.

[552] Behr, *Irenaeus of Lyons*, pp. 26–27.

[553] See Irenaeus, *AH*, III.4.3, p. 417.

[554] Tertullian, *Val. 4*; Behr, *Irenaeus of Lyons*, p. 27.

[555] Ptolemaeus, "Epistle to Flora", 33.7.3, in *The Panarion of Epiphanius of Salamis*, tr. P. R. Amidion (London: Oxford University Press, 1990); and Behr, *Irenaeus of Lyons*, p. 32.

[556] Behr, *Irenaeus of Lyons*, p. 33.

[557] Irenaeus, *AH* I.4.3, p. 321.

[558] Irenaeus, *AH* I.13.3, p. 334.

[559] Behr, *Irenaeus of Lyons*, p. 37.

[560] Eusebius, *HE* 18.8, p. 127.

[561] Behr, *Irenaeus of Lyons*, p. 67, drawing on the work of Charles E. Hill, *From the Lost Teaching of Polycarp*, 2006.

[562] Eusebius, *HE* 5:20, p. 169.

[563] Eusebius, *HE* 3:28, p. 92.

[564] Behr, *Irenaeus of Lyons*, p. 66.

[565] Ibid., p. 17.

[566] Irenaeus's list of bishops does not mention Peter. *AH* III.3.3, p. 416.

[567] Behr, *Irenaeus of Lyons*, p. 13.

[568] Ibid., p. 16.

[569] Irenaeus, *AH* 5.20.1, 4–8; and Behr, *Irenaeus of Lyons*, p. 13.

[570] Cleveland Cox, "Introduction" to *Against Heresies*, TANF, Vol I, p. 311.

[571] Cox, "Introduction", p. 313.

[572] Irenaeus, *AH* I.1, p. 315.

[573] Ibid. I.2, p. 315.

[574] Ibid. I.2, p. 315.

[575] Ibid. I.3, p. 316.

[576] Ibid. I, p. 316.

[577] Ibid. VI.3, p. 324.

[578] Ibid. I.6.4, p. 325.

[579] Ibid. I.8.1, p. 326.

[580] Ibid. I.10, pp. 331–332.

[581] Ibid. I.13.4, p. 335.

[582] Ibid. I.15.2, p. 339.

[583] Ibid. I.22–31, pp. 347–358.

[584] See the Chronology of Irenaeus's writings proposed by Behr in *Irenaeus of Lyons*, p. 69.

[585] Irenaeus, *AH* II.1, p. 359.

586 Ibid. II.1.1, p. 359.

587 Ibid. II.6, p. 366.

588 Irenaeus misrepresents Christ's age by saying that he is fifty when he dies, as he will by then have "recapitulated" every age of humanity (see *AH* II.22.4, p. 391).

589 Irenaeus, *AH* II.30 especially 9, p. 406.

590 Ibid. II.23.4, p. 412.

591 Ibid. III.20.2, p. 450; Behr, *Irenaeus of Lyons*, p. 161.

592 Irenaeus, *AH* IV.20.7, p. 490.

593 Robert M. Grant, *Irenaeus* (London: Routledge, 1997), p. 48.

594 Polybius, *Theon Progymnasmata* 1.2.1; Grant, *Irenaeus*, p. 48.

595 Irenaeus, *AH* I.8.1, p. 326.

596 Ibid. I.8.1, p. 326.

597 Ibid. I.8.5; Behr, *Irenaeus of Lyons*, p. 107.

598 Irenaeus, *AH* I.9.2, p. 329.

599 Already we are getting a foretaste of Gregory of Nazianzen's famous dictum that "what the Word has not assumed has not been healed".

600 1 Clement 7.2.5; Behr, *Irenaeus of Lyons*, p. 114.

601 Clement, *Stromata* 6.15.125.3; Behr, *Irenaeus of Lyons*, p. 114.

602 Irenaeus, *AH* II.25–28, pp. 396–402.

603 Ibid. II.25.2.

604 Ibid. I.9.3, p. 329.

605 Quintillian, *Inst.* 6.1.1; Behr, *Irenaeus of Lyons*, p. 137.

606 Grant, *Irenaeus*, p. 50.

607 Irenaeus, *AH* II.22.6, p. 392.

608 Ibid. III.21.10, p. 454; Behr, *Irenaeus of Lyons*, p. 163.

609 Irenaeus, *AH* III.19.3, p. 448.

610 Behr, *Irenaeus of Lyons*, p. 169.

611 Irenaeus, *AH* III.18.7, p. 448.

612 Ibid. V.16.2, p. 544.

613 Dem. 3; Behr, *Irenaeus of Lyons*, p. 173.

614 Irenaeus, *AH* III.22.4, p. 455.

615 Ibid. III.22.4, p. 455.

616 Behr, *Irenaeus of Lyons*, p. 175.

617 Irenaeus, *AH* V.20.2, p. 548.

618 Ibid. IV.18.5, p. 486.

619 Dem. 34; Behr, *Irenaeus of Lyons*, p. 135.

620 Irenaeus, *AH* III.22.3, p. 455.

621 Behr, *Irenaeus of Lyons*.

622 Irenaeus, *AH* V.1.3.

623 Ibid. V.6.1.

624 Ibid. IV.20.7, p. 490.

625 Behr, *Irenaeus of Lyons*, p. 209.

Chapter 6

626 See T. D. Barnes, *Tertullian* (London: Oxford University Press, 1985), p. 63.

627 Henry Chadwick, *The Early Church* (London: Penguin, 1993), p. 65.

628 Tertullian, *Apologeticum*, Ch. xxxvii, tr. S. Thelwall, TANF Vol III (New York: Cosimo Classics, 2007), p. 45.

629 Chadwick, *The Early Church*, p. 65.

630 Ibid.

631 Patrick Whitworth, *From Constantinople to Chalcedon: Shaping of the World to Come* (Durham: Sacristy Press, 2016), p. 282ff.

632 Barnes, *Tertullian*, p. 84.

633 Ibid., p. 86.

634 Ibid., p. 88.

635 See Tertullian, *Apologeticum*, TANF Vol III, Ch. xl, p. 47 (famous passage on the blaming of Christians for all ills).

636 Barnes, *Tertullian*, p. 89.

637 Ibid., p. 62.

638 Bart D. Ehrman, *After the New Testament: The Martyrdom of Perpetua and Felicitas* (London: Oxford University Press, 2015), p. 47.

639 Ehrman, *After the New Testament*, p. 48.

640 Ibid., p. 50.

641 Ibid., p. 50.

642 Ibid., p. 53.

643 Ibid., p. 54.

644 Ibid., p. 54.

645 Ibid., p. 55.

646 Ibid., p. 52; and Barnes, *Tertullian*, p. 78.

647 Barnes, *Tertullian*, pp. 83–84.

648 Ibid., p. 4.

649 Jerome, *De Viris Illustribus*, GCS, XLVII.212, cited in Barnes, *Tertullian*, p. 3.

650 Ibid., p. 21.

651 Eusebius, *HE* II.2, p. 38.

652 Barnes, *Tertullian*, pp. 22–29.

653 Ibid., p. 25.

654 Morwenna Ludlow, *The Early Church* (New York: I. B. Tauris, 2009), p. 89.

655 Barnes, *Tertullian*, p. 55.

656 Tertullian, *Apologeticum*, Ch 1, p. 2.

657 Ibid., Ch 1, p. 2.

658 Ibid., Ch 1, p. 2.

659 Ibid., Ch 2, p. 18.

660 Ibid., Ch 2, p. 18.

661 Ibid., Ch 2, p. 19.

662 Ibid., Ch 3, p. 20.

663 Ibid., Ch 16, p. 51.

664 Namely the law that compelled people to have children before they were allowed to enter matrimony under the Julian laws, see Ibid., Ch 4, p. 21.

665 Ibid., Ch 6, p. 22.

666 Ibid., Ch 10, p. 26.

667 Ibid., Ch 16, p. 31.

668 Ibid., Ch 17, p. 32.

669 Ibid., Ch 18, p. 32.

670 Ibid., Ch 21, p. 34.

671 Ibid., Ch 21, p. 35.

672 Ibid., Ch 21, p. 35.

673 Ibid., Ch 21, p. 35.

674 Ibid., Ch 21, pp. 35–36.

675 Ibid., Ch 39, p. 47.

676 Ibid., Ch 30, p. 42.

677 Ibid., p. 55.

678 Ibid., Ch 39, p. 46.

679 Ibid., Ch 39, p. 46.

680 Ibid., Ch 33, p. 43.

681 Tertullian, *Ad Sacuplam*, TANF Vol III (New York: Cosimo, 2007), Ch 2, p. 105.

682 Ibid., Ch 2, p. 105.

683 Ibid., Ch 5, p. 107.

684 Barnes, *Tertullian*, p. 55.
685 Tertullian, *De Spectaculis*, TANF Vol III, Ch 1, p. 79.
686 Ibid., Ch 5, p. 81.
687 Ibid., Ch 9, p. 87.
688 Ibid., Ch 11, p. 88.
689 Tertullian, *De Idololatria*, TANF Vol III, Chs 10, 11, 12, pp. 66–68.
690 Tertullian, *De Idololatria*, p. 99.
691 Barnes, *Tertullian*, p. 55.
692 Tertullian, *On the Apparel of Women*, TANF Vol IV (New York: Cosimo, 2007), Ch 4, p. 16.
693 Tertullian, *On the Apparel of Women*, Ch 11, p. 24.
694 Tertullian, *On the Veiling of Virgins*, TANF Vol IV, Ch 16, p. 37.
695 Tertullian, *On Repentance*, TANF Vol III, Ch 7, p. 662.
696 Tertullian, *On Prayer*, TANF Vol III, Ch 1, p. 682.
697 Ibid., Ch 9, p. 684.
698 Ibid., Ch 25, p. 689.
699 Tertullian, *On Prescription against Heresies*, TANF Vol IV, pp. 243ff.
700 Barnes, *Tertullian*, p. 126.
701 Tertullian, *Against the Valentinians*, TANF Vol III, p. 505.
702 Tertullian, *Against Marcion*, TANF Bk III, pp. 243–477.
703 Ibid., Bk II, Ch 5, pp. 300–301.
704 Ibid., Bk II, Ch 10, p. 305.
705 Ibid., Bk III, Chs 2–6, pp. 321–327.
706 Ibid., Bk IV, Ch 4, pp. 422–423.
707 Ibid., Bk V, Ch 6, p. 441.
708 Ibid., Bk V, Ch 19, pp. 470–471.
709 Barnes, *Tertullian*, p. 55.
710 Tertullian, *On the Flesh of Christ*, TANF Vol III, Ch 1, p. 520.
711 Ibid., Ch 4, p. 524.
712 Ibid., Ch 10, p. 530.
713 Ibid., Ch 18, p. 537.
714 Ibid., Ch 16, p. 535.
715 Tertullian, *On the Resurrection of the Flesh*, TANF Vol III, Ch 3, p 547.
716 Ibid., Ch 5, p. 549.
717 Ibid., Ch 7, p. 551.
718 Ibid., Ch 38, pp. 572–573.
719 Ibid., Ch 57, p. 590.
720 Ibid., Ch 51, p. 584.
721 Ibid., Ch 60, p. 592.
722 Ibid., Ch 61, p. 593.
723 Barnes, *Tertullian*, p. 55.
724 Cyprian, A*d Donatum*, TANF Vol V (New York: Cosimo, 2007), p. 275.
725 *Life and Passion of Cyprian*, TANF Vol V, Ch 5, p. 269, and CRES Vol 10 (New Jersey: Evolution Publishing), p. 6.
726 Tertullian, *Apologeticum*, p. 47.
727 Cyprian, *On the Unity of the Church*, CRES Vol 10, Ch 3, p. 20.
728 Ibid., Ch 4, p. 21.
729 Ibid., Ch 6, p. 22.
730 Ibid., Ch 15, p. 27.
731 Cyprian, *On the Lapsed*, CRES Vol 10; TANF Vol V, Ch 2, p. 51.
732 Cyprian, Letter 67, CRES Vol 10, p. 459.
733 See Letter 10: *To the Martyrs and Confessors who Sought that Peace Should be Granted to the Lapsed*, CRES Vol 10, p. 312.
734 See *On the Lapsed*, Chs 15, 24, 26, in which an unrepentant

woman who was an idolater
and who had sacrificed incense,
was struck down on taking
communion as though it were
poison! CRES Vol 10, p. 63.

735 Cyprian, *On the Dress of Virgins*,
CRES Vol 10, Ch 9, p. 41.

736 Ibid., CRES Vol 10, Ch 9, p. 41.

737 *From the Roman Clergy*, Letter
2, CRES Vol 10, pp. 292ff.

738 See also *To Januaris and the
Numidian Bishops on the
Baptism of Heretics*, Letter
69, CRES Vol 10, p. 471, and
Letters 73, 74 and 75 all on the
same issue, CRES Vol 10, pp.

491ff, and "Proceedings of the
Seventh Council of Carthage",
CRES Vol 10, p. 535.

739 Cyprian, *On Baptism, Against
the Donatists,* Bk V, Ch 23, p. 31.

740 *Complete Works of Cyprian: The
Seventh Council of Carthage*,
CRES, ed. Philip Campbell
(New Jersey: Evolution
Publishing, 2013), see p. 549.

741 Gerald Bonner, *St Augustine of
Hippo* (Norwich: Canterbury
Press, 2002), pp. 30–31.

742 See Patrick Whitworth, *From
Constantinople to Chalcedon,*
pp. 145ff.

Chapter 7

743 This was Origen's phrase, taken
from *Contra Celsum*, 5.59.

744 James D. G. Dunn, *Neither Jew
Nor Greek* (Grand Rapids, MI:
Eerdmans, 2015), p. 8.

745 John Behr, *Irenaeus of Lyon*
(London: Oxford University
Press, 2015), p. 4.

746 Dunn, *Neither Jew Nor Greek,*
p. 11.

747 Brakke, *The Gnostics,* p. 12,
quoted in Behr, *Irenaeus of
Lyons,* p. 8.

748 Brian Campbell, *The Severan
Dynasty,* TCAH Vol XII
(Cambridge: CUP, 2005), Ch 1,
p. 3.

749 Ibid., p. 19.

750 Ibid., p. 20.

751 Ibid., p. 25.

752 Ibid., p. 26.

753 John Drinkwater, *Maximinus
to Diocletian and The "Crisis",*
TCAH Vol XI (Cambridge:
CUP, 2005), Ch 2, p. 32.

754 Drinkwater, *Maximinus to
Diocletian,* p. 36.

755 Ibid., p. 40.

756 Novatian, *A Treatise of
Novatian Concerning the
Trinity,* TANF Vol V, pp. 611ff.

757 Eusebius, *HE* 6.43; *Cornelius'
Letter to Bishop Fabius of
Antioch,* p. 215.

758 Cyprian's Letter 40, *To Pope
Cornelius, on his Refusal to*

Receive Novatian's Consecration, CRES Vol 10, p. 365.

759 Chadwick, *The Early Church,* p. 119, fn.i.

760 Cyprian, *On the Unity of the Church,* TANF Vol V, p. 421.

761 Ibid., p. 422.

762 Chadwick, *The Early Church,* p. 120.

763 Cyprian, *Letters 70–75,* TANF Vol V, pp. 377–397.

764 Cyprian, Letter 70, *To Quintus, On the Baptism of Heretics,* TANF Vol V, p. 377 and CRES Vol 10, p 474.

765 Patrick Whitworth, *From Constantinople to Chalcedon* (Sacristy Press, 2017), pp. 145ff.

766 Ronald E. Heine, *Origen: Scholarship in the Service of the Church* (London: Oxford University Press, 2010), pp. 98–99.

767 Chadwick, *The Early Church,* p. 87.

768 Ibid., p. 87.

769 Ibid., p. 86.

770 Ibid., p. 86.

771 Eusebius, *HE* 6.21, p. 198.

772 See Hippolytus, *The Refutation of Heresies,* TANF Vol V, pp. 9–162. This translation is based on a manuscript discovered on Mt Athos in 1842 by Minoides Mynas, who was directed by the French government.

773 T. D. Barnes, *Tertulllian,* p. 55, 278 (Barnes dated *Adversus Praxean* in 208–9).

774 Tertullian, *Against Praxeas,* TANF Vol III, Ch 1, p. 587.

775 Ibid., p. 598.

776 Ibid., p. 599.

777 Ibid., p. 599.

778 Ibid., p. 602.

779 Ibid., pp. 606–7.

780 Ibid., Ch 30.

781 Ibid., Ch 31.

782 Ibid., p. 615.

783 Eusebius, *HE* 6.14.10–11, p. 193.

784 Heine, *Origen: Scholarship in the Service of the Church,* p. 98.

Chapter 8

785 Robin Lane Fox, *Alexander the Great* (London: Penguin, 2004), p. 197.

786 Ronald E. Heine, *Origen: Scholarship in the Service of the Church* (London: Oxford University Press, 2010), p. 3.

787 Heine, *Origen,* p. 13.

788 Ibid., p. 14, citing Timon, frg. 12 Diels, cited in Barnes, "Cloistered Bookworms in the Chicken-Coop of the Muses: The Ancient Library of Alexandria" in *The Library of Alexandria: Centre of Learning in the Ancient World,* ed. Roy

MacLeod (London/New York: I. B. Tauris, 2000), p. 62.

[789] Heine, *Origen*, p. 17.

[790] Ibid., p. 26.

[791] L. W. Barnard, *Studies in the Apostolic Fathers and their Background* (New York: Schoken Books, 1966), pp. 47–52.

[792] Eusebius, *HE* 2.16.1–17.24, p. 50.

[793] Ibid. 4.1, p. 105.

[794] Attila Jakab, *Ecclesia alexandrina* (Berlin: Peter Lang, 2001).

[795] Origen, *Comm. on John II.10* in Joseph W. Trigg, *Origen* (London: Routledge, 2008), p. 106.

[796] See Origen, *Comm. on John 1.10* in Trigg, *Origen*, pp. 106–107.

[797] Eusebius, *HE* 6.3.3.

[798] Heine, *Origen*, p. 61.

[799] Eusebius, *HE* 6.4.1–5.7.

[800] Ibid. 6.18, p. 194.

[801] Ibid. 6.8, p. 186. This section includes the account of Origen's self-castration to avoid sin, for which Demetrius, out of envy for Origen's growing prominence, later criticised him. This may have been one of the reasons for the falling out of Origen and Demetrius.

[802] Ibid. 6.24, p. 200.

[803] Heine, *Origen*, p. 47.

[804] Eusebius *HE* 6.6, p. 185.

[805] Ibid. 5.10, p. 156.

[806] Heine, *Origen*, p. 63; Origen's *Ep. Greg* 2.1, and Gregory's *Panegyric to Origen* (Ohio: Beloved Publishing, 2016), Argument IX, p. 23.

[807] Gregory the Wonderworker, *Dankesrede an Origenes*, tr. P Guyot FC 24 (Freiburg, 1996).

[808] Heine, *Origen*, p. 93.

[809] Ibid., p. 96.

[810] Origen, *First Principles*, tr. G. W. Butterworth (Notre Dame, IN: Ave Maria Press, 2013), Bk 1, ch ii.10, p. 31.

[811] Irenaeus, *Against Heresies*, 1.6.1.

[812] Heine, *Origen*, p. 128.

[813] See Origen, *First Principles*, Bk 1, ch v.5, pp. 64–65.

[814] Mandates 1.1, *The Shepherd of Hermas*; cited in Triggs, *Origen*, p. 19.

[815] Origen, *On First Principles*, p. 94.

[816] Porphyry, *Life of Plotinus*, 3.14, 20; cited in Triggs, *Origen*, p. 12.

[817] Origen, *On First Principles*, Bk 1, ch. ii.4, p. 42.

[818] Phillip Rousseau, *Basil of Caesarea* (Los Angeles: University of California Press, 1998), pp. 83–84.

[819] See Origen, *On First Principles*, p. 195.

[820] Trigg, *Origen*, p. 69.

[821] Ibid., p. 73.

[822] Ibid., p. 87, and Junod SC 226 (Paris: Cerf, 1976), pp. 130–166, 174–204.

[823] Trigg, *Origen*, p. 16.

[824] See Megan Hale Williams, *The Monk and the Book* (Chicago, IL: University of Chicago Press, 2006), p. 72.

[825] Williams, *The Monk and the Book*, p. 72.

826 Williams, *The Monk and the Book*, p. 175.
827 Ibid., p.150.
828 Trigg, *Origen*, p. 86.
829 Origen, *Commentary on Genesis*, Bk III, in *Philocalia* 21–27, Junod SC 226, pp. 130–166, 174–204, and cited in Trigg, *Origen*, p. 88.
830 Trigg, *Origen*, p. 89.
831 Bertrand Russell, *History of Western Philosophy* (London: Routledge, 1996), p. 279.
832 Trigg, *Origen*, p. 95.
833 Ibid., p. 97.
834 See Origen, *On First Principles*, p. 336.
835 See Ibid., p. 345.
836 See Ibid., Bk IV, Ch 2.4, pp. 363–364.
837 Ibid., Bk IV, Ch 2.7, p. 374.
838 Origen, *Commentary on the Psalms*, cited in Trigg, *Origen*, p. 71.
839 Trigg, *Origen*, p. 73.
840 Ibid., pp. 80–81.
841 Origen, *Commentary on Lamentations*, xlvi, cited in Trigg, *Origen*, p. 81, from the text of Pierre Nautin (Berlin, 1983), pp. 23–79.
842 Origen, *On First Principles*, p. 1.
843 Ibid., p. 2.
844 Ibid., p. 2.
845 Heine, *Origen*, p. 99.
846 Origen, *On First Principles*, p. 3.
847 Ibid., pp. 3–4.
848 Ibid., p. 4.
849 Ibid., Ch 1, p. 9.
850 Ibid., Bk I, Ch 1.5, p. 12.
851 Ibid., Bk I, Ch 1.5, p. 13.
852 Ibid., Bk I, Ch 1.6, p. 15.
853 Ibid., Bk I, Ch 1.7, p. 16.
854 Ibid., Bk I, Ch 1.7, p. 16.
855 Ibid., Bk I, Ch 1.9, p. 18.
856 See glossary for meaning of this term.
857 Origen, *On First Principles*, Bk I, Ch 2.1, p. 21.
858 Ibid., Bk I, Ch 2.2, p. 22.
859 Ibid., Bk I, Ch 2.3, p. 23.
860 Wisdom 7.25ff cited in Origen, *On First Principles*, Bk I, Ch 2.5, p. 25.
861 Origen, *On First Principles*, Bk I, Ch 2.6, p. 26.
862 Ibid., Bk I, Ch 2.6, p. 26.
863 Later Origen will describe this as effluence from the glory of the Father, see *On First Principles*, Bk I, Ch 2.11, p. 35.
864 Origen, *On First Principles*, Bk I, Ch 3, p. 39.
865 Ibid., Bk I, Ch 3.1, p. 39.
866 Ibid., Bk I, Ch 3, pp. 40–41.
867 Ibid., Bk I, Ch 3.4, p. 42.
868 Ibid., Bk I, Ch 3.5, p. 44.
869 Ibid., Bk I, Ch 3.7, p. 47.
870 Ibid., Bk I, Ch 2.8, p. 49.
871 Ibid., Bk I, Ch 3.8, p. 49.
872 Trigg, *Origen*, p. 8.
873 Origen, *On First Principles*, Bk III, Ch 5.3, p. 313.
874 Ibid., Bk III, Ch 5.3, p. 315.
875 Ibid., Bk III, Ch 5.6, p. 317.
876 Ibid., Bk III, Ch 1.5, p. 203.
877 Ibid., Bk III, Ch 1.6, pp. 208–209.
878 Ibid., Bk III, Ch 1.8.14, pp. 213–237.
879 Ibid., Bk I, Ch 6.2, pp. 70–71.
880 Ibid., Bk I, Ch 6.3, p. 73.
881 Ibid., Bk I, Ch 6.4, p. 75.

882 Ibid., Bk III, Ch 6.1, p. 323.

883 Heine, *Origen*, p. 145.

884 Lee I. Levine, *Caesarea under Roman Rule*, Studies in Judaism in Late Antiquity 7 (Leiden: Brill, 1975), cited by Heine, *Origen*, p. 147.

885 Heine, *Origen*, p. 147.

886 Ibid., p. 147.

887 Ibid., p. 151.

888 Eusebius, *HE* 5.23.

889 Pierre Nautin, *Origene: sa vie et son oeuvre* (Paris: Beauchesne, 1977).

890 Heine, *Origen*, p. 170.

891 Eric Junod, "L'impossible et le possible: Etude de la declaration preliminaire du De Oratione", in *Origena Secunda*, ed. H. Crouzel and A. Quacquarelli (Rome, 1980).

892 Origen, *HomJosh 6.2*, from Origen, *Homilies on Joshua*, FOTC 105 ed. C. White (Washington: Catholic University Press, 2002), cited by Heine, *Origen*, p. 183.

893 Trigg, *Origen*, p. 50.

894 Eusebius, *HE* 6.25, p. 200.

895 FOTC 94 tr. J. T. Lienhard (Washington: Catholic University of America Press, 1996).

896 PG 87.21545–1780 and PG 17.253–88 cited in R. P. Lawson, *Origen's Commentary and Homilies on the Song of Songs*, ACW No 26 (New York: Newman Press, 1956).

897 Eusebius, *HE* 6.32, p. 205.

898 Introduction to Lawson, *Origen's Commentary*.

899 Lawson, *Origen's Commentary*, pp. 46–50.

900 Ibid., p. 15.

901 Ibid., p. 29.

902 Ibid., p. 44.

903 Song of Songs 1:2.

904 Song of Songs 1:4; 2 Corinthians 12:1–4.

905 See Origen, *Dialogue with Heracleides*, tr. R. J. Daly, 7 ACW 54 (New York: Paulist Press, 1992), cited in Trigg, *Origen*, p. 41.

906 Origen, *Exhortation to Martyrdom*, ACW 19 (New York: Paulist Press, 1979), p. 12, cited in Trigg, *Origen*, p. 43.

907 Origen, *On Prayer*, tr. W. A. Curtis (Aeterna Press, 2015), Ch 4, p. 18.

908 Origen, *On Prayer*, Ch 5, p. 16.

909 Ibid., Ch 7, p. 23, my italics.

910 Ibid., Ch 9, p. 29.

911 Ibid., Ch 9, p. 29.

912 Ibid., Ch 11, pp. 35–37.

913 Ibid., Ch 13, p. 43.

914 Ibid., Ch 17, p. 61.

915 Ibid., Ch 17, p. 66.

916 Ibid., Ch 19, p. 72.

917 Ibid., Ch 19, p. 78.

918 Ibid., Ch 19, p. 78.

919 Ibid., Ch 20, pp. 80–83.

920 Patrick Whitworth, *The Shaping of the World to Come: The Years from Constantinople to Chalcedon and Beyond* (Durham: Sacristy Press, 2016), pp. 202ff.

921 Origen, *Contra Celsum*, tr. and introduced by Henry Chadwick (Cambridge: Cambridge University Press, 1953), p. ix.

922 Eusebius, *HE* 6.36, p. 207.

923 Ibid.

924 See Henry Chadwick, Introduction to *Contra Celsum*, pp. xxiv–xxvi.

925 Origen, *Contra Celsum*, Ch 7.42, p. 430.

926 Ibid., Ch 4.5, p. 188.

927 Ibid., Ch 5.18, 19, p. 278.

928 Ibid., Ch 3.5, p. 131.

929 Ibid., Ch 5.25, p. 283.

930 Ibid., Ch 7.42.

931 See Gregory Thaumaturgus, *The Oration and Panegyric Addressed to Origen* (Ohio: Beloved Publishing, 2016), p. 23.

932 Thaumaturgus, *The Oration* 9, p. 23.

933 Eusebius, *HE* VI.39, pp. 208–209.

Chapter 9

934 Stephen Williams, *Diocletian and the Roman Recovery* (London: Routledge, 2000), p.17.

935 Ibid., p. 18.

936 David Potter, *Constantine the Emperor* (London: Oxford University Press, 2015), pp. 8–9.

937 Potter, *Constantine the Emperor*, p. 21.

938 Ibid., p. 22.

939 Ibid., p. 23.

940 Williams, *Diocletian and the Roman Recovery*, p. 35.

941 Ibid., p. 430.

942 Ibid., p. 49.

943 Ibid., p. 73.

944 Ibid., p. 81.

945 Ibid., p. 86.

946 Potter, *Constantine the Emperor*, p. 61.

947 Ibid., p. 63.

948 Williams, *Diocletian and the Roman Recovery*, p. 91.

949 Potter, *Constantine the Emperor*, p. 219.

950 Williams, *Diocletian and the Roman Recovery*, p. 97.

951 Ibid., pp. 116–117.

952 Rescript *De Pretiis*, in Ibid., p. 129.

953 Ibid., p. 131.

954 Robin Lane Fox, *Pagans and Christians* (London: Penguin, 1986), p. 594; Williams, *Diocletian and the Roman Recovery*.

955 *Passio Marcelli*, 20: R. Knopf and G. Kruger, *Early Christian Hagiography* (Tubingen: 1929, revised 1965), quoted by Williams, *Diocletian and the Roman Recovery*, p. 170.

956 Eusebius, *HE* 8.4.

957 Lactantius, *Mortibus Persecutorum* 10, quoted by Williams in *Diocletian and the Roman Recovery*, p. 171, and

Fox, *Pagans and Christians*, p. 595.

958 Fox, *Pagans and Christians*, p. 596.

959 Williams, *Diocletian and the Roman Recovery*, p. 176.

960 Eusebius, *HE* 8.5, p. 261.

961 Ibid. 8.6, pp. 262–263.

962 Ibid. 8.12, p. 270.

963 Lactantius, *Institutiones Divinae* 8; quoted in Williams, *Diocletian and the Roman Recovery*, p. 181.

964 Potter, *Constantine the Emperor*, p. 102.

Chapter 10

965 Potter, *Constantine the Emperor*, p. 28.

966 Sam Moorhead and David Stuttard, *The Romans Who Shaped Britain* (London: Thames and Hudson, 2016), p. 187.

967 Potter, *Constantine the Emperor*, p. 111.

968 See Eusebius, *Vita Constantina*, Limovia.net ISBN 978–1490460659, pp. 23–24.

969 Potter, *Constantine the Emperor*, p. 117.

970 Ibid., pp. 120–121.

971 See the famous statue and head of Constantine taken from the Basilica of Maxentius, now in the Museum Capitolini, Rome.

972 Potter, *Constantine the Emperor*, p. 134.

973 Eusebius, *Vita Constantina*, Limovia.net, ISBN 978–1490460659, p. 27.

974 Latin Panegyrics, cited in Potter, *Constantine the Emperor*, p. 127.

975 Potter, *Constantine the Emperor*, p. 135.

976 Eusebius, *Vita Constantini*, pp. 36–38.

977 Potter, *Constantine the Emperor*, p. 136.

978 Ibid., p. 143.

979 Eusebius, *Vita Constantini*, Bk 1, p. 33.

980 Ibid., Bk 1, p. 35.

981 Ibid., Bk 1, p. 15.

982 Potter, *Constantine the Emperor*, p. 145.

983 Ibid., p. 149.

984 Ibid., p. 168.

985 Ibid., pp. 172–190.

986 Ibid., p. 178.

987 Ibid., p. 181.

988 Ibid., p. 181.

989 Sam Moorhead and David Stuttard, *The Romans who Shaped Britain*, p. 194.

990 Potter, *Constantine the Emperor*, p. 169.

991 Ibid., p. 169.

992 Ibid., p. 170.

993 Eusebius, *Vita Constantini,* p. 50.
994 Potter, *Constantine the Emperor,* p. 211.
995 Ibid., p. 244.
996 Ibid., p. 245, quoting Eutropius, *Breviarium ab urbe condita* 10.6.3, tr. Selby Watson, London, 1853.
997 Potter, *Constantine the Emperor,* p. 240.
998 David Potter, *Theodora: Actress, Empress, Saint* (London: Oxford University Press, 2015), p. 98.
999 See Jonathan Bardill, *Constantine, Divine Emperor of the Christian Golden Age* (Cambridge: Cambridge University Press, 2015), p. 260.
1000 Bardill, *Constantine, Divine Emperor,* p. 254.
1001 Potter, *Constantine the Emperor,* p. 260.
1002 Ibid., pp. 265–266.
1003 Ibid., p. 270.
1004 Ibid., p. 271.
1005 Ibid., p. 273.

Chapter 11

1006 Potter, *Constantine the Emperor,* p. 127; *Latin Panegyrics,* 6.21.4–5.
1007 Ibid., p. 180.
1008 Ibid., p. 198.
1009 Ibid., p. 198.
1010 Ibid., p. 195; Optatus of Milevis, *Against the Donatists,* tr. Mark Edwards (Liverpool, 1997).
1011 Potter, *Constantine the Emperor,* p. 202.
1012 Ibid., p. 203.
1013 Rowan Williams, *Arius* (London: SCM, 1987), p. 271, quoting Arius's "Statement of Faith" in Opitz's *Urkunden,* p. 12.
1014 Ibid., p. 9.
1015 Ibid., p. 19.
1016 Lewis Ayres, *Nicaea and its Legacy* (London: Oxford University Press, 2004), p. 22; Mark Edwards, *Religions of the Constantinian Empire* (London: Oxford University Press, 2015), pp. 256ff.
1017 Ayres, *Nicaea and its Legacy,* p. 22.
1018 Ibid., p. 24.
1019 Potter, *Constantine the Emperor,* p. 226, citing Williams, *Arius,* p. 30.
1020 Chadwick, *The Early Church,* p. 124.
1021 Edwards, *Religions of the Constantinian Empire,* p. 275.
1022 J. N. D. Kelly, *Early Christian Doctrines* (London: Adam & Charles Black, 1960), p. 228.
1023 Epistle c. Ar 1.6, cited by Kelly, *Early Christian Doctrines,* p. 229.
1024 Williams, *Arius,* pp. 48–49.
1025 Edwards, *Religions of the Constantinian Empire,* p. 277.
1026 Ibid., p. 279.
1027 Ibid., p. 280.

[1028] Eusebius, *Vita Constantini*, p. 102.

[1029] Ibid., pp. 116–117.

[1030] Ibid., p. 118.

[1031] Potter, *Constantine the Emperor*, p. 234.

[1032] Opitz's *Urkunden*, 1934A, no. 22; Socrates of Constantinople 5th Century, *HE* 1.8.4, cited by Potter, *Constantine the Emperor*.

[1033] The Apostles' Creed was first referred to by Bishop Ambrose of Milan in 390. Traditionally thought to have been written by the Apostles, it is probably much later than that, but its genesis is unknown.

[1034] Patrick Whitworth, *Three Wise Men from the East: the Cappadocian Fathers and the Struggle for Orthodoxy* (Durham: Sacristy Press, 2015), pp. 73–74 and 76–79.

[1035] Edwards, *Religions of the Constantinian Empire*, pp. 281–282.

[1036] Ibid., p. 280.

[1037] Williams, *Arius*, p. 75.

[1038] Ibid., pp. 75–76.

[1039] Edwards, *Religions of the Constantinian Empire*, p. 285.

[1040] Williams, *Arius*, p. 81.

[1041] Potter, *Constantine the Emperor*, p. 221.

[1042] Edwards, *Religions of the Constantinian Empire*, pp. 187–188.

[1043] Constantine, *Oration to the Saints*, NPNF Second Series, ed. Philip Schaff (New York: Eerdmans, 1993), Ch 3, p. 568.

[1044] Edwards, *Religions of the Constantinian Empire*, p. 189.

[1045] Ibid., p. 189.

[1046] Eusebius, *Constantine's Oration to the Saints*, Ch 11, p. 568.

[1047] And this many years before the term *theotokos*, mother or bearer of God, became a talisman in the Christological debates, see Whitworth, *Constantinople to Chalcedon*, pp. 305ff.

[1048] Eusebius, *Constantine's Oration to the Saints*, p. 569.

[1049] Eusebius, *The Oration of Constantine to the Saints*, Ch 19, pp. 575–576.

[1050] Ibid., Ch 22, p. 578.

[1051] Ibid., Ch 26, p. 580.

[1052] The Great Cameo, Geldsmuseum Utrecht, see Jonathan Bardill, *Constantine: Divine Emperor of the Christian Golden Age* (Cambridge: Cambridge University Press, 2012), p. 171.

[1053] Edwards, *Religions of the Constantinian Empire*, p. 173.

[1054] Bardill, *Constantine: Divine Emperor and the Christian Golden Age*, pp. 28ff. Part of this column is still visible in Istanbul today, see Bardill's photograph, p. 29.

[1055] Ibid., pp. 38–40, and p. 208.

[1056] Eusebius, *Vita Constantini* 4.48, p. 197; Bardill, *Constantine: Divine Emperor of the Christian Golden Age*, p. 339.

[1057] Bardill, *Constantine: Divine Emperor of the Christian*

Golden Age, p. 364; Eusebius,
Vita Constantini 4.62.
1058 Bardill, *Constantine: Divine
Emperor of the Christian
Golden Age,* p. 303.
1059 Potter, *Constantine the
Emperor,* p. 280.

1060 Eusebius, *Vita Constantini* 4.63,
p. 207.
1061 Ibid. 4.63, p. 207.
1062 Quite possibly now in the
Atrium of Hagia Eirene; see
Bardill, *Constantine, Divine
Emperor of the Christian
Golden Age,* pp. 187–194.

Chapter 12

1063 Tertullian, *Apologeticum* XL
TANF Vol III (New York:
Cosimo, 2007), p. 47.
1064 Ignatius, *Letter to the Romans*
4, tr. Bart D. Ehrman, Loeb
Classical Library (Boston,
MA: Harvard University Press,
2003), Vol 24, p. 275.
1065 Ignatius, *Epistle to Diognetus*
5.9, tr. Bart D. Ehrman, Loeb
Classical Library (Boston,
MA: Harvard University Press,
2003), Vol 25, p. 141.

Bibliography

A New Eusebius, ed. J. Stevenson (SPCK, 1975).

Augustine, *City of God*, tr. H. Bettenson (Penguin, 2003).

Bardill, Jonathan, *Constantine, Divine Emperor of the Christian Golden Age* (CUP, 2015).

Barnes, T. D., *Tertullian* (OUP, 1985).

Behr, John, *Irenaeus of Lyons: Identifying Christianity* (OUP, 2015).

Bonner, Gerald, *St Augustine of Hippo* (Canterbury Press Norwich, 2002).

Brakke, David, *The Gnostics—Myth, Ritual and Diversity in Early Christianity* (Cambridge, 2010).

Bruce F. F., *Paul, Apostle of the Free Spirit* (Paternoster Press, 1977).

Bruce, F. F., *New Testament History* (Oliphants, 1969).

Cassius Dio, *The Roman History: The Reign of Augustus*, tr. Ian Scott-Kilvert (Penguin, 1987).

Chadwick, Henry, *The Early Church* (Penguin, 1993).

Clement of Alexandria, *Exhortation to the Greeks*, tr. G. W. Butterworth, MA (Loeb Classical Library, 1960).

Clement of Alexandria, *Miscellaneous Stromata* (Beloved Publishing USA, 2014).

Clement of Alexandria, *The Instructor* (Lighthouse Publishing Minnesota, 2014).

Cyprian, *Complete Works*, ed. Phillip Campbell (Evolution Publishing NJ USA, 2013).

Dunn, James D. G., *Neither Jew nor Greek*, Christianity in the Making Vol III (Eerdmans Grand Rapids/Cambridge, 2015).

Edwards, Mark, *Religions of Constantinian Empire* (OUP, 2015).

Ehrman, Bart D., *After the New Testament* (OUP, 2015).

Eusebius, *The History of the Church*, tr. G. A. Williamson (Penguin, 1989).

Gamble, Harry Y., *The New Testament Canon* (Wipf and Stock Oregon, 2002).

Goldsworthy, Adrian, *Augustus: From Revolutionary to Emperor* (Weidenfeld and Nicholson, 2015).

Grant, Robert M., *Irenaeus of Lyons* (Routledge, 2003).

Griffin, Miriam T., *Nero, The End of Dynasty* (B. T. Batsford, 1987).

Heine, Ronald E., *Origen, Scholarship in the Service of the Church* (OUP, 2010).

Holland, Tom, *Dynasty, The Rise and Fall of the House of Caesar* (Little, Brown, 2015).

Holland, Tom, *Rubicon* (Abacus, 2010).

Horace, *The Complete Odes and Epodes*, tr. David West (Oxford World Classics OUP, 2008).

Jewett, *A Chronology of Paul's Life* (Fortress Press Philadelphia, 1979).

Josephus, *The Jewish War*, tr. G. A. Williamson (Penguin, 1969).

Kelly, J. N. D., *Early Christian Doctrines* (A & C Black, 1960).

Lane Fox, Robin, *Alexander the Great* (Penguin, 2004).

Lane Fox, Robin, *Pagans and Christians* (Penguin, 2006).

Ludlow, Morwenna, *The Early Church* (I. B. Tauris, 2009).

McLynn, F., *Marcus Aurelius* (Vintage, 2010).

Metzger, Bruce M., *The Canon of The New Testament* (Clarendon, 1997).

Opper, Thorsten, *The Emperor Hadrian* (British Museum Press, 2008).

Origen, *Contra Celsum*, tr. Henry Chadwick (CUP, 1980).

Origen, *First Principles*, tr. G. W. Butterworth, ed. John C. Caradini (Ave Maria Press Indiana, USA, 2013).

Origen, *On Prayer* (Aeterna Press, 2015).

Osborn, Eric, *Clement of Alexandria* (CUP, 2008).

Ovid, *Love Poems* (Oxford World Classics OUP, 2008).

Ovid, *The Art of Love* (Amazon, 2015).

Plato, *Timaeus and Critias*, tr. T. K. Johansen (Penguin, 2008).

Pliny the Younger, *Letters*, tr. Betty Radice (Penguin, 1969).

Potter, David, *Constantine the Emperor* (OUP, 2013).

Reeves, Michael, *The Breeze of the Centuries* (IVP, 2016).

Russell, Bertrand, *History of Western Philosophy* (Routledge, 2007).

Sebag Montefiore, Simon, *Jerusalem* (Weidenfeld and Nicholson, 2011).

Suetonius, *The Twelve Caesars*, tr. Robert Graves (Penguin, 2007).

Tacitus, Cornelius, *The Annals* (ISBN 9781512287189, Amazon, 2015).

TANF Vol I: The Apostolic Fathers with Justin Martyr and Irenaeus (Eerdmans USA, 1975).

TANF Vol III: The Ante-Nicene Fathers (Cosimo Press New York, 2007).

TANF Vol IV: The Ante-Nicene Fathers (Cosimo Press New York, 2007).

TANF Vol V: The Ante-Nicene Fathers (Cosimo Press, 2007).

Thaumaturgus, Gregory, *The Oration and Panegyric addressed to Origen* (Beloved Publishing Ohio, USA, 2016).

The Apostolic Fathers Vol I & II, ed. & tr. Bart D. Ehrman (Loeb Classical Library, 2003).

The Lives of the Caesars, tr. Anthony Birley (Penguin, 1976).

The Nag Hammadi Scriptures, ed. Marvin Meyer (HarperOne, 2007).

Trigg, Joseph W., *Origen* (Routledge London and New York, 2005).

Von Camphausen, Hans, *Ecclesiastical Authority and Spiritual Power* (A & C Black, 1969).

Williams, Rowan, *Arius (2nd Edition)* (SCM Press, 2001).

Williams, Rowan, *On Augustine* (Bloomsbury, 2016).

Williams, Stephen, *Diocletian and the Roman Recovery* (Routledge, 2000).

Wright, Tom, *Virtue Reborn* (SPCK, 2010).

Index

Abitinian Martyrs 310, 311
Achillas of Alexandria 319
Acra 27
Acte, slave girl and mistress of Nero 62
Actium, Battle of 16, 17
Acts of the Scillitan Martyrs 173, 175–7
Adam 148–9, 163, 168, 170–71, 195
Adrianople, Battles of 300, 302
Aelia Capitolina 118
Aemilian/Aemilianus, Emperor 213–14, 269
Africa, North *see* North Africa
Agabus, NT prophet 57
Agerinus 64
Agrippa, Herod *see* Herod Agrippa I; Herod Agrippa II
Agrippa, Marcus Vipsanius 15, 16, 20, 23, 29
Agrippa Postumus *see* Postumus Agrippa, grandson of Augustus
Agrippina the Elder 23, 31, 32–3, 51, 61
Agrippina the Younger (Agrippina II) 31, 53, 54, 55–6, 61, 62–4
Alamanni 211
Alans, Iranian tribe 270
Alaric, Gothic commander 295
Albinus, Clodius 210
Alexamenos 341
Alexander, Bishop of Alexandria 317–18, 319
Alexander, Bishop of Jerusalem 252
Alexander the Great 26, 224
Alexander, Severus, Emperor 211
Alexander, son of Herod the Great 29

Alexander, Tiberius 71
Alexander of Constantinople 319
Alexander Jannaeus 27
Alexandria 16, 17, 26, 71, 128, 129, 135, 138–9, 182, 210, 218, 224–7, 276, 302
    Brucheion museum 226
    Caesareum, Library 226
    church in 76, 77–8, 227–8, 229–31, 232
    Gnosticism 232–5, 338
    Jewish community 77, 232, 235, 238
    libraries 129, 226–7
    lighthouse, island of Pharos 225
    massacre under Caracalla 210, 252
    Origen in 223, 227, 228–36
    Platonic/neo-Platonist Schools 227, 230, 232, 235–6
    Pompey's death in 9
    Serapeon 226
Allectus 276, 290
Ambrose, patron of Origen, 230, 233, 258, 260, 262
Ambrose, Bishop of Milan, 191, 378
Ammonius Saccas 227, 230, 235
Ananias, High Priest 59
Ananias, husband of Sapphira 40
Ananias of Damascus 43
Ananus, High Priest 70
Anastasius 79
Anaximenes 132
Anenclatus 77
Anicetus 64
Annianus of Alexandria 77
Antigonids 224

Antinous 119, 131

Antioch, Pisidian 45

Antioch, Syrian 44, 45, 56, 76, 85, 106–8, 218, 224, 271, 281

Antiochus III (the Great) 26

Antiochus IV Epiphanes 26–7, 69

Antipas (Herod the Tetrarch) *see* Herod Antipas

Antipater II, son of Herod the Great 29

Antipater of Idumea, father of Herod the Great 27

Antonia Minor, daughter of Mark Antony and grandmother of Caligula 33, 53

Antoninus Pius, Emperor 113, 120, 128, 172

Antonius, Roman commander 69

Antony, Mark 9, 10, 12, 13, 14, 16–17, 22, 27–8, 61
    suicide 17

Anullinus, Prefect of Rome 294, 296, 311

Apollo, Constantine's association with 292, 305, 309

Apollonius, presbyter 87

Apollonius Dyscolus 229

Apollonius Molon of Rhodes 6

Apollos 227

Apologists 121, 124, 125–42, 157, 241, 261, 335–6

apostolic authority 105

Apostolic Fathers 79–94, 95, 97, 102–5, 108–9, 157, 335
    see also individuals by name

apostolicity 207–8

Apuleius 174, 183

Aquila (Christian in Acts) 56

Aquila, Bible translation 238

Aquitaini 158

Aratus 48

Archelaus the Ethnarch, son of Herod the Great 4, 29

Ardashir I, Shahanshah of Sassanian dynasty 211, 212, 270

Arianism 2, 247, 302, 314–19
    and Nicaea 320–24

Aristides 121

Aristobulus II, son of Alexander Jannaeus 27

Aristobulus III, Jonathan, High Priest, brother of Mariamme 28

Aristobulus IV, son of Herod and Mariamme 29

Aristotle 235

Arius vii, viii, 264, 314, 315, 317–19, 324, 325
    and Origen 315–16
    Thalia 318

Arles, Council of 312–13, 319–20, 337

Armenia 7, 69, 210, 212, 213, 270, 276, 330

Arminius 68

asceticism 78, 141
    false 142, 338
    of Marcion 154

Asia 41, 45, 56, 85, 89, 120, 143, 210, 275, 281, 333
    Jews from 58, 60

Asia Minor 216, 224, 272

Asiaticus, Decimus Valerius 53

Askelon 69

Assyrians 25, 26

Athanasius, bishop of Alexandria 3, 255, 317, 319, 324–5, 328, 330, 337, 339

Athenagoras 121, 261

Athens 21, 31, 46–7, 129, 213, 224
    Paul in 46, 47–9

Atia, mother of Augustus 11

Augustan age 18–25

Augustine of Hippo 20, 133, 138–9, 174, 183, 199, 204–5, 216, 234, 334
    On Baptism, Against the Donatists 205, 338
    The City of God 333
    and Origen 234, 265, 266
    De Trinitate 316

Augustus Caesar (born Octavian) 4, 5, 6, 11–16, 18, 19, 20, 21–2, 24–5, 27
    and Alexandria 225, 226
    death 25, 30
    as heir to Julius Caesar 10, 11, 13, 22
    and Julia and her sons 23–4
    marriage to Claudia 22

marriage to Livia 15, 22–3
marriage to Scribonia 15, 22
Postumus banished by 30
will 30
Aurelian, Emperor 269, 272–3, 278, 311
Aurelius, Marcus see Marcus Aurelius

Balbinus, Emperor 212
Balbus, Marcus Atius 11
Balkans 6, 270–71, 273, 299
baptism 223, 337–8
    Augustine on 204–5
    in Gnosticism 150
    Irenaeus on 169
    Justin on 126–7
    re-baptism 204, 216, 337
    and Stephen of Rome 216, 337–8
    Tertullian on 192–3
Bar Kochba, Simeon, Jewish Leader
    118, 119
Bar Qappara 252
Barbalissos, Battle of 271
Barbelo 146–7, 149, 150, 151
Barnabas 40, 44, 45, 46, 56, 228
Barnabas, Epistle of 98, 102–3, 227
Barnard, L. W. 227
Barnes, T. D. 181
Basil of Caesarea 191, 237, 242–3
Basilides (student of Origen) 229
Basilides of Alexandria,Gnostic
    teacher 96, 98
Bassianus 300
Bassus 87
Bauer, Walter: Orthodoxy and Heresy in
    Earliest Christianity 207
Behr, John 159–60
Berea 47
Berenice 60, 69
Beth Horon 69
Bethlehem 3, 35
Bible
    Alexandrian translations 238
    availability in early Church of records
        of Jesus' life and teachings 340
    Law of Moses see Law of Moses

and Marcion vii, 97, 152, 153–4,
        195, 238
    Muratorian Canon 97–8
    NT Apostolicity 207–8
    NT Canon 79, 94–7
    NT sources 95
    Septuagint 26, 129, 186, 237–9
    surrender of Scriptures under
        Diocletian's persecution 205
    Synoptic Gospels 81, 94–5, 340 see
        also individual Gospels
    unity 152, 238
    Vulgate 173
Bithynia 76, 115, 318
Boudicca, Queen 64, 69
Boulogne (Gesoriacum) 276, 290
Brakke, David 151, 209
Britain 64, 69, 271, 272, 274, 275, 276,
    290, 299
    Roman invasion under
        Claudius 54–5
    sea defences with coastal forts 278
Britannicus 55, 61, 62–3, 74
Britons 118
Brutus, Decimus Junius 13
Brutus, Lucius Junius 5
Brutus, Marcus Junias 9, 10, 12, 13,
    14, 21
Burrhus 86
Burrus (Prefect of the Praetorian
    Guard) 63, 64, 65
Byzacena 173
Byzantium 295–6, 297, 302, 304, 306
    see also Constantinople

Caecilian of Carthage 205, 310–11, 313
Caesar, Julius 5, 6–11, 12, 22, 174
    assassination 9, 10–11
    and Cleopatra 9
    crossing of Rubicon 8
    will 10
Caesarea Maritima 28, 50, 57, 59–60,
    69, 70, 252
    church in 252–3
    council at (AD 190) 253
    Jewish community 252, 256

library 239, 253
Origen in 223, 232, 251–5
paganism 252
Paul in 252–3
Rabbinic schools 252
theological school 264
Caesareum, Alexandria, library
Complex 226
Caesarion, son of Julius Caesar 9, 17
Caligula, Emperor 33, 34, 37, 51–3, 61
Callistus (civil servant) 54
Callixtus, Bishop of Rome 220, 223
Campenhausen, Hans von 106, 107
Candidus (Valentinian) 234
Candidus, Tiberius Claudius 210
Cappadocia 76, 213, 237, 253, 264
Cappadocian Fathers 237, 253, 264,
324, 339
Capri 32, 33, 34, 51, 52
Caracalla, Emperor 210, 252
Caratacus, British chieftain 55
Carausius 274, 276, 290
Carinus, Emperor 273
Carneades 261
Carnuntum, Council of 291
Carpi 213
Carrhae, battles of 68, 270
Carthage 78, 173, 174–5, 181, 182–3,
199, 218, 224, 276, 335
Donatist bishops assembled in 314
and Rome 204, 217
seventh Council of 204, 205
Carus, Emperor 273
Cassius 6, 9, 10, 12, 13, 14
catacombs 3, 214, 340
Catiline 11
Catullus, Valerius 53
Celsus the Epicurean 261–4
Celts 158, 161
censuses 4, 20
Cerdo 156
Chalcedon 214, 302
Charles I of England 79
Church
Apologists 121, 124, 125–42, 157,
241, 261, 335–6

apostolic authority 105
and the Apostolic Fathers see
Apostolic Fathers
Arian controversy see Arianism
challenge to pagan culture 185,
190–91, 333–4, 335–6
conduct in a pagan society 185–91
and Constantine viii, 117, 295–9,
304, 308–14, 319, 320–22, 324,
325–7
corporate life 40
deacons 105–6, 107–8, 228
discipline 201, 215, 216–17, 220,
223, 322–3, 324
Donatist controversy see Donatist
controversy
elders/overseers/bishops 45, 106–8
and false teachers 86, 88, 143, 153,
162, 194, 338 see also Gnosticism
formation 40, 75–110
gentile converts 42, 46, 319
Great Church in Rome 151, 153,
160, 171, 207–9, 223
the lapsed see lapsed Christians
local churches see specific place names
Meletian controversy 317
ministerial and leadership
structure 105–9, 228
mission and expansion 39–43,
44–51, 56–7, 75, 173, 332
Monarchist controversy see
Monarchianism
as mother 202
and Nicaea see Nicaea, Council of
North African expansion 173
and Pentecost 39–40
persecution see persecution
process of defining orthodoxy 151–3
and religio illiciata status of
Christianity 287
resilience 332–41
and Roman judicial system 50–51
ruling elders 108
sacraments see sacraments
Samaritan inclusion 26, 42

social outworkings of faith 49, 83, 340

and the Spirit *see* Holy Spirit

with temporal power 332

uniqueness of early Christian communities 340

unity 202, 341

worship *see* worship

Cibalae, Battle of 300

Cicero 8, 11, 12, 13–14, 20, 114, 183, 334

Circesium 214

Claudia, wife of Augustus 22

Claudius 52, 53–6, 61, 74, 175, 210
funeral 62

Claudius II 271–2

Clement of Alexandria 77, 97, 129–42, 165, 166, 167, 227, 261, 334, 336
The Exhortation to the Greeks 130–34
influence on Origen 231
Pedagogue 133, 134–8
The Stromata 138–42

Clement of Rome 77, 79–80, 85, 97, 108–9, 166

Clement, Epistles of 79–84, 95
First Letter 80–83, 108–9
Second Letter to the Corinthians 83–4

Cleopatra 9, 16–17, 28

Clodius Pulcher, Publius 12

Cniva (Gothic leader) 213

Codex Alexandrinus 79, 83

Codex Hierosolymitanus 83

Codex Sinaiticus 79

coinage 278

Colossae 143–4

Commodus, Lucius Ceionius 120, 129, 209

Constantia, wife of Licinius 299, 302, 309

Constantine vii, viii, 117, 272, 276, 288–308
administrative and judicial reforms 298–9
and Apollo 292, 305, 309
architectural legacy 297, 328–9

and the Church viii, 117, 295–9, 304, 308–14, 319, 320–22, 324, 325–7

and Constantinople 297, 302, 304–7, 328–9, 331

continuity and change under 296–9, 307–8, 327–8

and Council of Arles 312–13, 319–20, 337

death and burial 330–31

and Donatist controversy 310–14, 319–20, 337

and Edict of Milan 117, 296, 310

final years 328–9

and Licinius 293, 295, 296, 297, 299, 300–301, 302

march on Rome 294

as new Moses 295, 301

and Nicaea viii, 304, 319, 320–22

Oration to the Saints 325–7

reconciliation of imperial power and Christian humility 329

religious experience at Grand, Gaul 292–3

rise to power 289–92, 294, 295

as sole Emperor of East and West 295, 297, 299, 301, 302, 304–7

statues of 297, 300, 329

visions of Christ 294, 309

Constantine II 299, 300, 301, 330

Constantinople 216, 224, 295, 330
and Constantine 297, 302, 304–7, 328–9, 331
Council of 325
Hagia Sophia 305, 306
synod of AD 336 325

Constantius Chlorus, Constantine's father, 275–6, 286, 287, 288, 289, 290

Constantius II 324, 330

Corinth 46, 47, 50, 56–7, 76, 106, 224

Cornelia, wife of Pompey, daughter of Metellus Scipio 9

Cornelius (God-fearing centurion) 42, 252–3

Cornelius of Rome 200, 204, 214, 216, 223, 337

Cox, Cleveland 160
Crassus, Roman triumvirate 7–8, 16, 20, 68
Credo of Alexandria 228
Crementius (deacon) 204
Crescens 128
Crete 65
Crispus, Flavius Julius, son of Constantine 290, 300, 302–3, 328
Crocus 86
Cross of Christ 124, 168, 169–70, 222, 341
Ctesiphon 210, 212, 276
Cynics 183
Cyprian of Carthage viii, 174, 183, 191, 199–205, 214, 215, 216–17, 223, 310, 337
    Ad Donatum 200
    execution 335
    On the Lapsed 202–3, 310
    and re-baptism 204, 216–17
    and Stephen of Rome 216–17
    tracts 201–4
    On the Unity of the Church 201–2, 216–17
Cyril 315

Dacia/Dacians 74, 114, 115, 118, 213, 273
Dalmatae 16
Damas 87
deacons 105–6, 107–8, 228
Decebalus 114
Decius, Caesar Messius Quintus 200, 203, 213, 214, 223, 264–5, 269, 270–71, 335
Demetrius of Alexandria 223, 228, 229, 230, 235, 251
demiurge 147, 148, 156, 161, 162–3, 234
Derbe 45
devil 128, 149, 180, 195, 201, 234, 251, 265
Diana, goddess at Ephesus 49–50
Didache 98, 101–2, 108, 109
Dinocrates 180, 181, 225
Dio, Cassius 18, 211

Diocletian, Emperor vii, 205, 269, 271, 273–88, 289, 291, 293, 297, 307
    administrative, military and economic reforms 277–81
    persecution under vii, 205, 214, 274, 282–7, 310, 317, 335
    De Pretiis 279–80
Diodorus of Tarsus 317
Diogenes 183
Diognetus, Epistle to 103–5, 116
Dionysius (member of Areopagus) 49
Dionysius of Alexandria 83, 215, 217
Dobrudja, Battle of 271
Docetism 88, 144, 149, 338
    Marcionite Docetic tendencies 195, 196–7
Dolabella, Publius Cornelius 12
Domitian 74, 113
Domitius Ahenobarbus, Gnaeus 61
Donatist controversy 117, 178, 205–6, 214, 217, 286, 310–14, 336–8
    and Constantine 310–14, 319–20, 337
    and Council of Arles 312–13, 319–20
Donatus of Casae Nigrea 205–6, 310, 311
Doris, first wife of Herod the Great 29
Dover 276, 278
Druids 55
Drusilla, daughter of Herod Agrippa I 59
Drusilla, Julia, sister of Caligula 52
Drusus, Nero Claudius, brother of Tiberius 15, 22, 24, 210
Drusus Julius Caesar, son of Tiberius 30, 31, 33
dualism 145–6, 235, 236, 265
Dura 214

Eagle standards 8, 20, 68, 69
Easter date 253, 312, 323–4
economic reforms under Diocletian 279–80
Edom 69
Edomites 27
Egypt 4, 20, 27, 210, 272, 276
    as breadbasket of Empire 17, 29
    Jews deported by Ptolemy I to 26

Judaism's influence on Christianity in 227

Pompey in 9

Elagabalus, Emperor 211

elders 45, 106–8

  ruling elders 108

Eleazar ben Simon 69

Eleutherus of Rome 158, 160

Eliot, T. S. 336

Elvira, Council of 319

Elymas 44

Emesa, Battle of 272

Empedocles 132, 183

Emperor-worship 116, 117, 202, 335, 336–7

Ennius 5

Ephesus 49, 76, 85, 86, 224, 263, 333

  Ephesian elders vii, 57, 107, 333

Epicurus 132

Epimenides, Greek philosopher 48

Epiphanes 141

Epiphanius of Salamis 237, 250, 265

Essenes 36

Eucharist 127, 169, 207, 340

Euethius 285

Euripides 132, 165

Eusebius of Caesarea 42–3, 65, 73, 76, 77, 79, 89, 90–91, 207, 227–8, 229, 231, 253, 283, 286, 319, 328, 329

  and Nicaea 322

  and Origen 252, 255, 261

  on Tertullian 181, 182, 184

  Vita Constantini 291–2, 293, 294, 295, 301, 303, 309, 330

Eusebius of Nicomedia 302, 317, 319, 322, 324–5, 330

Euzoius 324

Eve 148, 149, 163

Evodius 76

Ezra 25

Fabian of Rome 200–201, 214

Fabius of Antioch 215

false teachers 86, 88, 143, 153, 162, 194, 338

  see also Gnosticism

Fausta, Flavia Maxima, wife of Constantine 291, 301, 303, 328

Felicitas, martyr Carthage, 178, 179, 180

Felix, Antonius 59, 60, 253

Felix of Abthugni 313

Festus, Porcius 60, 253

Florianus, Emperor 269, 273

Florinus 157

Florus, Gessius 69

Florus, poet 118

The Foreigner 151

Franks 270, 290

free will 249–50

Fulvia 14, 22

Gaetulicus 52

Gaius Caesar, grandson of Augustus 23, 24

Galba 52, 68, 71

Galerius, Gaius Caesar and Emperor, 275, 276, 286–7, 288, 289, 290, 293, 335

Galilee 69, 70

Gallandi, A. 103

Gallienus, Emperor 214, 271

Gallio, pro-consul 50

Gallus, Cestius 69

Gallus, Trebonianus, Emperor 200, 213–14, 216

Gamala 70

Gamaliel, Rabbi 332

Gaul 6, 7, 11, 13, 20, 118, 210, 271, 272, 273, 274, 275, 277, 292, 297

Gauls 158

Gemellus 52

Georgia 270

German tribes 19, 24, 30–31, 52, 68, 210, 211, 270, 274, 288

Germanicus, General 23, 31, 61

Germanicus of Smyrna 92

Germany 8, 30–31, 32, 53, 68, 114, 118, 186, 211, 270, 271

Gibbon, Edward: *Decline and Fall of the Roman Empire* 113

Gischala 70

Gnosticism vii, viii, 3, 95, 140, 142–56,
    157, 227, 230, 231, 314–15, 338–9
    in Alexandria 232–5, 338
    demiurge 147, 148, 156, 161, 162–3,
        234
    epigraph to Flavia Sophie 155–6
    The Foreigner 151
    Gnostic gospels 96, 141, 145, 154–5,
        231, 233, 338
    Ialdabaoth 147, 148, 162–3, 234
    and Irenaeus 158–64, 338–9
    and the Monarchists 219
    Ogdoad 162, 233
    and Origen 232–5, 255
    pleroma 161, 163, 165, 233
    in Rome 151–6
    Secret Book of John 146–7, 149–50
    Sophia 147, 148, 161, 163, 234
    Valentinians 156, 183, 234
Gordian I, Emperor 211–12
Gordian II, Emperor 212
Gordian III, Emperor 212, 270
Goths 201, 213, 214, 270–71, 275, 295,
    329
Gregory the Illuminator 284
Gregory Nazianzen 237, 242–3, 323, 339
Gregory of Nyssa 218, 255, 256
Gregory Thaumaturgus 232, 253, 264
Griffin, Miriam 62

Hadrian 113, 117–20, 129
Hannibal 174
Hasidim 36
Hatra 212
Heine, Ronald E. 265
Helena, mother of Constantine 275, 289,
    303–4, 328
Heraclas of Alexandria 229
Heracleon 154, 232
Heraclitus 128
Herais 229
Hermogenes 322
Herod Agrippa I 34
Herod Agrippa II 60, 69
Herod Antipas 20, 37
Herod the Great 4, 5, 7, 25, 27–30

and Caesarea 252
    death 29–30
    Second Temple 28–9
Herod, chief of police in Smyrna 93
Herodias 37
Herodotus 183
Hierapolis 76, 89
Hilarianus 179
Hill, Charles 157
Hippolytus of Rome 152, 172, 219–20,
    223, 244
    The Apostolic Tradition 220
Hirtius, Aulus 13
Hishaya 252
Holy Spirit
    anointing for leadership 106
    authority in Pauline churches 106
    charismata 181
    in Church's mission 39–40, 42, 75, 76
    Irenaeus on 169
    and Origen 245, 247–8
    and Pentecost 39–40
    and Tertullian 220–21
Homer 132
homoian party 324–5
homoios kat' ousian party 324
homoousios 222, 324, 328, 339
homosexuality 138
Horace, Roman poet 17, 21
Huns 270
Hyginus 154
hypostasis 218, 219–20, 222, 316
hypothesis 164–6
Hyrcanus, John 27
Hyrcanus II 7, 27
Hyrcanus the Tobiad 27

Ialdabaoth 147, 148, 162–3, 234
Iamblichus of Apamea 317
Iazyges, Sarmatian tribe 213
Iceni 64, 69
Iconium 45
idolatry 175, 189, 190
    see also Emperor-worship
Idumeans 70

Ignatius of Antioch viii, 3, 76, 85–9, 91, 97, 109, 153, 208, 335, 341
  Letters of 108, 341
Illyricum 16, 17, 32, 271, 275, 277
Irenaeus of Lyons viii, 3, 76, 89, 91, 96–7, 144–5, 151–2, 154, 156, 157–72, 208, 209, 219, 238
  Demonstration of the Apostolic Preaching 160, 164
  and Gnosticism 158–64, 338–9
  Against Heresies 95, 159–72
  letter to Florinus 157
  literary criticism tools of hypothesis, recapitulation and economy 164–71
  and Polycarp 157
Ishodad, 48
Islam 295, 332
Italy 14, 19, 21, 65, 271, 272, 275, 281, 293, 294, 300

Jakab, Attila 228
James, brother of Jesus 40, 44, 58, 73, 106, 107
James, son of Zebedee 333
Jason, High Priest 26
Jerome 66, 91, 191, 239
  and Origen 266
  on Tertullian 181–2
Jerusalem 26, 50, 69, 296
  Aelia Capitolina, built on site of 118
  and Antiochus III 26
  and Antiochus IV 26–7
  Council of 42, 46
  early Church in 39–42, 58, 107, 319
  fall to Pompey 7, 27
  Herod's building in 28–9
  Islam's victory in 332
  Jesus' triumphal entry 71
  and the Jewish rebellion 70, 72–3
  Maccabean Palace 28
  Paul's final stay and arrest in 57–9
  siege and destruction (AD 70) 72–3
  synod of AD 335 325
  temple *see* Temple of Jerusalem
Jeshua, High Priest 70

Jesus of Nazareth
  apostolic teaching about 40, 41, 45
  birth 3–5, 35
  and Celsus 263–4
  and Clement of Alexandria 133–5
  crucifixion 5, 34, 38, 169–70, 253, 341 *see also* Cross of Christ
  date of passion celebration 253
  Docetic view of 144, 149
  as Good Shepherd 340
  Justin, 125, 126
  life and ministry 35–8
  as *Logos* 86, 128, 139, 144, 186–7, 196, 263 *see also* Monarchianism
  as Messiah 35, 41, 43, 123, 195
  and recapitulation 167–70
  resurrection 34, 38, 332
  Second Coming 88
  Sermon on the Mount 81, 95, 102, 335
  and the Temple 37–8, 41, 72
  triumphal entry to Jerusalem 71
Jewish Law *see* Law of Moses
Jewish rebellion (AD 66) 69–70, 252, 253
John, apostle 41, 75, 76–7, 91, 144, 159, 333, 335
John, Gospel of 95–6, 165, 340
John the Baptist 35, 37
John Mark 44, 46
John of Gischala 70, 72, 73
Jonathan, High Priest (Aristobulus III) 28
Jordan 28
Joseph, husband of Mary 4, 35
Joseph the Tobiad 26
Josephus, Flavius, Jewish historian 69–70, 73, 243
Jotapata 70
Judaizers 87, 338
Judea 7, 25–7, 35, 37
  Jewish rebellion (AD 66) 69–70, 252, 253
  renamed Syria Palaestina 119
Julia the Elder, daughter of Augustus 15, 22, 23
  banishment 24, 32
  marriage to Agrippa 15, 23, 24, 29

marriage to Tiberius 23, 24
Julia Minor, sister of Caesar 12
Julia the Younger, granddaughter of
    Augustus 33
Julian from Bithynia 72
Julian Marriage Laws 21–2, 24, 298
Julianus, Amnius Anicius, Proconsul of
    Africa 282
Julianus, Didius 209
Julio-Claudian dynasty 51, 56
    see also specific Emperors
Julius, Imperial Regiment centurion 60,
    65
Junod, Eric 254
Justin Martyr viii, 120–28, 144–5,
    151–2, 156, 170, 261, 336
    Dialogue with Trypho the Jew 121–4,
        156
    First Apology 125–8
    and Monarchianism 218–19
    On the Resurrection 156
    in Rome 124–5, 208
    Second Apology 128
    On the Sole Government of God 156
Justinian, Emperor 265

Khalid ibn al-Walid, companion of
    Muhammad 332
Koetschau, Paul, classical philologis, 262

labarum standard 294–5, 302
Lactantius 274, 283–4, 286–7, 293, 294,
    309
lapsed Christians 223
    and Cyprian 201, 202–3, 310
    Donatist controversy see Donatist
        controversy
    Nicaea Canons on penance for
        inclusion of 323
    and persecution 172, 180–81, 202–3,
        205, 214, 310, 336–8 see also
    Donatist controversy
Law of Moses 37, 45, 58, 60, 65, 123,
    155, 163, 338
    false teaching about 143–4
Lawrence, St 214

Lebanon 28
Legio Martia 13
Lepida, Domitia, aunt of Nero 61
Lepidus, Marcus 10, 13, 17, 27, 53
Leptis Magna 175, 182
libellatici 202
libelli pacis 203
Licinius I 291, 293, 295, 296, 297, 299,
    300–301, 302, 319
Linus 77
Livia, Drusilla (later Julia Augusta) 15,
    18, 22–3, 25, 30, 32, 51
Livilla, Claudia Livia Julia, sister of
    Claudius 33
Livilla, Julia, sister of Caligula 53, 54
Logos 86, 126, 128, 139, 140, 144, 156,
    167, 170, 186–7, 196, 197, 230, 263,
    265
    and Monarchianism 218–23
    and Origen 230, 233, 242, 243,
        246–7
    and Song of Songs 256, 257
London 276
Loofs, Friedrich 159
Lucar, Cyril 79
Lucian 317
Lucius, Bishop of Rome 216
Lucius Caesar, grandson of Augustus 23,
    24
Lucius Verus 113
Lugdunum 157, 158, 210
Luke 59, 98
Luke's Gospel 35, 59, 71–2
    and Jesus' birth 4
Lupercalia 9
Lydia 47
Lysias, Claudius 58–9, 60
Lystra 45

Maccabee dynasty 27, 69
    John Hyrcanus 27
    Jonathan the Diplomat (Jonathan
        Apphus) 27
    Judah Maccabee/Judas
        Maccabeus 27
    Simon Maccabeus 26, 27

Macedonius 331
Macrinus, Marcus Opellius 210, 211
Macro 52
Maecenas, Gaius, patron of the Augustan
    arts 17, 20–21
Maesa, Julia 211
Magi 3, 4, 132, 141
Magnesians 87, 109
Majorinus 310, 311
Malta 61, 64
Malthace, third wife of Herod the
    Great 29
Mamaea, Julia 211
Mamre 296, 328
Mani, founder of Manichaeism, 270
Manichaeism 270, 282
Marcella, mother of Potamiaena 229
Marcellus, Marcus Claudius 23
Marcellus the centurion 282–3
Marcia, mistress of Commodius (Marcia
    Aurelia Ceionia Demetrias) 209, 220
Marcion (heretic) vii, 97, 152, 153–4,
    155, 156, 183, 194, 238
    book of Psalms 98
    Docetic tendencies 195, 196–7
    in Rome 152, 153–4, 156, 208, 209
    Tertullian against teachings of 194–8,
        339
Marcion, account of martyrdom of
    Polycarp 92
Marcus (Gnostic) 156, 158, 162
Marcus Aurelius, Emperor 113, 129, 155,
    158, 172, 186, 335
Mariamme I, second wife of Herod the
    Great 27, 28, 29
Mark the Evangelist 76, 77, 227–8
Mark's Gospel 95
marriage
    under Constantine 298, 307
    Julian Marriage Laws 21–2, 24, 298
    Justin on 140–42
Martianus 302
martyrdom 92, 139, 142, 180–81, 186,
    187–8, 205, 214, 258, 286, 287, 310,
    332
    Abitinan Martyrs 310, 311

of apostles vii, 67, 73, 333, 335
of Apostolic Fathers viii, 85, 88, 89,
    91–4, 157, 335
as a sacrament 88
    see also individual martyrs by name
Mary, mother of Jesus 4, 40, 169
Masada, Fortess near Dead Sea, 70
massacre of the innocents 4
Mattathias 27
Matthew, tax collector 35
Matthew's Gospel 4
Mauretania 173
Maxentius Augustus, Emperor 290–91,
    293, 294, 295, 296, 309
Maximian, Emperor 223, 274–5, 276,
    287–8, 289, 291
Maximinus, Julius Verus 211, 212
Maximinus II, Emperor 288, 293
Maximus the Confessor 255
Meletian controversy 317, 330
Meletius, Bishop of Lycopolis 317, 328
Melito of Sardis 121
Memphis 226
Menander (poet) 126, 132
Menander of Ephesus 183
Mensurius, Bishop of Carthage 286, 310
Mesopotamia 8, 42, 210, 211, 224
Messalina, Valeria 54, 55
Milan 271, 274, 281, 288, 290, 294, 304,
    313
    Edict of 117, 207, 296, 301, 310, 332
Miletus vii, 57, 333
Miltiades, Bishop of Rome 311
Milvian Bridge, Battle of 294, 296, 300
Minervina, wife of Constantine 290
Misenum 19
    Treaty of 14, 15
Mithradates VI enemy of Rome from
    Pontus 7
Mnason 57
Mnester, Marcus Lepidus, Pantomime
    artist 53, 55
modalism 219
Monarchianism 218–23, 244–5, 317
    and Gnosticism 219
    and Tertullian 199

Montanism 92, 158, 161, 175, 178–81, 183, 199, 220
Montanus 220
Moors 118
More, Henry 145
Moses 41, 60, 81, 124, 126, 132, 139, 140, 170, 261, 263
    Law of see Law of Moses
Muratori, Ludovico Antonio 97
Muratorian Canon 97–8
Mutina, Battle of 13

Nabateans 114
Nag Hammadi Library 96, 145, 151, 233, 338
Naissus, Battle of 271
Naples 67
Narcissus 54
Narses of Persia 276
Nautin, Pierre: Origen 254
Nehemiah 25
neo-Platonism 182, 230, 234, 235, 265, 314–15, 317
    see also Plotinus
Nero, Emperor 56, 61–8, 69, 71, 187
    persecution under vii, 66–7, 77, 187, 334, 335
Nero, Tiberius Claudius, first husband of Livia 15, 22
Nero Julius Caesar, son of Agrippina the Elder 33
Nerva 74, 113–14
Nestorius 315
New Prophecy 183, 199, 220
Nicaea, Council of 320–24
    background and road to 310–20
    Canons 1–20 322–3
    and Constantine viii, 304, 319, 320–22
    and the Novationists (Canon 8) 216, 323
Nicene Creed 322, 324–5, 328
Nicene Trinitarianism 316, 324
Nicodemus 36

Nicomedia 115–16, 214, 275, 281, 284, 285, 286, 288, 289–90, 301, 302, 327, 330, 331
Niger, Pescennius 210
Nisibis 210, 211, 270, 276
Norea 148
North Africa 271, 275, 276, 287, 293, 313–14
    Christianity 173–206, 210, 285–6, 313–14, 337 see also Donatist controversy
    Islam's spread in 332
Northern Kingdom of Israel 25–6
nous 234
Novatian 204, 214, 216, 223, 323, 337
Novatians 215–16, 323
Numerian, Emperor 273
Numidia 173

Octavia, Claudia, daughter of Claudius 55, 62, 63, 65–6
Octavia, sister of Augustus 14
Octavian see Augustus Caesar
Octavius, Caius, father of Augustus 11
Odaenathus 271
Odaenathus of Palmyra 213, 214, 271
Ogdoad 162, 233
oikonomia (economy) 164, 170–71, 221
Onesimus 86
Opitz, Hans-Georg 318
Origen 129, 138–9, 223–66, 334
    in Alexandria 223, 227, 228–36
    Alexandrian writings 237–51
    and Arius 315–16
    and Augustine 234, 265, 266
    biblical commentaries 230, 231, 232, 238, 239–41, 242–3, 245, 253, 255–7
    in Caesarea 223, 232, 251–5
    Caesarean writings 255–64
    Contra Celsum 253, 261–4
    Christology 233, 246–7, 315–16
    on creation 248, 265
    Decian persecution 264–5
    and Demetrius 223, 228, 229, 251
    Dialogue with Heracelides 257

and Epiphanius of Salamis 237, 250, 265

eschatology 250–51, 265

On First Principles 230, 232, 233–4, 235, 236, 237, 238, 241–2, 244–51

on free will 249–50

and Gnosticism 232–5, 255

as a *grammatikos* 229

and Hebrew 236, 252

Hexapla 229–30, 236, 238–9, 253

influences on 227, 231

and Jerome 266

On Natures 233

pastoral works 257–61

Philocalia 237, 239, 242–3, 262

Platonist/neo-Platonist tendencies 232, 234, 235–6, 237, 261, 265

on prayer 258–60

preaching ministry 253–4

On the Resurrection 230

on Song of Songs 255–7

and the soul 248–9, 265

Trinitarianism 245–8, 316

Ossius, Bishop of Cordoba 291, 298, 311, 319

Ostrogoths 270

Otho 63, 68, 71

ousia 316

Ovid 21–2

Paetus 54

paganism 45, 49–50

of Caesarea 252

Christian challenge to pagan culture 185, 190–91, 333–4, 335–6

Christian conduct in a pagan society 185–91

and Diocletian's persecution 281–7

Emperor-worship 116, 117, 202, 335, 336–7

idolatry 175, 189, 190

Justin's critique 125

pagan Rome and Empire and Constantine's revolution 295–9

pagan temples 102, 186, 296, 298, 305–6, 330

Paul's use of pagan literature and poetry 47, 48–9

and public shows 189–90

punishment for refusal to participate in pagan practices 117, 186, 281–7

worship in pagan temples 186

Pallas, brother of Felix 54, 59

Palmyra 213, 270, 271, 272

Pansa, Gaius Vibius 13

Pantaenus 129, 231

Paphos 44

Papias of Hieropolis 76, 85, 89–91

Parthamaspates 117

Parthians 7–8, 12, 16, 19, 20, 68, 117, 174, 201, 210, 211

Passion of Perpetua 178–81

paterfamilias 18

Patripassianism 219

Paul, apostle 43–50, 51, 75, 76, 143, 152–3, 170, 260, 341

appeal to Caesar 60

in Caesarea 252–3

conversion 43, 51, 60, 106

execution vii, 67, 335

final stay and arrest in Jerusalem 57–9

and the Law of Moses 58

at Miletus vii, 57, 333

missionary journeys 44–51, 56–7, 75

and Peter 44, 106

in Rome vii, 61, 64, 65, 67

as Saul 42, 43

trials 59–60, 65, 253

Paul of Samosata 222, 273, 317, 323

Paulus, Sergius 44

Pax Romana 18, 19

Pelagianism 250

Pentecost 39–40

Perpetua, Vibia 178, 179–81, 200, 210, 310, 335

persecution 3, 40, 76, 91, 92, 172, 333

in Antioch 85

Apologists' stimulation through 335–6

and the Church's resilience and
     growth 332–41
and the 'crisis of the Empire' 211
under Decius 200, 203, 214, 215,
     223, 264–5, 269, 310, 335
under Diocletian vii, 205, 214, 274,
     282–7, 310, 317, 335
under Domitian 74
and Donatist controversy see
     Donatist controversy
with expansion of Church 42
under Galerius 286–7, 293, 335
under Gallienus 214
under Gallus 200
and lapsed Christians 172, 180–81,
     202–3, 205, 214, 310, 336–8 see
     also Donatist controversy
in Lyons 172
under Marcus Aurelius 158, 335
and martyrdom see martyrdom
under Nero vii, 66–7, 77, 187, 334,
     335
in North Africa 173–4, 175–81, 210,
     285–6
and Pliny the Younger 116–17
punishment for refusal to participate
     in pagan practices 117, 186, 281–7
and scapegoating 66, 334
under Severus 223, 229, 335
systematic, middle of third
     century 200–201, 223
and Tertullian's writings 184–8
under Valerian 200, 205, 214, 223,
     335
in Vienne 172, 186
by Zealots 73
Persians 201, 269–70, 271, 273, 274,
     275, 276, 329–30
Pertinax, Emperor 209
Peter, apostle 38, 40, 41, 42, 75, 76, 333,
     335
     Cyprian and Petrine
          authority 201–2, 216–17
     execution 67
     and Paul 44, 106
Peter of Alexandria 317

Petra 114
Petronius 68
Pharisees 36–7
Pharsalus, Battle of 8, 12
Philip the Arab, Emperor 212, 213, 270
Philip the evangelist and deacon 41, 57,
     89, 106
Philippi, Macedonia 46, 47, 49, 50, 333
     Battle of Philippi 14, 17, 21
Philippus, Lucius Marcius 12
Philo of Alexandria 77–8, 129, 227, 230
philosophy, as handmaid to
     theology 139–40
Philostratus 182
Photius 159
Phraates IV 20
Picts 290
Pilate, Pontius 34
Pionius 92
Piso, Gaius Calpurnius 67
Piso, Gnaeus Calpurnius, Prefect of
     Syria 31, 67
Pius I 98
Plancus 5
Plato 20, 77, 132, 139, 140, 183, 235,
     334, 336
     and Justin 121, 125, 126
     and Origen 263
Platonism 49, 77, 122, 146, 197, 235–6,
     261, 262
     Middle 144, 197, 235, 314–15, 338
     Platonic/neo-Platonist Schools 227,
          230, 232, 235–6
     Platonic dualism 235, 236, 265
     see also neo-Platonism
Plautius, Aulus, jnr 67
pleroma 161, 163, 165, 233
Pliny the Elder 114–15, 183
Pliny the Younger 114, 115–17, 185
Plotinus 140, 182, 227, 230, 235
Plutarch, brother of Heraclas of
     Alexandria 229
Polybius 87
Polycarp viii, 3, 76, 85, 86, 87, 88, 89,
     91–4, 97, 157, 159, 335
     and Irenaeus 157

Letter to the Philippians 91–2, 108
Pompeianus, Rauricius 294
Pompeii 74, 115
Pompeius, Sextus 14–15, 16
Pompey 7, 8, 9, 12, 27
Pomponianus 115
Pomponius (deacon) 179, 180
Pontic Kingdom 7
Pontus 76, 115
Poppaea Sabina 63, 66, 67
Porphyry 235
Postumus Agrippa, grandson of
    Augustus 23, 25, 30
Potamiaena 229
Pothinus of Lyons 160
Praetorian Guard 19, 53, 54, 55, 56, 62,
    63, 114, 212, 291
Praxeas 220
prayer
    Lord's Prayer 193, 259–60
    Origen on 258–60
    Tertullian on 193
Primus, Antonius 71
Prisca, Empress, wife of Diocletian 285,
    286
Priscilla 56
Priscus, Marius 115
Probus, Emperor 273
Propertius 21
prosopa 219–20
Ptolemaeus 154, 155, 156
Ptolemaic dynasty 224
    early Ptolemies 225, 226
    see also specific pharaohs
Ptolemias 70
Ptolemy I Soter 26, 225
Ptolemy II Philadelphus 26
Ptolemy XIII 9
Ptolomaeus 156, 232, 233
Pupienus, Emperor 212
purgatory 251, 265
Pythagoras 183

Quadi 213
Quirinius 4
Qumran community 36

Rakotis 225
recapitulation (anakephalaiosis) 164,
    166–70
Regulus, Publius Memmius 33
religious intolerance
    persecution see persecution
    punishment for refusal to participate
        in pagan practices 117, 186, 281–7
religious tolerance 117, 290, 296, 307,
    330, 332
    freedom of worship 188–9, 301,
        307, 310
Remus 9, 21
repentance 48, 80, 84, 98–9, 140, 192–3
Resaena, Battle of 270
resurrection 198, 341
    of Jesus 34, 38, 332
Revocatus, martyr Carthage, 179, 180
Roman army 8–9, 14, 16, 35, 68, 71,
    213, 271, 273, 288
    under Augustus 12–13, 15, 18–19
    under Caligula 52
    Christianity spreading within 75
    Diocletian's reforms 277–8
    Eagle standards 8, 20, 68, 69
    invasion of Britain, under
        Claudius 54–5
    and the Jewish rebellion 69–70, 72–3
    labarum standard 294–5, 302
    Legio Martia 13
    Legio XII Fulminata 69
    Praetorian Guard see Praetorian
        Guard
    under Severus 210
    veterans in Carthage 174
Roman Wars 270–71
Rome
    and administrative reforms of
        Empire under Constantine 298–9
    and administrative reforms of
        Empire under Diocletian 277–81
    Basilica Constantiniana 297
    building projects under Octavian 16
    under Caligula 52–3
    and Carthage 204, 217
    catacombs 3, 214, 340

Christian challenge to way of
    life 333–4, 335–6
Christian community in 56, 57, 66,
    76, 77–8, 88–9, 309–10 see also
    Rome: Great Church
church under Constantine 309–10
City Prefect 281
Constantine's march on 294
and Constantinople 304
and the 'crisis of the Empire' 210–14
fire of AD 64 66, 67, 334
games 9, 11, 12, 189–90
Gemonian Steps 34, 71
Gnosticism in 151–6
Golden House 67, 68
Great Church 151, 153, 160, 171,
    207–9, 223
and Herod 29
Ignatius in 208
interest rates 18
Justin in 124–5, 208
Lupercalia 9
Marcion in 152, 153–4, 156, 208, 209
as a microcosm 208
under Nero 61–8, 77
pagan Rome and Empire and
    Constantine's revolution 295–9
Paul in vii, 61, 64, 65, 67
Peter in 67, 77
proscriptions 13
Santa Croce church 297
Senate see Senate
Severus's march on 210
Sol Invictus cult 273
and the tetrarchy 275–6, 289
under Vespasian 74
Victory Arch 297
Romulus 9, 21
Rubicon 8
Rufinus, Tyrannius 237, 249, 255, 266

Sabellius, theologian Rome,
    modalist 219
Sabinus 72
Saccas, Ammonius see Ammonius Saccas
sacraments 126–7

martyrdom as a sacrament 88
    validity 204–6, 216, 337–8
    see also baptism; Eucharist
Sadducees 69
Salamis 44
Salome I, Herod the Great's sister 29
Salome, daughter of Herodias 37
Salome Alexandra (Hasmonean ruler of
    Jerusalem) 7, 27
Samaria 25, 42
Samaritans 25–6, 42
Sanhedrin 36, 41, 42, 59, 60, 73, 332, 333
Sapor I of Persia 269, 270, 271
Sapor II of Persia 329–30
Sapphira 40
Sarmatians 118, 270, 276, 329
Sassanids 270, 271
Saturninus (catechumen) 179, 180, 181
Saturninus, Vigellus 175–7
Saxons 270
Scapula, Proconsul 188
Scipio Aemilianus Africanus, Publius
    Cornelius (Scipio the Younger) 174
Scipio Africanus, Publius Cornelius
    (Scipio the Elder) 174
Scribes 36
Scribonia, wife of Augustus 15, 22
Scripture see Bible
Sebasteni 28
Secret Book of John 146–7, 149–50
Secundulus of Carthage 179
Sejanus, Prefect 19, 32–3, 52
Seleucids 224
Senate 5, 10, 11, 12, 13, 18, 20, 24, 25, 31,
    32, 33, 34, 74, 128, 209, 211, 212, 281
    and Caligula 52, 53
    at Constantinople 307
    and Nero 62, 64, 68
    New Regulations against
        Christians 210
    and Severus 210
Seneca, tutor to Nero 50, 62, 64, 67, 183
Septuagint, tr. of OT by 70 Scholars,
    Alexandria 26, 129, 186, 237–9
Serapis, cult of 226, 230
Serdica, Treaty of 300

Serenus 229

Sermon on the Mount 81, 95, 102, 335

Seth 148–9, 163

Severus, Flavius Valerius 288, 290

Severus, Julius 119

Severus, Septimius 174–5, 182, 209–10, 223, 229, 290, 335

Shakespeare, William
Antony and Cleopatra 16–17
Julius Caesar 10

Shapur I 212–13, 214

Shepherd of Hermas 79, 98–101, 208, 231, 235

Sibylline Oracles 132

Silanus 52, 54

Silas, companion of Paul 46, 49, 50

Silius, Gaius 55

Silvester I of Rome 319

Simon ben Giora, Jewish leader 70, 72

Simon Magus 145, 163

Simon the High Priest (Simon Maccabaeus) 26, 27

Sirmium 274, 299, 301, 304

Sixtus II, pope and martyr 214, 217

Smyrna 76, 86, 87–8, 91, 109

Socrates 125, 128

Sol Invictus 272, 273, 291

Song of Songs 202, 255–7

Sophia, wisdom, 147, 148, 161, 163, 234

Sophocles 165

Spain 9, 20, 65, 68, 272, 275, 319, 332

'Sporus' 67, 68

Spurinna 10

Stephen, St 41–2, 44, 106, 333

Stephen I, Bishop of Rome 200–201, 204, 205, 216, 223, 337

Stoics/Stoicism 121, 128, 132, 172, 235, 261

subordinationism 317

Suetonius 7, 10, 19, 22, 51, 56, 61, 74

Suetonius Paulinus, Gaius 64

Symeon, son of Clopas 76

Symmachus 238

Synagogue of the Freedmen 41

syncretism 78, 230

Syria 4, 7, 19, 20, 28, 35, 271, 275

Tacitus, Marcus Claudius, Emperor 269, 273

Tacitus, Publius Cornelius (historian) 31, 33–4, 66, 183

Tanakh 26

Tatian 121, 124, 261

Tatiana 258, 260

taxation 4, 69, 114, 211, 274, 279
clergy exemption 309
and Jesus 35
registration 4, 35
Temple taxes 38

Temple of Jerusalem
and Antiochus III 26
desecration by Antiochus IV 27
desecration by Florus 69
destruction (AD 70) 73
and the early church 40
Herod's Second Temple 28–9
and Jesus 37–8, 41, 72
and the Jewish rebellion 70
Paul at 58, 59–60
Pompey's violation of 7
and Stephen 41–2

temples, pagan 102, 186, 296, 298, 305–6, 330

Terence, playwright, 174

Tertius (deacon) 179

Tertullian, Quintus Septimius Florens viii, 3, 97, 152, 154, 165, 173, 174, 178–9, 181–99, 208, 209, 238, 334, 336
Apologeticum 184–8, 201
De Ectasi 199
On the Flesh of Christ 196–7
De Idololatria 190
Adversus Marcionem 194–6
against Marcionites 194–8, 339
and Monarchianism 199, 220–22
and the New Prophecy 183, 199, 220
Adversus Praxean 199, 220–22
on prayer 193
To Scapula 188–9
De Spectaculis 189
tracts 192–3, 199
Against the Valentinians 194
On the Veiling of Virgins 191, 192

on women's dress 191–2
Tertullus 59
Teutoborg Pass 68
Thales of Miletus 132
Theoctistus, Bishop of Caesarea 251, 252
Theodora, daughter of Maximian 275, 289
Theodore of Mopsuestia 255, 317
Theodoret of Cyrus 255
Theodosius I 325, 328
Theodotion 238
Theognis of Nicaea 324
Theophilus of Antioch 121, 165, 261
Theophrastus 132
Thessalonica 46, 47, 75, 302
Thomas, apostle 42–3, 75
Thomas, Gospel of 96
Thugga 174
Tiberius, Emperor (born Tiberius
    Claudius Nero, son of Livia) 15, 23,
    24–5, 30–34, 51
    death 51
Tigellinius 65
Timesitheus, Gaius Furius 212
Timothy 46, 108
Tiridates 69
Titus, Emperor, son of Vespasian 69, 70,
    71, 73, 74
Trajan 113, 114, 115, 116, 117, 185
Trallians, church in east, 87
Trier 271, 281, 290, 292, 297, 304
Trinitarianism
    and the Monarchist
        controversy 218–23
    Nicene 316, 322, 324
    and Origen 245–8, 316
Tyre 57
    Council of 328

Vahram of Persia 275
Valens 300
Valentinians 156, 183, 234
Valentinus of Rome 96, 98, 152, 153,
    154–5, 156, 157, 158, 161, 194, 208,
    209, 230, 232, 338
    Gospel of Truth 154–5, 338

Valeria, Galeria, daughter of
    Diocletian 275, 285, 286
Valerian, Emperor 200, 205, 214, 223,
    269, 271, 335
Varro 183
Varus, Publius Quinctilius 8, 19, 31,
    54, 68
Verus, Lucius, co-emperor 21, 113
Vespasian 68, 69–70, 74, 186
Vesuvius, Mount 74, 115
Victor, Bishop of Rome 220
Vienne 172, 186
Vindex 68
Vipsania Agrippina 23, 24, 32
Virgil 13, 21
virgins 191, 192, 193, 202, 203–4
Visigoths 270
Vitellius 68, 71
Volusianus, son of Gallus 213–14
Vulgate, Latin bible, 173

worship
    Emperor-worship 116, 117, 202, 335,
        336–7
    freedom of 188–9, 301, 307, 310
    Justin on 127
    in pagan temples 186
    punishment for refusal to participate
        in pagan practices 117, 186, 281–7

Yarmuk, Battle of 332
York 290
Young, Patrick 79

Zama, Battle of 174
Zealots 69, 70, 72, 73
Zenobia of Palmyra 226, 272
Zenodorus 67
Zephyrinus of Rome 218, 219, 223, 244
Zoroastrianism religion of Persia 270
Zosimus 303
Zostrianos, gnostic teacher 148, 150–51

Lightning Source UK Ltd.
Milton Keynes UK
UKHW010615221218
334426UK00005B/81/P